The Office Professional's Guide

THE Office Professional's Guide

OXFORD

UNIVERSITY PRESS

2003

Oxford University Press

Oxford   New York
Auckland   Bangkok   Buenos Aires   Cape Town   Chennai
Dar es Salaam   Delhi   Hong Kong   Istanbul   Karachi   Kolkata
Kuala Lumpur   Madrid   Melbourne   Mexico City   Mumbai
Nairobi   São Paulo   Shanghai   Taipei   Tokyo   Toronto

Published by Oxford University Press, Inc.
198 Madison Avenue, New York, New York, 10016
http://www.oup-usa.org

Oxford is a registered trademark of Oxford University Press

Library of Congress Cataloging-in-Publication Data

The office professional's guide / senior editor, Erin McKean.
   p. cm.
Includes bibliographical references and index.
   ISBN 0-19-516519-5
   1. Office practice.   2. Office management.   3. Business etiquette.   I.
McKean, Erin
   HF5547.5 .O344 2003
   651—dc21

                                              2003003655

Printing number: 9 8 7 6 5 4 3 2 1

Printed in the United States of America
on acid-free paper

Staff:

Senior Editor: Erin McKean	*Contributing Editors*: Joseph Gerharz
Managing Editor: Constance Baboukis	Orin Hargraves Sandra Ban
Staff Editor: Christine A. Lindberg	Linda Costa Beth Ann Koelsch
Manuscript Editor: Julia Penelope	Joseph Patwell Marina Padakis

Chapter 9, Making Presentations, and tips in chapters 1, 2, 3, and 5 were written by Evan
Schnittman

Contents

Foreword

Edward P. Bailey

Years ago, when my daughter was very young, I saw her sitting quietly in the family room. She was at that age when her feet didn't touch the floor as she sat on the couch. She had a book in her lap and was bravely trying to make her way through the first page.

"Jeannette," I said, "would you like me to read that to you?"
"Oh, yes!" she said. Who could resist? I couldn't!

I didn't even notice what book I was reading and just started in. After a page or two, I thought to myself, "Whoa! This is some book! It's great!" And it was. It was E. B. White's children's classic, *Charlotte's Web*. Somehow I'd missed it as a child, and that time with my daughter was my first experience reading it. I soon turned to other books and essays by E. B. White.

One thing that makes E. B. White wonderful is the power he can pack into simple language—ordinary words, unpretentious words. My favorite sentence of his comes from a letter he wrote soon after his wife died. White had been happily married for many years, and his wife's death devastated him. This is what he wrote: "She seemed beautiful to me the first time I saw her, and she seemed beautiful when I gave her the small kiss that was good-bye." All simple words, but in the hands of a master, they make a powerful and emotional sentence.

PREFER ORDINARY WORDS

E. B. White's mastery doesn't come from using bigger words than other authors. It comes from *putting words together* better than most other authors do. That's an important concept for all writing, but especially for business writing.

My professional specialty and fascination is Plain English. How can people in business write complex ideas clearly? There are many requirements for Plain English, but one is to prefer ordinary words. Some people, for example, always say *commence* when they write and never say *begin*; they *utilize* but never *use*; they *implement* but never *do*. Plain English says it's better to prefer *begin*, *use*, and *do*.

Does that mean we should reduce our vocabulary to that of a kindergartener, that words of more than one or two syllables are inappropriate and ineffective in business writing? No, of course not, although that's a common misconception about Plain English. Actually, Plain English doesn't suggest doing away with any words at all. It's bureaucratic writing that suggests doing away with words: it wants us to do away with words like *begin*, *use*, and *do*.

Notice that the Plain English requirement is to *prefer* ordinary words. That means you should set your default for the ordinary word and use the others when they're appropriate—that is, you should use common words commonly and uncommon words, well, when they work.

Good writers, like E. B. White, set their default for the common word and use a less common word when it's more precise. All too often in business, though, people set their default for the uncommon word and use a common one only when they can't think of something more impressive.

AN EXAMPLE OF GOOD WORD CHOICE

Let me illustrate what I mean. Another of my favorite writers is Russell Baker. I've quoted the first paragraph of his best-selling book, *Growing Up*, many times in my books. Here that paragraph is. Notice the power of the ordinary word:

At the age of eighty my mother had her last bad fall, and after that her mind wandered free through time. Some days she went to weddings and funerals that had taken place half a century earlier. On others she presided over family dinners cooked on Sunday afternoons for children who were now gray with age. Through all this she lay in bed but moved across time, traveling among the dead decades with a speed and ease beyond the gift of physical science.

Wonderful writing! Do you think Russell Baker has a good vocabulary? Let's consider his résumé: best-selling author, columnist for the *New York Times*, host of *Masterpiece Theatre*—the guy has an impressive résumé! And, of course, he has mastery over our language's vocabulary.

When you write for business, do what Russell Baker and E. B. White do: trust the power of the ordinary word; use other words when they work. For example, notice that Baker uses the word *presided* in the middle of that paragraph. It's not a common word, but here it's the perfect word, isn't it? It suggests that his mother, now helpless in bed, was a matriarch, a power in the family. It makes a wonderful contrast between what she once was and what she now is, between what she once was and never can be again.

CLEAR BUSINESS ENGLISH

As you use *The Office Professional's Guide*, keep Russell Baker and E. B. White in mind. Good writing, of any kind, communicates from the author to the reader.

Though no guide will make a Baker or a White out of us, it can:

- make us aware of problems in our own writing;
- enable us to make better choices of words and sentence structures;
- help us to keep our audience in mind when we write.

CHAPTER 1

Your Office Environment

The office of the twenty-first century is still vastly different from that of the twentieth century. Most of the obvious differences have been introduced by rapidly changing technologies that have altered the way office records are updated and maintained and how office space is utilized. In the offices of large and small businesses, medical establishments, and institutions, virtually all of the information required for efficiently running and maintaining the organization is now processed and stored in computer memory, eliminating the need for rows of file cabinets and the time involved in handling paper documents. Branches and divisions of organizations are connected by large area networks (LANs), eliminating the time and expense of exchanging information using postal services. Keyboards have replaced manual typewriters and adding machines. Every aspect of conducting any kind of business or institution is now done electronically, and familiarity with the software required for working successfully in any office is a necessity.

BASIC TECHNOLOGIES

In the twentieth century, the telephone was the technological breakthrough in the workplace. It connected the outside world to the business world, giving salespeople a running start. That same technology plays another role in today's business world. Telephone lines give our computers extra "connecting" power through the use of e-mail, voice mail, faxes, scanners, modems, printers, and the Internet, making business transactions more convenient and cost-effective. Where once, not so long ago, business meetings required sometimes lengthy and expensive travel plans, business can be conducted via e-mail, fax, teleconferencing, and even videoconferencing, connecting business-people and their prospective clients all over the globe.

Computer chips are finding their way into everything from cash registers, calculators, and cameras to stoves and refrigerators, medical equipment, and airplane cockpits. Increased memory in computers offers the office professional greater diversification in the workplace through a variety of software programs. Through the use of sophisti-cated computer programs and printers, offices can save money by cre-ating printed brochures and other materials with offset printing quality in-house.

Computers

The computer, a device that processes information through **input** and **output** of data, has become the central feature of the workplace. Com-puters in all shapes, sizes, and capacities are now available. An orga-nization can choose an industrial-size mainframe computer, or one or more personal computers (PCs), depending on the size of the com-pany. The larger PC that sits on a desk and has multiple components is called a **desktop**. Individuals may also have the more compact and portable **laptop** PC available to them. Laptops (or notebooks) are especially useful for businesspeople who travel frequently and need to be able to connect to their home office or to clients or to work while they travel. Business travelers also may use **PDAs** (personal digital assistants) or **tablet PCs** when they travel. These are smaller than lap-tops and used mostly for quick access to information rather than for serious work. A laptop or desktop computer that is not connected to other computers is called a **stand-alone**. A **network** can link together several computers for the purpose of sharing information, and printers and communicating with other computers. The main computer in such a network is called a **server**.

The computer's **memory** stores data. There are two types of memory: **RAM** and **ROM**. RAM (random-access memory) is the temporary storage of memory. When the computer is turned off, temporarily stored data is lost unless it is stored on floppy disks or on the hard drive. ROM (read-only memory) is unalterable, permanent memory, encompassing such information as the internal instructions for the computer's operation.

Computers have varying amounts of RAM and ROM, depending on the model or make of the computer—the more the better. Eight binary digits (**bits**) equal a **byte**, which can represent a single character, digit, or letter. The amount of information a computer can store is expressed in bytes:

    1 kilobyte (KB)   = 1 thousand bytes
    1 megabyte (MB) = 1 million bytes
    1 gigabyte (GB)   = 1 billion bytes
    1 terabyte (TB)   = 1 trillion bytes

Printers

The three most common types of printers are ink-jet, dot matrix, and laser. Cost and the particular needs of an office must be considered when deciding which type of printer to buy. Is a printer that uses only a black ink cartridge all you need? Color printers provide eye-catching graphics when making presentations to prospective clients or colleagues, but is the extra cost of such a printer warranted? Is speed or appearance a factor? If not, a dot matrix printer may suffice. If quality or speed is important, then the expense of a laser printer is justified. These are all factors to be considered before buying a printer.

Here's a brief overview of what each type of printer can do:

laser: A laser printer operates by electrostatically charging a photosensitive drum that attracts toner particles. These

Do You Need a PDA?

You've seen them and they look seductive, those tiny electronic devices that are half appointment book and half *Star Trek* tricorder. But do you really need one?

1. Do you already have an organizer that works? If you're committed to your paper planner or to a calendar function on your desktop computer, it may be more trouble than it's worth to switch to a PDA.
2. Do you travel often? Travelers often find PDAs attractive for two reasons: their small size and the automatic backup of data to a computer at home or work. Losing a paper planner while traveling can be traumatic. Losing a PDA is a little less so, since at least you know that you haven't lost the information, just the information container.
3. Are you happy with gadgets? If your VCR is unprogrammed and you regularly swear at your desktop computer, a PDA might be more than you want to wrestle with. However, most PDAs have good interfaces and can be learned quickly, even by the most tech-averse of users.
4. What kind of information do you need to access? If you only need a basic calendar, names and phone numbers, and a calculator, there are smaller and cheaper devices that might meet your needs at any office supply store. Check them out before springing for a larger PDA.
5. Will your desktop computer support a PDA? Many older computers may not have the USB (universal serial bus) connectors that modern PDAs require. Adapters are available but are an extra expense and may add to your setup and troubleshooting time. You don't want to have to upgrade your entire system just to use a PDA.

particles are heat fused onto paper in the form of the image being copied. These printers offer fast, attractive print images.

ink-jet: An ink-jet printer sprays tiny droplets of ink onto the paper to form the type or graphics being printed. While

6. Will your desktop software support a PDA? One of the main advantages to using a PDA is being able to synchronize data from your desktop applications to the PDA. If your company mandates a particular e-mail, meeting coordination, or calendar software, make sure that it will 'sync' with your PDA. Otherwise, you'll spend a lot of time manually entering information, or wishing you had.

7. Do you already carry another electronic device? If you carry a cell phone or digital camera for work, you might want to look into multipurpose PDAs. However, make the switch only if the multipurpose device fulfills all your requirements for both devices.

8. Do you lose things? If you go through a dozen pens a week, two pairs of reading glasses a month, and replace your keys twice a year, you may not be the best candidate for a PDA.

9. Do you need specialized information regularly? There are many add-on software titles for PDAs that deliver everything from prescription drug interaction information to the location of the closest Chinese restaurant to stock portfolio management. If having such information on-the-go would be useful to you, consider a PDA.

10. Will it improve your life? If a PDA is just one more thing to keep track of and worry about, stick to your paper planner or current system. However, if you think you would use a PDA to the fullest—including reading e-books or playing games or keeping track of your personal finances—there are many Web sites that will guide you through buying the one that's right for you.

not as fast as the laser printer, it offers good quality print images. Because of its compact size, it can be easily transported for laptop users.

dot matrix: A dot matrix printer has pins that strike the paper through a ribbon, making dots on the paper that form the type or graphics. These printers work well with multipage forms such as invoices and purchase orders. They also use continuous-feed paper with holes on the sides that fit into tracks to help the feeding process. After the page is printed, the form can be separated at the perforations at the bottom and the sides. The dot matrix printer is not a high-quality printer, but it's economical and useful in the workplace.

Copiers

The copier, like the telephone and computer, has become an essential item in the workplace. The kind of copier to buy is determined by the volume it will handle, along with the speed at which it produces copies. Other decisions regarding the capabilities needed in the office include:

- color copies or black-and-white?
- collating?
- stapling?
- enlarging/reducing?
- automatic feed?
- ability to handle pages larger than 8½" x 11" (11" x 17", blue prints, etc.)?

The number of special features usually determines the cost and size of the copier.

Scanners

The central function of a scanner is similar to that of a fax machine or copier: it reproduces an image. The difference is that the scanner can duplicate a photo that can then be transferred to a computer document, making it more polished, professional, informative, and visually appealing. A scanner can also take a typeset text and place it into a word-processing document, eliminating the need to rekey and reformat. Scanners are capable of handling black-and-white text, color, or gray for photographs, depending on the model.

Not long ago dismissed as superfluous equipment, the scanner has increasingly become a standard fixture in the modern office. If its value had to be expressed in three words, they would be *time, space,* and *aesthetics*.

Time. Scanning a document of prepared text and/or graphics is an electronic imaging process that replicates the document into, for instance, a word-processing program, making it directly accessible for review or revision. Eliminating the need for rekeying and reformatting not only saves time, but assures the exactitude of the copy as well.

Space. After only a few years of operation, the typical office has any number of file cabinets, boxes, and shelves brimming with inactive printed material. Although many accumulated documents could probably be discarded, this is certainly not a task to be done carelessly, as "inactive" is by no means synonymous with "unnecessary" or "disposable." The electronic storage facilitated by the technology of scanning provides an efficient alternative to the often unwieldy physical storage of documents.

Aesthetics. Until recently, it was a matter of simple discernment to recognize the difference between expensive farmed-out "professional" graphics and economical in-house "do-it-yourself" graphics. The distinction is becoming less dramatic with the rising availability of affordable high-performance scanners. From brochures to newsletters to portfolios to major presentations, the impact of artwork is a worthy consideration.

SCANNER FEATURES.

For the best results in the reproduction of photographic material, choose a scanner that fits your needs, inquiring into such features as:

- high resolution
- automatic sheet feeder
- speed
- software
- correction

SCANNING TIPS.

Once a document has been scanned into the computer, it should always be backed up (for example, on a diskette). Before disposing of the paper pages, it is wise to confirm that they were scanned successfully and that they are electronically retrievable.

Fax Machines

The fax machine has given the workplace a tremendous boost, enabling businesses to cut expenses and save time by faxing documents rather than using postal services ("snail mail") or overnight delivery services. The fax machine scans an image of a document, transmits it via telephone lines, and duplicates it at the recipient's fax machine in a matter of seconds. The unit may be a stand-alone version or one that operates through the computer or via the Internet. When choosing a fax machine, print quality and speed are important factors to consider. Checking into special features that may be available, along with monthly telephone or provider fees, is important as well.

Multifunction Machines

Some machines are capable of handling more than one function, such as a telephone/answering machine/fax/copier unit. In an office where space is limited, the multifunction machine offers compactness and cost-effectiveness while delivering useful and necessary technology. A desktop PC can come equipped with an internal modem that connects the user to the Internet, enables the user to make and receive phone calls, and provides faxing capabilities.

THE INTERNET

The Internet, created by the U.S. Department of Defense in the 1960s, consists of thousands of connected networks of computers that share information. Businesses, schools, libraries, organizations, governments, and individuals use it worldwide for innumerable purposes, especially to send and receive e-mail, to access and retrieve stored documents, information, games, and music, and to conduct such transactions as banking and shopping. **Cyberspace** refers to the environment through which all this information is processed and transferred.

Internet Connections

The computer connects to the Internet through telephone lines via a piece of hardware in the computer called a **modem**. The modem converts the computer information from digital to analog form so that it can be carried by the telephone lines. It is the most common and least expensive form of "dialing up" the Internet. An Internet service provider (ISP), such as AOL, Earthlink, or AT&T, provides such a service for a monthly fee, though there are a few free Internet services available. When Internet use is completed, there is a disconnect feature to click on, which is the equivalent of hanging up the receiver of a telephone. A digital subscriber line (DSL) is more costly but is very fast because the telephone line is always open, much the same as leaving a telephone off the hook after connecting to another party. It requires, however, a different type of modem. Another option is having a television cable hooked to the personal computer, rather than going through the telephone lines. This requires extra hardware. Monthly fees are similar to that of DSL, and the connection is also faster than the dial-up option.

The software required to use the Internet is called a **browser**. This provides the PC user with a means to connect to information stored on the Web in places called **Web sites**. Microsoft Internet Explorer or Netscape is sometimes already installed in newer computers; e-mail capability is usually part of the browser package. Common e-mail programs include Microsoft Outlook and Eudora.

THE WORLD WIDE WEB

The "World Wide Web," or "the Web," is the most used aspect of the Internet. It contains an unlimited source of information that is accessed by keying in a uniform (or universal) resource locator (URL), the unique domain name assigned to each site. The URL is also called the "address" of a Web site. The domain name identifies where the site can be found on the Internet. A typical URL contains several different elements, each of which provides specific information, and might look like this:

http://www.sdsu.edu

Many URLs begin with http://, which stands for hypertext transfer (or transport) protocol and identifies the address as a Web site; www. indicates that the site will be found on the World Wide Web. Some URLs begin with ftp:// (file transfer protocol) or gopher:// (individuals and organizations around the world have set up several thousand Gopher computers, or servers, that provide Internet users with a wide variety of information presented as menus, or lists, written in plain language). The address ends with one of the following, which identifies the kind of site:

.com   (commercial)
.net   (network)
.org   (non-profit)
.gov   (government)
.edu   (educational)

These elements of URLs are read "dot-com," "dot-net," "dot-org," and so on. In the example provided, "sdsu" tells users that this is the address for San Diego State University, and ".edu" identifies it as an educational institution.

Occasionally the core of an address is shared by two different domains. The United States Postal Service is at www.usps.com, but the United States Power Squadrons is at www.usps.org. The computer will display a prompt requiring the user to choose the proper domain.

If the user does not know a specific Web site address, a search can be made using a **search engine**. When a key phrase or word is keyed in, the search engine is activated to locate any sites that may be linked to that topic. For example, if the user is looking for publishers, keying

Setting Favorites (Internet Explorer) or Bookmarks (Netscape)

The modern office relies on the Internet in numerous ways, not the least of which are for the gathering and dissemination of information. The Internet has become essential in business research: for observing competition, for profiling clients, for accessing industry news, for following worldwide trends, and so on. With so many sources to track, an online bookmark system can be a useful tool. Here are some tips to setting up and organizing a directory of Web site favorites:

1. Bookmark (that is, save a link to) every Web site that may be of use to you at a later time. This insures simple retrieval of an address that may otherwise become lost or forgotten. For sites that are visited daily, bookmarking is especially convenient.

2. To save a link to the page you are viewing in Internet Explorer, click "Favorites" on the toolbar at the top of the screen. Within the Favorites menu, click on "Add to Favorites." You may click "OK" to add the link to a running list, or you may assign it to an appropriate folder. You can manage the content of your Favorites folders at any time by clicking "Organize Favorites."

3. To save a link to the page you are viewing in Netscape, click "Bookmarks" on the toolbar and then "Add to Bookmarks." If you want to move it to a folder, open the Bookmarks menu and click on "Organize Bookmarks."

4. Create a logical taxonomy for your Favorites/Bookmarks. Broad subjects can be organized by primary folders with titles like "Marketing" and "Competition." As relevant Web sites are added, subfolders may be created. For example, if your Marketing folder has 20 bookmarks, you may want to organize them further in subfolders such as "Online," "Direct Mail," and "Outdoor Advertising."

—*Evan Schnittman*

in "publishers" will result in millions of Web matches. If the user wants to narrow the search, the phrase "publishers in New York" will result in a more specific listing. (Using quotation marks around the request tells the search engine to restrict its search only to those words in that order, although the protocols for different search engines may differ.) Many Web pages have their own search engine, but users can choose from dozens of others, including AltaVista, Excite, Google, Lycos, Yahoo!, and Dogpile. Because of the volume of information stored on the Internet, not every keyword or Web site has been indexed by a search engine, resulting in incomplete listings, and search engines frequently turn up unrelated, therefore useless, information. The more specific the request to a search engine, the fewer the irrelevant Web sites listed.

Web Page Formats

Hypertext Markup Language (HTML) is a coding system that produces readable text but also contains hidden text that tells the browser where to display bold text or where to put graphics. Also, HTML lets the user know where to find more information on certain subjects within the text by highlighting words or phrases, often by underlining them. By clicking on the underlined word or phrase, the browser sends the user to another Web page or **link**. The first page of a Web site is called the **home page**. Web sites consisting of more than one page to browse through usually provide a link that will take the reader back to the **home page**.

CHAPTER 2

You and Your Career Development

CAREER DEVELOPMENT

Computers and the Internet have made business more efficient, but the new technologies have also speeded up ordinary business processes and made them more complicated. The business of any typical company requires support for its computers, telephone system, and e-mail, fax, and Internet capabilities. The modern office professional can choose from among several different career paths, from specializing in technical support, data management, or telecommunications to being a generalist and doing a little bit of everything. Even in specialized fields like information management, you can learn a lot on the job, but you will first need formal education to acquire systematic, expert knowledge.

As a beginner, you may choose to be a generalist. Because the generic duties of an office are easier to grasp than those requiring specialized training and knowledge, you can be immediately productive, while learning new skills along the way. Establishing your usefulness will open doors to expanding your responsibilities. By so doing, you

13

may discover that you have an aptitude for research or data management. Perhaps you'll find that you like and are good at keeping track of times, events, people, and places—in short, managing. Duties and responsibilities vary from business to business, but the fundamental duties typically include:

- answering and routing telephone calls;
- receiving, distributing, and answering mail;
- scheduling meetings and appointments;
- attending meetings and conferences;
- preparing the minutes of meetings;
- making travel arrangements and planning itineraries and schedules;
- operating computers and other equipment;
- doing word processing.

As you acquire experience, your duties may come to include:

- using the Internet for research and purchasing;
- coordinating business and office functions with telecommuters, other departments, and other businesses;
- processing contracts and leases;
- maintaining company books and records;
- managing desktop publishing of business documents;
- managing in-house or outside publishing of business documents;
- purchasing office supplies, equipment, and furniture;
- preparing budgets and financial statements.

At the senior level, your duties probably will include:

- setting work and office standards and being in charge of quality control;
- interviewing, hiring, training, and supervising temporary workers and assistants;
- performing job evaluations;
- setting up and maintaining electronic and traditional filing systems;

- setting up online databases;
- designing, developing, and managing projects.

PREPARING YOUR RÉSUMÉ

Before you begin work on your résumé, take the time to do a thorough, honest self-evaluation. It will be beneficial to assess your marketable skills before applying for a job. Begin by making a simple list, writing down your strengths and weaknesses. Outline your skills and abilities and your work experience as well as your hobbies and other interests. Having such information helps narrow the job-search field and indicates which positions you can realistically apply for with the expectation of being perceived as a serious candidate. (If you're having trouble evaluating yourself, a placement agency has staff qualified to help in this assessment.) Now you're ready to prepare a résumé that will present your skills and experience in the best light.

A résumé is a one- or two-page summary (no more) of your education, skills, accomplishments, and work experience. If you think that the purpose of a résumé is to land you a job, you're wrong. A résumé's purpose is to get you in the door. If you're called for that first interview, your résumé has successfully served its purpose.

Form and Design

Your résumé (along with a cover letter) is your first contact with prospective employers, so keep it simple and keep it clean. The following suggestions will make your résumé easy to scan into a company's database.

- Use white or off-white paper (no colored paper).
- Use 8 1/2" x 11" paper.
- Print on one side of the paper only.
- Use a font size of 10 to 14 points.
- Use a large, clear (nondecorative) typeface.
- Choose one typeface and stick to it.
- Avoid italics, bold print, script, and underlined words.

- Do not use graphics, horizontal or vertical lines, or shading.
- Do not use lines or borders.
- Do not fold or staple your résumé.
- Use a large manila envelope if you must mail your résumé.

The preceding suggestions are designed to make a résumé scannable, which is often a necessity. However, you may wish to create a separate version of your résumé, especially if you know for certain that your prospective employer does not scan submitted résumés. In this version you can be more flexible about formatting and aesthetics, but the final product should still have a clean look to it.

All of your contact information—name, address, telephone, e-mail address, Web-site address—should be centered at the top of the first page:

Elaine Bertolli
1234 Grosse Point Court
Hartford, CT 06655
203-925-0032
ebertolli@yahoo.com

Here are some additional dos and don'ts to help you present yourself professionally:

- Avoid nicknames.
- Use a permanent address. If you don't have one yet, use your parents' or a friend's address.
- Use a permanent telephone number and include the area code. (If you have an answering machine, record a neutral greeting.)
- Choose an e-mail address that sounds professional.
- Include your Web site only if it reflects your professional goals.

Content

Businesspeople say that your résumé is a critical tool in evaluating potential candidates' qualifications. They look for key phrases and words, they review accomplishments, and they are critical in assessing the quality of your written document. Your résumé must be perfect in its visual presentation and the quality of the written word.

OBJECTIVE/SUMMARY.

Your objective (or summary) tells potential employers the kind of work you hope to do. Be specific about the job you want, and tailor your objective to each employer you target and every job you seek. This will take some time, but it will be worth your effort.

EDUCATION.

If you're a recent graduate without much work experience, then list your education first. (If you have significant work experience, list that first, followed by your education.) Begin with your most recent educational information and go back in time. Include your degree(s) (A.S., B.S., B.A., M.A., M.S., etc.), your major, the institution(s) attended, and any minor or concentration. If your grade-point average (GPA) is higher than 3.0, include it. Remember to list any academic honors you may have received.

WORK EXPERIENCE.

Give the employer an overview of work that has taught you skills, and use action words (*achieved, acquired, composed, formed, founded, set up, supervised,* etc.) to describe your job duties. List your work experience in reverse chronological order, as you did with your education: put your last job first and go backward to your first relevant job. Include the following information for each job you list: title of position, name of the organization/business, location of work (town, state), dates of employment, and a description of your work responsibilities emphasizing specific skills and achievements.

OTHER INFORMATION.

If you think it is relevant to the job you're applying for, you may want to include additional information, such as special skills or competencies, leadership experience in volunteer organizations, and sports participation. If you have access to a career services office, someone there can advise you on the kinds of information that might be important enough to mention.

REFERENCES.

Before you give anyone's name as a reference to a potential employer, ask that person if he or she is willing to give you a reference. Do not include your references on your résumé. At the end of your résumé add: References furnished on request. Or, if your references are available from a career placement office, provide that information.

Reviewing Your Work

You've written your résumé, but you aren't finished yet. It's important to check it for spelling and grammatical errors. Before anyone looks at your résumé, run it through a spell-check on your computer. Next, ask someone whose opinion you respect to read it over and comment on it. Ask another friend to proofread your work. The more people who read your résumé, the more likely it is that misspelled words and awkward phrases will be noticed (and corrected).

A Sample Résumé

LI-YANG MAI
4446 River Ridge Road
Topeka, KS 66600
785-272-0102
LIYM0016@mindspan.com

OBJECTIVE
An entry-level position in the U.S. Department of Agriculture, especially one related to genetics research

EDUCATION
Bachelor of Science in Agriculture, 2002
Texas A&M University, College Station, TX

RELATED EXPERIENCE
- Collected samples of insects found in Central Mexican cornfields (summer, 1998)
- Identified and catalogued Central Mexican insects (Carney Research Lab, 1998–1999)
- Gained thorough knowledge of insect identification during summer studies at Central Kansas State Agricultural Station (1999)
- Worked as undergraduate research assistant (Carney Research Lab, 1999—2001)

ORGANIZATION/COORDINATION
- Coordinated and wrote research reports for Carney Research Lab
- Designed a study of corn fungi in a research project
- Coordinated research projects for beginning agriculture students

PROFESSIONAL PROFILE
- Highly organized and motivated
- Excited about genetics research in agricultural science
- Able to work carefully and attend to minute details
- Accustomed to long hours in the lab

EMPLOYMENT HISTORY
Library Assistant, Texas A&M University, College Station, TX (1999–Present)
Night Manager, Patch Convenience Store, College Station, TX (1997–1998)
Cashier, Bright Days Discount Store, Topeka, KS (summers, 1996–1998)

JOB TITLES AND JOB DESCRIPTIONS

As companies, organizations, and institutions evolve, job titles change, as do the job descriptions associated with them. For example, the old job title "secretary" was used in such a broad and generic sense for so long that the title eventually took on a demeaning connotation, especially for secretaries who had reached a high level of responsibility. Today, those with specific secretarial skills and various levels of experience can enjoy more appropriate titles, such as "administrative assistant" and "executive secretary."

Sample Cover Letter

Employers expect a résumé to be accompanied by a cover letter, which should be written in a formal style, but without sounding stuffy or awkward. A conventional cover letter is also part of selling yourself to a potential employer. It should identify the position for which you're applying, contain a brief outline of your skills and experience, indicate that you know something about the organization, and inform the employer when you'll be available. (For additional information on writing conventional business letters, see Chapter 8.)

José Hernández-Hidalgo
603 Ventura Court
Santa Barbara, CA 94512
June 17, 2002

Ms. Elizabeth Corning
Personnel Manager
Artemis Publishing
1601 Avenue of the Americas
New York, NY 10011

Dear Ms. Corning:
    I am applying for the position of editorial assistant advertised in the Career Services Center at New York University. The position seems to fit well with my education, experience, and career interests.

As traditional secretarial duties have become more and more dependent on electronic resources, the once clear line between secretarial jobs and non-secretarial jobs has become less distinct. In the past, for instance, good typing skills were hardly a concern for someone with no interest in secretarial work. Today, most office employees rely daily on their computers; hence, reliable keying is now a skill required at virtually all levels of office work. Conversely, those whose responsibilities are primarily secretarial may find themselves dealing with such diverse issues as electronic communications and compliance with state and federal regulations.

Certain job titles include words that specify ranks within the company hierarchy. The most common are "assistant," "associate,"

According to the advertisement, the position requires excellent communication skills, computer literacy, and a B.A. degree in the sciences or humanities. I have just graduated from New York University this month with a B.A. degree in English, with a concentration in technical and scientific writing, and with minors in biology and chemistry. My studies have included courses in computer science, vertebrate and invertebrate biology, organic chemistry, and modern literature. I understand that the position also requires a candidate who works well with people, is attentive to detail, works well under the pressure of deadlines, and is able to deal with many different kinds of people. These are skills I developed both in my coursework and in my summer work at Goldentree Books, Inc., in Garden City, New York.

My background and career goals match your requirements well, and I am confident that I can perform the job effectively. I am excited about the possibility of working for a high-profile publishing house well-known for the quality of its publications. If you would like to schedule an interview with me, please call me at 914-997-1642. I am available at your convenience.

Thank you for your consideration.

Sincerely,

[Signature]

José Hernández-Hidalgo
Encl: Résumé

"senior," and "executive" (in order from lowest to highest in the hierarchy). In job postings, more general designations are often used, usually "entry-level," "intermediate," and "advanced."

Entry-level positions typically require basic skills in keyboarding and communication (written and verbal). The work is closely supervised and is usually repetitive. Many office professionals begin at the entry level as a way of "paying their dues" and adapting the general skills learned in school to the style of a particular company. An intermediate position is offered to an individual who is able not only to fulfill the obligations of an entry-level position, but who is ready to take on more responsibilities, presumably with the intention of working toward a promotion to an advanced position.

An advanced position requires an excellent command of English, speed and accuracy in keyboarding, computer literacy, and knowledge of the company's standard operating procedures. Workers in advanced positions have much more autonomy and responsibility; they work with minimal supervision and are expected to be able to supervise others, especially those in entry-level and intermediate positions.

Advanced positions also require specific traits of character or temperament in addition to technical proficiency, depending on the nature of the business or the function of a department within a company. For instance, a publishing house that publishes textbooks or other hardcover books needs assistants with proven experience in copyediting and proofreading. These tasks, which can be exacting and tedious, are well-suited to a detail-oriented individual with a high threshold for concentration and tedium. In a magazine publishing house, however, or at a newspaper, there are nonstop deadlines, so an attention to detail must be balanced with the ability to work well under pressure.

There are advanced positions in specialized fields such as medicine and law (the "learned professions") that require knowledge and understanding of the technical vocabulary and language usage of the profession, knowledge of the professional ethics of the learned profession, knowledge of federal and state laws, regulations, and guidelines affecting these professions, and knowing how to work with and process the numerous medical, legal, and insurance documents and forms. Such knowledge can be acquired either by formal schooling or by long experience working in one of the learned professions. In addition to mastery of these very demanding intellectual technical skills, which must be performed with perfect accuracy and great speed, an advanced office professional in a learned profession may also be expected to manage the office as well, a position that requires great organizational skill, efficiency, tact, and discretion.

In sum, the proper matching of job to individual is vital to any company's success. When on a job search, make the effort to match yourself to appropriate job opportunities. Honest self-evaluation and clear career objectives will help both you and those from whom you seek employment.

CAREER PATHS

As an example of how complicated office work has become and how fast an advanced professional career in a learned field has grown, consider that the career of a paralegal and one in the field of information technology (IT) did not exist thirty years ago and probably could not have been predicted. The work that paralegals now do was done by lawyers, which was very expensive for their clients, or by office staff who often did not have the necessary skill or experience. The position of the paralegal was created in order to keep lawyers' fees affordable for clients. The work that a paralegal does in a law office can be learned on the job, but an advanced office professional in another field (say, in insurance), might find it advisable to earn a paralegal certificate or degree in order to begin work at a law office at the same level of responsibility and salary as in the insurance industry. Many community and four-year colleges offer paralegal courses that can be taken full-time during the day (usually for one full academic year), on an accelerated basis (two semesters of courses taught in one semester), at nights, or on weekends. Such flexibility allows the aspiring paralegal to select a schedule of courses that fits in with his or her business, personal, and financial requirements. In addition, the schools and colleges provide professional contacts for their graduates with employment agencies and law firms.

Information technology (IT) is already of vital importance to all businesses and will become even more critical in the future; IT is, therefore, an excellent choice for a career path. By definition, "information technology" is the study or use of systems—especially of computers and telecommunications systems—for storing, retrieving, and sending data, sound, and video. Every business function nowadays has physical tasks and corresponding IT functions: computers and telecommunications are used to perform routine tasks such as accounting, record keeping, payroll preparation, and the processing and fulfillment of orders. In addition, IT allows companies to collect and analyze more data than ever before, which results in streamlining production, marketing, and distribution within a company and between a company and its customers or suppliers. Using IT, a company can develop new products and services or modify existing products and services more rapidly for its customers, thereby gaining a competitive advantage.

The most common business uses for computers are: (1) word processing, (2) communications, (3) developing and maintaining databases, (4) accounting, (5) spreadsheets, and (6) graphics. All companies will use the first three applications and, depending on the size and nature of the business, most companies will use some or all of the others.

Word processing is a facility that enables users to compose, edit, reformat, store, and print documents.

Communications using computers is the sending and receiving of data from computer to computer; it also includes Internet research, videoconferencing, and person-to-person communication via e-mail.

Databases are organized, structured sets of data in a computer, accessed by a database management system (DBMS). A database consolidates and stores information from many separate files so that a common pool of information serves as a central file for data processing.

Accounting procedures (that is, bookkeeping, maintaining and auditing a company's books, analyzing the financial position of a business) can be done either within a business or by an outside firm, depending on the size of a company.

Spreadsheets are computer programs used especially for budgets and general accounting. A spreadsheet consists of horizontal rows and vertical columns, with the boxes (called "cells") containing numerical information and formulae or text. Each time the value within a cell is changed, the values of all the other cells whose values depend on it are changed.

Graphics (in full, **computer graphics**) are visual elements of text made, displayed, and manipulated using a special computer program. Graphics applications include:

- *paint programs*, which allow the user to make rough freehand drawings that can be stored and edited;
- *illustration/design programs*, also called "draw programs," which are more advanced than paint programs and allow the user to draw precise curved lines;
- *presentation graphics software*, which allows the user to make bar charts, pie charts, and other images for printed reports and slideshow presentations;
- *desktop publishing* (DTP), which is the use of a computer and a page printer to perform many of the functions of a print shop, including page layout and design, choice of fonts and type size, and the inclusion of diagrams and pictures. Many companies will use outside printers for full-size books or magazines, but will use in-house DTP for advertisements, brochures, or newsletters.
- *computer-aided design* (CAD), which allows the user to design a product or manipulate a specific kind of design, especially in architecture, in electronics, and in electrical, mechanical, and aeronautical engineering.

Within IT there are many different careers to choose from, depending on one's aptitude and interest. The word-processing and communications functions are nearly universal at home, school, and business; they are relatively simple and easy to learn. Other functions can be learned, at least in part, on the job, but in order to gain proficiency to learn a new career or advance your current one, formal study is necessary.

If, for instance, you have good organizing skills, database management is a possible career choice. A database is somewhat like a library's card catalog or a filing system in that the books, papers, or data are organized into a system for easy access and retrieval. A database is made up of fields, records, and files. A **field** is a space set aside for a piece of information. In a phone book entry, for example, there are three fields: one for the name, one for the address, and one for the phone number. The **record** consists of all the fields in the phone book entry. All the records in the phone book, from AAA Auto to Zyza, are, in computing terms, the **file**. The data in a database are accessed by a DBMS, a collection of programs for the retrieval, modification, and storage of data.

You can learn some aspects of database management on the job—for example, by helping a technical expert set up an electronic filing system or by sorting and updating files. Eventually, however, you will need to know something about programming languages, for which you will have to go to school. Nearly all community and four-year colleges offer certificate or degree programs in database management.

If you are creative and have visual skills, then computer graphics may interest you. Skills in the various applications of computer graphics are valuable for marketing and advertising, and for using desktop publishing to produce employee handbooks, instruction manuals, house organs, and magazines. Word-processing skill is essential, and you can also acquire some on-the-job experience in setting up columns and charts, creating graphs, drawing pictures, and using shade and colors. Many of the applications of computer graphics, however, need computers with a powerful central processing unit (CPU) and a very large memory. Moreover, the software for computer graphics requires a graphics monitor and support for the graphics standards. Many, or most, companies will not have computer graphics because of the special requirements and will have such work done by outside contractors.

Many computer graphics professionals prefer Apple computers ("Macs") rather than the PCs used in nearly all businesses and at home. If a career in computer graphics, appeals to you, you may have to become proficient on both types of computer. In any case, it will be necessary to take courses in computer art and graphics, and it would also be helpful to study public relations, advertising, and marketing principles.

EDUCATION

Physicians, lawyers, scientists, and professors continue their professional education throughout their working lives by conducting their own research and writing up the results for publication and by reading journals in their fields. So, too, businesspeople will—and must—continue their education for the rest of their careers. For most, frequent or daily reading of the business and other sections of newspapers such as the *New York Times*, the *Washington Post*, and the *Wall Street Journal* will keep them abreast of recent developments in business, politics, and computer technology.

The daily reading of well-written material has the added advantage of providing a model for writing good, clear English. Indeed, all the courses you can take—computer science, accounting, paralegal studies, computer graphics, finance, database management, advertising, marketing—will not advance your career unless you can write clear, simple English. The effectiveness of an expensive, glossy, well-researched, four-color brochure will be undone if it contains such howlers as "It's application to our system ...," "There expectations were not met," or "Please join Lee and I for lunch." Many law firms require writing samples from paralegals applying to their firms, and many publishing houses administer tests in copyediting for even relatively senior positions, not to determine whether or not the applicants know legal terminology or usage or how to edit a manuscript, but to ascertain how well the applicants can read, write, and edit Standard English.

For those interested in accounting, business administration, database management, or computer systems theory, courses in mathematics above introductory calculus are necessary.

THE JOB SEARCH

In the ups and downs of the job market, it is imperative that job seekers know what is available in order to avoid the pitfalls of wasted time and energy in their search for the perfect job. After assessing what skills you can offer, check various sources to see if the occupation you are interested in is viable. Oftentimes certain career choices become saturated in the marketplace while there are insufficient qualified applicants for other positions. Here are some sources for finding out which positions are most in demand:

- employment agencies
- the Internet
- newspapers
- trade journals
- libraries
- word-of-mouth
- cold calls to area businesses

OPPORTUNITIES IN OTHER COUNTRIES.

Don't overlook the possibility of working in another country. The Internet offers many listings for foreign job opportunities. Multinational companies will also list overseas jobs in newspapers and trade journals. Be aware that certain criteria must be met, and a background check is usually done before an applicant is seriously considered for a position.

PROFESSIONAL ASSISTANCE.

The professional with lofty goals has a much greater chance at success and climbing the corporate ladder through a mentor or a good working relationship with another successful professional. Sound advice from someone who has "been there" is invaluable, whether it is in regard to deciding whether to make a career change or to accept new responsibilities or promotions. The "who you know" game may have been around a very long time, but it is still extremely valid.

YOUR FIRST JOB

Taking on that first job out of school is very exciting but can also bring uncertainty and insecurity. It's the true test of how much was absorbed in class and can now be applied in the workplace, in addition to the problem of fitting in with a whole new environment. Finding that perfect job, however, will take some planning. Unfortunately, if the job market is slow, there may be few choices. On the other hand, a booming economy will open the field in such a way that a job prospect can be identified by answering a few questions:

- Am I willing to relocate? How far?
- What size company would I like to work in?
- Do I want a job that deals with the public?
- What kind of job will highlight my strengths?
- What are my salary requirements?
- What kind of work schedule will fit my lifestyle?

If the answers to any of these questions aren't immediately obvious, perhaps an employment agency can help find the perfect job fit. Being uncertain about the perfect career may also warrant a look at a temporary employment agency. Some companies require extra help at

---

Returning to the Workforce after an Absence

Looking for a job is always challenging. It can feel especially daunting for people who have not been getting a paycheck for a while, whether by choice or not. If this is your situation, here are some tips to help you with the job hunt:

1. Take time to think about what you want to do. You are a different person now than you used to be. Are you interested in the same things you were the last time you were in the job force? Consider attending workshops or talking to a career counselor.
2. Find out what is new in your job field. Read professional journals. Learn about the current issues being discussed by

(continued)

your peers. Pick up on the latest jargon. Talk to people who are currently working in the field you are interested in.

3. Evaluate your skills. The work world has changed while you've been gone. You probably need to update your skills, especially technology and computer skills. Take courses at community colleges or job centers.

4. Call up your former employers and colleagues and all of your friends and let them know you are looking for work again. Network!

5. Build a support system. You don't have to do this alone. Attend workshops for job seekers or form a support group with others.

6. Consider doing temporary work, freelancing, or even volunteering to get your foot back in the door.

7. Be prepared to explain the time gap in your résumé. Prospective employers will want to know what you have been doing in your "time off." Be honest, but emphasize your desire to return to the workforce.

8. Consider doing a "functional" instead of a chronological résumé. Highlight your skills rather than simply list each job you have held. What have you learned in your time away? Many experiences and skills learned at home, in school, through volunteer activities, or even in the pursuit of hobbies are transferable to the workplace.

9. Act confident even if you don't feel that way. Many people re-turning to the workforce are stymied by their fears. A positive attitude is essential. Apply for jobs even if you don't feel you have all of the necessary credentials for a particular position.

10. Don't be discouraged by job leads and opportunities that don't pan out. Finding the right job takes time. Be persistent and expect a favorable outcome.

busy times of the year, don't want the expense of hiring a full-time employee, or just want to evaluate whether a position is necessary on a regular or more permanent basis later on. Whatever the reason, working at a job as a "temp" has great advantages for people unable to decide on the type of job they are best suited for. Also, new skills are developed with each temporary position, which adds to your résumé. Trying several temporary jobs also provides you with a firsthand look

Finding Free or Inexpensive Career Advice

Job got you down? Hate what you're doing but you don't know what else to do? Laid off and sick and tired of your industry? Try finding some free or inexpensive career advice online, at the library, and/or in bookstores. A great way to jump-start this process is to take a career assessment test. There are several legitimate career assessments out there, such as the Strong Interest Inventory, the Birkman Career Assessment, and the Myers-Briggs Interest Inventory. Each has its own unique methods and outcomes. Avail yourself of a free assessment, and from there get a few books on the career type you are leaning toward. For starters, check out these resources:

1. http://www.jobhuntersbible.com/counseling/ctests.shtml
   Read this article before you take any test.

2. http://www.quintcareers.com/online_assessment_review.html
   A helpful review of online career assessments that rates them and lists prices.

3. http://www.allthetests.com/career.php3?katb=0640
   An alternative review of career assessments.

4. http://discovery.skillsone.com/strong/Default.asp
   A free Strong Interest Inventory with a report.

5. http://www.advisorteam.com/user/ktsintro1.asp
   A Myers-Briggs type of test.

6. http://www.princetonreview.com/cte/quiz/default.asp
   A Birkman style quiz.

7. http://www.tenspeedpress.com/catalog/all/item.php3?id=1260
   Order the bible of the career hunt, *What Color Is Your Parachute?* by Richard N. Bolles.

8. http://www.monster.com
   Post your résumé and search for jobs.

—*Evan Schnittman*

at the types of jobs available and the skills required to perform them. Sometimes a company that hires a temp decides to fill that position permanently, especially if the temp handles the job efficiently and works well with others.

Whether the first job is temporary, part-time, or full-time, new skills can be acquired and honed, and confidence can be boosted. It's a stepping-stone for greater opportunities, as long as the individual is willing to be open to new challenges and thought processes.

PROFESSIONAL ORGANIZATIONS AND ASSOCIATIONS

American Society of Corporate Secretaries (ASCS)
521 Fifth Avenue
New York, NY 10175
Phone: 212-681-2000
Fax: 212-681-2005
E-mail: webmaster@ascs.org
Web: www.ascs.org

Home Office Association of America (HOAA)
PO Box 51
Sagaponack, NY 11962-0051
Phone: 212-588-9097 / 800-809-4622
Fax: 212-286-4646
E-mail: hoaa@aol.com
Web: www.hoaa.com

International Association of Administrative Professionals (IAAP)
10502 NW Ambassador Drive
PO Box 20404
Kansas City, MO 64195-0404
Phone: 816-891-6600
Fax: 816-891-9118
E-mail: service@iaap-hq.org
Web: www.iaap-hq.org

National Association of Executive Secretaries & Administrative
    Assistants (NAESAA)
900 S Washington Street, Suite G-13
Falls Church, VA 22046
Phone: 703-237-8616
Fax: 703-533-1153
Web: www.naesaa.com

National Association of Home Based Businesses, Inc. (NABB)
10451 Mill Run Circle, Suite 400
Owings Mills, MD 21117
Phone: 410-363-3698
E-mail: nahbb@msn.com
Web: www.usahomebusiness.com

National Association of Legal Secretaries (NALS)
Resource Center
314 East 3rd Street, Suite 210
Tulsa, OK 74120
Phone: 918-582-5188
Fax: 918-582-5907
E-mail: info@nals.org
Web: www.nals.org

National Association of Working Women (9to5)
1430 W Peachtree Street, #610
Atlanta, GA 30309
Phone: 800-522-0925
Web: www.9to5.org

National Business Association (NBA)
5151 Beltline Road, Suite 1150
Dallas, TX 75254
Phone: 800-456-0440 / 972-458-0900
Web: www.nationalbusiness.org

Office & Professional Employees International Union (OPEIU), AFL-
    CIO, CLC
265 West 14th Street, 6th Floor
New York, NY 10011
Phone: 212-675-3210 / 800-346-7348
E-mail: opeiu@opeiu.org
Web: www.opeiu.org

Professional Secretaries International World Headquarters
10502 NW Ambassador Drive
PO Box 20404
Kansas City, MO 64195-0404
Phone: 816-891-6600
Fax: 816-891-9118

CHAPTER 3

You and Your Colleagues

BUSINESS ETHICS

Many companies specify in their company or employee handbooks the mutual obligations between employer and employee and minimal standards of behavior and procedure. The "learned professions" (medicine, law) have their own standards of professional ethics founded on centuries-old custom and nowadays enforced by federal and state law. In addition, businesses such as banks and brokerage houses are regulated by various federal and state agencies. Some of the rules to be followed are common sense; others must be learned either on the job or by outside reading or classes or by in-house classes and lectures. In general, business ethics require employees:

1. to keep confidential their employer's private business matters and information regarding customers and clients;
2. not to slander or damage the reputation of another or engage in unfair competition with others;
3. to acknowledge a colleague's accomplishments and not claim them for themselves;
4. to take responsibility or blame for their own mistakes and not pass the blame to another;
5. not to use company equipment such as telephones, copiers, and computers for personal matters without

permission and to be aware that personal e-mails sent
and received on company equipment are not private or
protected by the First Amendment;

6. not to take business supplies for personal use;
7. not to leave private or confidential materials on their
   desks or other unsecured areas;
8. to lock or secure desk drawers, filing cabinets,
   computers, storage areas, and offices overnight;
9. to ensure that confidential documents are disposed of or
   destroyed properly and in accordance with state and
   federal regulations on burning and shredding;
10. to observe copyrights when reproducing paper or
    electronic documents.

WORKING WITH AND FOR OTHERS

Working in an office or a business means that you will work with people from many different backgrounds with different skills, educations,
and limitations. There may, for instance, be someone in the "back
room" who does remarkably good and thorough technical analysis and
can write clear, succinct reports, but is uncomfortable at company
parties and functions. Good sales representatives typically like to be
their own boss and set their own schedules; they enjoy traveling and
meeting strangers, as part of their sales routine. Neither the retiring
analyst nor the extroverted sales representative is likely, usually, to be
a good manager. Neither the analyst nor the sales representative
needs or wants to be supervised or to supervise others. The analyst's
reserved temperament may make interaction with employees
strained and artificial; the sales rep, because of a free-and-easy style,
is likely to be unsuited to the daily procedures of office work. Yet, both
the technical analyst and the sales representative are essential for the
success of a business.

At the beginning of your career as an office professional, you can
expect—even welcome—training and supervision so that you can
learn standard procedures as quickly and efficiently as possible. As

you acquire experience and seniority, you will work more and more on your own without direction and, finally, probably train and supervise new employees yourself.

The willingness to contribute to a cooperative work environment is something you should demonstrate at all levels of your career. As a matter of custom, you should:

1. know exactly, from your supervisor, what the standards for your work or a project are;
2. make clear to those you supervise what the standards are, and be eager to help them understand what is expected;
3. maintain close contact with others working on a project so that everyone knows what parts of the project are ahead of schedule, on schedule, or behind schedule;
4. maintain good humor and morale, especially over a long or complex project;
5. use the first person plural pronouns (*we, our, us*) and not the singular (*I, my, me*) to reinforce the fact that everyone is included;
6. compliment others publicly for good work;
7. never criticize the work of someone else in public;
8. acknowledge your own mistakes;
9. know your strengths and weaknesses and those of your colleagues, and exploit the strengths and help to improve the weaknesses;
10. pitch in when extra help is needed, and ask for extra help if you need it.

Working for an executive is an acknowledgment of and compliment to your professionalism and competence, but it has its own peculiar difficulty in that your personality and the executive's personality must mesh almost as a single unit. If you and the executive get along, your job will be exciting and personally and professionally rewarding; if not, you will be personally miserable and your career stymied or even ruined.

The executive may be a hands-on manager, closely directing everything and demanding constant feedback, or may prefer to delegate responsibility and keep a watchful eye on long-term developments. The executive may be easy-going and patient or hard-driving and explosive.

Assuming that you and the executive you work for get along, you will become privy to a great deal of important business and personal information. Some of the information may be open and public or may be rumor in the office, but in all cases you must be scrupulously discreet and loyal to your boss. The well-being, even the survival, of the company, the executive's career, and your career, may well depend on your discretion and tact.

The higher up the ladder you go, the less you are told; this applies to men and women, young and old. If you enjoy socializing with your colleagues, you may find that you and they have less occasion to socialize with each other and they may not be so willing as before to talk shop. You will have to make compromises between your career and life outside work.

If you work for several executives, managing your time among them will probably be your most important problem. If it should turn out that you simply do not have enough time to arrange or manage all your executives' affairs, you owe it to them and to yourself to tell them exactly what the problems are and to suggest solutions. Perhaps the executives will arrange among themselves how much of your time each of them will use; perhaps they will decide to hire more assistants or an assistant for you.

Telecommuting

You may work for someone who travels a lot at regular or irregular intervals or is away at another office or branch for considerable periods. He or she will not be present for many routine managerial or executive matters, which will then be your responsibility. If you find yourself in such a position of greater responsibility and authority, and work unsupervised for much or most of the time, you and your supervisor or executive should be certain that several aspects of the situation are clear to both of you. At the very least, you should:

1. establish clear limits of your responsibilities and authority—for example, in signing letters, documents, and checks;
2. set up a system of communication, with a backup, by telephone (landline, cell phone, and voice mail), faxing, and e-mail;
3. determine whom you should contact in emergencies or for matters beyond your authority when your superior is unavailable.

There should already be in place standard operating procedures for routine office tasks.

Working with Temporary Assistants

Many companies outsource their work in order to save money. Companies may hire full-time or part-time assistants or temporaries to work in-house for, say, keyboarding, or freelancers to work off the business premises. Your company may hire its outside help through an employment contractor such as Kelly Services or Manpower, or it may have its own roster of temps for seasonal work, such as extra sales staff for a large retail store from Thanksgiving till Christmas or extra clerical help during tax season for an accounting firm. If your company has a standard procedure for hiring temps through an agency or a list or roster of temps, all you need do is contact the agency or the temps and fill them in on the latest developments since their last employment.

If your company has no procedure for hiring temps, you may be responsible for interviewing, recommending for hiring, or even hiring temps or assistants. You may also be responsible for training and breaking in assistants and temps, from showing them where to hang their coats and where to find restrooms and the cafeteria to explaining the nature of the project and what they'll be doing. You may even be obliged to relinquish some of your routine duties in order to orient and train temporary assistants.

Training Assistants or Temporary Workers

If you are dealing with skilled temporary workers or assistants, you need only give them specific instructions because they will be familiar with typical office routines and the equipment they will be using. Be sure, however, to show them where your office or work station is and give them your phone extension in case a problem should arise.

If your company is hiring an assistant who has just graduated from school or who is new to the business world, the human resources department will select a list of suitable candidates from which you or your supervisor can choose for further consideration. If your company does not have a human resources department, you or your supervisor will have to make your own selection.

The first test is a negative one: read the applicants' cover letters carefully for spelling, grammar, punctuation, and coherent syntax; if the cover letter has incorrect spelling, grammar, or punctuation or is confusing, consider the candidate no further. If the letter is correct in spelling, grammar, and syntax, then consider whether the letter is a "shotgun blast" with no particular target or whether the letter is directed to your type of business or even to your firm. Obviously, the closer the cover letter comes to the "bull's-eye" of your company's requirements, the more suitable the candidate is.

Next consider the candidate's résumé. If the candidate has prior work experience, check the kinds of businesses for compatibility with your firm. Also take note of the lengths of employment; is there a pattern of reliability? Check references; if none are listed, contact the applicant's former employers. A recent graduate entering the workforce for the first time will likely have little or no work experience; therefore, check the courses the applicant has taken to see if they are relevant to the needs of your business. If the applicant has done any internships, check with the organization for references.

Training experienced temporary workers or assistants is relatively easy; they will need relatively little supervision and have enough experience to recognize an unusual or special problem with which they need help. Recent graduates, however, may be nervous and unsure of themselves no matter what their technical strengths are; everything and everyone is new to them. Your job is to help them settle in and do productive work as quickly as possible. In order to accomplish this, you must:

- be friendly, helpful and patient;
- be aware that many procedures in a business office are simple and logical but not obvious and that what is second nature to you must be learned by new employees;
- introduce new assistants to their coworkers and make them welcome;
- show the new worker the physical layout of the office;
- instruct the new worker regarding the standard business procedures of the office and of office etiquette (make sure the new worker has a copy of the employee manual or office handbook);
- make sure all pertinent equipment is hooked up and operating (computer, telephone and voice mail, Internet and e-mail), and that the new worker has appropriate supplies (pencils, paper, etc.), and explain the company policy on personal calls and e-mails (remind the person that e-mail is not private and is not protected by the First Amendment);
- set up brief, regular sessions with the new worker—such as one session at the end of the workday for review of the day's work, and one in the morning for instruction about that day's work;
- use positive language in critiquing the new employee's work;
- encourage the new employee to ask questions and show initiative;
- watch for the new employee's strong and weak points and concentrate on improving the latter.

Managing Telecommunications and Telecommuting

Experience shows that teleworkers generally enjoy greater productivity, reduced stress, and improved quality of life over their workplace counterparts. The following ten tips will help you make your teleworking arrangement a success:

1. **Create your work environment:** It's still a job, even if you're doing it in your pajamas. The home workplace has a different set of distractions than the traditional one, and it is not unusual for the teleworker to find the distractions of home far more compelling and attractive, even demanding, than those of the office. Make a place for yourself at home that is reserved for work, and set aside the time that you are going to be there. If necessary, establish a protocol for others in the household who may be tempted to take you away from your work. Get a separate telephone line to take your work calls, put it in your office, and get the household telephone out of there.

2. **Be clear on what your job is:** If your employer already has a teleworking policy and agreement, familiarize yourself with them. If you're starting from scratch, check out some of the agreements and policies published on the Internet in order to formulate your rules. Be sure that you understand your responsibilities and your employer's expectations. Take special care over any part of your teleworking job that is going to create an expense, and be sure that you know who is paying for what.

3. **Make a schedule and keep it:** You need to be available for your colleagues when they expect you to be working, and they need to know if you're not going to be available at a time when you normally would be. Rumors about your activities may start very easily if you're not in the office to set matters straight, so it's important to signal any deviations from your routine in advance via e-mail. Don't forget to build into your daily schedule the breaks that you need from work, especially breaks from sitting at your computer.

4. **Maintain your voice links:** Working at home enables you to streamline communication with your colleagues, cutting out a lot of what is unnecessary and focusing on conveying significant information. But don't let the principle of "out of sight, out of mind" apply to you. Friendly chats with your boss and colleagues are necessary for maintaining your good relations with them, in addition to dealing with matters that are strictly business. When you are not physically present in the office, you need to ensure by

(continued)

the way you communicate that you remain a vivid and positive presence in the minds of those you work with. This is especially important when you need to thank or encourage someone; your phone voice has to do all the work. Remember that the best way to combat the isolation of teleworking some people feel is to maintain close relationships with your workmates.

5. **Maintain your data links:** The data link from your computer to your employer's computer or server is as vital as your voice link. Get the fastest and most reliable data link available for your home, and invest the time to understand how it works and how to troubleshoot it. Make sure that you have a backup link, such as a dial-up modem, to connect you in case the main link fails. Educate yourself as much as you can about your e-mail client software and any other electronic link between you and your employer; you will be a star in the eyes of technical personnel if you can meet them halfway in ironing out any problems that occur.

6. **Respond in real time:** Timely communication with all of your colleagues is the key to assuring them of your competence and effectiveness. You cannot easily dismiss someone inquiring at your office door, and you should not easily dismiss the inquiring e-mail from one of your colleagues or your boss if this is the only way they have of getting in touch with you. Make it a point to respond as quickly as possible to all of those who legitimately require your attention, even if all you can do for the moment is to acknowledge that you hear them. Solicit feedback from your key communication contacts about their contact with you; it is better for you to hear it from the horse's mouth than for it to arrive on your desk weeks later or indirectly in the form of a complaint.

7. **Demonstrate your effectiveness:** In the minds of many employers, the jury is still out on the benefits of teleworking. If you like the home setup, it is up to you to show that your effectiveness is not compromised by not working at the office. Even if your most effective contributions are made quietly and behind the scenes, there should be no doubt in anyone's mind that you are doing your job, and you should have at hand the means of proving it. Make sure that your being at home is not going to make more work for someone in the office, or more expense for your employer, and be ready to document it. When you are not physically present in the office, your employer knows your effectiveness only by your results.

8. **Monitor your effectiveness:** If your work at home isn't at least as productive as your work at the office would be, your employer is not getting a good deal. Keep track of your productivity; if necessary, identify and eliminate the distractions that are keeping you from meeting your

production goals or deadlines. You need to look at the technical side of things, as well as your time-management habits, your workload, and the real-time demands that others make on you. Don't hesitate to propose changes in your way of working if you think they will lead to an improvement, and don't hesitate to ask the big question, whether teleworking is really the best solution for you in this job.

9. **Exploit technology:** Constantly advancing developments in electronics and telecommunications are what make teleworking possible. Now that you are teleworking, be sure that you're using all the conveniences and devices that allow you to be virtually present in the workplace. Keep abreast of new developments that will make you even more effective, and don't hesitate to ask for the technology you need to do your job. Check the Internet for forums, sites, and software for and about teleworking; there's a lot more out there than you might think!

10. **Provide your own safety net:** All the elements in the infrastructure of an office need to be duplicated in the home workplace, and you need to feel confident that these are in place and reliable. Make sure that you give attention to how your work will be backed up; think about the kind of reception a caller gets when you're not there; consider a power source backup if your house is subject to electrical outages. Familiarize yourself with the occupational safety aspects of your employer's workplace and ask yourself whether your home office is completely in compliance with them.

BUSINESS ETIQUETTE

You should treat others the way you would like to be treated. Courtesy is a two-way street: treat others well and expect to be treated well yourself. Courtesy reflects favorably on you personally and on your company. It will be welcomed by those of good nature and may mollify those who are angry or difficult. Courtesy need not be, nor should it be, elaborate or forced, but simple and unaffected; with practice it becomes almost second nature.

Many people want to be courteous but simply do not know the rules of courtesy in the business world, where young and old, superiors and inferiors, familiar faces and strangers are mixed in all sorts of combinations. The rules for courtesy at the workplace are simple, logical, and flexible.

Doors and Elevators

The opening of a door for another is no longer a matter of a gentleman's proper gesture to a woman. Everyone, male or female, is grateful for this small courtesy, regardless of who has extended the kindness. Men and women hold doors for each other; whoever gets to the door first holds the door open. It is only common sense, and therefore common courtesy, to hold doors open especially for someone carrying packages, using a cane or crutches, or otherwise encumbered.

Elevators are usually crowded at the beginning and the end of the business day. Since there are so many women working in business, the traditional "ladies first" rule no longer applies in getting on and getting off elevators; whoever is closest to the elevator doors gets on or off first. It is courteous to hold the door for others coming toward the elevator and to thank those who hold the door for you.

Introductions

It is important to you in social functions and in business to project friendliness, interest, and self-confidence when introducing yourself or when you are being introduced. For all introductions, whether social or business, shake hands firmly, look into the eyes of the person you are being introduced to, and smile. Do not turn your face away or look down: that implies shyness or diffidence and may upset or annoy the person you are being introduced to. After being introduced, repeat the name of the person you were introduced to and say something like, "I'm very pleased to meet you, Ms. Jewett."

There is a protocol for making introductions. The person to whom someone is introduced will be older or more senior in rank than the person being introduced—for example, "Professor Barnes, I'd like you to meet my daughter Mary." In social situations, introduce a man to a woman: "Ms. Andersen, I would like you to meet Martin Parwell." Introduce a younger person to an older one: "Mom, I'd like you to meet Johnny Culhane." In business situations, introduce a junior employee to a senior employee or manager or executive regardless of gender—for example, "Mr. Prokop, I would like you to meet Pauline

Abbas." Introduce a fellow employee or colleague to a customer or client: "Mr. Hanrahan, this is John Kernahan, the head of our legal department. John, this is Michael Hanrahan, the publisher of the Lynn *Daily News*." Do not presume to use first names; wait till the person to whom you are being introduced suggests it or asks you to: "I'm pleased to meet you, Mr. Kernahan; call me 'Mike.'"

Always use the names of both (or all) people in an introduction, for example, "Ms. Jewett, I'd like you to meet Mr. Seki." It is common, but no longer necessary, except in very formal situations, to repeat the introduction in reverse order: "Ms. Jewett, I'd like you to meet Mr. Seki; Mr. Seki, this is Ms. Jewett." "Mr." is the usual courtesy title for a man, and "Ms." for a woman unless she specifies "Miss" or "Mrs." Professional titles such as "Doctor" or "Professor" are used for both sexes. If you are introducing people of equal rank, titles are unnecessary.

In informal situations, names alone are sufficient, but more formal occasions and many business situations require using a person's title or rank to identify him or her. If a person is a former public official, he or she is introduced by that title, for example, "former senator Jacob Mandrel"; if the person is retired from the military, use that person's title or rank: "Colonel O'Brien." It is helpful, too, if the person making the introductions gives some information about each person to make small talk easier: "Mr. Contarini, this is Francis Jones, professor of French and German at Regis. Professor Jones, Mr. Contarini's son James is a freshman at Regis."

If a man is sitting, he always stands up for introductions. If a woman is sitting, she usually sits for introductions unless she is meeting a government official or other important person, and then she should stand up. A young woman should always stand up when meeting an older man or woman. Men always shake hands with other men. Formerly it was the custom that a man did not shake hands with a woman unless she extended her hand first. Some older men still follow that custom, which may cause them to hesitate slightly. Nowadays, however, it is nearly universal that a woman extend her hand to be shaken.

Do not hesitate to reintroduce yourself or repeat your name if someone seems to have forgotten it: "Hello again, I'm Catherine Bellantonio—Kate." Likewise, be frank if you have forgotten a name, and simply say, "I'm sorry—I've forgotten your name."

SPECIFIC SITUATIONS.

When introducing yourself to a receptionist, say hello, state your name and the purpose of your visit, and offer the receptionist your business card if you have one—for example, "Hello, I'm Myrna Jacobson, and I'm here to meet Mr. Canavan." If you are the first person to greet a visitor, introduce yourself, "Hello, I'm Kevin Carpenter, Ms. Costello's assistant. Can I help you?"

If you are introducing a person to a group, address the new person unless those in the group outrank him or her, allowing the individual enough time to shake hands with each member of the group—for example, "Bob, I'd like you to meet some of my colleagues: Peter Wang, Joyce Zorara, and Jim Griffith. This is Bob Winkin, the owner of Winkin Musical Instruments." If you are being introduced to several people at the same time, repeat each person's name as you shake her or his hand unless you feel there isn't sufficient time for this nicety. (Repeating someone's name as you shake hands is one way of ensuring that you remember it.) If you are introducing a group of people to a group of people, make the introductions in descending order of seniority and use titles.

Introduce your spouse to a superior, regardless of gender: "Mr. Lattimore, I'd like you to meet my husband, Chu."

Answering Invitations

Most invitations for business functions are sent by e-mail or photocopy to the entire company, division, or department, and not to individuals. Such invitations are not meant to be answered. A formal invitation, whether for a business function, a social function, or a combination of the two, addressed and sent to you personally, must be answered as a matter of courtesy and for the practical task of planning and seating. If the invitation has a reply card enclosed, send it with your acceptance or regrets. If the invitation does not have a reply card but has an RSVP printed on it, send a handwritten note for a social function (typed notes are acceptable for business functions) with your acceptance or regrets. If a telephone number or an e-mail address is printed with the RSVP, you may reply by telephone or e-mail.

In your reply you should use the same third-person style of the invitation. Do not wonder whether you may take a guest with you, let alone assume that you may; the invitation will specify whether you may take a guest with you. If you have accepted an invitation and something happens that prevents your attendance, notify your host immediately.

Business Lunches

Business lunches, where everyone can relax away from the workplace, are good venues for becoming acquainted with new or potential employees or clients. Some common sense considerations will help make the lunch successful:

1. Let the guest choose the time for lunch (he or she may have deadlines, travel reservations, or other appointments).
2. Ask the guest for culinary preferences (Italian, Indian, vegetarian, seafood) or dietary restrictions (for example, due to allergies or diabetes).
3. If necessary, arrange to pay for the guest's parking fees and coat check.
4. If the host and guest arrive separately, the host should arrive first.
5. In many states, counties, or cities, smoking is not permitted in restaurants. If, however, smoking is allowed, ask the guest to decide where to sit.
6. The guest should have the seat of honor or the best seat, and the host should sit opposite for good eye contact and ease of conversation.
7. If someone orders an alcoholic drink, you may order an alcoholic drink for yourself, but only if you want to.

Otherwise, ask the other diners whether anyone cares if you have a drink.

8. A 15-percent tip is the minimum at most restaurants; a 20-percent tip is usual at expensive restaurants. Many restaurants automatically add a minimum tip onto a check for a party of six or more people.

Business Cards

Business cards are essential whether you are a self-employed steno-typist or an employee of a multinational corporation. The business card identifies you, your company, and your position within the company. You can attach your card when sending a newspaper article or an article from a technical journal to a client (clip it onto the upper left-hand corner of the reading material) or when sending a colleague a gift or flowers (write a short message on the back of the card, and sign it with your first name). Business cards may also be exchanged at social occasions, especially for networking. Your card should contain:

- the company logo;
- the full legal name of the company
- the business address of the company (post office box numbers should follow the street address)
- the company's phone number and your extension number (also include any toll-free numbers)
- fax numbers
- your office e-mail address
- the company's Web-site address
- your name and job title
- your business days and hours, if they are unusual (that is, your regular hours are not Monday through Friday, 9:00–5:00)

The business card should be of heavy paper and be about 3½ by 2 inches. Engraved cards are expensive and usually unnecessary unless you are an executive; offset or letterpress printing is attractive and is used for most business cards. The fonts used on the card must be clear and easy to read so that the card does not look cluttered. If your company uses color on its letterhead, then use that color on your card; otherwise, use black or blue type on white stock. If you are responsible for ordering business cards, you must be sure to proofread the order before it goes to the printer and after it comes back.

Domestic Partners

A "domestic partner" is a live-in lover of either sex. This is no longer shocking at the social level, at least in big cities, but there has been much agitation in recent years for state and federal legal recognition of such partnerships for medical, social security, and survivor benefits, all of which is controversial and may generate a lot of heat in a casual conversation. Therefore, to avoid embarrassment and the possibility of misunderstanding, use "guest" instead of "spouse" in sending out invitations to a company function or party, and treat the domestic partner as you would a spouse.

Cards and Gifts

The basic rules of etiquette for business and social introductions are clear, simple, and universal throughout North America. There are, however, no standard rules for sending cards and giving gifts, and many companies have their own policies regarding such. The most sensible thing is to follow the procedures or customs of your workplace.

Many executives give cards and/or gifts to their assistants or take them out to lunch on birthdays and holidays. In such cases, all the assistants need do is thank the executive; it is inappropriate to reciprocate. Many managers will give nominal gifts (candies, calendars) to their subordinates in December. Again, all the subordinates need do is say "thank you." It is not necessary for them to send cards or give gifts to their managers or executive officers.

Many companies send cards and/or gifts to customers and clients in December. The cards should be secular, not religious, in order to be appropriate for recipients of all beliefs. Likewise, the inside of the card should proffer a neutral greeting such as "Happy Holidays" or "Season's Greetings." Gifts may also be sent to long-term or valuable clients and customers. An up-to-date list must be kept of those to whom cards and gifts are sent. Cards should be ordered well in advance (two months) and contain a personal message from the sender (CEO, president, branch manager) or personally signed.

DIVERSITY IN THE WORKPLACE

Today's workplace reflects the diversity of today's society. You work with and socialize at lunch and after work with people from all over the country and all around the world. In addition there is federal and state legislation protecting the rights of people based on their race, gender, age, national origin, ethnicity, language, religion, physical disability, and sexual orientation. The important thing for you to remember is to treat others as you would like to be treated; be friendly, open-minded, and willing to learn, and you will avoid friction at the office, not to mention inadvertently violating someone's civil rights.

Different cultures have different norms of greeting, casual conversation, body language, facial expression, and eye contact. For a man from a culture where men and women are more or less segregated and a man does not look at or talk to a woman who is not his relative, it will be a real and constant effort for him, at least initially, to associate with women in a friendly, professional, business setting. Someone from a very hierarchic culture may find it very difficult to begin a conversation with his or her boss and would prefer to speak only after being spoken to.

People like talking about how things are done back home or in the "old country." Friendly curiosity about another culture and friendly explanations of how things are done in the United States will break the ice and avoid mutual misunderstanding, and you will learn how other people look at things. In addition, you can attend workshops devoted to teaching diversity in the workplace and pick up reading material about diversity from these workshops.

UNBIASED LANGUAGE

Everyone is aware of the changes in vocabulary and usage in English with regard to gender, race, and disability over the past 30 years or so, and everyone has different reactions to these changes, from automatic acceptance of the most extreme proposals to scorn or bewilderment. People who express their distaste for such simple linguistic courtesies often try to pass off their lack of concern for others' feelings by referring to such changes in terminology scornfully as "political correctness." This dodge, however, reveals only that the individual intends to harbor her or his delusions of superiority to other people. The issue is not about what is "correct" or "incorrect," but about acknowledging the diversity of our society and our individual differences with respect.

It is very easy to write good Standard English and offend no one without lapsing into euphemisms or awkward constructions. Just remember that language changes constantly, and no one can predict whether a new form or usage will become part of the standard language, be uneasily accepted, or simply die. Nevertheless, there are some commonly accepted usages that will demonstrate courtesy and consideration for the various groups with which people identify. When in doubt, ask, if you can, how individuals prefer to be described.

Both *African American* and *black* (sometimes, but not usually, capitalized) are standard. *People of color*, but not *colored*, is also acceptable, and acknowledges that people of ethnic identities come in many shades and colors, including those who lack distinctive pigmentation.

Hispanic (always capitalized) is the usual, generic term for those of Spanish or Spanish-American ancestry. If possible, however, use the specific national term, such as *Cuban* or *Cuban American* or *Peruvian*. *Latino* or *Latina* is also standard in English as an adjective (as in "Latino culture"), but is a little problematic as a noun referring to a person since *Latino* (plural *Latinos*) is specifically masculine (with corresponding *Latina* and *Latinas* for women), a distinction not usually made in English. The same distinctions apply to *Chicano* and *Chicana*, but the terms properly refer only to Mexican Americans and are, therefore, inaccurate when used to refer to someone of Nicaraguan or Bolivian heritage.

Do not use *oriental*, which has connotations of inscrutability or deviousness. Also, because it means 'eastern,' in contrast to *western*, it is descriptively inaccurate because our world is a sphere. What is "west" or "east" from one position on the planet is also "east" or "west" from another position, so the outdated putative distinction is not only false but potentially confusing. Alternatively, *Asian*, which is the most generic term, refers to the continent of origin, and can be qualified by *East Asian* for Koreans, Chinese, and Japanese; by *South Asian* for Indians, Pakistanis, and Afghanis; and by *Southeast Asian* for Thais, Laotians, Cambodians, and Vietnamese. Of course, as with *Hispanic*, it is preferable to use the specific national term.

Indian, *American Indian*, and *Native American* are all acceptable, although individuals may have a personal preference. In Canada, it is common to speak of the people who first dwelled in North America as *First Peoples*, a term that acknowledges their claim to precedence. Again, as with *Hispanic*, use the specific term (*Cheyenne, Inuit, Mohawk*) if you know the person's group of origin.

"Ms." is now standard when referring to women. If a woman prefers "Miss" or "Mrs.," she will tell you so.

The most common difficulty in writing is with *he, his,* and *him* when used generically to refer to an unspecified individual, as in "Every employee must show *his* ID card to the guard at the gate." Many older people in the United States were taught that it is correct to refer to an indefinite person using the masculine pronoun forms, but this supposed grammatical "rule" originated, not in the English language itself, but in an 1850 Act of Parliament. Its continued use as though it included women as well as men is, therefore, sexist. One solution, common in spoken and informal varieties of English is "singular *they*," "Every employee must show *their* ID card to the guard at the gate." This familiar usage can be found in Chaucer, Shakespeare, and many other writers, yet pundits continue to discourage its use in formal contexts. Others reject the use of both pronouns, "Every employee must show *his or her* ID card to the guard at the gate," because it's "awkward," but this argument, too, is disingenuous. The simplest solution, however, is using plural nouns: "All employees must show their ID cards to the guard at the gate," which will put you beyond the reach of critics of any stripe.

The use of nouns ending in -*man* (for example, *policeman*, *fireman*, and *mailman*) is also discouraged, and for the same reasons that the pseudogeneric use of the masculine pronoun forms were criticized: such nouns position males alone as agents, exclude women from specific careers, and, as well, make women in those careers invisible. Objections to gender-neutral forms merely exposes a lack of creativity on the part of the speaker because English makes so many options available—for example, *police officer*, *firefighter*, and *letter carrier*. Instead of *salesman* or *saleswoman*, *salesperson* and *sales representative* are commonly used; in fact, *sales representative* has become so well established that *sales rep* is now common in informal usage. *Spokesperson* for *spokesman*, may sound "awkward" to some, but it is becoming more common and may become standard. (Of course, there is absolutely nothing wrong with sex-specific terms like *spokesman* and *spokeswoman* when the sex of the individual is known.)

Occupations that once had two forms, one for women with an identifying suffix (-*ess* or -*ette*) and one for men (without a suffix)—for example, *steward* and *stewardess*, have either been replaced entirely (*flight attendant*), or the specifically female forms have been abandoned; thus *poet* and *author* are used for both men and women, and *poetess* and *authoress* are obsolescent. Sometimes, however, the specifically feminine form can be used for economy, as in, "There are relatively few jobs for middle-aged and older actresses," when the alternative, "There are relatively few jobs for middle-aged and older women actors," requires an extra word. In fact, some writers prefer to use forms that make women more visible as agents in the world. Using *actor* or *poet* to refer to women, they argue, implicitly accepts the idea that men are properly at the center of the universe because the neutralization has shifted to the formerly male-only term. Avoid the female nouns with the suffixes *-ess* and *-ette*, however, because they suggest that women are inferior to men, a trivialization explicit in pairs of terms like *major* and *majorette*, where the female-specific term is clearly applied to a vocation perceived as less significant.

Do not make irrelevant references to race, gender, religion, or ethnicity, as in, "Mr. James McPherson, the new CFO, is an African American from King of Prussia, Pennsylvania, and a graduate of the Wharton School of Business." Mr. McPherson's being an African American is no more relevant to his new position than, say, Mr. Michael Canavan's being a red-haired Irishman is to his.

There simply are no terms with positive connotations for referring to people with physical, mental, or emotional handicaps, and the euphemisms that have been suggested (for example, *physically challenged* and *differently abled*) are demeaning. *Disabled* and *disability* remain the most widely accepted terms, but do not make tactless distinctions that treat nondisabled people as "normal" and disabled people as freaks or "abnormal" as in, "The automatic doors are only for the disabled; the 'normals' are supposed to use the revolving doors." Instead, say something like, "The automatic doors are only for the disabled; others should use the revolving doors."

Try to avoid specifically religious terms. The traditional "Christmas holiday" has been changed to "the holidays." Yet many businesses are closed for Rosh Hashana and Yom Kippur, which are Jewish observances, and for Good Friday, which is Protestant and Roman Catholic, but not usually for other holy days. As Eastern Orthodox Christians, Muslims, and Hindus become more prominent in the United States, ways of recognizing religious holidays on the office calendar will have to change because it is inappropriate to acknowledge only the observations of Protestants, Catholics, and Jews. It is an unfortunate habit, for example, for salespeople and receptionists to end a transaction in December by saying "Merry Christmas," but saying "Have a happy holiday" or "Happy holidays" is neutral yet still conveys the speaker's good wishes, which is the intent.

OFFICE POLITICS

Many people believe that human beings were born in order to gossip, and wherever there are three or more people, there will be politics. People are usually interested in other people and their lives— spouses, families, friends, neighbors, colleagues. Not to be interested in at least some people and curious about them is unusual. Success at work and promotion depend not only on how well you do your job but also on how well you get along with your colleagues. Nevertheless, you must be discreet and avoid the extremes of the loner and gossipmonger. A little common sense and consideration for the feelings of others, as with other office mores, will enable you to be genuinely interested in and caring of other people without being nosy or unduly prying .

- Realize that anything you say can become public knowledge in the office.
- Do not lose your temper in public.
- Keep confidential what was told to you in confidence, whether of a business or a personal nature.
- Correct gossip or a rumor that you *know* to be false.
- Do not criticize a subordinate in public.
- Do not inquire about the private lives of colleagues who are ordinarily reticent about their lives outside work.

HARASSMENT

All businesses have a fundamental responsibility, enforced by federal and state laws (through the U.S. Equal Employment Opportunity Commission [EEOC]), to treat employees with dignity and respect and to ensure that employees are not harassed because of their race, ethnic origin, sex, sexual orientation, age, religion, or disability. Should such harassment occur, it must result in immediate and effective disciplinary action. Managers in particular have the explicit responsibility to forbid and prevent the occurrence of harassment and to take immediate action when harassment is brought to their attention. Any complaints or instances of harassment should be immediately reported to management. The following guidelines identify the nature of harassment:

1. Harassment is written material, speech, or conduct that belittles or shows hostility or aversion to a person because of his or her race, ethnic origin, religion, sex, national origin, sexual orientation, age, or disability or that of his or her friends, relatives, or associates.
2. Harassment has the purpose or effect of creating a hostile, intimidating, or offensive working environment.
3. Harassment has the purpose or effect of unreasonably interfering with a person's performance at work or with a person's employment opportunities.
4. Harassment includes, but is not limited to, epithets, slurs, and negative stereotyping, as well as threatening, intimidating, or hostile acts relating to race, ethnic origin, religion, sex, national origin, sexual orientation, age, or disability.
5. Harassment also includes displayed or circulated graphic material such as photographs, pictures, or cartoons that belittles or shows hostility or aversion to a person because of race, ethnic origin, religion, sex, national origin, sexual orientation, age, or disability.

Someone who has been harassed, should:

- tell the harasser to stop the behavior (otherwise the harasser may think that the harassment will be tolerated);
- document the harassment, recording dates, times, places, circumstances, the kinds of behavior, and the attempts made to discourage or stop the harassment;
- keep evidence of harassment, such as offensive jokes or cartoons posted on a bulletin board;

- if the harassment persists, write to the harasser, complaining against the offensive behavior and demanding that it stop (and keep a copy of the letter or e-mail);
- if the harassment continues even after the letter, report the harassment to a supervisor (or to the person specified in the company handbook);
- if the harassment continues even after it has been reported to the company, file a complaint with the local EEOC office (employees who report harassment cannot be demoted or fired);
- if all else fails, consult an attorney about bringing a suit against the harasser.

SUBSTANCE ABUSE

Substance abuse includes excessive or illegal use of alcohol, pre-scription medications, and street drugs. Substance abuse is wide-spread throughout the United States and, therefore, in the workplace, and it results in millions of hours of lost productivity, inferior perfor-mance, absenteeism, and decline in office morale. The treatment of substance abuse is properly reserved for physicians, psychologists, and other health-care professionals, and, often, for legal authorities as well. There is very little, therefore, that a professional office worker can or should do except to suggest that individuals who seem to have a substance abuse problem seek help. The human resources depart-ments of many companies have brochures listing various health-care professionals who specialize in helping people with substance abuse problems.

ILLNESS AND INJURY

Illness and injury at work can range from fingers smashed in a door or a sprained ankle to a heart attack or diabetic coma. Many compa-nies have instructions in their employee handbook for dealing with medical emergencies. If your company has an in-house nurse, either take the victim to the nurse or, if the condition is serious enough, have the nurse treat the victim and arrange for ambulance or other services. If your company has no nurse on staff and the sick or injured person is able to report to a medical facility on his or her own, notify the manager or supervisor of the absence and arrange to have the individual's work duties covered by someone else. If the sickness or injury is serious, notify the manager or supervisor and call paramedics or a hospital emergency room or EMTs (emergency medical technicians). The manager will then notify the next of kin or human resources or legal departments in the company for possible insurance claims, workman's compensation, or negligence lawsuits.

DIFFICULT PEOPLE

Some employees and coworkers are difficult to work with or unpleasant to be around. As a result, morale, efficiency, and productivity suffer. The best thing, though not always possible, is to ignore chronic complainers and troublemakers and concentrate on your own work. If, however, the complainer is complaining to you and ignoring him or her is impossible, try to deflect the individual, not by agreeing, but by suggesting a positive alternative. If that doesn't work, politely say that you must concentrate on your work and cannot be distracted.

Do not become antagonistic or try to argue with complainers: that gives them the attention they want and the audience they need for further sounding off. If the person keeps directing his or her complaints to you to the point that you can no longer stand it or your work is adversely affected, report the problem to your supervisor or human resources department; a reprimand may stop the complaints. Under no circumstances should you lose your temper; that would only create a second problem. If a coworker or colleague is so disaffected by everything in the office or business, he or she will eventually quit or be fired.

Many businesses have public access. This means that you may at some time encounter someone who is mentally disturbed or irrationally angry with your company and who focuses attention on you

Coping With Difficult People

Every company has them. They come in every size and shape and age. Their behavior is marked by such unwelcome characteristics as brutishness, laziness, fearfulness, and pettiness. They make your job more difficult and less pleasant. The following are some personality types you will encounter, and some tips for coping with them:

1. **The Bear:** The bear has a vicious roar and roams the office trying to intimidate. To deal with the bear, use caution and a steady voice. Avoid office bears as much as possible, but when forced to deal with them, approach with firm resolve and an unflappable expression. If they know you aren't scared by them, they are less likely to use you as a target for their intimidation.

2. **The Slacker:** The slacker has somehow managed to work an unofficial three-day week for years and avoids all possible responsibility for anything. When you must depend on the slacker, firm consistency is the ticket to success. The sooner slackers realize that you won't stop your sweet but dogged pursuit of what you need, the sooner they react. CC'ing your boss or theirs in appropriate correspondence can be an effective tool, as slackers live to be perceived as useful in management's eyes.

3. **The Keeper:** To get anything done right, you have to work through the keeper. The keeper will never tell you how to do something. The keeper will never explain. Keepers think their jobs are protected because they keep what they know to themselves. Friendliness and a sympathetic ear are usually the best way to deal with keepers. They need to know that you are not a threat to their livelihood.

4. **The Credit Thief:** In the movie *Working Woman*, Sigourney Weaver takes credit for the ideas of her assistant, Melanie Griffith. In the end, Griffith winds up with Harrison Ford and a better job. Why? Because she could explain how she came up with the ideas. Sure, that's a Hollywood ending, but there is some wisdom there. Credit thieves indeed exist in the real world, but if you have a creative nature and you enjoy crafting solutions to problems, keep plugging away and you will be

(continued)

recognized. Don't worry about Sigourney Weaver...she will eventually shave her head and get impregnated by the Alien ...

5. **The Harasser:** This may be the worst kind of creature in the office world. The harasser often preys on those of lower rank and can be inappropriate in every way. Harassment can come in the form of racial or religious baiting or in sexual innuendos and advances. Do not let harassers go past the first step. Cut them off at the knees. If they make one single comment that you feel is inappropriate, immediately ask to speak with them in private and tell them that you took what they just said as offensive. More than likely, they will claim they never meant things that way, and perhaps you both can smile and shake hands before walking away. Chances are they will never bother you again. However, it is important that you detail this experience in writing and send a copy to yourself at home. Never open the envelope. Should the harassment be repeated at a later date, this sealed, postmarked letter is your proof that harassment occurred before and that you attempted to address it by confronting the person.

—*Evan Schnittman*

because you are accessible. If you cannot reason with a distracted or angry person and feel likely to be overwhelmed or even threatened, call for assistance from a coworker, a supervisor, or security.

MANAGING YOUR TIME

Professional success depends on your personality—how well you cooperate, take orders, follow instructions, and instruct others—and on your technical efficiency—how well you do your work and how quickly.

Experienced office professionals have built-in schedules. They know how much time to devote to daily or weekly tasks and short- or long-term projects; yet even they will feel the need to set up a work schedule when there is a major reorganization within the company, a change in supervisors, or a new project to begin.

Office professionals who have less experience or who are new to the company should set up a schedule of tasks. The schedule should be a grid made on graph paper or a legal pad and cover two or three weeks of tasks. Make a separate page for each working day (10 or 15 for two or three weeks). In a vertical column running down the left-hand side, list the times of your workday in 15-minute segments. Do not forget to put on your list your two 15-minute breaks (they follow federal guidelines, and, besides, you'll need them). Across the top of the page, list your daily tasks in a horizontal row (mail processing, correspondence, staff meetings, scheduling appointments, etc.). Put an "x" or a check mark under each task in the corresponding time-column. If you are new on the job, give yourself plenty of time for each task.

You may find a daily, weekly, or even monthly pattern in your work. Monday mornings, for example, may be especially busy for incoming mail, and therefore you may need more time on Monday morning to process mail than on any other day of the week. Friday afternoons may be relatively slow, and you can then allot several blocks of uninterrupted time for tasks requiring long periods of concentration (preparing budget reports, annual reports, etc.).

You may be able to combine similar tasks, such as sorting incoming mail and writing correspondence, into the same time periods or spread out similar routine tasks that are too numerous or boring to do at one stretch over several different periods in one day or over several days. Eventually, as you acquire experience and proficiency, you will require less time to perform your tasks and you will be able to set aside blocks of time. You can either volunteer for extra work or study some aspect of your business, such as how the computer network operates or the history and development of the business and its accounts. Either option will benefit you personally and help your career.

Realize, too, that you are not locked into an established schedule no matter how efficient it makes your work. Flexibility is necessary to accommodate routine occurrences such as the illness of a coworker or an unexpected business development.

Do not ignore your break times. Walking around the block, enjoying a solitary cup of coffee, or joking and chatting with coworkers will refresh you physically and mentally, and you will work more smoothly and efficiently.

Time Wasters

Even the most dedicated employees will find themselves wasting time during working hours. At times, a brief diversion from the demands of the job can be just what you need to stay fresh and focused throughout the day. However, it is important to keep those diversions in check and never to lose sight of the fact that you're being paid to work, not to kill time. Familiarize yourself with the specific policies that your company may have regarding time-management issues and be compliant. Some of the most common time-wasting activities are listed below. It's not the occasional indulgence in any of these that is problematic. It is the cumulative effect of "a little time here, a little time there" that can eat into an otherwise productive day. So think about what the company is expecting from you when you engage in any of the following:

1. Talking to friends and family on the phone.
2. Exchanging "instant messages" with friends and family.
3. E-mailing friends and family.
4. Playing Internet games or participating in Internet chat rooms or bulletin boards.
5. Customizing your desktop background and screensaver.
6. Taking extended breaks and wandering around the office.
7. Visiting with co-workers. (Remember: positive, friendly interactions with colleagues should be encouraged, but should never turn into lengthy or frequent gabfests.)
8. Running errands.
9. Conducting personal business.
10. Daydreaming at your desk.

—Evan Schnittman

CHAPTER 4

Telecommunications

After more than a century of use, the telephone has undergone remarkable advances in technology that provide the workplace with more options and conveniences than could have been imagined even a generation ago. Much of today's business is conducted over telephone lines, from push-button systems, to computers, to cell phones. It is important to know the kind of system that will best accommodate your business's rate of growth. Depending on the size of your business, you may want to consider, for example, whether you need an automated operator or attendant, or a receptionist to handle incoming calls.

TELEPHONE TECHNOLOGY

There are several telephone systems available that will meet the needs of most businesses, depending on several factors:

• *Intercom:* This system works best in a company that has fewer than ten people working in the same vicinity. A receptionist answers a call and announces who it is for over the intercom: "Christine, you have a call on line 1." Each employee has an extension at his or her desk for taking calls. This system is very limited and doesn't allow for growth, such as the addition of voice mail, call waiting, and so forth.

• *Single or multiline:* This system incorporates the push-button system, which allows anyone to place or receive calls from his or her extension. It works well for small- to medium-sized businesses.

• *Exchange:* This is an advanced system. Incoming calls are handled through a receptionist or an automated attendant. A private branch exchange (PBX) offers features such as automatic call distribution, call forwarding, call waiting, conference call capabilities, and voice mail. It requires extensive wiring and equipment. A central office exchange service (CENTREX) is a more costly option, with a price-per-minute charge, but existing phones can be used and no rewiring is necessary. It also handles such features as call forwarding, call transferring, conference calls, and voice mail.

TELEPHONE FEATURES

Telephones and telephone systems offer many convenient features for the workplace. Reviewing the benefits of each feature with a telephone company representative before incorporating any of them into your system will help you to avoid wasting money on unnecessary features.

• *Answering machines:* Answering machines offer you the ability to record messages when you are not available to answer the phone, and to play them back at your convenience. Messages can be digitally recorded or recorded onto cassette tapes. Many models offer extra features such as caller ID, remote access, call waiting, and message protection.

• *Automatic attendant:* Automatic attendant plays a recorded message to handle incoming phone calls, replacing a live operator. It is especially useful during nonbusiness hours. It can be frustrating to callers, though, if the outgoing messages are long and the options are numerous. Be sure your options do not lead to dead ends. During business hours, callers should be able to speak to someone, so be sure that that option is available if at all possible.

• *Automatic call distribution:* Companies dealing with numerous incoming calls often have a central location or server that handles them initially and then transfers each call to the first available person who can handle it, usually with an automated message such as "Please hold for the next available representative."

• *Automatic speed dialing:* This feature lets you program frequently called numbers for quick access. It may be accessed by entering a code or by pushing a button, depending on your system.

• *Beepers and pagers:* Beepers and pagers offer the ability to be available to receive calls even when you are not in the office. The beeper chirps or beeps when someone is calling you. The signal goes first to the beeper service, and the message is transmitted to the beeper, which signals you to call in. The more advanced units, often called pagers, can also vibrate to let you know you have a message, a signal that is less intrusive in public than the beeping sound. Pagers can also display a number to call or a short message. As cell phones became more common and multifunctional, beepers and pagers may eventually be phased out.

• *Buzzer:* This telephone feature, with the push of a button, signals the recipient of a call to pick up the receiver.

• *Call accounting:* Call accounting allows you to monitor outgoing calls, usually to safeguard against the misuse of business phones for personal use. Outside providers offer a feature called station message detail recording (SMDR) for such telephone traffic analysis.

• *Call blocking:* This option allows you to specify phone numbers you'd like to prevent from coming through. You can also prevent your name and telephone number from appearing on others' caller-ID displays when you call them, although some companies require that you unblock this feature before they will accept your call.

• *Call forwarding:* Call forwarding allows you to forward all your calls to another number. This feature is especially helpful if you will be away from your desk for a long period of time. You can forward your call to another extension or phone number.

• *Call sequencing:* For businesses with a high volume of incoming calls, this feature is useful for monitoring the sequence of calls and lets you know which one should be taken next.

• *Call transferring:* This feature allows you to transfer a call to another number.

- *Call waiting:* Call waiting alerts you when someone is trying to call you while you're talking to someone else. The recipient has the option of placing the first call on hold to answer the second, ending the first call to take the second, or ignoring the second call.
- *Caller ID:* With caller ID, you know when important calls are coming through, even if you're on another call. Caller ID identifies the number or name of the person trying to get through, providing that caller does not have call blocking.
- *Conference calls:* This feature allows you to communicate with two or more people at the same time, with just one call, no matter where they are located.
- *Continuous redial:* If you reach a busy signal, the continuous re-dial feature will continue to dial the number until it becomes available.
- *Cordless phones:* A cordless phone offers the convenience of being able to talk into a receiver and walk around without the hindrance of wires or cords, but you are often limited in how far you can be from the base unit that recharges the battery.
- *Dial safeguards:* A device can be added to your telephone system to prevent unauthorized long-distance calls or access to restricted numbers.
- *Direct inward dialing (DID):* Direct inward dialing provides direct access to incoming calls to individual phones, eliminating the need for an attendant to connect every call.
- *Direct inward system access:* This feature allows employees to access long-distance company lines, even when they are not in the building, by using an authorization code.
- *Headsets:* Headsets offer hands-free communication, a useful feature for offices handling many phone calls that require the keying of information into computer databases or the handling of paperwork.
- *Hold:* Putting a caller on hold by pushing a button gives the recipient the opportunity to notify other people that they have calls or to find information for the caller. Callers often listen to preprogrammed music, a message, or a signal while they wait.
- *Last-call return:* This feature allows you to redial the last number you called by pressing a button.

- *LCD display:* Many telephones feature this display window. It may show the number you have dialed, the name or number of an incoming call, or the date and time.
- *Least-cost routing:* An outside provider can offer this feature, which finds the most cost-effective route for long-distance calls.
- *Line-status indicator:* Many telephones feature a button that lights up to indicate if a particular line is busy (often a solid light) or on hold (often a blinking light). When a call is on hold, often there is an intermittent beeping as a reminder to the recipient.
- *Message waiting:* Some telephones have a light or signal to alert you that the receptionist or attendant has a message for you.
- *Messaging:* This feature allows you to leave brief messages on someone's telephone display. A sophisticated line of PC messaging devices is also now available.
- *Music on hold:* This feature provides music, on tape or through a radio station, for callers to listen to while on hold.
- *Paging:* This feature allows you to announce a call or relay a message for a particular person through speakerphones if that person is away from his or her desk.
- *PC cordless phones:* With this feature, your cordless phone is connected to your personal computer to manage incoming calls, and offer voice mail, caller ID, call blocking, and so forth.
- *Picturephones:* If both caller and recipient have this feature, you can see the person to whom you are speaking through a small screen on your telephone.
- *Priority calls:* This feature enables you to assign a distinctive ring to selected numbers.
- *Remote-station answering:* This feature allows you to answer someone else's telephone from your own.
- *Speakerphones:* This feature allows you to speak and listen to a caller without lifting the receiver.
- *Speed calling:* With this feature, you can program frequently dialed telephone numbers and access them quickly, often with a two-digit code number of your choice.

- *Toll restriction:* This feature allows you to restrict the types of long-distance calls being made to specific kinds of telephone numbers, such as 900 numbers, international calls, Operator, Caribbean area codes, and so on.
- *Voice mail:* Voice mail acts as a personal answering machine on your telephone. It records incoming calls and plays them back at your discretion. It may be part of your telephone system or be provided by an outside source.

TELEPHONE COST CONTROL

Every company, whether large or small, is concerned with cost-effectiveness. Cutting costs significantly can often help ward off downsizing. One way to do this is to actively and consistently monitor outgoing long-distance telephone calls. It may even be advantageous to advise, in the employee handbook, that personal use of the company telephone for long-distance calls is forbidden and may result in unpleasant consequences.

Companies should also check their phone bills regularly to be sure they are not being charged for features or services they do not have. Cost control can also include keeping employees informed as to what services are more costly than others, or the most inexpensive way to place certain calls.

TELEPHONE COMPANY SERVICES

Check with your local telephone company for the services they provide. Those services usually include some of the following:

- *Calling cards:* Some companies provide calling cards to their employees, enabling them to place calls away from the office and charge them to the company. Long-distance providers offer international calling cards as well. For infrequent travelers, prepaid phone cards is a solution that avoids monthly invoicing. A specific number of minutes is purchased in advance, to be used as needed.

- *Cell phones:* Cell phones have become a popular and valuable means of communication, providing a mobile connection to the working world through strategically located transmission towers. The signal is routed from one tower to another as the cell phone user travels from one area to another. It is important to check competing cellular services before signing up, because each has different requirements, options, and geographic limitations, and higher fees may be charged when a call is placed outside the service area. Buy a digital cell phone. It offers less interference, high-quality sound, and greater privacy than the analog type. If you use a cell phone while driving, be knowledgeable about applicable state laws. In some states, for example, it is illegal to hold a cell phone while driving. Many cell phones can be equipped with a voice recognition feature for hands-free communication. Some units also have the capacity for hookups to e-mail, fax machines, and the Internet.

- *Teletypewriter (TTY):* A TTY device (sometimes referred to as a TDD—telecommunication device for the deaf) enables people who are deaf, hard of hearing, or speech impaired, to communicate by typing their messages back and forth. A TTY device is required at both ends of the conversation. If only one person has such a device, a call can still be made by using a telecommunications relay service.

- *Telecommunications relay service (TRS):* A TTY user types a message that is then intercepted by an operator provided by a TRS. The operator then reads the message to the recipient, who answers by voice, and types the return message to the TTY user.

- *Wide area telephone service (WATS):* This service allows a company to make an unlimited number of long-distance telephone calls within a specific service area for a monthly fee, or to receive calls from specific areas at no charge to the caller.

TELEPHONE TECHNIQUES

As soon as you pick up a telephone, you are setting the tone for your company. Being pleasant to those on the other end of the line can mean the difference between bringing in a new client or turning someone away.

Using the telephone effectively in a business context is the equal responsibility of the caller and the recipient of the call. In business, as in any other area of daily life, people expect and deserve courtesy in their dealings with others, and the golden rule still applies: treat other people as well as you expect (and deserve) to be treated.

TELEPHONE ETIQUETTE

Answering the Phone

Never walk past a ringing telephone; an unanswered phone call is an opportunity lost. Take a message or transfer the call to someone who can help. The caller could be a new customer who has never done business with your company or could be your oldest and best customer. People will judge your competence and the quality of your service and product by how promptly the phone is answered and how their calls are handled. A few simple rules of courtesy will keep everyone happy.

1. Try to answer the phone by the third ring.
2. Put a smile in your voice when you answer the phone (no matter how you feel) and speak clearly, identifying the company, the department, and yourself: "Good morning/afternoon, Westville Widgets Customer Service. This is Howard Stein. How can I help you?"
3. Avoid using jargon or slang. Speak simply and in complete sentences.
4. Sound interested in what the caller has to say and listen carefully. If you have to take a message, write down the caller's name, company, telephone number, and reason for calling, and repeat the information to the caller to be sure you have written everything correctly. Record your name and the date and time of the call, and be sure that

the message gets to the person for whom it is intended or to someone who can respond appropriately.

5. If you must put the caller on hold, ask for permission. If you know that you'll be away from the phone for more than five minutes, be honest and tell the person that. This gives him or her the option of calling back.

6. If you have to transfer the call, tell the caller so and provide the correct telephone number or extension for his or her future use. Be sure that you know how to transfer calls correctly. Nothing is worse than inadvertently disconnecting callers or sending them to the wrong individual or department.

7. Be especially patient and courteous when handling customer who is upset. Let the person say whatever is bothering him or her before you respond. When the person has finished, acknowledge his or her dissatisfaction and offer to do what you can to help. Be honest and realistic with the customer about what you can or cannot do, and ask the customer if he or she is satisfied with your proposed solution.

8. Never say "I don't know" to a customer. If you don't have an answer or know what to do, ask the customer to wait, put him or her on hold, and quickly find someone who can help or resolve the problem.

Making a Call

In business, how you make a call is just as important as how you receive calls, and similar rules apply.

1. Sound cheerful and confident. Speak clearly, and identify yourself, the company you represent, the department (if appropriate), and your reason for calling.

2. If the person you are calling is out of the office or unable to take your call, leave a message with your name, your company, and your reason for calling. Be sure that the

person taking the message has written everything down correctly.

3. Don't use jargon or slang, and speak in simple, clear sentences.

4. If the person answering your call says that he or she has to put you on hold, ask how long you can expect to be on hold. If you don't want to be on hold, say so, and either ask to leave a message or tell the person that you'll call again later.

5. If the person who has answered your call has to transfer the call, ask for the correct telephone number or extension so that you can call the appropriate individual directly in the future.

6. Never call anyone when you're angry. Wait until you have calmed down and are able to speak calmly and coherently. If you have a problem or complaint but cannot describe it clearly, the person who takes your call will be unable to understand what has happened and, as a result, may be ineffective in responding to the situation. Describe the situation or occurrence that has upset you, and ask to speak to someone who can help resolve the problem.

7. Be gracious and patient, and most people will respond in kind.

CELL PHONES

A cell phone, like a noncellular telephone, has tremendous interruptive potential: we cannot control its use at the caller's end. It is aggravating enough to be constantly interrupted by your own ringing telephone. It is even more aggravating when it is someone else's phone. Many people regard cell phones as handy devices for staying in touch, while others, especially businesspeople whose work requires them to be out of the office frequently, have come to think of them as indispensable adjuncts. But there are also people who consider cell phones to be nuisances that increase the noise pollution in public places. More than 100 million people in the United States use cell phones regularly, and that number increases daily by 46,000. As the number of cell phones increases, so does the potential for unwanted noise in public spaces and aggravation on the part of those imposed on by their discourteous use. As a result, a lack of courtesy on the part of cell phone users has created a backlash, and demands for legal restrictions on cell phone use continue to escalate.

Observing a few common-sense rules will make the people around you much happier and you can still get that critical call you're waiting for.

1. Turn off your cell phone in public places—theaters, restaurants, schools, concert halls, churches, and so forth—or use the phone's silent or vibration options. No matter how important that call may be, a ringing phone in the middle of a meal, during the playing of a symphony, or at the most intense moment in a movie is rude and intrusive. Either leave your phone at home or, if you're expecting an important call while you're in a public place, set the phone to vibrate. Should the call come through, leave your seat, and take the call where no one else can hear your conversation. Otherwise, let voice mail take the message.

2. Never accept a call during a business meeting or while you're involved in a face-to-face conversation with a client or customer. To do so tells other people that they are less important than the individual who called you, and you risk alienating your colleagues and losing customers. If you expect to receive a call that you must take during a meeting with other people, tell them in advance that you're expecting an important call and will excuse yourself in order to take it. Better, tell the person who is going to call you that you'll be unable to take the call for a specific period and arrange a time for the

conversation when you are not otherwise occupied. Or,
let your voice mail take the message.

3. Never conduct business in a public social setting. If you
take your work with you to a movie or a concert, you
won't enjoy yourself and neither will those around you.
Leave your phone at home or in your car.

4. Do not turn your back on a colleague or client in order to
accept a call. If it's a call that you absolutely must take,
set your phone to vibrate, explain to the individual(s) that
you're expecting an urgent call, and excuse yourself in
order to take it. And make it brief!

5. If your work requires you to spend a great deal of time in
your car and away from your office, and you need your
cell phone in order to stay connected, do not use it while
you're driving. If you're talking on the phone, your mind
is not fully focused on your driving or the conversation. If
you must make or receive a call while driving, pull off to
the side of the highway. If you're driving in town, find a
parking lot and have your conversation. No phone call is
worth endangering your life or the lives of other people.

6. If you use your phone while in a public conveyance (a
cab, bus, train, etc.), speak at a normal level. Do not shout
or yell when using your phone. Forcing other people to
endure your noise is inconsiderate. Most cell phones are
equipped with sensitive microphones. If there's
interference or static, yelling won't help anyway.

ANSWERING MACHINES AND VOICE MAIL

When putting messages for incoming calls on an answering machine
or voice mail, keep your greeting brief. Ask callers to leave their
name, a phone number, the date and time, and the reason for the call.
When your call is answered by an answering machine or voice mail,
speak slowly and leave your name, phone number, the date and time,

and a brief message. In any case, don't waste time with clichés like "Have a nice day."

SPEAKER PHONES

If you use a speaker phone, inform callers of that fact and ask whether they mind if you use it. If other people are nearby and will be forced to overhear your conversation, ask their permission as well before turning it on.

PAGERS

Although there are fewer pagers (beepers) in service than cell phones (approximately 40 million), their use still requires courtesy and respect for other people. For recipients of messages, the same rules apply that have been described for cell phones. For callers, however, a couple of additional considerations will improve your calling manners. First, keep your message very brief. Most pagers can only receive numeric messages anyway. Second, some companies will refuse to transmit any words they regard as obscene or offensive. Therefore, you should avoid potentially offensive language when addressing a client or a colleague as a matter of principle.

FAXES

Fax machines have made it possible to send and receive text quickly, a plus for businesspeople who often need information faster than any delivery service can manage. As with other kinds of electronic communications, the ability to transmit information through telephone lines requires sensitivity to what is and is not appropriate behavior. Above all, be respectful of the people to whom you send faxes and considerate of their time. Readability and brevity are essential. A few dos and don'ts will keep your recipients happy and make you look good.

1. Never send a fax without first contacting the recipient. Make sure that your recipient wants to receive the document and is prepared for its transmission. Sending an unsolicited fax is annoying. Sending one to a machine that isn't turned on is futile.

2. Use a cover sheet that includes: the recipient's name and both the telephone and fax numbers; your name and telephone and fax numbers; the date of the transmittal; the total number of pages (including the cover sheet) that you're transmitting. Indicate which number is the telephone number and which is the fax number—for example, Phone: 212-555-1212, Fax: 212-555-1213.

3. Start your text with a clear sentence that informs the recipient(s) of your purpose for sending the fax, the topic to be discussed, and the response you're expecting.

4. If the document is more than one page, provide headings. Headings make your text look more professional and, in addition, make it easier for the recipients to read (and respond to) the text quickly.

5. Simplify the text you're sending as much as possible. Keeping it simple saves time and money for everyone involved. Always remove graphics that aren't essential to your text, including cartoons, clever sayings, and any shading. Limit your use of dark colors in particular. Because such material takes a lot of time to transmit, it runs up your telephone bill and ties up your recipient's fax machine. Also, the recipients will not appreciate the unnecessary depletion of ink from their fax cartridges.

6. Keep your text as brief as possible. As a general rule, don't fax any document that is longer than five pages. If it runs more than five pages and it's really important, fax only the crucial information your recipient must have immediately and send the entire text by overnight delivery. If you send a very long document, say 30 pages, the recipient's fax machine may run out of paper and the

entire text will not be received, which defeats your purpose.

7. Use a large font size, at least 12-point, and avoid fancy or italic typefaces because their delicacy makes them difficult to read in a fax. Clear, simple typefaces, such as Times Roman, will make your document much easier to read. In addition, leaving sufficient white space around the text improves its readability.

8. Make it easy for your recipient to respond, especially to international faxes. For example, in an overseas fax number, a 0 (zero) may appear in front of the city code (for example, 046). When dialing from the United States, the 0 is unnecessary.

CHAPTER 5

The Mail

POSTAL MAIL: THE UNITED STATES POSTAL SERVICE

For up-to-date postal rates and guidelines on size and weight restrictions, visit www.usps.com, the Web site of the United States Postal Service (USPS). This informative site also provides a calculator for both domestic and international shipments. One simply keys in weight and measurements and the calculator figures the postage required. Pickup service is available for a flat rate (regardless of number of pieces being shipped) on certain postal categories, such as Priority Mail and Express Mail. The Web site offers a toll-free number to call for details about pickup options.

First-Class Mail

First-Class Mail is used for personal correspondence, bills and statements of account, items sealed or otherwise closed against inspection, and items wholly or partly in writing or typewriting. A piece of first-class mail may not measure less than 5 inches long, 3.5 inches high, and 0.007 inch thick, and its weight must not exceed 13 ounces.

Priority Mail

Priority Mail offers two-day service to most domestic destinations but is not intended for overnight service. The item being sent cannot weigh more than 70 pounds and must be clearly marked "Priority Mail." Priority Mail envelopes and boxes, as well as "Priority Mail" stickers, are available through the USPS.

Express Mail

Express Mail offers next-day delivery by noon to most destinations in the United States and is delivered 365 days a year. Express Mail envelopes, labels, and boxes are available, free of charge, from the USPS. Items must weigh 70 pounds or less.

Parcel Post

Books, circulars, and catalogs may be sent Parcel Post, provided they weigh no more than 70 pounds. Each package must be marked "Parcel Post" in the postage area.

Bound Printed Matter

According to the USPS, Bound Printed Matter must meet certain criteria. It must:

- consist of advertising, promotional, directory, or editorial material (or any combination thereof);
- be securely bound with permanent fastenings such as glue, staples, or stitching (loose-leaf binders and similar fastenings are not considered permanent);
- not be personal correspondence of any kind;
- not be stationery, such as pads of blank forms;
- not exceed 15 pounds.

Rates vary according to weight and destination. Check the USPS Web site for dimension restrictions and other criteria.

Media Mail (Book Rate)

This category of mail includes books, film, printed music or test materials, sound recordings, scripts, educational charts, loose-leaf pages and binders consisting of medical information, and computer-readable media. Be sure to check the Web site for restrictions on advertising. Mark each package "Media Mail" in the postage area.

Standard Mail (A)

Formerly known as third-class mail, this category is used for circulars, catalogs, booklets, printed matter, and photographs. It can be used for items weighing less than one pound each, 200 pieces or 50 pounds per mailing, and is available to businesses and nonprofit organizations. USPS personnel can inspect this type of mail, whether sealed or unsealed. Individuals can also use it for mailing parcels weighing less than one pound. There are certain restrictions for sorting, bundling, or labeling, so check with the USPS in your area.

Standard Mail (B)

Formerly known as fourth-class mail, this category is used for mailing packages weighing more than one pound. There is no guaranteed delivery time and USPS personnel can inspect this type of mail also. Check with the USPS for size and weight restrictions. Rates vary depending on weight and destination.

Special Services

CERTIFICATE OF MAILING.

A Certificate of Mailing is purchased at the time of mailing and is used as proof of mailing, not delivery. No receipts are involved.

CERTIFIED MAIL.

This service provides the sender with a receipt. The USPS keeps a record of this transaction, but no insurance coverage is provided. It can be used with first-class mail and priority mail.

COLLECT ON DELIVERY (COD).

COD allows senders to collect the price of goods and/or postage on merchandise ordered by the recipient when it is delivered. It can be used for items shipped first-class mail, express mail, priority mail, parcel post, bound printed matter, and media mail. A record of this service is kept by the USPS, and it can be combined with other services but cannot be used for international mail, APO, or FPO addresses.

INSURED MAIL.

This service provides coverage against loss or damage of shipped goods. Insurance coverage must not exceed the value of the item(s) being shipped.

RETURN RECEIPT AND RETURN RECEIPT FOR MERCHANDISE.

Return receipt can be requested before or after mailing and provides proof that the item was delivered, and it indicates to whom it was delivered and when it was delivered. It can be used for express mail, certified mail, COD, registered mail, and mail insured for over $50. It can also be combined with other restricted mail options, as documented on the USPS Web site.

Return receipt for merchandise provides the sender with a mailing receipt and a return receipt. A record is kept by the USPS and provides the sender with the correct address information, if different from the address originally used by the sender.

REGISTERED MAIL.

Registered Mail offers the maximum protection and security for valuables, providing a mailing receipt and delivery record maintained by the USPS. Postal insurance is provided for items with a declared value up to a maximum of $25,000. Items over $25,000 are subject to a handling charge.

RESTRICTED DELIVERY.

Restricted Delivery gives the sender the ability to mail an item directly to a specified individual. It may be used for first-class mail, priority mail, parcel post, bound printed matter, media mail that is sent certified mail, COD, registered mail, and mail insured for more than $50.

SPECIAL HANDLING.

This service provides preferential care and handling of items requiring delicate treatment. It does not provide preferential delivery.

Postage Meters

Many businesses choose to use postage meters because they offer convenience and expediency in handling mail. You can print postage for first-class, priority, express, parcels, and international mail. Once the item to be mailed is weighed on an authorized postage scale, the proper postage rate can be found by logging onto the USPS Web site [www.usps.com]. A business envelope may be scanned through the postage meter for the proper postage amount, or a label may be fed through and affixed onto the envelope or package.

Service and leasing fees for postage meters are set by the manufacturers. The USPS has four authorized providers:

Ascom Hasler Mailing Systems, Inc.
19 Forest Parkway
Shelton, CT 06484-6140
800-243-6275
www.ascom-usa.com

Francotyp-Postalia, Inc.
140 N. Mitchell Court, Suite 200
Addison, IL 60101-5629
800-341-6052
www.fp-usa.com

Neopost
30955 Huntwood Avenue
Hayward, CA 94544-7084
800-624-7892
www.neopostinc.com

Pitney Bowes, Inc.
1 Elmcroft Road
Stamford, CT 06926-0700
800-322-8000
www.pitneybowes.com

International Mail

International Mail should be addressed in English as follows:

Line 1: name of addressee
Line 2: street address or post office box number
Line 3: city or town name, other principal subdivision
(i.e., province, state, country, etc.), and postal code
(Note: In some countries, the postal code may precede the
city or town name, as in Canada.)
Line 4: country

Be sure to print in uppercase letters the sender's address, including country, in the upper left corner of the package or envelope. As a precaution, senders should place a piece of paper inside the package with the entire address printed on it.

International mail is subject to customs examination when it arrives at its destination. There are exemptions, and individual countries may have specific requirements for mail handling, which are listed at the USPS Web site. There are four basic categories of international mail:

1. *Global Express Guaranteed™ (GXG):* This service is the product of an alliance between the USPS and DHL Worldwide Express, Inc. It provides high-speed, reliable delivery service to principal locations in more than 200 countries and territorial possessions. If destination-specific delivery standards are not met, postage will be refunded. Shipments are insured against loss, damage, or rifling, at no additional charge, up to a value of $100, and there is optional insurance for up to a maximum of $2,499. The maximum weight limit for GXG shipments is 70 pounds.

2. *Global Express Mail™ (EMS):* EMS is a high-speed, reliable service for mailing time-sensitive items to more than 175 countries and territorial possessions. It provides "on demand" handling and delivery. Insurance is available at no additional charge for values up to $100. Optional insurance is available for values over $100 on merchandise only. EMS does not offer a money-back service guarantee. A return-receipt service for EMS shipments is available to certain countries at no additional charge.

3. *Global Priority Mail™ (GPM):* A GPM envelope or sticker furnished by the USPS provides the customer with an accelerated airmail service. It is an economical means of sending correspondence, business documents, printed matter, and lightweight merchandise to areas such as Canada, Mexico, and other specified destination countries. These items receive priority handling in the United States and the destination country. As with domestic priority mail, senders have the option of flat-rate or variable-weight postage. The maximum weight limit is four pounds.

4. *Letter-post:* "Letter-post" is the accepted term for classes of international mail formerly referred to as LC (Letters and Cards) and AO (Other Articles). It may include letters, packages, postcards, printed matter, and small packets, and can be sent as airmail or economy (surface) mail. The maximum weight is four pounds.

PRIVATE DELIVERY SERVICES

While the USPS is the leading carrier of mail—delivering to over 130 million addresses, including over 20 million post office boxes—several well-established companies (Federal Express, UPS, and Airborne, to name a few) provide delivery services as well. They offer the convenience of pickup and delivery of letters and packages, along with listings of drop-off locations. Supplies of stickers, mailing envelopes, and boxes are offered free of charge by many of these companies, and an account can be opened with them (some charge a monthly fee). They also offer online services and information: drop-off and pick-up times, packaging requirements, rates, and options such as overnight, next-day air, two-day delivery, and so on.

MAIL SAFETY AND SECURITY

After the anthrax incidents that followed the terrorist attacks of September 11, 2001, many people became concerned about the safety of the mail they receive. However, most corporations have had mail safety procedures in place for some time. If your company does not, you may want to take a few precautions when handling the mail:

1. Accept packages for current employees only.
2. Refuse packages without an employee's name, and either discard them or return them to sender.
3. Accept mail only from postal employees, special delivery employees, or courier services known to you. If a courier arrives with a suspicious package, ask to call the courier's dispatcher. If the courier refuses, refuse the package.
4. Learn to be suspicious of certain physical attributes of envelopes and parcels. Certainly, a ticking sound or protruding wires would concern the most careless person, but an alert mail handler will watch for these other signs as well:

    > oily stains, leaks, or discoloration
    > excessive postage
    > handwritten, poorly typed, or cut-and-paste lettering
    > an incomplete or generic address, such as "President" or "CEO" but with no name
    > misspellings of common words
    > no return address
    > unusual heaviness
    > uneven or lopsided packaging
    > excessive wrapping material such as masking tape, string, etc.
    > unusual artwork or pictures on the package
    > an excessive marking of "Personal" or "Confidential"
    > a postmark that does not match the return address

If you do receive a suspicious letter or package, report the package to building security and your supervisor. They should notify local police or other law enforcement officials. Do not shake or open the letter or package. Put the package or letter in a plastic bag, and wash

Reducing Mail Theft

A few simple precautions can reduce mail theft:

1. Create a trail for each package that enters the building. Each person who takes possession of a package on and after delivery should sign for it.
2. If a package cannot be delivered immediately to an employee, it should be kept in a secure place with limited access.
3. Do not place new employees in the mail room. New employees should pass their probationary period before handling the mail.
4. Keep outgoing mail in a secure place, and limit access to it.
5. Limit access to the postage meter and account for its use.

your hands with soap and water. You should make a list of all the people in the room or area when the package was received, and give this list to an official investigator.

If a suspicious package or envelope spills powder or other suspicious substances, do not try to clean it up. Cover the spill immediately with paper or a trash can. Turn off any fans or ventilation systems in the area, if possible. Leave the room and close it off, and wash your hands with soap and water. Notify building security and your supervisor. If powder or another substance has contaminated your clothing, remove the clothing as soon as possible and put it in a plastic bag. Give the bag to law enforcement personnel when they arrive. Shower as soon as possible, but do not use harsh detergents, disinfectant, or bleach on your skin.

E-MAIL

As computer use in the workplace has become increasingly more commonplace, so has the custom of communicating via electronic mail, known more familiarly as "e-mail."

Although hard copy is still kept on file in certain cases, e-mail has largely replaced typewritten, photocopied, and hand-distributed interoffice memos, along with typewritten correspondence sent via the postal service to outside parties. E-mail correspondence saves paper, and a record can be kept of the e-mail by storing it in a customized computer file. Most companies offer the option for, or even encourage, prospective employees to submit their résumés through e-mail.

Among the general guidelines that apply to the drafting and sending of e-mails is the advice not to key the text of a message in all uppercase letters, which is the equivalent of yelling at the recipient. Another advisable practice is to be concise, remembering that many professionals receive a multitude of e-mails throughout the day and often don't have the time to read thoroughly each piece of correspondence. Because the recipient may have to evaluate which incoming messages have the greatest priority, it may be to the sender's advantage to use the subject line as an attention grabber, especially if the objective is to get a response as soon as possible. Also, the subject line can be used to identify the sender, as sometimes the reading of e-mail may be delayed because the recipient does not recognize the sender's name or address. If the sender is unknown, or the subject-line message is particularly obscure or cryptic, there is a chance that the recipient may, as a precautionary measure against viruses, disregard the e-mail altogether and delete the message without opening it.

E-mail messages being sent off-site should end with a closing signature that includes the sender's full name and business affiliation. Most e-mail programs provide an option whereby a closing signature may be created and automatically appended to all outgoing messages.

It is good business practice to use the "reply" option to an existing message rather than opening a "new message" page. The "reply" gives the recipient a link, commonly called a thread, to the original message, and a path to follow if several replies to one message pile up. Or, if the incoming message is lengthy and only certain items require a response, the sender can copy only those relevant parts and paste them into a "new message," then key in the appropriate responses. A standard technique (often performed automatically by e-mail software) for indicating which text was excerpted from the original is to precede that text with a greater-than symbol (>), for example:

>Will you be available for a meeting on Tuesday, March 19? [from
the original incoming message]
Yes, that's fine. [response]

It is important to remember that the e-mail system in the workplace is the property of the employer. It should not be used to send
personal messages. It is not private. While passwords safeguard privacy to some extent, they are not a guarantee. (For additional information on business correspondence, see Chapter 8.)

E-Mail Dos and Don'ts

Dos:

1. *Be sure that the people with whom you plan to communicate are
comfortable receiving e-mail.* Not everyone is.

2. *Consider your readers.* Ask yourself how they might react to what
you've written.

3. *Provide a clear, specific subject line.* Be sure it's meaningful at a
glance. If the recipient has an in-box replete with messages (some people
receive more than 100 a day), he or she will decide which to read based on
the relative importance of senders and subjects. Users often respond to
the volume of their e-mail by using filters and rules-based agents. If your
message has been filed, the recipient can find it quickly by checking the
subject area.

4. *Use excerpts from previous messages to clarify what you're replying
to.* To distinguish the earlier text from your current responses, insert the
">" symbol in front of the quoted material and follow it with your
response. This example shows how such a text will look on your screen:

>How about 3:00 p.m. on Thursday for the meeting?
That will work for me.
>Can we count on a report from you concerning your group's progress?
Yes. It'll take about five minutes.

This technique is preferable to quoting an entire message and adding
"OK," "Me, too," or "I agree."

5. *Remove long lists of recipients' names and addresses.* These require
the recipient to scroll down in order to get to your message, and some of
your correspondents might not like having their e-mail addresses made
available to other people. Use the BCC ("blind carbon copy") feature to
suppress the names of other recipients.

6. *Strike a balance between formal and casual language.* Your message creates an image of your company and you. When communicating with upper management or customers, use a business letter format, complete sentences, and a spell-checker. Misspelled or omitted words indicate a lack of attention to detail. If you're just trying to set up a meeting with your colleague in the next cubicle, casual language is appropriate.

7. *Read and then reread your message before you send it.* Be sure that your message is clear and grammatical. Attention to detail is as important in e-mail as it is in other forms of written communication. Double-check the spelling of recipients' addresses. A missed keystroke will result in undelivered mail. After sending e-mail, check back in case you've received an "undeliverable" error message. Save a sender's address to your address book, which allows you to avoid retyping the address and introducing errors.

8. *Key in your name at the end of your message.* It identifies you as the sender, and it's common courtesy.

9. *Be careful how you present your message.* Double check your formatting. Your message may look quite different on your recipient's screen than it does on yours. Avoid fancy fonts and the use of special characters which may result in a garbled message.

10. *Acknowledge receipt of messages promptly.* If you're going to be out of the office, use auto-response messages.

11. *Observe the common practices of your company.* Every company has its own "culture." If you're not familiar with a new system, ask someone who is before sending messages.

Don'ts:

Most of these rules are practices that are inappropriate in any form of business communication because they are either rude or unprofessional. With so many new (and inexperienced) e-mail users going online every day, the rules need to be made explicit.

1. *Never substitute e-mail for necessary face-to-face meetings,* especially when praising work well done, reprimanding someone, or firing someone. Such communications should be handled in person.

2. *Never assume that e-mail is private.* Something can go wrong with any software program, and your e-mail might be misdirected. Also, many companies monitor their employees' e-mail. Don't send anything via e-mail that you wouldn't post to the company bulletin board. If your message is personal, ask for a face-to-face meeting or send it via regular mail.

(continued)

3. *Don't assume that everyone reads e-mail immediately.* E-mail travels quickly, but speed of transmission does not guarantee speed of communication. Some people don't check their e-mail in-box every day. Others may set aside a particular time of the day to check their e-mail, but respond only to messages that require immediate attention. Sometimes days or weeks can pass between when a message is sent and when it is read. If you need an immediate response, put "urgent" or "please read immediately" in the subject line, preceding the specific subject of the message.

4. *Never send an angry message via e-mail.* There's no time in business when such correspondence is appropriate.

5. *Never send an e-mail message written in capital letters, LIKE THIS!* Using all capital letters in any context is regarded as the e-mail equivalent of shouting.

6. *Never forward jokes, spam, chain letters, or advertisements.* They will annoy colleagues and potential customers.

7. *Do not reply to everyone who received an e-mail unless it's relevant to them.* If you're simply acknowledging receipt or confirming the time of a meeting, respond only to the sender.

8. *Do not send anyone a large attached file unless the person is expecting it.* If a document is really important, send it by overnight delivery.

9. *Do not send files in HTML unless it's requested.* Some servers cannot handle messages in HTML, and your message will arrive garbled. Such documents can actually cause the recipient's software program to crash.

10. *Do not use e-mail for any illegal or unethical purpose.* This should go without saying.

The Biggest E-Mail Mistakes

E-mail is a great tool but can sometimes be a bit perilous. Sloppiness, and carelessness can not only get you in trouble, they can lead to your company's e-mail system crashing. Anyone who uses e-mail should avoid the following mistakes:

1. *Giving confidential information in an e-mail.* Your credit card number, for instance, can easily be sent throughout in the world.

2. *Opening attachments from strangers.* Never open an e-mail that has an attachment that is vague or says "Check this out!" A virus may spread by invading the contact list on a computer and sending itself to every e-mail address on the list.

3. *Opening unsolicited e-mail without first scanning for viruses.* There are several free anti-virus programs available. Check with your company's IT or MIS department to see what they recommend.

4. *Hitting "reply" to an unsolicited e-mail when asking to be taken off the sender's list.* By hitting "reply" you may be opening up your account to a deluge of spam.

5. *Hitting "reply all" when only the sender needs a response.* If you receive an e-mail from someone in the company who asks for feedback on an issue, remember to hit "reply."

6. *Sending "all@" e-mails.* Being able to send e-mail to everyone in your organization at once is not a right. Very few companies in the world allow employees the right to send e-mails to the entire company without some approval process. So remember, just because you are desperate to sell your 1997 Geo Prism, that doesn't mean the CEO needs an e-mail about it.

7. *Sending an e-mail without a signature.* Your business e-mail should have a preset signature at the bottom. Make sure you use company colors and logos if provided. Never use a virtual business card attachment (unless it is a company protocol). It may be mistaken for a virus.

8. *Sending an e-mail without spell-checking it.* E-mail is official correspondence. Most e-mail systems spell-check as you type or have a "spell-check before sending" setting.

9. *Sending e-mail without a "subject" line or sending e-mail with a vague subject line.* Be specific. A subject that reads "Lastest Info on Johnson Account" will get more attention than one that reads "FYI" or "new data." A blank subject line may get no attention at all.

—*Evan Schnittman*

CHAPTER 6

Creating Documents

WORD-PROCESSING SKILLS

In this highly technical age, it is becoming more difficult to find an office without a computer. Businesses depend a great deal on office professionals with word-processing skills, whether to create a complicated form, a report, or a simple business letter. Typing speed and accuracy play an important role in document creation, but understanding the word-processing program you are using is just as important. These programs offer many useful features, like choices of typefaces and font size, the cutting and pasting of data, and grammar- and spell-checking. But it still takes a keen eye to proofread the final document before printing. The spell-checking feature will not pick up an error such as "he" in place of "the" because it recognizes both as acceptable words.

These word-processing programs give the business office the capability of creating documents that were once sent out to a local print shop. Keeping such work in-house saves time and money. It offers the convenience of making corrections on-screen without having to redo the document from scratch, another money-saving feature. There is the added benefit of being able to store many documents in a computer file, making searches and retrieval quicker and easier.

Computer Production

Becoming familiar with computer basics, along with the capabilities of your word-processing program, are critical to maintaining cost-efficiency and professionalism in your office. It's up to you to tell the computer what you want it to accomplish for you.

Computer Capabilities

RECEIVING INFORMATION (INPUT).

Input is the information (data) the computer receives, via the keyboard, a mouse, a trackball (for laptop computers), or a scanner. More sophisticated systems may also receive input by voice. Once the computer receives this information, it waits for a command to tell it how to process the information.

PROCESSING INFORMATION.

Once the computer receives information (data), it must process it in some way. In order to process information, computers need software. Depending on the software programs installed in the computer, it can calculate, draw, create graphics for presentations, keep financial records through accounting systems, communicate, and write. The writing feature is the most common use of the computer. Reports, tables, or documents can be keyed and formatted to give an appealing look using various typefaces, point sizes, bold or italic print, justified lines, indents, bulleted or numbered lists, columns, and boxed or lined sections. Multipaged documents can be formatted to include consecutive page numbers. Headers and footers are also a helpful feature. The header, or running head, is placed in the top margin of the page and repeated on each page thereafter. The footer is in the bottom margin and may include the page numbers or even filing information, such as the name of the folder the document is stored in on the hard drive.

RETRIEVING INFORMATION (OUTPUT).

Once the data is processed, it can be retrieved. This is often accomplished by using a printer to produce the information (hard copy), or it can be attached to an e-mail message and sent to a coworker or to a client outside your firm.

STORING INFORMATION.

In most cases, a document is saved on a computer's hard drive in a file you create, much like a manila folder used in a file cabinet. By copying the data onto a floppy disk (diskette), you also create a backup in the event the original file is accidentally deleted or the computer fails.

DESKTOP PUBLISHING

Desktop publishing (DTP) is a step above word processing and enables organizations to produce camera-ready brochures, documents, newsletters, complex reports, calendars, business cards, books, and more, on a computer. The best feature of such a software program is that it shows on-screen exactly what your data will look like in printed form. The initial cost of a DTP program is more than made up in the eventual savings for typesetting, printing, and time. But do some research first to determine if such a program is right for your office. DTP programs require lots of memory and fast processors. A good laser printer is essential in producing high-quality printouts as well.

Those who will be using the program should become familiar with DTP terminology, such as *font, leading, point size, justified type, ragged right, Roman, italic, bold, serif, sans serif,* and so on. Because of the complexity of DTP, it is wise to invest in a training course for such a program. Be sure your office already has the DTP program in place. It is important to have hands-on experience in order to retain what is learned in class.

REPORT PREPARATION

The report plays an important role in the workplace, whether you are preparing one for your supervisor, the executive staff, board of directors, or clients. It may be short and simple, in the form of a memo or e-mail, or it may be more formal and several pages long.

Reports require more preparation time than letters or memoranda, especially if you are creating them from one of the many software programs available for such tasks, and require careful proofreading for accuracy. They often contain tables and graphics, which offer readers facts at a glance, but also break up the monotony of solid text and provide visual appeal. Whatever its length, content, or destination, the end result is the same: a report must be informative, factual, understandable, and neatly presented. This requires research, focus, and patience.

Research

Research for a report may be as simple as questioning key people within the workplace, gathering numbers and information from documents on file, or even pulling data from past minutes of meetings. In some cases, however, contacting other organizations, using the resources of the local library, or browsing the Internet will be necessary. You may even have to enlist the help of others, and, depending on the amount of research needed, assigning specific tasks to each helper.

Before you begin, it is important to have a clear picture of what you need to know. If you are interviewing someone, have a list of questions ready, so as not to waste time. If you are planning to use books, magazines, newspapers, or the Internet for answers, have the topics needing investigation written out, with key questions listed. Sometimes the answer to one question leads to another question not even on your list. It is wise to keep track of your sources, even on the Internet, in case you have to go back to that source for any reason. You'll also need a record of your sources in order to prepare a bibliography for a formal report.

Informal Reports

An informal report may be one or two pages in length and formatted as a letter or memo. It may even be distributed via e-mail. Your company may have a specific format to be followed, so using past reports as a guide will help. Or you may choose a style with headings and subheadings, numbered lists, or an outline style to make reading easier. The title of the report should be introduced as a subject line. Keep in mind who will be receiving your report and use vocabulary and tone appropriate for your audience. Simplicity and accuracy, however, remain key factors.

Formal Reports

The formal report is usually more complex and runs several pages long. Accuracy of facts, spelling, and grammar is a must. Also, if more than one person writes the report, be sure it has continuity (no sudden jumps from one topic to another) and a consistent voice (no jarring contrasts in style). Your company may have its own report format, or you may have to develop one of your own. Whatever the case, some or all of the following sections will probably be required.

COVER PAGE.

Always provide a cover page for a formal report, not only to improve its appearance but to keep it neat as well. Your cover page should usually be of heavier stock paper than the body of the report; it can be any color, or clear or colored plastic. Whatever you choose, the cover page should have a label with the title and author(s) of the report. Your company name should also be provided if the report is going off-site.

FLYLEAF.

A flyleaf is a blank page inserted both after the front cover and before the end cover. The purpose of these pages is to protect the report, but they are also useful for jotting down notes.

TITLE PAGE.

The title page should include the title of the report, the author, the name of the company or organization responsible for it, the name of the company or organization the report was compiled for (if appropriate), and the date. Center all the information, keeping in mind that a wider left margin may be necessary for binding the report. Generally, the title is typed in uppercase, about two inches from the top of the page. All other information is typed in initial caps, centered below the title. The date is usually typed two inches from the bottom of the page.

Sample Title Page:

COMPETITORS' PRICING OF SOAP PRODUCTS

Lisa Yu, Jim Martinez, and Wendy Fitzgerald
Four-Way Protection Soap Company
Marketing Division

September 23, 2003

Letter of Transmittal.

A letter of transmittal acts as an introduction to the report. It may give the reason the report was written, who originally had the idea, and a summary of the report's content. It can be typed on business letterhead or in memorandum style and signed by the person(s) who wrote it.

Acknowledgment Page

If several people, departments, or outside sources contributed to the compilation of your report, you should acknowledge them on this page.

Table of Contents.

The table of contents is the last page to be typed, after the entire report is finished and its pages are numbered. List the chapter or section headings exactly as they appear in the report. If headings are prefaced by Roman numerals, Arabic numbers, capital letters, and so on, be sure to follow that format as well in the table of contents. Each major heading should be listed also, with the corresponding page number. Leaders are also helpful, connecting the entry heading with the page number.

Sample Table of Contents:

Contents

LIST OF ILLUSTRATIONS.

Tables, charts, and figures all fall in the category of illustrations. Each illustration should be numbered, listing the caption or title exactly as it appears in the report. If there are several of each, they may each have a separate page, listing them, in the same format as the table of contents. If they can fit nicely on one page, head each section with the proper title, for example, "List of Tables," "List of Figures," and so on.

PREFACE.

The preface allows the author to provide a personal message or explanation that is not otherwise incorporated in the body of the report. It is not a common feature in a report, but it is an option, nonetheless.

SUMMARY.

The summary has the same purpose as, and would supersede, the preface in most cases. It gives the authors the opportunity to discuss their research methods and offer a brief synopsis of the report's conclusions.

BODY.

The body of the report may be single- or double-spaced, depending on the length. The margins should be no less than one inch on each side, and top and bottom, but allow at least an extra half inch where the binding will be.

A heading or subheading usually begins each section. You may choose to use Arabic numbers, Roman numerals, or the alphabetical system to preface each heading. Be consistent throughout.

If you are incorporating illustrations within the body of the report, be sure they are identified in some way, such as with a title or a figure number. The placement should coincide with the corresponding text for easy referral by the reader.

APPENDIX.

If you choose to keep all charts, illustrations, tables, and so forth together, they are placed in an appendix, which follows the body of the report. Supporting material such as maps, notes, or summaries of data may also go here. If you have several items appended, they would be headed as Appendix A, Appendix B, and so on.

FOOTNOTES/ENDNOTES.

The use of reference notes validates the authority of your work and gives proper credit to those whom you quote. A footnote appears at the bottom of the page to which its reference belongs. The numbering of footnotes usually begins with "1" on each new page. Instead of footnotes, you may prefer endnotes, the references to which are numbered consecutively to the end of each chapter or to the end of the entire report. The endnotes thus appear in correspondingly numbered lists at the end of each chapter or at the end of the report. If you choose the latter method, keep in mind that, if you change the number of a note near the beginning of the report, it will affect the numbers thereafter. Note numbers are placed after the appropriate text and are indicated by a superscript, or raised, numeral:

Human Resources reported a decline in applications that summer.[1]

Footnotes and endnotes that refer to published text should follow a conventional style. A good source of information on acceptable formats is the *Chicago Manual of Style* (14th edition).

Sample Footnotes/Endnotes

1. Irving Blankenship. Index of Soap Manufacturers (Portsmouth, NH: Reference Books, 1986).
2. Irving Blankenship, Mildred Wu, and Darlene Saltzstern. Marketing Soap (New York: Acme Publishing, 2002.
3. Mildred Wu, "The Use of Chemicals in Soap Manufacturing," Journal of Soap and Bath Manufacturers 68 (1966): 9–33.
4. Ken Starbright, "You and Your Soap," Redbook, March 1983, 44–50, 66, 104.
5. Sharon McCoy, "Soap Takes a Bath," Los Angeles Times, 6 July 1991, sec. D, p. 2.

If your report will have numerous reference notes, it may be advantageous to the keyer and the reader to set them as endnotes, after the appendix. While it may sometimes be annoying to the reader to have to flip back and forth from the body of the report to the endnotes, it keeps notes contained in one area and keeps the text flowing without the clutter of footnotes at the bottom of pages.

If you are not familiar with the features of your word-processing software that facilitate the placement and numbering of footnotes and endnotes, consult the help menu or ask an experienced user for assistance. Letting the word processor handle the organization and numeration of notes is both time-saving and accurate.

GLOSSARY.

If your report uses many technical or uncommon terms, a glossary can provide readers with an alphabetical listing with definitions. If you include a glossary of terms, using boldface type to draw your readers' attention to glossary terms in the body of your text will alert them that the term is included in the glossary.

BIBLIOGRAPHY.

The bibliography lists, in alphabetical order, all published resources used in the compilation of your report. The author's surname is typed first, followed by first name or initials or a period if there is no initial.

The year of publication comes immediately after the author's name, also followed by a period. If the source has more than three authors, type the first author, followed by *et al.* If there are several sources by the same author, type the first one according to the usual format. Each source thereafter, use three em-dashes, followed by a period, (or a comma if there is more than one author), to take the place of the author's name. Then proceed with the title of the publication, and so on. In the bibliography, book titles are in italics, and only the first word is capitalized. The rest of the title is lower case, except for proper nouns and the first word following a colon in the title. Article and essay titles are in roman type, and capitalization of words is the same as that for books. A good source of style for the bibliography is the *Chicago Manual of Style* (14th edition).

Sample Bibliography

Books

    Single author

        Blankenship, Irving. 1986. *Index of soap manufacturers. Portsmouth*, NH: Reference Books.

    Two or Three Authors:

        ———, Mildred Wu, and Darlene Saltzstern. 2002. Marketing soap. New York: Acme Publishing.

Articles

    In a journal:

        Wu, Mildred. 1966. The use of chemicals in soap manufacturing. *Journal of Soap and Bath Products Manufacturers* 68: 9–33.

    In a magazine:

        Starbright, Ken. 1983. You and your soap. *Redbook*, March, 44–50, 66, 104.

    In a newspaper:

        McCoy, Sharon. 1991. Soap takes a bath. *Los Angeles Times*, 6 July, sec. D, p. 2.

REFERENCE LIST.

The reference list takes the place of the bibliography and the use of footnotes. Instead of using superscripts within the text, you place the author's name and publication year in parentheses after the quoted material. The detailed reference list is placed at the end of the report in place of a bibliography. The style for the reference list can be the same as that of a bibliography.

INDEX.

Very long reports may require an index. Major headings, sections, or topics are listed in alphabetical order with corresponding page numbers listed. This may be compiled by an outside firm, by available software packages for your computer, or manually.

HEADERS/FOOTERS.

Headers and footers are used to aid the reader in locating specific information or sections. The header is placed at the top of the page, outside the top margin. It may contain the title of the report along with subheadings for that particular section, for example:

LAUNDRY DETERGENTS / Powder

The footer is placed at the bottom of the page, outside the bottom margin, and may contain the page number, date, or other pertinent information. The header and footer may also be keyed in a slightly smaller point size than the text.

COPYRIGHT.

If your report will be distributed outside your company or organization, it should be copyrighted to protect the material from being used without permission by others. If a report isn't copyrighted, it is in the public domain, which means that the material may be used without permission from the publisher or writer.
There are two parts to copyright: the registration and the printed copyright notice. For the most up-to-date information about registering

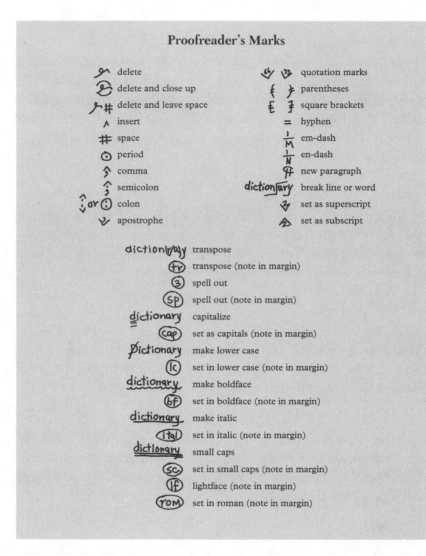

Proofreader's Marks

Mark	Meaning	Mark	Meaning
	delete		quotation marks
	delete and close up		parentheses
	delete and leave space		square brackets
	insert	=	hyphen
	space		em-dash
	period		en-dash
	comma		new paragraph
	semicolon		break line or word
	colon		set as superscript
	apostrophe		set as subscript

dictionary — transpose
transpose (note in margin)
spell out
spell out (note in margin)
capitalize
set as capitals (note in margin)
make lower case
set in lower case (note in margin)
make boldface
set in boldface (note in margin)
make italic
set in italic (note in margin)
small caps
set in small caps (note in margin)
lightface (note in margin)
set in roman (note in margin)

copyright, contact the Copyright Office, Library of Congress, Washington DC, or visit the Web site at http://www.copyright.gov.

In general, you can print a copyright notice without registering the copyright. This notice usually takes the form:

©2002. Amalgamated Holdings, Inc. All Rights Reserved.

This notice should go on a separate page following the title page in a printed book or report, or at the bottom of the home page and at the end of each section of a Web site.

If you need to use original material from a copyrighted source, you must get the permission of the copyright holder. If the material is in the public domain, permission is not needed, but credit should be given to the original source. When a copyright holder gives you permission to use his or her material in your work, you must use the exact wording for the permissions credit as supplied by the copyright holder. This credit can be positioned in text footnotes, in a separate permissions section, or underneath a figure or table.

CHAPTER 7

Business Writing

INTRODUCTION TO BUSINESS WRITING

Writing is not a gift. It is a skill, learned in the same way as any other activity: by trial and error over a long period of time. Everyone begins as an inexperienced novice who longs for a simple formula: if you follow these six easy steps, you will (presto!) become a fluent writer. While there are formulas for writing specific types of content, for example, the elements that must go into a thank-you letter or a letter of resignation, you will become a skilled writer only by writing, and writing, and writing some more. It is one of the most important skills you will need in the world of business, regardless of the specific culture in which you work.

Writing is not a linear process. It is messy and, frequently, time-consuming. When you confront that blank piece of paper, or, more likely these days, a blank computer screen, you will often find that your mind is just as blank, and that can be frustrating when your boss wants that report on her desk by 5:00 p.m. Gather your wits, the facts and figures you'll need, something to write with and something to write on, and get started. Be prepared to spend a lot of time thinking, not writing—thinking about what you need to say and what you want to say. If you can think well, you can write well. And, take comfort in this: only a few, a very few, writers can truthfully claim that they get "it" right on the first try. Good writing is the product of revising, rereading, revising, . . . you get the idea.

Writing, the process of using written language to communicate, can be intensely personal, as when we write in a diary or write a letter to a loved one, but more often it is a public, social event. That is, although we may sometimes write for our own pleasure we usually write in order to provide a specific group of people with information on a topic we know about. Where do you begin?

There are several identifiable steps in the writing process: define your purpose, audience, and subject; jot down ideas as they come to you; gather information; organize your ideas; prepare a first draft; revise; prepare a second draft; revise. Repeat the drafting and revision steps as many times as you need to. Then type what you hope is a final draft, edit it once more and, if you are satisfied, proofread it. (Yes, neatness counts.) Although not one of these steps can be omitted, they need not be done in a specific order. (Remember, writing is not a linear process.) You will probably find, as you become more and more experienced, that some of the steps do seem to follow logically one from the other.

Identifying Your Purpose

Most of us rarely write without a purpose in mind, and business writing, in particular, always has a goal, something to be accomplished. Clarifying for yourself the reason(s) for your writing will immediately put you on the right track. You can do this by asking yourself three questions:

- Do I want to explain an idea or provide information? (*expository* writing)
- Do I want to convince others that my point of view is the best perspective or persuade them to act? (*argumentative* or *persuasive* writing)
- Do I need to describe a detailed process or an experiment? (*scientific* or *technical* writing)

Scientific (technical) writing is the most straightforward because it describes the methodology and steps performed in an experiment or it lays out, point by point, the course of a process from beginning to end. Both expository and persuasive writing can be approached in numerous ways, giving you some latitude in deciding exactly how you want to approach your topic. That decision depends on your assessment of your audience.

Identifying Your Audience

Much of the time, when you write letters or memorandums, you know exactly who your audience is: a customer who requested information about a product or informing colleagues about Thursday's meeting. In other situations, however, you will need to think more thoroughly about your audience, what kinds of people might comprise your audience and what their needs and expectations are. Identifying your audience early in the writing process will help you determine what kind of information they need and how much you need to tell them. One of the crucial aspects of writing is deciding what information you must provide and what you can safely omit.

Answering a few questions before you begin to write will provide you with an initial profile of your audience:

- Who is going to read what I am writing?
- What might a general reader know about my topic, and what will I need to explain in some detail?
- What might a reader expect to find in terms of purpose, subject matter, presentation (format), length, level of formality (tone), and date of delivery?
- How can I interest my reader(s) in what I am saying and make reading what I produce an enjoyable, rather than frustrating, experience?

Writing for a general audience is quite different from writing for a group of specialists. While general readers might know a few terms in a specific field, you will obviously need to provide them with more detail and explanation than you would a group of colleagues who share your training and expertise. You don't want to lose general readers' interest by assuming they know as much as you do about the topic or overwhelming them with technical jargon. A bit of humor might lighten the reading for a general audience, but it would be out of place in a formal report to the board of directors. Most readers of Standard English, regardless of their interests or expertise, expect informative and persuasive prose to have six characteristics:

1. a clearly stated main point—a central *thesis* that governs and unifies the piece of writing;
2. several clearly articulated points that support your thesis;
3. several paragraphs, each with its own main idea, often explicitly stated;
4. specific details that support or illustrate the main idea of each paragraph;
5. concrete language;
6. a more-or-less formal tone that avoids slang or colloquial language without sounding stuffy or stilted.

Gathering Your Ideas

You've identified the purpose of your writing and the audience for whom you're writing, but what are you going to say and how are you going to organize it? Remember that pen and pad of paper you took out? If you haven't already begun to jot down ideas as they occur to you, start now.

Where do ideas come from? Obviously ideas can come out of your own mind or from reading and talking to others about your topic, but almost anything can ignite that spark of creativity you'll need to generate ideas for your project. Be prepared to have that brilliant realization happen at any time and in any situation. You'll be amazed at the way your subconscious mind continues to work on issues and problems associated with your topic long after you've turned off your PC or put your notepad aside, even while you're asleep! (Some professional writers keep a pen [or pencil] and paper on the table beside their bed so that they can record solutions and flashes of insight when they come during the night. And those ideas must be recorded at the moment they occur. No, you won't remember them, at least not easily, when you awaken.)

There are also more organized ways of generating ideas. Some people find that keeping a journal in which to record observations, references, and quotations is helpful. Others use a method called "freewriting," writing sessions during which they just start writing whatever comes to mind, allowing the words already on the page to generate still more words, without worrying about grammar, organization, or spelling. (Those can be attended to later.) Another way of getting started is to construct an outline, (1) beginning with a broad description of your subject area, and gradually narrowing that area to (2) a topic to explore within that subject area, (3) formulating a question about that topic that interests you, and (4) stating your thesis, an opinion or main point that answers the question.

Two other methods you can try are brainstorming (most fruitful when done in a group) and mapping. When you brainstorm, you make a list of ideas as they come to you, whether or not they seem irrelevant or "off the wall" and without worrying about how you might organize them or connect them. The purpose is to generate ideas at this stage, and the more ideas you have, the more likely you are to end up with some that will be useful when you begin to write. Mapping, which can also be done individually or in a group, is a way of using words to construct a conceptual map around your topic. You begin by writing your topic (subject area) in the middle of a page, think of concepts related to your topic and write them down around your topic. As you begin to perceive relationships among those concepts and your topic, you draw lines connecting the supporting details to your main idea.

Finally, there are those reliable standbys—Who? What? When? Where? Why? and How?—used by journalists to make sure that they've answered all of the questions that their readers might ask.

Formulating Your Thesis

Your *thesis* is the main idea you will be writing about, the central point about your topic that you want your audience to remember. Generally, you are prepared to state your thesis after you've chosen a topic, developed a question or opinion to answer or elaborate, and generated ideas from your experience or research.

Your thesis is what all of your preparation has been leading up to, and a good thesis accomplishes several important writing objectives:

- it narrows your topic to one central idea you will write about;
- it states your position clearly;
- it expresses your opinion about or attitude toward the topic;
- it makes a generalization you will support with details, facts, and examples;
- it stimulates the interest of your readers in what you have to say.

Depending on the kind of writing you are doing, for example, expository or persuasive, a good thesis should also do one or more of the following:

- make a firm, controversial statement;
- express a "call to action";
- ask a question that will be answered in the body of your text;
- provide a preview of how your text will be organized.

At some point in the writing process, you will have to decide whether to state your thesis explicitly or leave your readers to infer it from the details, facts, examples, and other information you provide.

Expository writing

The purpose of expository writing is to provide readers with information. For this reason, it usually contains facts, concrete examples, and specific details about the topic in an objective tone. In this kind of writing, the thesis is usually stated explicitly near the beginning of the essay (or report), and it functions as a touchstone for you as you prepare your first draft—keeping you from straying too far—and prepares your readers for what you will tell them.

PERSUASIVE WRITING

The purpose of persuasive writing (as you would guess) is to convince your readers to agree with you on some point regarding your topic, to adopt your perspective on the topic as the one that best addresses the issues you raise and the questions you ask. In a persuasive piece of writing, the thesis takes a stand on an issue, and, although you should present alternative and competing arguments for your readers' consideration, you will reach a conclusion and clearly state your position on the issue.

Eventually, you will decide where to place your thesis if it's going to be stated explicitly. That placement is up to you. It can be placed at or close to the beginning, especially if it's expository writing, or at the conclusion of your essay if your purpose is to persuade. You state your thesis *after* you've presented all of your evidence and built your case, and it functions as the climax and final outcome of the evidence you've presented.

One other thing to remember: your thesis is not, and should not, be thought of as "engraved in stone." Because writing is a process of discovery, you will probably find that your thesis will change during that process, as it should. It is not unusual for writers to find, at the end of a first draft, that their thesis has changed. If that happens, begin your second draft by focusing on the thesis that emerged at the end of your first draft. Never try to squeeze your evidence into tight boxes to try and make it fit a thesis that doesn't work. It's much easier to change your thesis so that it fits the evidence than to mangle your evidence in an effort to retain an erroneous thesis.

Writing Your Drafts

One of the rewarding outcomes of the writing process is a polished piece of writing of which you can be proud. Unlike speaking, writing gives us the opportunity to refine the way we express our ideas and revise until we are satisfied (within whatever time limit we face). As you learn methods that enable you to produce your best writing and extend the range of your writing ability, you, and your readers as well, will find the results of your hard work highly satisfying. Don't let this go to your head. Note that plural, *drafts*, in the heading. You haven't begun yet, and several drafts (probably) lie between you and that superb piece of writing.

GETTING STARTED

First things first: do not begin at the beginning. The introduction (or first paragraph) is the hardest part of your report or essay, for one simple reason: you have no idea at this point what you're going to say, and your introduction should be the last thing you write, after you know what you've said. You've probably heard the simple formula for writing: (1) Tell your readers what you're going to tell them; (2) tell your readers; (3) tell your readers what you've told them.

Well, yes and no. In actual practice, begin by saying what you want to say. Start by writing those parts of your essay for which you have the most material to write about. After you have something down on paper, you can begin to consider how you want to organize your material.

Next, write that first draft just as quickly as you can. Fill those pages without stopping to worry over spelling, commas, or sentence fragments. This one is for your eyes only, so don't waste your valuable time searching for just the right word or the most eloquent statement of an idea. If you are stymied along the way, make a note to yourself in the margin, leave a space, or insert a blank to remind you that something is missing. If an idea suddenly comes to you that belongs somewhere else, jot it down on that notepad and note approximately where you think it will fit.

Although this first draft will be written quickly, you don't want to write without thinking. Ideally, what appears in this draft should support your thesis. If you find yourself straying from your central idea—what this is all about—stop and ask yourself whether what you're saying is a digression or something that might lead to a more interesting thesis. If you have the time, pursue it and see where it takes you. If not, make a note to yourself and return to your original idea and stick with it.

At this point, don't worry about your language or about being extreme in stating your ideas. What is important now is getting your ideas down on the page. You can tone down your language and adopt a more restrained stance in your next draft, if that's what you decide to do.

Once you're sure you've gotten down everything that you want to say, read through your work, paying particular attention to how you've developed your thesis paragraph by paragraph. Is each sentence in a paragraph related both to what precedes it and what follows it? How does each paragraph relate to the one that immediately precedes it and the one that follows? Is each paragraph coherent, moving smoothly from one sentence to the next, and does each paragraph follow from those before it and provide a link to those that follow? If not, now is the time to pay attention to organizing your ideas in the most logical relationships and ensuring that the entire essay coherently addresses your thesis and presents sufficient examples and specific details to support it.

The Final Work

When you've completed your first draft, you can begin the long process of polishing, rewriting, and rethinking. It is important in business writing to follow the rules of Standard English (which are laid out for you in the next section). Reread your draft several times, preferably several hours to a day after writing it. Check any and all words that you are uncertain about in a dictionary, and ask a trusted friend or colleague to read your work and give you feedback, not only about your grammar and spelling, but also about your word choice and the expression of your thesis and evidence.

Make sure that you've put your final document in the format that was required, and be sure to read it at least once on paper, even if—or perhaps especially if—you have written the entire report on the computer.

Ten Tips for Better Business Writing

1. Use ordinary words. Write *begin* instead of *commence*, and *help* instead of *assist*, for example.
2. Use personal pronouns. It's friendlier and more direct.
3. Use contractions in all but the most formal writing.
4. Use the active voice rather than the passive. Write "We did it," not "It was done."
5. Don't be a slave to certain rules (e.g., "never split an infinitive," "never end a sentence with a preposition") that may make your writing stiff and unfriendly.
6. Put your main point first. (You can reiterate it in your conclusion if necessary.)
7. Use headers and lists to organize your thoughts.
8. Avoid being abstract. Use concrete examples and brief stories to make your points.
9. Avoid fancy fonts.
10. Always proofread your work. (Don't rely on spell-checkers: they can't identify common errors like *your/you're* and *there/their/they're* or omitted words.)

Guide to Composition: Rules of English Grammar

Grammar is the system and structure of a language. It embodies all the principles by which the language works. All good writing begins with an understanding of the fundamentals of grammar:

- parts of speech
- parts of sentences
- sentence structures
- sentence functions

PARTS OF SPEECH

Noun

A **noun** is a word that identifies or names a person, place, thing, action, or quality. There are two types of nouns: proper and common.

PROPER NOUNS

A noun that names a particular person, place, or thing is a **proper noun**. It always begins with a capital letter:

Benito Mussolini
Cairo
Chrysler Building
Jell-O
Mount Everest

COMMON NOUNS

A noun that names a type of person, place, or thing is a **common noun**. There are three kinds of common nouns: concrete, abstract, and collective.

A **concrete noun** names someone or something that you can see or touch:

arm
giraffe
hamburger
lake
stapler

An **abstract noun** names something intangible (that is, something that cannot be seen nor touched):

assistance
bravery
disappointment
flavor
wit

A collective noun names a group of persons or things:

audience
colony

herd
platoon
set

SINGULAR AND PLURAL NOUNS

A noun that names one person, place, or thing is **singular**. A noun that names more than one person, place, or thing is **plural**. The spelling of a singular noun almost always changes when it becomes a plural. Most plurals can be formed by adding *–s* or *–es*, but many nouns do not follow this format.

beach/beaches
bean/beans
hairbrush/hairbrushes
leaf/leaves
mouse/mice
party/parties
school/schools
woman/women

If the spelling of a plural noun is in doubt, it is always advisable to consult a dictionary.

APPOSITIVES

An **appositive** is a noun (or a unit of words that acts as a noun) whose meaning is a direct copy or extension of the meaning of the preceding noun in the sentence. In other words, the appositive and the preceding noun refer to the same person, place, or thing. The appositive helps to characterize or elaborate on the preceding noun in a specific way.

The wedding cake, a chocolate <u>masterpiece</u>, was the hit of the reception.
[The noun *cake* and the appositive *masterpiece* are the same thing.]

His primary objective, <u>to write the great American novel</u>, was
never realized.
[The noun *objective* and the appositive *to write the great
American novel* are the same thing.]

Eleanor's math teacher, <u>Mrs. Kennedy</u>, is retiring next year.
[The noun *teacher* and the appositive *Mrs. Kennedy* are the
same person.]

POSSESSIVES

A **possessive** is a noun whose form has changed in order to show possession. Certain rules can be followed to determine how the form
should change for any given noun.

In the case of a singular noun, add an apostrophe and an *s*:

<u>Lincoln's</u> inaugural address
the <u>baby's</u> favorite blanket

Exception: Most singular nouns that end in *s* follow the preceding
rule with no difficulty (e.g., Chris's, Dickens's), but some singular
nouns that end in *s* may be exempted from the rule because the pronunciation of the plural is less awkward with just an apostrophe and
no final *s*:

<u>Ramses'</u> dynasty
<u>Aristophanes'</u> great comedic works

In the case of a plural noun that ends in *s*, add just an apostrophe:

the <u>Lincolns'</u> summer home
our <u>babies'</u> double stroller

In the case of a plural noun that does not end in *s*, add an apostrophe
and an *s*:

<u>men's</u> footwear
the <u>fungi's</u> rapid reproduction

In the case of a compound noun (a noun made of more than one word), only the last word takes the possessive form:

> my sister-in-law's house
> the commander in chief's personal staff

In the case of joint possession (that is, two or more nouns possess the same thing together), only the last of the possessing nouns takes the possessive form:

> Ryan and Saul's nickel collection
> [There is only one nickel collection, and *both* Ryan and Saul
>   own it together.]

> Gramma and Grampa's photo albums
> [However many photo albums there may be, they all belong
>   to *both* Gramma and Grampa *together.*]

In the case of individual possession by two or more nouns (that is, two or more nouns possess the same type of thing, but separately and distinctly), each of the possessing nouns takes the possessive form:

> Lenny's and Suzanne's footprints on the beach
> [Lenny and Suzanne *each* left *their own distinct* footprints on
>   the beach.]

> Strauss's and Khachaturian's waltzes
> [Strauss and Khachaturian *each* composed *their own distinct*
>   waltzes.]

Pronoun

A **pronoun** is a word that represents a person or thing without giving the specific name of the person or thing. There are five classes of pronouns: personal, relative, demonstrative, indefinite, and interrogative.

A **personal pronoun** is used to refer to the person speaking (first person), the person spoken to (second person), or the person or thing spoken about (third person). A pronoun formed from certain personal pronouns by adding the suffix –*self* (singular) or –*selves* (plural) is called "reflexive."

PERSON	SINGULAR	PLURAL	REFLEXIVE SINGULAR	REFLEXIVE PLURAL
first person	*I*	*we*	—	—
	my	*our*	*myself*	*ourselves*
	mine	*ours*	—	—
	me	*us*	—	—
second person	*you*	*you*	—	—
	your	*your*	*yourself*	*yourselves*
	yours	*yours*	—	—
	you	*you*	—	—
third person masculine	*he*	*they*	—	—
	his	*their*	—	—
	his	*theirs*	—	—
	him	*them*	*himself*	*themselves*
third person feminine	*she*	*they*	—	—
	her	*their*	—	—
	hers	*theirs*	—	—
	her	*them*	*herself*	*themselves*
third person neuter	*it*	*they*	—	—
	its	*their*	—	—
	its	*theirs*	—	—
	it	*them*	*itself*	*themselves*

Note that the gender designations of masculine, feminine, and neuter apply only to the third person singular.

Reflexive personal pronouns are so-called because they reflect the action of the verb back to the subject. It is incorrect to use a reflexive pronoun by itself; there must be a subject to which it refers.

incorrect: Denise and <u>myself</u> will fix the car.
          [The reflexive pronoun *myself* has no subject to refer to; the wording should be "Denise and I."]

correct: I will fix the car <u>myself</u>.
          [The reflexive pronoun *myself* refers to the subject *I*.]

A reflexive pronoun that adds force or emphasis to a noun or another pronoun is called "intensive:"

> You <u>yourself</u> must return the ladder.
> Terri and Phil want to wallpaper the kitchen <u>themselves</u>.

A **relative pronoun** introduces a descriptive clause. The relative pronouns are *which, that, who, whoever, whose, whom,* and *whomever*.

> Wendy was the pianist <u>who</u> won the scholarship.
> Is Mr. Leonard the teacher <u>whose</u> book was just published?
> <u>Whoever</u> wrote the speech is a genius.
> I attended the morning meeting, <u>which</u> lasted for three hours.

A **demonstrative pronoun** is specific. It is used to point out particular persons, places, or things. The demonstrative pronouns are *this, that, these,* and *those*.

> <u>These</u> are the finest fabrics available.
> I'll look at <u>those</u> first.
> What is <u>this</u>?

An **indefinite pronoun** is nonspecific. It is used to refer to persons, places, or things without particular identification. There are numerous indefinite pronouns, including the following:

all	everyone	none
any	everything	no one
anybody	few	other
anyone	little	others
anything	many	several
both	most	some
each	much	somebody
either	neither	someone
everybody	nobody	something

George brought two desserts, but I didn't try <u>either</u>.
<u>Many</u> are called, but few are chosen.
Can <u>somebody</u> please answer the phone?

An **interrogative pronoun** is used to ask a question. The interrogative pronouns are *who*, *which*, and *what*.

<u>Who</u> wants to buy a raffle ticket?
<u>Which</u> of the two applicants has more practical experience?
<u>What</u> is the purpose of another debate?

PRONOUN CASES

The case of a pronoun is what determines its relation to the other words in the sentence. There are three pronoun cases: nominative, objective, and possessive.

Nominative case
The nominative pronouns are *I, we, you, he, she, it, they, who,* and *whoever*.

A pronoun that is the subject (or part of the subject) of a sentence is in the nominative case:

<u>They</u> loved the movie.
Mark and <u>I</u> are going to the Bahamas.

A pronoun that is a predicate is in the nominative case:

It was <u>she</u> who wrote the poem.
The winner will probably be <u>you</u>.

Objective case
The objective pronouns are *me, us, you, him, her, it, them, whom,* and *whomever*.

A pronoun that is the direct object of a verb is in the objective case:

Stephen already invited <u>them</u>.
Should we keep <u>it</u>?

A pronoun that is the indirect object of a verb is in the objective case:

> Captain Mackenzie told <u>us</u> many seafaring tales.
> I'll give <u>you</u> the recipe tomorrow.

A pronoun that is the object of a preposition is in the objective case:

> Does she think this job is beneath <u>her</u>?
> To <u>whom</u> was it addressed?

Possessive case

A possessive pronoun shows ownership.

The possessive pronouns used as predicate nominatives are *mine, ours, yours, his, hers, its, theirs,* and *whose*.

> The blue station wagon is <u>mine</u>.
> None of the cash was <u>theirs</u>.

The possessive pronouns used as adjectives are *my, our, your, his, her, its, their,* and *whose*.

> <u>Whose</u> test scores were the highest?
> I believe this is <u>your</u> package.

TIP

A possessive pronoun never has an apostrophe. Remember, the word *it's* is the contraction of *it is* or *it has*—not the possessive form of *it.*

- possessive: Life has its ups and downs.
- contraction: It's good to see you.

SINGULAR AND PLURAL AGREEMENT

It is important to identify a pronoun as singular or plural and to make certain that the associated verb form is in agreement. The pronouns that tend to cause the most problems for writers and speakers are the indefinite pronouns.

Some indefinite pronouns are always singular and therefore always require a singular verb. These include *everybody*, *everyone*, *some-body*, *someone*, *nobody*, *one*, *either*, and *neither*.

Nobody <u>wants</u> to leave.
Don't get up unless <u>someone</u> <u>knocks</u> on the door.
<u>Either</u> of these two colors <u>is</u> fine.

Other indefinite pronouns may be singular or plural, depending on the particular reference. These include *any*, *all*, *some*, *most*, and *none*.

If <u>any</u> of these marbles <u>are</u> yours, let me know.
[The noun *marbles* is plural.]

If <u>any</u> of this cake <u>is</u> yours, let me know.
[The noun *cake* is singular.]

<u>Most</u> of the potatoes <u>are</u> already gone.
[The noun *potatoes* is plural.]

<u>Most</u> of the evening <u>is</u> already gone.
[The noun *evening* is singular.]

Verb

A **verb** is a word that expresses an action or a state of being.

An **action verb** expresses a physical or mental action:

break	operate
eat	unveil
intercept	wish

A **state of being verb** expresses a condition or state of being:

be	lack
become	seem
is	smell

TRANSITIVE VERBS

A **transitive verb** expresses an action that is performed on someone or something. The someone or something is the **direct object.** Notice in each of the following examples that the direct object receives the action of the verb.

Ingrid <u>restores</u> antique <u>furniture</u>.
[transitive verb: *restores*; direct object: *furniture*]

Hernandez <u>pitched</u> the <u>ball</u>.
[transitive verb: *pitched*; direct object: *ball*]

Did you <u>feed</u> the <u>animals</u>?
[transitive verb: *feed*; direct object: *animals*]

Sometimes a transitive verb has both a direct object and an indirect object. An **indirect object** is the person or thing to whom or for whom the verb's action is being performed. Notice in each of the following examples that the direct object receives the action of the verb, while the indirect object identifies who or what the action affected.

The captain <u>handed us</u> our <u>orders</u>.
[transitive verb: *handed*; direct object: *orders*; indirect object: *us*]

TIP

Remember: A direct object answers *what?* An indirect object answers *to whom?* (or *to what?*) or *for whom?* (or *for what?*).

direct objects:	*What* does Ingrid restore?	furniture
	What did Hernandez pitch?	ball
	Did you feed *what*?	animals
	What did the captain hand?	orders
	Did you give *what*?	water
	What did I toss?	pen
indirect objects:	*To whom* did the captain	us
		hand orders?
	Did you give water *to what*?	plants
	To whom did I toss a pen?	Herman

Did you <u>give</u> the <u>plants</u> some <u>water</u>?
[transitive verb: *give*; direct object: *water*; indirect object:
   plants]

I <u>tossed</u> a <u>pen</u> to <u>Herman</u>.
[transitive verb: *tossed*; direct object: *pen*; indirect object:
   Herman]

INTRANSITIVE VERBS

An **intransitive verb** does not have an object. Notice in each of the
following examples that the verb expresses an action that occurs without needing to be received.

We <u>marched</u> in the parade.
The tea kettle <u>whistled</u>.
Heidi <u>sleeps</u> on the third floor.

TIP

Remember: Because an intransitive verb does not have an object, the
question *what?* will be unanswerable.

What did we march?
What did the kettle whistle?
What does Heidi sleep?

These questions simply cannot be answered; therefore the verbs are
intransitive.

LINKING VERBS

A **linking verb** joins a word (or unit of words) that names a person or
thing to another word (or unit of words) that renames or describes the
person or thing. It is always intransitive and always expresses a state
of being. The most common linking verbs are *to be* and all the forms
of *to be*, which include *am*, *are*, *is*, *was*, and *were*. Other common linking verbs include the following:

act	feel	remain	sound
appear	grow	seem	taste
become	look	smell	turn

The air <u>seemed</u> humid yesterday.
What <u>smells</u> so good?
The days <u>grow</u> shorter.
I <u>am</u> a registered voter.
Kim <u>remains</u> a devout Catholic.
Butch and Sundance <u>were</u> the title characters.

Predicate adjectives and nominatives

The word (or unit of words) that a linking verb joins to the subject can be either an adjective or a noun, but its function is always the same: to tell something about the subject. An adjective that follows a linking verb is a **predicate adjective**. A noun that follows a linking verb is a **predicate nominative**.

predicate adjective: The air seemed <u>humid</u> yesterday.
What smells so <u>good</u>?
The days grow <u>shorter</u>.

predicate nominative: I am a registered <u>voter</u>.
Kim remains a devout <u>Catholic</u>.
Butch and Sundance were the title <u>characters</u>.

VOICE

The subject of a transitive verb either performs or receives the action. A verb whose subject performs is said to be in the **active voice**. A verb whose subject receives is said to be in the **passive voice**.

active voice: Brainerd & Sons <u>built</u> the storage shed.
[The subject *Brainerd & Sons* performed the action of building.]

Lydia <u>will curry</u> the horses.
[The subject *Lydia* will perform the action of currying.]

passive voice: The storage shed <u>was built</u> by Brainerd & Sons.
[The subject *shed* received the action of building.]

The horses will be curried by Lydia.
[The subject *horses* will receive the action of currying.]

MOOD

Verbs have a quality that shows the attitude or purpose of the speaker. This quality is called the **mood**. There are three verb moods: indicative, imperative, and subjunctive.

The **indicative mood** shows a statement or question of fact:

Does Paula <u>know</u> the combination to the safe?
Dr. Sliva <u>is</u> my dentist.

The **imperative mood** shows a command or request:

<u>Make</u> the most of your situation.
<u>Proceed</u> to the third traffic light.

The **subjunctive mood** shows a condition of doubtfulness, possibility, desirability, improbability, or unreality:

<u>Should</u> you <u>decide</u> to return the blouse, you will need the
receipt.
If I <u>were rich</u>, I'd quit my job.

PERSON AND NUMBER

The **person** (first, second, or third) of a verb depends on to whom or to what the verb refers: the person speaking (first person), the person spoken to (second person), or the person or thing spoken about (third person).

The **number** (singular or plural) of a verb depends on whether the verb refers to a singular subject or a plural subject.

For nearly all verbs, the form of the verb changes only in the third person singular.

PERSON	SINGULAR	PLURAL
first person	I *know*	we *know*
second person	you *know*	you *know*
third person	he *knows* she *knows* it *knows*	they *know*
	Chris *knows* Mrs. Hansen *knows* God *knows* the teacher *knows* the heart *knows*	Chris and Pat *know* the Hansens *know* the gods *know* the teachers *know* our hearts *know*

TENSE

The **tense** of a verb shows the time of the verb's action. There are six verb tenses: present, present perfect, past, past perfect, future, and future perfect.

The **present tense** shows action occurring in the present:

I <u>smell</u> fresh coffee.

The present tense can also show the following:

action that is typical or habitual:	I <u>design</u> greenhouses. Stuart <u>daydreams</u> during math class.
action that will occur:	Lynne <u>retires</u> in six months. Our plane <u>lands</u> at midnight.
facts and beliefs:	March <u>follows</u> February. Greed *destroys* the spirit.

The **present perfect tense** is formed with the word *has* or *have*. It shows action begun in the past and completed by the time of the present:

James <u>has checked</u> the air in the tires at least three times.
I <u>have read</u> the book you're talking about.

TIP

Yet another function of the present tense is what is called the **historical present**. This usage allows the writer or speaker to relate past actions in a present tone, which may enhance the descriptive flow of the text.

> The United States <u>acquires</u> the Oklahoma Territory from France in 1803 as part of the Louisiana Purchase. Following the War of 1812, the U.S. government <u>begins</u> a relocation program, forcing Indian tribes from the eastern United States to move into certain unsettled western areas, including Oklahoma. Because of their opposition to the U.S. government, most of these native people <u>lend</u> their support to the Confederate South during the American Civil War. In 1865, the war <u>ends</u> in utter defeat for the Confederacy, and all of the Oklahoma Territory soon <u>falls</u> under U.S. military rule.

When using the historical present, writers and speakers must be careful not to lapse into the past tense. For example, it would be an incorrect mix of tenses to say, "In 1865, the war <u>ended</u> in utter defeat for the Confederacy, and all of the Oklahoma Territory soon <u>falls</u> under U.S. military rule."

The **past tense** shows action that occurred in the past:

> Greg <u>memorized</u> his speech.
> The mouse <u>scurried</u> across the room.

The **past perfect tense** is formed with the word *had*. It shows action that occurred in the past, prior to another past action:

> Eugene <u>had finished</u> his story by the time we got to the airport.
> The parrot <u>had flown</u> into another room long before we noticed an empty cage.

The **future tense** is formed with the word *will*. It shows action that is expected to occur in the future:

> The president <u>will address</u> the nation this evening.
> Tempers <u>will flare</u> when the truth comes out.

The **future perfect tense** is formed with the words *will have*. It shows action that is expected to occur in the future, prior to another future or expected action:

> Noreen <u>will have finished painting</u> by the time we're ready to
>   lay the carpet.
> The candidates <u>will have traveled </u>thousands of miles before
>   this campaign is over.

VERBALS

A verb form that acts as a part of speech other than a verb is a **verbal**. There are three types of verbals: infinitives, participles, and gerunds.

An **infinitive** is a verb form that can act as a noun, an adjective, or an adverb. It is preceded by the preposition *to*:

noun: <u>To steal</u> is a crime.
            [The infinitive *to steal* is the subject.]

            Our original plan, <u>to elope</u>, was never discovered.
            [The infinitive *to elope* is an appositive.]

adjective: Those are words <u>to remember</u>.
            [The infinitive *to remember* modifies the noun *words*.]

adverb: The hill was too icy <u>to climb</u>.
            [The infinitive *to climb* modifies the predicate adjective *icy*.]

            He lived <u>to golf</u>.
            [The infinitive *to golf* modifies the verb *lived*.]

A **participle** is a verb form that has one of two uses: to make a verb phrase ("they <u>were trying</u>"; "the car<u> has died</u>") or to act as an adjective. A participle is a verbal only when it acts as an adjective.

A **present participle** always ends in *–ing*:

> catching
> laughing
> winding

A **past participle** usually ends in *–ed*, *–en*, or *–t*:

> given
> lost
> toasted

In the following examples, each participle acts as an adjective and is therefore a verbal:

> Does the zoo have a <u>laughing</u> hyena?
> We live on a <u>winding</u> road.
> It was a <u>lost</u> opportunity.
> Add a cup of <u>toasted</u> coconut.

A **gerund** is a verb form that acts as a noun. It always ends in *–ing*:

> <u>Reading</u> is my favorite pastime.
> The next step, <u>varnishing</u>, should be done in a well-ventilated area.
> The doctor suggested guidelines for sensible <u>dieting</u>.

TIP

Remember: Both gerunds and present participles always end in *–ing*, but their functions are quite distinct. Also remember that a present participle is only a verbal when it acts as an adjective, *not* when it acts as a verb phrase.

verbal:	Her <u>singing</u> has improved this year. [Used as a noun, *singing* is a gerund, which is always a verbal.]
	Peterson hired the <u>singing</u> cowboys. [Used as an adjective, *singing* is a present participle that is also a verbal.]
not a verbal:	The birds <u>are singing.</u> [Used as a verb phrase, *singing* is a present participle, but not a verbal]

Adjective

An **adjective** is a word that modifies a noun. There are two basic types of adjectives: descriptive and limiting.

DESCRIPTIVE ADJECTIVES

A **descriptive adjective** describes a noun. That is, it shows a quality or condition of a noun:

> She is an <u>upstanding</u> citizen.
> Josh has invited his <u>zany</u> friends.
> That was a <u>mighty</u> clap of thunder.
> I prefer the <u>white</u> shirt with the long sleeves.

LIMITING ADJECTIVES

A **limiting adjective** shows the limits of a noun. That is, it indicates the number or quantity of a noun, or it points out a certain specificity of a noun. There are three types of limiting adjectives: numerical adjectives, pronominal adjectives, and articles.

A **numerical adjective** is a number. It may be cardinal ("how many") or ordinal ("in what order"):

cardinal: We have served <u>one million</u> customers.
            There are <u>three</u> prizes.
            After Arizona was admitted, there were <u>forty-eight</u> states.

ordinal: You are the <u>one millionth</u> customer.
            We won <u>third</u> prize.
            Arizona was the <u>forty-eighth</u> state to be admitted.

A **pronominal adjective** is a pronoun that acts as an adjective. A pronominal adjective may be personal (*my, our, your, his, her, their, its*), demonstrative (*this, that, these, those*), indefinite (*all, any, few, other, several, some*), or interrogative (*which, what*).

personal: We loved <u>her</u> goulash.
                  The squirrel returned to <u>its</u> nest.

demonstrative: <u>Those</u> directions are too complicated.
                  <u>This</u> window is broken.

indefinite: Pick <u>any</u> card from the deck.
                  <u>All</u> luggage will be inspected.

interrogative: <u>Which</u> radios are on sale?
                  <u>What</u> color is the upholstery?

There are three **articles** in English: *a, an,* and *the.* Articles are classified as either indefinite (*a, an*) or definite (*the*).

indefinite: At dawn, <u>a</u> helicopter broke the silence.
                  <u>An</u> usher seated us.

definite: <u>The</u> paintings lacked imagination.

Comparison of adjectives

Descriptive adjectives are able to indicate qualities and conditions by
three degrees of comparison: positive, comparative, and superlative.
Adjectives may be compared in downward or upward order.

TIP

Never "double compare" an adjective. Remember:

• Sometimes a descriptive adjective may use either *–er* or *more,*
  but it never uses both.

correct: The red grapes are <u>sweeter</u> than the green ones.
            The red grapes are <u>more sweet</u> than the green ones.

incorrect: The red grapes are <u>more sweeter</u> than the green ones.

• Sometimes a descriptive adjective may use either *–est* or *most,*
  but it never uses both.

correct: Samson is the <u>friendliest</u> dog in the building.
            Samson is the <u>most friendly</u> dog in the building.

incorrect: Samson is the <u>most friendliest</u> dog in the building.

For **downward comparisons**, all adjectives use the words *less* (comparative) and *least* (superlative).

DOWNWARD COMPARISONS

positive (the quality or condition)	comparative (a degree lower than the positive)	superlative (the lowest degree of the positive)
intelligent	less intelligent	least intelligent
kind	less kind	least kind
salty	less salty	least salty

For **upward comparisons**, there are three different formats:

UPWARD COMPARISONS

positive (the quality or condition)	comparative (a degree higher than the positive)	superlative (the highest degree of the positive)

1. Almost all one-syllable adjectives use the endings *–er* (comparative) and *–est* (superlative). Some adjectives with two or more syllables follow this format as well.

kind	kinder	kindest
straight	straighter	straightest
salty	saltier	saltiest

2. Most adjectives with two or more syllables use the words *more* (comparative) and *most* (superlative). Most one-syllable adjectives may use this format as an optional alternative to using *–er* and *–est*.

harmonious	more harmonious	most harmonious
impatient	more impatient	most impatient
talkative	more talkative	most talkative
kind	more kind	most kind

3. Some adjectives have irregular forms.

bad/ill	worse	worst
good/well	better	best
far	farther/further	farthest/furthest
little	less	least
many	more	most

Adverb

An **adverb** is a word that modifies a verb, an adjective, or another adverb.

ADVERB MEANINGS

An adverb usually describes how, where, when, or to what extent something happens.

An **adverb of manner** describes *how*:

> They argued <u>loudly</u>.

An **adverb of place** describes *where*:

> Please sit <u>near</u> me.

An **adverb of time** describes *when*:

> I'll call you <u>later</u>.

An **adverb of degree** describes *to what extent*:

> The laundry is <u>somewhat</u> damp.

ADVERB FUNCTIONS

A **relative adverb** introduces a subordinate clause:

> I'll be out on the veranda <u>when</u> the clock strikes twelve.

A **conjunctive adverb** (also called a **transitional adverb**) joins two independent clauses:

> Dinner is ready; <u>however</u>, you may have to heat it up.

An **interrogative adverb** introduces a question:

> <u>Where</u> did Lisa go?

An **independent adverb** functions independently from the rest of the sentence. That is, the meaning and grammatical correctness of the sentence would not change if the independent adverb were removed:

> <u>Besides</u>, I never liked living in the city.

COMPARISON OF ADVERBS

Like adjectives, adverbs of manner may be compared in three degrees: positive, comparative, and superlative.

Most adverbs, especially those that end in *–ly*, take on the upward comparing words *more* and *most*:

positive	comparative	superlative
nicely	more nicely	most nicely
diligently	more diligently	most diligently

Some adverbs take on the upward comparing suffixes *–er* and *–est*:

positive	comparative	superlative
early	earlier	earliest
soon	sooner	soonest
close	closer	closest

Some adverbs have irregular upward comparisons:

positive	comparative	superlative
much	more	most
little	less	least
badly	worse	worst
well	better	best
far	farther	farthest
far	further	furthest

Almost all adverbs take on the downward comparing words *less* and *least*:

positive	comparative	superlative
nicely	less nicely	least nicely
diligently	less diligently	least diligently
early	less early	least early
soon	less soon	least soon
close	less close	least close

TIP

Adverbs ending in –*ly*

A great number of adverbs are created by adding the suffix –*ly* to an adjective:

hesitant + -*ly* = hesitantly
strong + -*ly* = strongly

This does not mean, however, that all adverbs end in –*ly*.

adverbs: fast, seldom, now

Nor does it mean that all words ending in –*ly* are adverbs.

adjectives: friendly, homely, dastardly

The way to determine if a word is an adverb or an adjective is to see how it is used in the sentence:

* If it modifies a noun, it is an adjective.
* If it modifies a verb, an adjective, or another adverb, it is an adverb.

Preposition

A **preposition** is a word or group of words that governs a noun or pronoun by expressing its relationship to another word in the clause.

The suspects landed <u>in</u> jail.
[The relationship between the noun *jail* and the verb *landed* is shown by the preposition *in*.]

Please hide the packages <u>under</u> the bed.
[The relationship between the noun *bed* and the noun *packages* is shown by the preposition *under*.]

The guitarist playing <u>with</u> our band is Samantha's uncle.
[The relationship between the noun *band* and the participle *playing* is shown by the preposition *with*.]

I already knew <u>about</u> it.
[The relationship between the pronoun *it* and the verb *knew* is shown by the preposition *about*.]

Common prepositions:

aboard	beneath	in front of	past
about	beside	in lieu of	per
above	besides	in place of	prior to
according to	between	in regard to	regarding
across	beyond	in spite of	round
after	but	inside	since
against	but for	instead of	thanks to
ahead	by	into	through
along	by means of	like	throughout
along with	by way of	near	till
amid	concerning	next to	to
around	contrary to	of	toward
as	despite	off	under
as far as	down	on	underneath
as for	during	on account of	unlike
as to	except	on behalf of	until
aside from	for	onto	up
at	from	opposite	upon
because of	in	out	up to
before	in addition to	out of	with
behind	in back of	outside	within
below	in case of	over	without

TIP

Many words used as prepositions may be used as other parts of speech as well.

The closest village is <u>over</u> that hill.	[preposition]
He leaned <u>over</u> and whispered in my ear.	[adverb]
I told no one <u>but</u> Corinne.	[preposition]
We played our best, <u>but</u> the other team won.	[conjunction]
She is <u>but</u> a shadow of her former self.	[adverb]

Conjunction

A **conjunction** is a word (or unit of words) that connects words, phrases, clauses, or sentences. There are three kinds of conjunctions: coordinating, subordinating, and correlative.

COORDINATING CONJUNCTIONS

A **coordinating conjunction** connects elements that have the same grammatical rank—that is, it connects words to words (nouns to nouns, verbs to verbs, etc.), phrases to phrases, clauses to clauses, sentences to sentences. A coordinating conjunction is almost always one of these seven words: *and, but, for, nor, or, so, yet.*

> Would you prefer rice <u>or</u> potatoes?
> [The coordinating conjunction *or* connects the two nouns *rice* and *potatoes*.]
>
> I have seen <u>and</u> heard enough.
> [The coordinating conjunction *and* connects the two verbs *seen* and *heard*.]
>
> Vinnie's cat lay on the chair purring softly <u>yet</u> twitching its tail.
> [The coordinating conjunction *yet* connects the two participial phrases *purring softly* and *twitching its tail*.]
>
> O'Donnell is the reporter whose name is on the story <u>but</u> who denies having written it.
> [The coordinating conjunction *but* connects the two subordinate clauses *whose name is on the story* and *who denies having written it*.]
>
> We wanted to see batting practice, <u>so</u> we got to the stadium early.
> [The coordinating conjunction *so* connects the two sentences *We wanted to see batting practice* and *We got to the stadium early*, creating one sentence. Notice that a comma precedes the conjunction when two sentences are joined.]

SUBORDINATING CONJUNCTIONS

A **subordinating conjunction** belongs to a subordinate clause. It connects the subordinate clause to a main clause.

> I could get there on time <u>if only</u> the ferry were still running.
> [The subordinating conjunction *if only* connects the
>   subordinate clause *if only the ferry were still running* to the
>   main clause *I could get there on time*.]

Common subordinating conjunctions:

after	but	since	until
although	even if	so	when
as	even though	so that	whenever
as if	how	than	where
as long as	if	that	whereas
as though	if only	though	wherever
because	in order that	till	while
before	rather than	unless	why

TIP

A noun clause or an adjective clause may or may not be introduced by a subordinating conjunction, but an adverb clause always is introduced by a subordinating conjunction.

- noun clause introduced by subordinating conjunction:
  Jack asked the question <u>even though he knew the answer</u>.

- noun clause with no subordinating conjunction:
  We gave <u>every single detail</u> our fullest attention.

- adjective clause introduced by subordinating conjunction:
  This is the farm <u>where we boarded our horses</u>.

- adjective clause with no subordinating conjunction:
  The people <u>we met last night</u> are Hungarian.

- adverb clause with subordinating conjunction (as always):
  I will speak <u>as soon as the crowd quiets down</u>.

CORRELATIVE CONJUNCTIONS

Two coordinating conjunctions that function together are called a pair of correlative conjunctions. These are the most common pairs of **correlative conjunctions**:

both . . . and	not only . . . but
either . . . or	not only . . . but also
neither . . . nor	whether . . . or

The site in Denver offers the potential for <u>both</u> security and expansion.
[The pair of correlative conjunctions *both . . . and* connects the two nouns *security* and *expansion*.]

I'm running in tomorrow's race <u>whether</u> it is sunny <u>or</u> rainy.
[The pair of correlative conjunctions *whether . . . or* connects the two adjectives *sunny* and *rainy*.]

TIP

It would be incorrect to say:
    Their dog is <u>neither</u> quiet <u>nor</u> obeys simple commands.
    Why? Because the pair of correlative conjunctions *neither . . . nor* is being used to connect the adjective *quiet* to the verb phrase *obeys simple commands*. This is not a grammatically valid connection.
    Remember: A pair of correlative conjunctions is comprised of two coordinating conjunctions, and a coordinating conjunction must connect elements that have the same grammatical rank—that is, it must connect words to words (nouns to nouns, verbs to verbs, etc.), phrases to phrases, clauses to clauses, sentences to sentences.
    Therefore, the sentence must be reworded to make the grammatical ranks match. Here are two such corrected versions:

Their dog is <u>neither</u> quiet <u>nor</u> obedient.
[The adjective *quiet* is connected to the adjective *obedient*.]

Their dog <u>neither</u> stays quiet <u>nor</u> obeys simple commands.
[The verb phrase *stays quiet* is connected to the verb phrase *obeys simple commands*.]

Interjection

An interjection is a word or phrase that expresses emotion, typically in an abrupt or emphatic way. It is not connected grammatically to the rest of the sentence. When the emotion expressed is very strong, the interjection is followed by an exclamation point. Otherwise it is followed by a comma:

<u>Stop</u>! I can't let you in here.
<u>Yeah</u>! Dempsey has won another fight.

<u>Ah</u>, that was a wonderful meal.
<u>Oh no</u>, I left my sweater on the train.

TIP

Interjections occur more often in speech than in writing. It is not wrong to use interjections in writing, but writers should do so sparingly. Remember, an interjection is essentially an interruption, and too many may disrupt the flow of the text.

PHRASES, CLAUSES, SENTENCES, AND PARAGRAPHS

Phrases

A **phrase** is a unit of words that acts as a single part of speech.

NOUN PHRASES

A phrase made up of a noun and its modifiers is a **noun phrase**:

<u>The biggest pumpkin</u> won <u>a blue ribbon</u>.
<u>A magnificent whooping crane</u> flew overhead.

Most noun phrases can be replaced with a pronoun:

Give the tickets to <u>the tall, dark-haired gentleman</u>.
Give the tickets to <u>him</u>.

VERB PHRASES

A phrase made up of a main verb and its auxiliaries is a **verb phrase** (also called a **complete verb**):

> We <u>have been waiting</u> for three hours.
> What type of music <u>do</u> you <u>prefer</u>?

ADJECTIVE PHRASES

A phrase made up of a participle and its related words is an **adjective phrase** (also called an **adjectival phrase** or a **participial phrase**). Acting as a single adjective, it modifies a noun or pronoun:

> <u>Awakened by the siren</u>, we escaped to safety.
> [The adjective phrase *Awakened by the siren* modifies the
>   pronoun *we*.]

> <u>Following his grandmother's directions</u>, Harry baked a
>   beautiful apple pie.
> [The adjective phrase *Following his grandmother's directions*
>   modifies the noun *Harry*.]

PREPOSITIONAL PHRASES

A phrase that begins with a preposition is a **prepositional phrase**. It can act as an adjective or an adverb:

adjective: The car <u>with the sunroof</u> is mine.
             [The noun *car* is modified by the prepositional phrase *with the
             sunroof*.]

adverb: <u>After the storm</u>, we gathered the fallen branches.
             [The verb *gathered* is modified by the prepositional phrase
             After the storm.]

Clauses

A clause is a unit of words that contains a subject and a predicate.

INDEPENDENT CLAUSES

A clause that can stand by itself as a complete thought is an **independent clause**. Any independent clause can stand alone as a complete sentence:

> The Milwaukee Brewers joined the National League in
>   November 1997.
> It is snowing.
> Vitus is the patron saint of actors.
> Bob called.
> The Celts were highly ritualistic.
> Read what child development experts have to say.

SUBORDINATE CLAUSES

A clause that cannot stand by itself as a complete thought is a **subordinate clause** (also called a **dependent clause**). It cannot be a part of a sentence unless it is related by meaning to the independent clause. Essentially, it exists to build upon the information conveyed by the independent clause. A subordinate clause can relate to the independent clause as an adjective, an adverb, or a noun:

adjective: The Milwaukee Brewers, who play at Miller Park, joined the National League in November 1997.

adverb: Bob called when you were at the store.

noun: Read what child development experts have to say about the virtues and drawbacks of homeschooling.

ELLIPTICAL CLAUSES

An **elliptical clause** deviates from the rule that states "a clause contains a subject and a predicate." What an elliptical clause does is *imply* both a subject and a predicate, even though both elements do not in fact appear in the clause:

<u>While vacationing in Spain</u>, Jo received word of her
    promotion.
[The elliptical clause implies the subject "she" and the
    predicate "was vacationing"—that is, it implies "While she
    was vacationing in Spain."]

Myers arrived on Saturday the 12th; <u>Anderson, the following
    Monday</u>.
[The elliptical clause implies the predicate "arrived the
    following Monday"—that is it implies "Anderson arrived
    the following Monday."]

Elliptical clauses are valuable devices, as they allow the writer to
avoid excessive wordiness, preserve a sense of variety, and enhance
the rhythm of the text.

RESTRICTIVE CLAUSES

A clause that is essential to the meaning of the sentence—that is, it
restricts the meaning of the sentence—is a **restrictive clause**. The
content of a restrictive clause identifies a particular person, place, or
thing. If the restrictive clause were to be removed, the meaning of
the sentence would change. A restrictive clause begins with the relative pronoun *that, who*, or *whom*. It should never be set off with
commas.

I'm returning the coat <u>that I bought last week</u>.
[The identification of the coat is important. It's not just any
    coat. It's specifically the one and only coat "that I bought
    last week." Without the restrictive clause, the
    identification would be lost.]

The president <u>who authorized the Louisiana Purchase </u>was
    Thomas Jefferson.
[The point of this sentence is to identify specifically the one
    and only president responsible for the Louisiana Purchase.
    Without the restrictive clause, the point of the sentence
    would be lost.]

Nonrestrictive clauses

A clause that is not essential to the meaning of the sentence—that is, it does *not restrict* the meaning of the sentence—is a **nonrestrictive clause**. The content of a nonrestrictive clause adds information to what has already been identified. If the nonrestrictive clause were to be removed, the meaning of the sentence would not change. A nonrestrictive clause begins with the relative pronoun *which*, *who*, or *whom*. It should always be set off with commas.

I'm returning my new coat, <u>which doesn't fit</u>.

President Jefferson, <u>who authorized the Louisiana Purchase</u>, was the third U.S. president.

[The clauses *which doesn't fit* and *who authorized the Louisiana Purchase* are informative but not necessary. Without them, the meaning of each sentence is still clear.]

Sentences

Properly constructed sentences are integral to good communication. By definition, a sentence is "a set of words that is complete in itself, typically containing a subject and predicate, conveying a statement, question, exclamation, or command, and consisting of a main clause and sometimes one or more subordinate clauses." Simply put, a sentence is a group of words that expresses a complete thought.

Subject and predicate

The primary building blocks of a sentence are the subject and the predicate.

The **subject** (usually a noun or pronoun) is the part that the sentence is telling about. A **simple subject** is simply the person, place, or thing being discussed. A **complete subject** is the simple subject along with all the words directly associated with it:

<u>The large tropical plant in my office</u> has bloomed every summer.

[Here, the simple subject is *plant*. The complete subject is
The large tropical plant in my office.]

Two or more subjects that belong to the same verb comprise what is
called a **compound subject**:

Stan Garrison and the rest of the department are relocating
next week.
[Here, the compound subject consists of *Stan Garrison* and
the rest of the department. They share the verb phrase *are
relocating*.]

The **predicate** (a verb) is the "action" or "being" part of the sentence—
the part that tells something about the subject. A **simple predicate** is
simply the main verb and its auxiliaries. A **complete predicate** is the
simple predicate along with all the words directly associated with it:

The setting sun has cast a scarlet glow across the skyline.
[Here, the simple predicate is has cast. The complete
predicate is *has cast a scarlet glow across the skyline*.]

Two or more predicates that have the same subject comprise what is
called a **compound predicate**.

I wanted to buy some art but left empty-handed.
[Here, the compound predicate consists of *wanted to buy
some art* and *left empty-handed*. They share the subject *I*.]

FOUR SENTENCE STRUCTURES

A **simple sentence** contains one independent clause. Its subject
and/or predicate may or may not be compound, but its one and only
clause is always independent:

Paula rode her bicycle. [subject + predicate]
Honus Wagner and Nap Lajoie are enshrined in the Baseball
Hall of Fame. [compound subject + predicate]
The correspondents traveled across the desert and slept in
makeshift shelters. [subject + compound predicate]
Lunch and dinner are discounted on Sunday but are full price
on Monday. [compound subject + compound predicate]

A **compound sentence** contains two or more independent clauses. The following examples show the various ways that coordinating conjunctions (e.g., *and, but, yet*), conjunctive adverbs (e.g., *however, therefore*), and punctuation may be used to join the clauses in a compound sentence:

Ken made the phone calls and Maria addressed the envelopes.

The war lasted for two years, but the effects of its devastation will last for decades.

Judges and other officials should sign in by noon; exhibitors will start arriving at 2:00.

I have decided to remain on the East Coast; however, I am willing to attend the monthly meetings in Dallas.

FDR initiated the New Deal, JFK embraced the New Frontier, and LBJ envisioned the Great Society.

A **complex sentence** contains one independent clause and one or more subordinate clauses:

Even though I majored in English, I was hired to teach applied physics.

We can have the party indoors if it gets too windy.

Before I agree, I have to read the final report that you drafted.

[The independent clauses are *I was hired to teach applied physics; We can have the party indoors; I have to read the final report.* The subordinate clauses are *Even though I majored in English; if it gets too windy; Before I agree; that you drafted.*]

A **compound-complex sentence** contains two or more independent clauses and one or more subordinate clauses:

Because the candidates have been so argumentative, some voters are confused and many have become disinterested.

We will begin painting tomorrow if the weather's nice; if it rains, we will start on Thursday.

[The independent clauses are *some voters are confused; many have become disinterested; We will begin painting tomorrow; we will start on Thursday.* The subordinate clauses are *Because the candidates have been so argumentative; if the weather's nice; if it rains.*]

FOUR SENTENCE FUNCTIONS

A **declarative sentence** states a fact, an assertion, an impression, or a feeling. It ends with a period:

> Florence is a beautiful city.
> Lewis Carroll died in 1898.
> I'm sorry I missed the end of your speech.

An **interrogative sentence** asks a question. It ends with a question mark:

> Did you read the article about migrating geese patterns?
> How do spell your last name?
> Mr. Young owns a kennel?

An **imperative sentence** makes a request or gives an order. It typically ends with a period but occasionally may end with an exclamation point:

> Please lock the doors.
> Do not throw trash in the recycling bins.
> Think before you speak!

An **exclamatory sentence** expresses surprise, shock, or strong feeling. It ends with an exclamation point:

> Look at this mess!
> I can't believe how great this is!
> I lost my purse!

Paragraphs

A paragraph is a series of sentences that conveys a single theme. Paragraphs help writers organize thoughts, actions, and descriptions into readable units of information. The paragraph, as a unit of text, may have one of several functions. It may be descriptive, giving certain details or impressions about a person, thing, or event. It may be instructive, explaining a method or procedure. It may be conceptual, stating thoughts, feelings, or opinions.

Every paragraph should contain a sentence that states the main idea of the paragraph. This is called the **topic sentence**. The other sentences in the paragraph are the **supporting sentences**, and their function is just that—to support or elaborate on the idea set forth in the topic sentence. Most paragraphs begin with the topic sentence, as in the following example:

> Each Thanksgiving we make place cards decorated with pressed autumn leaves. After gathering the smallest and most colorful leaves from the maples and oaks in our backyard, we place the leaves between sheets of blotter paper, which we then cover with a large, heavy book. In just a day or two, the leaves are ready to be mounted on cards. We use plain index cards, folded in half. Using clear adhesive paper, we put one leaf on each card, leaving room for the guest's name.

Try reading the preceding paragraph without the topic sentence (the first sentence). The supporting information becomes less unified because it has no main idea to support. Now imagine adding to the paragraph the following sentence:

> Last year, three of our guests were snowed in at the airport.

This would be a misplaced addition to the paragraph, as it is unrelated to the topic sentence (that is, it has nothing to do with making Thanksgiving place cards). Because it introduces a new and distinct idea, it should become the topic sentence for a new and distinct paragraph.

SENTENCE DEVELOPMENT: AVOIDING PROBLEMS

Sentence style

Getting one's ideas across in words is the core of communication. Sentences provide the means to arrange ideas in a coherent way. Certainly, the rules of grammar should be observed when constructing a sentence, but the general rhythm of the sentence is also important.

Sentences may be categorized into three general types: loose, periodic, and balanced. Good writers typically use a combination of these styles in order to create a flow of ideas that will hold the reader's interest.

A **loose sentence** gets to the main point quickly. It begins with a basic and complete statement, which is followed by additional information:

> The power went out, plunging us into darkness, silencing the
> drone of the television, leaving our dinner half-cooked.
> [The basic statement is *The power went out*. Everything that
> follows is additional information.]

A **periodic sentence** ends with the main point. It begins with additional information, thus imposing a delay before the basic statement is given:

> With no warning, like a herd of stampeding bison, a mob of
> fans crashed through the gate.
> [The basic statement is *a mob of fans crashed through the
> gate*. Everything that precedes is additional information.]

A **balanced sentence** is comprised of grammatically equal or similar structures. The ideas in the sentence are linked by comparison or contrast:

> To visit their island villa is to sample nirvana.

As writers become more comfortable with the basic rules of grammar and the general patterns of sentence structure, they are able to remain compliant with the rules while getting more creative with the patterns. Many well-constructed sentences will not agree precisely with any of the three preceding examples, but they should always evoke an answer of "yes" to two fundamental questions:

- Is the sentence grammatically correct?
- Will the meaning of the sentence be clear to the reader?

Flawed sentences

Three types of "flawed sentences" are sentence fragments, run-on sentences, and sentences with improperly positioned modifiers.

SENTENCE FRAGMENTS

A **sentence fragment** is simply an incomplete sentence. Fundamental to every sentence is a complete thought that is able to stand on its own. Because a phrase or subordinate clause is not an independent thought, it cannot stand on its own as a sentence. To be a part of a sentence, it must either be connected to an independent clause or be reworded to become an independent clause. Consider this sentence fragment:

My English guest who stayed on for Christmas.

Here are three possible ways to create a proper sentence from that fragment:

Everyone left on Tuesday except Dan, my English guest who
   stayed on for Christmas.
[The fragment is added to the independent clause *Everyone
   left on Tuesday except Dan.*]

My English guest stayed on for Christmas.
[The fragment becomes an independent clause by removing
   the word *who.*]

Dan was my English guest who stayed on for Christmas.
[The fragment becomes an independent clause by adding the
   words *Dan was.*]

RUN-ON SENTENCES

A **run-on sentence** results when two or more sentences are improperly united into one sentence. Characteristic of a run-on sentence is the absence of punctuation between the independent clauses or the use of incorrect punctuation (typically a comma) between the independent clauses:

> Our flight was canceled we had to spend the night in Boston.
> Our flight was canceled, we had to spend the night in Boston.

Here are three possible ways to correct the preceding run-on sentences:

> Our flight was canceled; we had to spend the night in Boston.
> [A semicolon provides a properly punctuated separation of
>   the two independent clauses.]

> Our flight was canceled, so we had to spend the night in Boston.
> [A comma followed by a conjunction (*so*) provides a properly
>   worded and punctuated separation of the two independent
>   clauses.]

> Our flight was canceled. We had to spend the night in Boston.
> [The creation of two distinct sentences provides an absolute
>   separation of the two independent clauses.]

MODIFIER PROBLEMS

The improper placement of modifying words, phrases, and clauses is a common mistake. The result is a sentence in which the modifier unintentionally refers to the wrong person or thing. The three principal culprits are dangling modifiers, misplaced modifiers, and squinting modifiers. Writers must be careful to avoid these troublesome errors in sentence construction. Review the following examples to see how an improperly placed modifier can be confusing to the reader. It is important to recognize the subtle differences between the incorrect sentences and their corrected versions.

A **dangling modifier** is an adjectival phrase or clause that lacks a proper connection because the word it is supposed to modify is missing.

dangling: While waiting for my son, a cat jumped onto the hood of my car.
               [This wrongly implies that "a cat was waiting for my son."]

correct: While I was waiting for my son, a cat jumped onto the hood of
            my car.
            While waiting for my son, I saw a cat jump onto the hood of my
            car.
            A cat jumped onto the hood of my car while I was waiting for my
            son.
            [The word that was missing is "I."]

dangling: At age seven, her grandfather died of diphtheria.
            [This wrongly implies that "her grandfather died when he was
            seven."]

correct: When she was seven, her grandfather died of diphtheria.
            Her grandfather died of diphtheria when she was seven.
            At age seven, she lost her grandfather when he died of
            diphtheria.
            [The word that was missing is "she."]

A misplaced modifier is a phrase or clause that is not positioned close
enough to the word it is supposed to modify. It will seem to the reader
that a different word is being modified.

misplaced: There was an outbreak in our school of chicken pox.
            [This wrongly implies that there is "a school of chicken pox."]

correct: There was an outbreak of chicken pox in our school.
            In our school there was an outbreak of chicken pox.
            Our school experienced an outbreak of chicken pox.

misplaced: I was stopped by a policeman without a driver's license.
            [This wrongly implies that there was "a policeman without a
            driver's license."]

correct: Driving without a license, I was stopped by a policeman.
            I was stopped by a policeman, and I did not have a driver's
            license.

A squinting modifier is an adverb placed between two verbs. For the
reader, it is often difficult to determine which verb the adverb is supposed to modify.

squinting: The stack of chairs she had arranged carefully collapsed in the
                 wind.
                 [Was the stack of chairs "arranged carefully" or did it "carefully
                 collapse"?]

correct: The stack of chairs she had carefully arranged collapsed in the
                 wind.
                 [Of the two possible meanings, this is only one that makes
                 sense.]

squinting: The stack of chairs she had arranged quickly collapsed in the
                 wind.
                 [Was the stack of chairs "arranged quickly" or did it "quickly
                 collapse"?]

correct: The stack of chairs shc had quickly arranged collapsed in the
                 wind.
                 The stack of chairs she had arranged collapsed quickly in the
                 wind.
                 [Either meaning could make sense, so only the writer would
                 know which version is correct.]

Guide to Spelling

Any reader or writer knows that spelling is an important component
of writing. Some individuals seem to have little or no trouble spelling
words correctly, while others seem to struggle with spelling, often
misspelling the same words over and over.

TIP

Keep a list of words that you find difficult to spell. Use a dictionary to confirm the correct spellings. Add to your list whenever you encounter a troublesome word. Refer to your list often, and quiz yourself. Make up
sentences that include words from the list, writing them without going
back and forth to double-check the spelling. Compare the words in your
sentences to the words on your list. Make a note of the words that continue to give you trouble, and write these words in sentences every day
until you have learned to spell them.

For those who have experienced the struggle, it is important to remember that spelling is a skill that improves with practice. Regular reading and writing, accompanied by a dictionary for consultation, are the best methods for improving one's spelling. Anyone who has encountered trouble with spelling knows that the English language contains numerous irregularities. Even so, there are basic spelling rules that can be followed in most cases.

[For spelling guidelines for plural nouns and possessive nouns, refer to the "Noun" section under "Parts of Speech."]

COMPOUND ADJECTIVES AND NOUNS

A compound adjective or noun is a single term formed from two or more distinct words. There are three spelling formats for compounds: open, hyphenated, and closed.

In an **open compound**, the component words are separate, with no hyphen (*well fed; wagon train*).

In a **hyphenated compound**, the component words are joined by a hyphen (*half-baked; city-state*).

In a **closed compound**, the component words are joined into a single word (*hardheaded; campfire*).

Compound Adjectives

For most cases of open compound adjectives, there is a general rule of thumb: the compound is left open when it is not followed by the modified noun; the compound is hyphenated when it is followed by the modified noun:

She was well known in the South for her poetry.
[The compound *well known* is open because it is not followed by the modified noun *She*.]

In the South, she was a well-known poet.
[The compound *well-known* is hyphenated because it is followed by the modified noun *poet*.]

A notable exception occurs when the first part of the compound adjective is an adverb that ends in *–ly*. In this case, the compound remains open, even when it is followed by the noun:

The <u>woman</u> who met us in the lobby was <u>beautifully dressed</u>.
A <u>beautifully dressed woman</u> met us in the lobby.

Compound Nouns

For spellers, the least troublesome compound nouns are familiar closed compounds:

briefcase   downstairs
cupcake   fireplace

Other compound nouns can be troublesome. Although certain ones, such as *mother-in-law*, are always hyphenated, many compound nouns commonly occur in more than one acceptable format, such as *ice cap* or *icecap* and *vice president* or *vice-president*. For most spelling questions, the best resource is a dictionary; for questions pertaining specifically to compounds, an unabridged edition is recommended.

TIP

Different dictionaries often disagree on the preferred spelling formats for a number of compounds, so writers are well advised to consult just one dictionary when establishing a spelling style.

PREFIXES

A prefix is group of letters added to the beginning of a word to adjust its meaning.

In most cases, prefixes are affixed to the root word without hyphenation:

antibacterial
postwar
semicircle

Often, however, a hyphen is customary, necessary, or preferable.

Certain prefixes almost always take a hyphen: *all-*, *ex-*, *full-*, *quasi-*, *self-*:

   all-encompassing   quasi-liberal
   ex-partner   self-confidence
   full-bodied

When the root word begins with a capital letter, the prefix takes a hyphen:

   anti-American
   pre-Conquest

Sometimes, without a hyphen, a word could be easily confused with another:

   We <u>recovered</u> our furniture.

Does this mean we *found our missing* furniture? Or did we *put new coverings on* our furniture? If the latter is meant, a hyphen would have avoided confusion:

   We <u>re-covered</u> our furniture.

Sometimes, a hyphen is not necessary but preferable. Without it, the word may look awkward. One such circumstance is when the last letter of the prefix and the first letter of the root word are both vowels, or when an awkward double consonant is created. For each of the following pairs of words, either spelling is acceptable:

   antiknock / anti-knock
   preadapt / pre-adapt
   semiindependent / semi-independent
   nonnegative/non-negative

TIP

Regarding the use of optional hyphens, the writer should establish a preferred style. Keeping a running list of hyphenated terms can help writers keep track of which spellings they have already used in their text, thus making the style consistent.

SUFFIXES

A suffix is group of letters added to the end of a word to create a deriv-ative of the word. There are exceptions to the following guidelines on how to spell with suffixes, but in most cases these rules apply:

A root word that ends in *e* drops the *e* when the suffix begins with a vowel:

> rehearse / rehearsing

However, most words that end in *ce* or *ge* keep the *e* when the suffix begins with *a* or *o*:

> service / serviceable
> advantage / advantageous

A root word that ends in *e* keeps the *e* when the suffix begins with a consonant:

> wise / wisely

A root word that ends in a *y* preceded by a consonant changes the *y* to *i* when the suffix begins with any letter other than *i*:

> satisfy / satisfies / satisfying

A root word that ends in *ie* changes the *ie* to *y* when the suffix is *–ing*:

> lie / lying

A root word that ends in *oe* keeps the *e* when the suffix begins with a vowel, unless the vowel is *e*:

> toe / toeing / toed

A one-syllable root word that ends in a single consonant preceded by a single vowel doubles the consonant when the suffix is *–ed, –er,* or *–ing*. This rule also applies to root words with two or more syllables if the accent is on the last syllable.

> stir / stirred
> refer / referring

WORD DIVISION

Sometimes it is necessary to "break" a word when the line on the page has run out of space. Dividing a word at the end of a line is perfectly acceptable, as long as two conditions are met: the word must be divisible, and the division must be made in the right place.

When a word is properly divided, a hyphen is attached to its first part, so that the hyphen is at the end of the line:

> At the conclusion of the interview,
> I had two minutes to sum-
> marize my management experiences.

What words are never divisible?	*for example:*	
• one-syllable words	catch; flutes; strange; through	
• contractions	didn't; doesn't; wouldn't; you're	
• abbreviations	Calif.; NASCAR; RSVP; YMCA	
• numbers written as numerals	1776; $2,800; 9:45; 0.137	

Where is a correct place to divide a word?	*good break:*	*bad break:*
• after a prefix	inter-national	interna-tional
• before a suffix that has more than two letters	govern-ment	gov-ernment
• between the main parts of a closed compound	nut-cracker	nutcrack-er
• at the hyphen of a hyphenated compound	gender-neutral	gen-der-neutral
• after double consonants if the root word ends in the double consonants	address-ing	addres-sing

Where is a correct place to divide a word?

	good break:	bad break:
• otherwise, between double consonants	rib-bon	ribb-on
• in general (for words that don't fall into the previous categories), between syllables	whis-per	whi-sper

Where is an incorrect place to divide a word?

	good break:	bad break:
• before a two-letter suffix	——	odd-ly
• after the first syllable if it has only one letter	Ameri-can	A-merican
• before the last syllable if it has only one letter	nu-tria	nutri-a
• before the ending –ed if the –ed is not pronounced	——	abash-ed

---

TIP

When dividing a word at the end of a line, it is always a good idea to use a dictionary to verify the word's proper syllabification.

NUMBERS

Numbers are an important part of everyday communication, yet they often cause a writer to stumble, particularly over questions of spelling and style. The guidelines on *how* to spell out a number are fairly straightforward. The guidelines on *when* to spell out a number are not so precise.

How to spell out numbers

CARDINAL NUMBERS

The most common problem associated with the spelling of whole cardinal numbers is punctuation. The rules are actually quite simple:

Numeric amounts that fall between twenty and one hundred are always hyphenated. No other punctuation should appear in a spelled-out whole number, regardless of its size.

26	twenty-six
411	four hundred eleven
758	seven hundred fifty-eight
6,500	six thousand five hundred
33,003	thirty-three thousand three
972,923	nine hundred seventy-two thousand nine hundred twenty-three

Note: The word *and* does not belong in the spelling of a number. For example, "758" should not be spelled "seven hundred and fifty-eight."

ORDINAL NUMBERS

The punctuation of spelled-out ordinal numbers typically follows the rules for cardinal numbers.

> What should we do for their <u>fifty-fifth</u> anniversary?
> He graduated<u> two hundred twenty-ninth</u> out of a class of two hundred thirty.

When ordinal numbers appear as numerals, they are affixed with –th, with the exception of those ending with the ordinal *first*, *second*, or *third*.

1st	581st
2nd	32nd
3rd	73rd
4th	907th

Note: Sometimes *2nd* is written as *2d*, and *3rd* as *3d*.

FRACTIONS

A fraction can appear in a number of formats, as shown here:

$^3/_8$	case fraction (or split fraction)
3/8	fraction with solidus
0.375	decimal fraction
three-eighths	spelled-out fraction

When acting as an adjective, a spelled-out fraction should always be hyphenated.

The Serbian democrats have won a <u>two-thirds</u> majority.

When acting as a noun, a spelled-out fraction may or may not be hyphenated, according to the writer's or publisher's preferred style.

At least <u>four-fifths</u> of the supply has been depleted.
or
At least <u>four fifths</u> of the supply has been depleted.

When to Spell Out Numbers

When to spell out a number, whole or fractional, is as much a matter of sense as of style. Text that is heavy with numbers, such as scientific or statistical material, could become virtually unreadable if the numbers were all spelled out. Conversely, conventional prose that occasionally makes mention of a quantity may look unbalanced with an occasional numeral here and there.

Often, the decision to spell or not to spell comes down to simple clarity:

Our standard paper size is 8½ by 11.
Our standard paper size is 8 1/2 by 11.
Our standard paper size is eight and a half by eleven.
Our standard paper size is eight and one-half by eleven.

The preceding four sentences say exactly the same thing, but the best choice for readability is the first.

Even the most comprehensive books of style and usage do not dictate absolute rules regarding the style of numbers in text. When writing, it is most important to be as consistent as possible with a style once one has been established. For example, some writers or publishers may adopt a policy of spelling out the numbers zero through ten. Others may prefer to spell out the numbers zero through ninety-nine. Either style is perfectly acceptable, as long as the style is followed throughout the written work.

Sometimes, even after adopting a basic number style, the writer may wish to incorporate certain style allowances and exceptions. Perhaps the decision has been made to spell out only the numbers zero though ninety-nine. But in one paragraph, a sentence reads, "There must have been more than 1,000,000 people there." In this case, it may be better to write, "There must have been more than a million people there."

SYMBOLS

In most contexts of formal writing, the use of symbols should be strictly limited, but there are occasions when a symbol may be a better choice than a word. Text that deals largely with commerce, for instance, may rely on the use of various monetary symbols to keep the text organized and readable. In any text, mathematical equations and scientific formulas are much easier to read if written with symbols rather than words. Also, it is usually appropriate to use symbols within tables and charts; as symbols conserve space, they prevent a "cluttered look."

Here are some of the most common symbols found in print:

@	at	$\approx$	is approximately equal to
c/o	care of	$\neq$	is not equal to
$	dollar	<	is less than
¢	cent	>	is greater than
Can$	Canadian dollar	$\leq$	is less than or equal to
£	pound sterling	$\geq$	is greater than or equal to
¥	yen	$\sqrt{}$	square root
#	number or pound	∞	infinity
/	per *or* solidus	©	copyright
%	percent	®	registered
°	degree	™	trademark
+	plus	¶	paragraph
−	minus	§	section
÷	divided by	*	asterisk
×	times	†	dagger
±	plus or minus	‡	double dagger
=	equals	‖	parallels or pipes

Symbols are sometimes used to point out note references to the reader. In a table or chart, for instance, the writer may wish to indicate that an item is further explained or identified elsewhere on the page. A symbol placed with the item signals the reader to look for an identical symbol, which precedes the additional information. Sometimes, numerals are the symbols of choice, but if the material within the table or chart consists of numerals, it is probably better to use non-numeric symbols for the note references. The conventional set of symbols used for this purpose, in the conventional sequence in which to use them, is *, †, ‡, §, ||, #.

TIP

Numerals and other symbols should never begin a sentence. If the symbol should not or cannot be spelled out, the sentence needs to be reworded.

19 students have become mentors.
should be:
Nineteen students have become mentors.

2004 is the year we plan to get married.
should be:
We plan to get married in 2004.

$10 was found on the stairs.
should be:
Ten dollars was found on the stairs.

6:00 is the earliest I can leave.
should be:
Six o'clock is the earliest I can leave.
or:
The earliest I can leave is 6:00.

$y = 2x + 1$ is a line with a slope of 2.
should be:
The line $y = 2x + 1$ has a slope of 2.

FOREIGN TERMS

Foreign words and phrases that are likely to be unfamiliar to the reader should be set in italics. When such terms are to be included in writing or speech, a dictionary should be consulted by the writer to insure proper placement of accents and other diacritical marks and by the speaker to insure correct pronunciations. Each of the following sample terms gives the literal translation, the English-usage definition, and an example sentence.

annus mirabilis: [Latin, 'wonderful year'] a remarkable or auspicious year.
This has been our team's *annus mirabilis*.

cause célèbre: [French, 'famous case'] a controversial issue that attracts a great deal of public attention.
The trial of Lizzie Borden became a *cause célèbre* throughout New England.

Weltschmerz: [German, 'world pain'] a feeling of melancholy and world-weariness.
A sense of *Weltschmerz* permeated his later works of art.
[Note that it is correct to capitalize a German noun.]

Familiar Foreign Terms

Many foreign terms have become so familiar and well-established in standard English usage that it is not necessary to put them in italic type. For most of these words, it is also not necessary to use accents and other diacritical marks, but in certain cases the inclusion of diacritics remains customary. There are, however, no absolute rules regarding when to italicize and when not to italicize, when to use diacritics and when not to use diacritics. Some foreign words may be more familiar to one group of readers than to another; therefore, targeted readership should be considered. Often, the style adopted is a matter of preference. As always, it is important for the writer to be consistent once this preference has been introduced.

Some familiar foreign terms:

ad absurdum
ad hoc
ad infinitum
ad interim
ad lib
ad nauseam
aficionado
à la carte (or a la carte)
à la king (or a la king)
à la mode (or a la mode)
al fresco
alter ego
annus mirabilis
Anno Domini
apartheid
aperitif
a priori
apropros
au contraire
au courant
au fait
au fond
au gratin
au jus
au naturel
au pair
avant-garde
ballet
basmati
bas-relief
baton
beau
beau monde
belle
bête noire

billet doux
bona fide
bonbon
bon mot
bon vivant
bouclé
boudoir
bouffant
bouillabaisse
bouillon
bouquet
bouquet garni
bourgeois
bric-a-brac
burka (or burkha)
burrito
cabaret
café (or cafe)
camisole
canapé
capo
carafe
carpe diem
carte blanche
cause célèbre
chaise longue
chalet
chamois
chapeau
chateau (or château)
chauffeur
chic
ciao
cognac
coiffeur
connoisseur
consommé

contretemps
corps
crepe (or crêpe)
croquette
cul-de-sac
de facto
déjà vu
de jure
de rigeur
dolce vita
Doppelgänger
élan
elite
enchilada
enfant terrible
en masse
en route
entourage
entrée (or entree)
entre nous
eureka
ex cathedra
ex post facto
fait accompli
fajita
faux
faux pas
fiancé (or fiance)
fiancée (or fiancee)
fiesta
flagrante delicto
glasnost
gourmand
gourmet
hacienda
haute cuisine
hoi polloi

hors d'oeuvre
incognito
ingénue
in loco parentis
in re
in situ
in toto
in vitro
in vivo
jabot
judo
julienne
karma
karate
kasha
kibitz
kitsch
laissez-faire
lanai
lèse-majesté
loco
lorgnette
madame
mademoiselle
maître d' (or maitre d')
mañana
masseur
masseuse
materiel (or matériel)
mea culpa
modus operandi
monsieur
mot juste
née
ne plus ultra
nom de guerre
nom de plume
non sequitur

nota bene
nouveau riche
objet d'art
objet trouvé
pace
par excellence
pasha
pâté de foie gras
patio
per capita
persona non grata
pièce de résistance
pied-à-terre
piccolo
poncho
portière (or portiere)
post mortem
prima donna
prima facie
pro bono
pro forma
pronto
protégé (or protege)
purée (or puree)
quid pro quo
qui vive
raisond'être
re
rendezvous
repertoire
résumé (or resume)
revue
roué
roulette
sachet
salsa
samovar
samurai

sang froid
sans souci
savoir faire
seance
serape
siesta
sine die
sine qua non
sombrero
soufflé
status quo
sub judice
suede
tableau
table d'hôte
tabula rasa
taco
tango
terra incognita
tête-à-tête
tour de force
tout le monde
trompe l'oeil
trousseau
verboten
vice versa
villa
viva voce
viz.
vox populi
Wanderjahr
Weltanschauung
Weltschmerz
yin/yang
yoga
Zeitgeist

Commonly Misspelled Words

abbreviated	anesthetic	believe
absence	angel	benefit
absolutely	angle	benefited
acceptance	annihilation	bicycle
accessible	annually	bouillon
accidentally	answer	boundary
accommodate	anticipate	bulletin
accompany	anxiety	bureau
accuracy	apartheid	buried
ache	aperitif	business
achieve	apology	cafeteria
achievement	apparatus	calendar
acquaintance	apparent	campaign
acquire	appearance	cancellation
acre	appetite	captain
across	appreciate	carburetor
actually	approach	career
administration	appropriate	ceiling
admittance	approximately	cemetery
adolescent	argue	census
advantageous	argument	certificate
advertisement	arithmetic	chamois
advisable	arrangement	changeable
affectionate	ascend	character
affidavit	ascertain	characteristic
aficionado	assistant	chauffeur
afraid	athletic	chic
again	attendance	chief
aggravate	authority	chocolate
aghast	auxiliary	choice
aisle	available	choose
allege	awkward	chose
allotment	bachelor	Christian
ally	because	clothes
amateur	beggar	collateral
analysis	beginning	colonel
analyze	behavior	color

column	decision	equipped
commercial	definite	escape
commission	dependent	especially
committee	describe	essential
community	despair	et cetera
compel	desperate	(abbreviated *etc.*)
competitor	despise	exaggerate
completely	develop	excellent
conceivable	difference	exciting
concentrate	dilemma	exercise
condemn	diphthong	exhilarating
confidence	disappearance	exhort
confidential	disappoint	existence
confusion	disastrous	expense
connoisseur	discipline	experience
conscience	discrepancy	experiment
conscious	disease	extraordinary
continuous	diuretic	extremely
controlled	doctor	facsimile
controversial	duplicate	familiar
conversant	easily	fantasy
convertible	ecclesiastical	fascinate
cooperate	ecstasy	fashionable
copyright	effect	fasten
corps	efficient	fatal
correspondence	eighth	favorite
counterfeit	elementary	February
courageous	eligible	field
courteous	embarrass	fiery
criticism	eminent	finally
criticize	emphasize	financial
cruelly	encouragement	fluorescent
curiosity	encumbrances	forehead
curious	enforceable	foreign
cylinder	entirely	forfeit
dealt	entourage	fortunately
debtor	envelope	forty
deceive	environment	forward

Commonly Misspelled Words (*cont.*)

fourth	hysterical	lieutenant
freight	ignorance	lightning
friend	illiterate	likely
fulfill	imagine	liquefy
further	immediately	liquidate
gauge	impossible	listener
genius	incidentally	literature
gourmet	increase	livelihood
government	indefinite	lively
governor	independent	loneliness
gracious	indictment	luxury
grammar	indispensable	magazine
guarantee	individually	magnificent
guerrilla	inevitable	maintenance
guess	influence	maneuver
guidance	ingredient	manufacturer
gymnasium	innocence	marriage
gypsy	inoculate	marvelous
handsome	insurance	mathematics
hangar	intelligence	meant
hanger	intelligent	mechanic
happened	interference	medical
happiness	interrupt	medicine
harass	iridescent	melancholy
Hawaii	irrelevant	merchandise
heavily	itinerary	millionaire
height	jealous	miniature
heinous	jewelry	minimum
heroine	knowledge	minuscule
hors d'oeuvre	laboratory	minute
hospital	laborer	miscellaneous
humor	laid	mischief
humorous	legitimate	mischievous
hungrily	leisure	Massachusetts
hygiene	liaison	misspell
hypocrisy	library	mortgage
hypocrite	license	muscle

mysterious	peculiar	psychic
narrative	performance	psychology
naturally	permanent	pumpkin
necessary	perseverance	punctual
nickel	personality	punctuation
niece	personnel	pursuit
ninety	perspiration	questionnaire
noisily	persuade	quiet
non sequitur	pessimistic	quite
noticeable	phenomenal	quotient
obstacle	Philippines	raspberry
occasionally	philosophy	realize
occurrence	physical	really
offensive	picnicking	realtor
official	pleasant	realty
often	politician	receipt
omission	Portuguese	recipe
omit	possession	recognize
omitted	possibility	recommend
once	practically	referred
operate	practice	reign
opponent	prairie	relevant
opportunity	preferred	relieve
optimistic	prejudice	religious
orchestra	preparation	removal
ordinarily	presence	rendezvous
organization	pressure	repertoire
originally	pretension	repetition
outrageous	privilege	rescind
pageant	probably	reservoir
paid	procedure	resistance
parallel	proceed	resource
paralleled	procure	responsibility
paralyze	professor	restaurant
parliament	proffered	rheumatism
particular	promissory	rhythm
pastime	pronunciation	ridiculous
peaceful	propaganda	roommate

Commonly Misspelled Words (*cont.*)

sachet	specimen	tomorrow
sacrifice	sponsor	tragedy
sacrilegious	statistics	transferred
safety	straight	traveled
satisfied	strength	tremendous
scarcely	stretch	truly
scarcity	strictly	twelfth
scene	stubborn	typical
schedule	substitute	unanimous
scholar	subtle	unnecessary
scissors	succeed	useful
scurrilous	successful	useless
seance	suede	usually
secretary	sufficient	vacillate
seize	summary	vacuum
semester	superintendent	vague
separate	supersede	valuable
sergeant	surgeon	variety
shepherd	surprise	various
siege	susceptible	vegetable
similar	suspense	vengeance
sincerely	swimming	vilify
skein	sympathetic	villain
skiing	synonym	warrant
skillful	temperamental	weather
sophomore	temperature	Wednesday
soufflé	tendency	weird
source	therefore	whether
souvenir	thorough	whole
specialty	though	yacht
specifically	thoughtful	yield

Guide to Capitalization and Punctuation

CAPITALIZATION

Beginnings

The first word in a sentence is capitalized:

<u>Dozens</u> of spectators lined the street.

The first word in a direct quotation is capitalized:

Andy stood by the window and remarked, "<u>The</u> view from here is spectacular."

If a colon introduces more than one sentence, the first word after the colon is capitalized:

We went over our findings, one piece of evidence at a time: <u>The</u> custodian had discovered the body just before midnight. The keys to the victim's office were found in the stairwell. In the adjoining office, three file cabinets had been overturned.

If a colon introduces a formal and distinct statement, the first word after the colon is capitalized:

All my years on the basketball court have taught me one thing: <u>Winning</u> is more of a process than an outcome.

If a colon introduces a complete statement that is merely an extension of the statement preceding the colon, the first word after the colon is usually lowercased:

Everything in the house was a shade of pink: <u>the</u> sofa was carnation blush, the tiles were misty mauve, and the carpet was dusty rose.

If a colon introduces an incomplete statement, the first word after the colon is lowercased:

The caterer provided three choices: <u>chicken</u>, beef, and shrimp.

Proper names

Proper names are capitalized. This is true of all proper names, including those of persons, places, structures, organizations, vessels, vehicles, brands, etc. Notice from the following examples that when a properly named entity is referred to in a "non-named" general sense, the general sense is almost always lowercased:

Eleanor Roosevelt
J. D. Salinger
Carson City / a city in Nevada
Ural Mountains / a view of the mountains
New York Public Library / borrowing books from the public
   library
Washington Monument / our photos of the monument
Calvin Leete Elementary School / the rear entrance of the
   school
Amherst Historical Society / when the society last met
Boeing 747
USS *Missouri* [note that the names of specific ships, aircraft,
   spacecraft, etc., are italicized]
Chevy Malibu
Slinky

Titles

The titles of works are capitalized. Titled works include:

- written material (books, periodicals, screenplays, etc.)
- components of written material (chapters, sections, etc.)
- filmed and/or broadcast works (movies, television shows, radio programs, etc.)
- works of art (paintings, sculptures, etc.)
- musical compositions (songs, operas, oratorios, etc.)

There are certain rules of convention regarding which words in the titles are capitalized.

Capitalize:

- first word in the title
- last word in the title
- nouns and pronouns
- adjectives
- verbs
- adverbs
- subordinating conjunctions (*although, as, because, if, since, that, whenever*, etc.)

Do not capitalize (unless they are first or last words in the title):

- articles (*a, an, the*)
- coordinating conjunctions (*and, but, for, nor, or, so, yet*)
- prepositions (although some guides suggest capitalizing prepositions of more than four letters)
- the word *to* in infinitives

The King, the Sword, and the Golden Lantern
A Room within a Room
Seventy Ways to Make Easy Money from Your Home
The Stars Will Shine Because You Are Mine

If a subtitle is included, it typically follows a colon. It follows the capitalization rules of the main title, thus its first word is always capitalized:

Aftermath Explored: The Confessions of a Nuclear Physicist

The first element in a hyphenated compound is always capitalized. The subsequent elements are capitalized unless they are articles, prepositions, or coordinating conjunctions. But if the compound is the last word in the title, its final element is always capitalized, regardless of its part of speech:

Nineteenth-Century Poets
Over-the-Top Desserts
The Love-in of a Lifetime
The Year of the Love-In

An element that follows a hyphenated prefix is capitalized only if it is a proper noun or adjective:

Pre-Columbian Artifacts
Memoirs of a Semi-independent Child

TIP

Which titles should be set in italics, and which should be set off by quotation marks? In printed material, the distinction can be significant. Here's a handy list of the most common categories of titles and their standard treatments in type:

italics:

- books
  Crossroads of Freedom: Antietam, by James M. McPherson
- pamphlets
  Thomas Paine's *Common Sense*
- magazines
  Popular Mechanics
- newspapers
  USA Today
- movies
  One Flew Over the Cuckoo's Nest
- television or radio series
  This Week in Baseball
- plays
  Neil Simon's *Lost in Yonkers*
- long poems
  Beowulf
- collections of poems and other anthologies
  The Collected Poems of Emily Dickinson
- operas, oratorios, and other long musical compositions
  Madame Butterfly
- painting, sculptures, and other works of art
  Thomas Cole's *Mount Etna from Taormina*

quotation marks:

- articles
  "How to Remove Wallpaper"
- chapters
  "Betsy Saves the Day"
- short stories
  "The Pit and the Pendulum," by Edgar Allan Poe
- short poems
  "Tree at My Window," by Robert Frost
- essays
  Emerson's "Spiritual Laws"
- television or radio episodes
  "Lucy Does a TV Commercial"
- songs and other short musical compositions
  "Are You Lonesome Tonight?"

Education

An academic title is capitalized (whether it is spelled out or abbreviated) when it directly accompanies a personal name. Otherwise, it is lowercased:

Professor Sarah McDonald
Assoc. Prof. Brown
my chemistry professor

An academic degree or honor is capitalized (whether it is spelled out or abbreviated) when it directly accompanies a personal name. Otherwise, it is lowercased:

Harold L. Fox, Ph.D.
Charles Gustafson, Fellow of the Geological Society
working toward her master's degree

Academic years are lowercased:

the senior prom
he's a sophomore
the fourth grade

The course name of a particular school subject is capitalized. A general field of study is lowercased (unless the word is normally capitalized, such as "English"):

Astronomy 101
Algebra II
taking classes in psychology, French literature, and chemistry

Calendar terms and time

The names of the days of the week and months of the year are capitalized:

Sunday   September
Monday   October
Tuesday   November

The names of the four seasons are lowercased:

winter   fall
spring   autumn
summer

The names of holidays (religious and secular) and periods of religious observance are capitalized:

Arbor Day
Easter
Halloween
Lent
Memorial Day
Ramadan

The names of time zones and the time systems they designate are lowercased (except for any words that are proper names). Their abbreviations are capitalized:

eastern daylight time (EDT)
Greenwich mean time (GMT)
Pacific standard time (PST)

Legislation, treaties, etc.

The formal name of a policy, treaty, piece of legislation, or similar agreement is capitalized. A general reference to such is lowercased:

Volstead Act
the act sponsored by Congressman Volstead
Treaty of Versailles
the treaty at Versailles
Bottle Bill
Articles of Confederation
Connecticut Constitution
Connecticut's constitution
North American Free Trade Agreement

Military service

A military title or rank is capitalized (whether it is spelled out or abbreviated) when it directly accompanies a personal name. Otherwise, it is lowercased:

Gen. George Patton
Ensign Irene Mahoney
promoted to admiral
James Kirk, captain of the USS *Enterprise*

There are two significant exceptions to the preceding rule: the U.S. military titles "Fleet Admiral" and "General of the Army" should always be capitalized, even when not directly accompanying a personal name:

became General of the Army in 1950
a visit from the Fleet Admiral

The full official name of a military group or force is capitalized. A general reference to a military group or force is lowercased:

the Royal Air Force
the British air force
the Army Corps of Engineers

the Third Battalion
our battalion
the U.S. Navy
joined the navy

The full name of a battle or war is capitalized. A general reference to a battle or war is lowercased:

the Russian Revolution
fought in the revolution
the Spanish-American War
the war in Vietnam
the Battle of the Bulge
the first battle of the campaign
the Norman Conquest

The official name of a military award or medal is capitalized:

the Purple Heart
the Silver Star
the Victoria Cross
the Congressional Medal of Honor

Science

The capitalization rules governing scientific terminology cover a wide range of categories and applications. Some of the basic rules are discussed here.

Taxonomic nomenclature—that is, the scientific classification of plants and animals—follows specific rules for both capitalization and italics.

The names of the phylum, class, order, and family of a plant or animal are capitalized and set in roman type. This format also applies to the intermediate groupings (suborder, subfamily, etc.) within these divisions:

The North American river otter belongs to the phylum
    Chordata, the subphylum Vertebrata, the class Mammalia,
    the order Carnivora, and the family Mustelidae.

The divisions lower than family—that is, genus, species, and sub-species—are set in italic type. Of these, only the genus is capitalized. When a plant or animal is identified by its "scientific name" or "Latin name," the name given is the genus and species (and, when applicable, the subspecies):

> The scientific name of the river otter is *Lutra canadensis*.
> The Manitoban elk (*Cervus elaphus manitobensis*) is a
> subspecies of the North American elk.

The common names of plants and animals, as well as their hybrids, varieties, and breeds, are lowercased and set in roman type. A part of the name may be capitalized if that part is a term normally capitalized (that is, a proper name). If there is doubt, a dictionary should be consulted.

> Alaskan malamute
> Christmas cactus
> Johnny-jump-up
> maidenhair fern
> rainbow trout
> rose-breasted grosbeak
> Swainson's hawk
> Vietnamese potbellied pig

The names of astronomical entities, such as planets, stars, constellations, and galaxies, are capitalized:

> Alpha Centauri
> Canis Major
> Crab Nebula
> Ganymede
> Mercury
> Milky Way
> Orion
> Sirius

TIP

The names *sun, moon,* and *earth* are frequently lowercased. It is customary to capitalize them only when they are being referred to as components of the solar system. Also noteworthy is the fact that, in any context, the words *sun* and *moon* typically are preceded by the definite article, *the*. In non-astronomical contexts, the word *earth* often is preceded by *the*, but it is never preceded by *the* when used specifically as the name of a planet. Hence, *the Earth* would not be an appropriate use of capitalization.

We enjoyed the warmth of <u>the sun</u>.
The glow of <u>the moon</u> has inspired poets for centuries.
Countless species inhabit <u>the earth</u>.
What on <u>earth</u> are you doing?
In size, Venus is comparable to <u>Earth</u>.
The eclipse of <u>the Moon</u> will be visible from the night side of <u>Earth</u>.
They made observations of Neptune's orbit around <u>the Sun</u>.

The names of geological eras, periods, epochs, etc., are capitalized. When included with the name, the words *eras, periods, epochs,* etc., are lowercased:

Mesozoic era
Quaternary period
Oligocene epoch
Upper Jurassic

Abbreviations

Although the use of abbreviations in formal writing should be limited, abbreviations are legitimate components of the language and deserve the same attention to spelling as do other words. Certain capitalization guidelines for a few types of abbreviations are given below. Because the possible variations are numerous, a standard dictionary should be consulted for more thorough guidance on the spelling, capitalization, and punctuation of a specific abbreviation.

When a capitalized term is abbreviated, the abbreviation is capitalized. If the abbreviation is comprised of initials, all the initials are capitalized:

Professor J. Leggett / Prof. J. Leggett
Sergeant David Potter / Sgt. David Potter
Master of Business Administration / MBA
United States Marine Corps / USMC

When a lowercased term is abbreviated as a simple shortening, the abbreviation is usually lowercased. But if the abbreviation is comprised of initials, all the initials are usually capitalized. When there is a compound word in the term, the initials may include the first letter of the root word:

especially / esp.
teaspoon / tsp.
deoxyribonucleic acid / DNA
monosodium glutamate / MSG
most favored nation / MFN

Usually, an abbreviation that ends in a capital letter is not followed by a period. An abbreviation that ends in a lowercase letter usually is followed by a period, although the period may be optional, depending on the prevailing style of the particular piece of writing.

One group of abbreviations that never ends with a period is the set of chemical symbols. Also, these abbreviations are always initially capitalized even though the terms they represent are lowercased:

Ar	argon	Na	sodium
Dy	dysprosium	Sb	antimony
H	hydrogen	Sn	tin
Kr	krypton	U	uranium
Lr	lawrencium	Xe	xenon

Note that some chemical symbols appear to be straightforward abbreviations (*Ca* for *calcium*) while others seem unrelated to their corresponding terms (*Au* for *gold*). In fact, these symbols are abbreviations of the official scientific, or Latin, names (*Au* for *aurum*, which is Latin for *gold*).

TIP

If the name of an entity such as an organization, institution, or movement is to be abbreviated, its full name should be identified. Upon first mention, both abbreviation and full name should appear together, with either one being set within parentheses. (Usually the lesser known format goes in the parentheses.) Thereafter in the text, only the abbreviation need appear:

In February 1909, a group of activists founded what would become the NAACP (National Association for the Advancement of Colored People). For more than ninety years, the NAACP has persevered to honor its founders' vision of racial equality and social justice.

Plans to rebuild at the site of the World Trade Center (WTC) are being discussed today. Various designs for new office space are expected to be considered. Thousands of suggestions for a WTC memorial have already been submitted.

PUNCTUATION

Punctuation is an essential element of good writing because it makes the author's meaning clear to the reader. Although precise punctuation styles may vary somewhat among published sources, there are a number of fundamental principles worthy of consideration. Discussed below are these punctuation marks used in English:

comma
semicolon
colon
period
question mark
exclamation point
apostrophe
quotation marks
parentheses
dash
hyphen

Comma

The comma is the most used mark of punctuation in the English language. It signals to the reader a pause, which generally clarifies the author's meaning and establishes a sensible order to the elements of written language. Among the most typical functions of the comma are the following:

1. It can separate the clauses of a compound sentence when there are two independent clauses joined by a conjunction, especially when the clauses are not very short:

   It never occurred to me to look in the attic, and I'm sure it didn't occur to Rachel either.

   The Nelsons wanted to see the Grand Canyon at sunrise, but they overslept that morning.

2. It can separate the clauses of a compound sentence when there is a series of independent clauses, the last two of which are joined by a conjunction:

   The bus ride to the campsite was very uncomfortable, the cabins were not ready for us when we got there, the cook had forgotten to start dinner, and the rain was torrential.

3. It is used to precede or set off, and therefore indicate, a nonrestrictive dependent clause (a clause that could be omitted without changing the meaning of the main clause):

   I read her autobiography, which was published last July.
   They showed up at midnight, after most of the guests had gone home.
   The coffee, which is freshly brewed, is in the kitchen.

4. It can follow an introductory phrase:

   Having enjoyed the movie so much, he agreed to see it again.
   Born and raised in Paris, she had never lost her French accent.
   In the beginning, they had very little money to invest.

5. It can set off words used in direct address:

   Listen, people, you have no choice in the matter.

   Yes, Mrs. Greene, I will be happy to feed your cat.

6. It can separate two or more coordinate adjectives (adjectives that could otherwise be joined with *and*) that modify one noun:

   The cruise turned out to be the most entertaining, fun, and relaxing vacation I've ever had.

   The horse was tall, lean, and sleek.

   Note that cumulative adjectives (those not able to be joined with *and*) are not separated by a comma:

   She wore bright yellow rubber boots.

7. It is used to separate three or more items in a series or list:

   Charlie, Melissa, Stan, and Mark will be this year's soloists in the spring concert.

   We need furniture, toys, clothes, books, tools, housewares, and other useful merchandise for the benefit auction.

   Note that the comma between the last two items in a series is sometimes omitted in less precise style:

   The most popular foods served in the cafeteria are pizza, hamburgers and nachos.

8. It is used to separate and set off the elements in an address or other geographical designation:

   My new house is at 1657 Nighthawk Circle, South Kingsbury, Michigan.

   We arrived in Pamplona, Spain, on Thursday.

9. It is used to set off direct quotations (note the placement or absence of commas with other punctuation):

   "Kim forgot her gloves," he said, "but we have a pair she can borrow."

There was a long silence before Jack blurted out, "This must be the world's ugliest painting."

"What are you talking about?" she asked in a puzzled manner.

"Happy New Year!" everyone shouted.

10. It is used to set off titles after a person's name:

Katherine Bentley, M.D.

Martin Luther King, Jr., delivered the sermon.

Semicolon

The semicolon has two basic functions:

1. It can separate two main clauses, particularly when these clauses are of equal importance:

   The crowds gathered outside the museum hours before the doors were opened; this was one exhibit no one wanted to miss.

   She always complained when her relatives stayed for the weekend; even so, she usually was a little sad when they left.

2. It can be used as a comma is used to separate such elements as clauses or items in a series or list, particularly when one or more of the elements already includes a comma:

   The path took us through the deep, dark woods; across a small meadow into a cold, wet cave; and up a hillside overlooking the lake.

   Listed for sale in the ad were two bicycles; a battery-powered, leaf-mulching lawn mower; and a maple bookcase.

Colon

The colon has five basic functions:

1. It can introduce something, especially a list of items:

   In the basket were three pieces of mail: a postcard, a catalog, and a wedding invitation.

Students should have the following items: backpack, loose-leaf notebook, pens and pencils, pencil sharpener, and ruler.

2. It can separate two clauses in a sentence when the second clause is being used to explain or illustrate the first clause:

We finally understood why she would never go sailing with us: she had a deep fear of the water.

Most of the dogs in our neighborhood are quite large: two of them are St. Bernards.

3. It can introduce a statement or a quotation:

His parents say the most important rule is this: Always tell the truth.

We repeated the final words of his poem: "And such is the plight of fools like me."

4. It can be used to follow the greeting in a formal or business letter:

Dear Ms. Daniels:

Dear Sir or Madam:

5. It is used (in the U.S.) to separate minutes from hours, and seconds from minutes, in showing time of day and measured length of time:

Please be at the restaurant before 6:45.

Her best running time so far has been 00:12:35.

Period

The period has two basic functions:

1. It is used to mark the end of a sentence:

It was reported that there is a shortage of nurses at the hospital. Several of the patients have expressed concern about this problem.

2. It is often used at the end of an abbreviation:

On Fri., Sept. 12, Dr. Brophy noted that the patient's weight was 168 lb. and that his height was 6 ft. 2 in.

Note that another period is not added to the end of the sentence when the last word is an abbreviation.

Question Mark and Exclamation Point

The only sentences that do not end in a period are those that end in either a question mark or an exclamation point.

Question marks are used to mark the end of a sentence that asks a direct question (generally, a question that expects an answer):

Is there any reason for us to bring more than a few dollars?

Who is your science teacher?

Exclamation points are used to mark the end of a sentence that expresses a strong feeling, typically surprise, joy, or anger:

I want you to leave and never come back!

What a beautiful view this is!

Apostrophe

The apostrophe has two basic functions:

1. It is used to show where a letter or letters are missing in a contraction.

The directions are cont'd [continued] *on the next page.*
We've [we have] *decided that if she can't* [cannot] *go, then we aren't* [are not] *going either.*

2. It can be used to show possession:

The possessive of a singular noun or an irregular plural noun is created by adding an apostrophe and an s:

the pilot's uniform
Mrs. Mendoza's house
a tomato's bright red color
the oxen's yoke

The possessive of a plural noun is created by adding just an apostrophe:

the pilots' uniforms [referring to more than one pilot]
the Mendozas' house [referring to the Mendoza family]
the tomatoes' bright red color [referring to more than one tomato]

Quotation Marks

Quotation marks have two basic functions:

1. They are used to set off direct quotations (an exact rendering of someone's spoken or written words):

    "I think the new library is wonderful," she remarked to David.

    We were somewhat lost, so we asked, "Are we anywhere near the gallery?"

    In his letter he had written, "The nights here are quiet and starry. It seems like a hundred years since I've been wakened by the noise of city traffic and squabbling neighbors."

    Note that indirect quotes (which often are preceded by *that, if*, or *whether*) are not set off by quotation marks:

    He told me that he went to school in Boston.

    We asked if we could still get tickets to the game.

2. They can be used to set off words or phrases that have specific technical usage, or to set off meanings of words, or to indicate words that are being used in a special way in a sentence:

    The part of the flower that bears the pollen is the "stamen."

    When I said "plain," I meant "flat land," not "ordinary."

    Oddly enough, in the theater, the statement "break a leg" is meant as an expression of good luck.

    What you call "hoagies," we call "grinders" or "submarine sandwiches."

*He will never be a responsible adult until he outgrows his
"Peter Pan" behavior.*

Note that sometimes single quotation marks, rather than double quotation marks may be used to set off words or phrases:

The part of the flower that bears the pollen is the 'stamen.'

What is most important is to be consistent in such usage. Single quotation marks are also used to set off words or phrases within material already in double quotation marks, as:

"I want the sign to say 'Ellen's Bed and Breakfast' in large gold letters,"she explained.

Parentheses

Parentheses are used, in pairs, to enclose information that gives extra detail or explanation to the regular text. Parentheses are used in two basic ways:

1. They can separate a word or words in a sentence from the rest of the sentence:

   On our way to school, we walk past the Turner Farm (the oldest dairy farm in town) and watch the cows being fed.

   The stores were filled with holiday shoppers (even more so than last year).

   Note that the period goes outside the parentheses' because the words in the parentheses are only part of the sentence.

2. They can form a separate complete sentence:

   Please bring a dessert to the dinner party. (It can be something very simple.) I look forward to seeing you there.

   Note that the period goes inside the parentheses, because the words in the parentheses are a complete and independent sentence.

Dash

A dash is used most commonly to replace the usage of parentheses within sentences. If the information being set off is in the middle of the sentence, a pair of long (or "em") dashes is used; if it is at the end of the sentence, just one long dash is used:

On our way to school, we walk past the Turner Farm—the oldest dairy farm in town—and watch the cows being fed

The stores were filled with holiday shoppers—even more so than last year.

Hyphen

A hyphen has three basic functions:

1. It can join two or more words to make a compound, especially when so doing makes the meaning more clear to the reader:

   We met to discuss long-range planning.

   There were six four-month-old piglets at the fair.

   That old stove was quite a coal-burner.

2. It can replace the word "to" when a span or range of data is given. This kind of hyphen is sometimes keyed as a short (or "en") dash:

   John Adams was president of the United States 1797–1801.

   Today we will look for proper nouns in the L–N section of the dictionary.

   The ideal weight for that breed of dog would be 75–85 pounds.

3. It can indicate a word break at the end of a line. The break must always be between syllables:

   It is important for any writer to know that there are numerous punctuation principles that are considered standard and proper, but there is also flexibility regarding acceptable punctuation. Having learned the basic "rules" of good punctuation, the writer will be able to adopt a specific and consistent style of punctuation that best suits the material he or she is writing.

WORDS: MAKING THE RIGHT CHOICES

The building blocks of written or spoken communication are, of course, words. When we speak informally to one another throughout the day, we use our familiar vocabulary and patterns of expression without giving the individual words much thought. When our communication is more formal—as in a letter, an article, or a speech—our choice of words becomes more important.

Synonyms

Knowing which words to choose depends largely on knowing how to use synonyms. A **synonym** is a term that means exactly or nearly the same as another term in the same language. For example, *glad* is a synonym of *pleased*. By exploring synonym choices, writers are likely to keep their writing fresh and interesting.

Thoughtfully selected words not only convey the writer's message, they can enhance readability and demonstrate the writer's competency. It is usually well worth the writer's time to be guided by such resources as thesauruses and synonym studies.

USING THESAURUSES

A thesaurus, essentially a book of synonyms, can be an indispensable tool for the writer. There are two conventional types of thesauruses: one arranges the material by theme; the other arranges the headwords in an A-to-Z format, much like a dictionary. Most modern thesauruses are compiled in the latter format.

There are several reasons that one might consult a thesaurus. Perhaps "the right word" is somewhere in the writer's mind, but it just isn't coming to the writer at that moment. The writer thinks, "The word means something like *to pause*." When the writer looks up *pause* in the thesaurus, there in a list of synonyms is the very word! The writer is relieved and thinks, "Yes, that's what I was thinking of—the word *hesitate*."

Another valuable function of a thesaurus is to help the writer avoid repetition. Using the same word over and over again can be monotonous to the reader and may suggest weak vocabulary skills on the part of the writer. Consider the following paragraph:

> The movie we saw last night was very exciting. It started with an exciting car chase, and it just got more and more exciting as the plot developed. There were many moments that had me on the edge of my seat, but the scene in the train station was definitely the most exciting part of the story.

The writer risks losing the reader's attention because the reader may be thinking, "Doesn't this person know any word other than *exciting*?" If the writer were to consult a thesaurus, the paragraph could be greatly improved. One such revision might read as follows:

> The movie we saw last night was very <u>exciting</u>. It started with a <u>sensational</u> car chase, and it just got more and more <u>thrilling</u> as the plot developed. There were many moments that had me on the edge of my seat, but the scene in the train station was definitely the most <u>electrifying</u> part of the story.

A thesaurus can expand a writer's use of vocabulary and perk up a piece of writing, but it is the writer's responsibility to make certain that the words chosen are appropriate for the intended context. If a writer is not certain of the precise meaning or correct usage of a term listed in a thesaurus, a dictionary should be consulted as well.

USING SYNONYM STUDIES

Many dictionaries feature synonym studies, which expound on the usage of synonyms for selected terms. They offer an analytical treatment of the nuances of meaning that distinguish a set of closely related synonyms. If a synonym study were to appear at the dictionary entry for *despise*, for example, it might look like this:

> **SYNONYM STUDY: distinguish**
> DESCRY, DIFFERENTIATE, DISCERN, DISCRIMINATE. What we **discern** we see apart from all other objects (*to discern the lighthouse beaming on the far shore*). **Descry** puts even more emphasis on the

distant or unclear nature of what we're seeing (*the lookout was barely able to descry a man approaching*). To **discriminate** is to perceive the differences between or among things that are very similar; it may suggest that some aesthetic evaluation is involved (*to discriminate between two singers' styles*). **Distinguish** requires making even finer distinctions among things that resemble each other even more closely (*unable to distinguish the shadowy figures moving through the forest*). *Distinguish* can also mean recognizing by some special mark or outward sign (*the sheriff could be distinguished by his badge*). **Differentiate**, on the other hand, suggests the ability to perceive differences between things that are easily confused. In contrast to *distinguish*, *differentiate* suggests subtle differences that must be compared in some detail (*the color of the first paint sample was difficult to differentiate from the third sample*).

Ten Tips to Improve Your Vocabulary

1. Decide why you need new words. Do you need new words in a particular area or subject, so that you can learn more about that subject? Do you want to improve your writing, or your speaking, or both? Do you want to replace overused words in your vocabulary? Make a plan first, so that you can get the most out of your new words.
2. READ! You will learn more new words, faster, by seeing them in their natural habitats, rather than in dull lists. Choose subjects that interest you or ones you aren't already familiar with. When you see an unfamiliar word, guess what it means from its context. If it still doesn't make sense, look it up in a dictionary. Keep a list of words you find and might like to use.
3. Use your new words right away. When you find one you like, make a point of using it in writing or in conversation that very day. If you don't use it, you'll lose it. Even if you have to write it in an e-mail to yourself, make sure to use it that day.
4. Subscribe to a word-a-day e-mail list. The biggest and best-known is A Word A Day, at www.wordsmith.org. Many dictionary sites have their own word-a-day lists or pages as well, including the Oxford English Dictionary (www.oed.com). Print out or write down the words you especially like—and use them.

(continued)

5. Buy and use a good dictionary. Look up a word every day. You can even look up words you think you know the meaning of already. You might be surprised to find that the word you think you know has additional meanings you aren't familiar with. Then you can make that word do twice the work in your vocabulary.

6. Ask your friends and family to help you by using new words with you. Ask them to tell you words they use in their work, or their favorite words. When you associate those new words with the people who told them to you, they will be easier to remember.

7. Set little word-hunt goals for yourself. Decide that you will find a word that you don't know that rhymes with "mellow," or a word that has to do with buildings, for instance, and keep looking for them until you find them. Then you can cross them off your list and add them to your vocabulary.

8. Buy and use a good thesaurus. Look up a word that you use too often and memorize the first five synonyms, and any antonyms. Be sure to look them up in a dictionary so that you know exactly what they mean. Then use them to replace the word you use too often. Some good words to replace: very, great, good, beautiful.

9. Watch TV, especially TV news programs, with the closed-captioning on. This will show you how words you may have only heard are spelled. (Caution: Often captioning has typographical errors. Check words in a dictionary before you use them.)

10. Don't forget to check the pronunciation of new and difficult words in your dictionary. While you're there, check out the etymology of the word, too. A good word history will often help you to remember the meaning of your new word.

Commonly Confused Words

Certain words in the English language are commonly confused with other words that are in some way similar. Some of the most frequently confused terms are listed here, accompanied by brief usage notes.

CONFUSED TERMS	PROPER USAGE
accept	*Accept* is a verb, meaning "consent to receive" or "agree to undertake."
	I am pleased to <u>accept</u> your generous offer.
except	*Except* is usually a preposition, meaning "not including" or "other than."
	Everyone <u>except</u> Ursula has made reservations.
advice	*Advice* is a noun meaning "guidance" or "recommendations."
	May I ask your <u>advice</u> on a personal matter?
advise	*Advise* is a verb meaning "offer suggestions," "give an opinion," or "warn."
	We were <u>advised</u> to take an alternate route.
affect	*Affect* is a verb meaning "influence" or "produce an effect on."
	The rise in gas prices has <u>affected</u> our travel plans.
effect	*Effect*, as a noun, means "the result or consequence of an action."
	The rise in gas prices has had an <u>effect</u> on our travel plans.
	Effect, as a verb, means "bring about" or "cause to occur."
	Exactly what circumstances have <u>effected</u> these rising gas prices?
already	*Already* means "before now" or "by now."
	Evelyn <u>already</u> fixed the leak.
all ready	*All ready* means "completely ready."
	Are you <u>all ready</u> to leave?
all together	*All together* means "all in one place" or "all at once."
	For the first time in years, we were <u>all together</u>.
altogether	*Altogether* means "in total."
	<u>Altogether</u>, there are six bedrooms.

CONFUSED TERMS	PROPER USAGE
allusion	*Allusion* is used to refer indirectly to someone or something. The <u>allusion</u> to Jesus in his poetry is fairly obvious.
illusion	*Illusion* means "a false or misleading appearance or impression." His mother created the <u>illusion</u> of a happy family.
adverse	*Adverse* means "unfavorable" or "harmful." Drought has had an <u>adverse</u> effect on the crops.
averse	*Averse* means "having a strong dislike of or opposition to." I am not <u>averse</u> to the idea of moving.
as	*As* is sometimes a preposition, used to refer to function or character. He landed a job <u>as</u> an editor. *As* is sometimes a conjunction, used to indicate the concurrence of events. The fans went wild <u>as</u> Elvis walked onto the stage.
like	*Like*, as a preposition, takes an object. It means "similar to." That dog looks <u>like</u> a bear. *Like* is not a conjunction, yet it is frequently used as one. Especially in formal speech or writing, be careful to avoid this incorrect usage: I don't have a big kitchen <u>like</u> you do. [incorrect] I don't have a big kitchen <u>like</u> yours. [correct] Sammy goes to bed by eight, just <u>like</u> children should. [incorrect] Sammy goes to bed by eight, just <u>as</u> children should. [correct]

CONFUSED TERMS	PROPER USAGE
beside	*Beside* is a preposition meaning "next to" or "alongside." Please put the tray on the table beside my bed.
besides	*Besides*, as a preposition, means "in addition to." Besides the free room, we were given a lavish breakfast. *Besides*, as an adverb, means "furthermore." I'm too tired to go to a restaurant. Besides, I'm not hungry.
can	*Can* expresses ability Cheetahs can run at a remarkable speed.
may	*May* expresses permission or possibility. The children may have more pizza. [permission] I may join you later. [possibility] Note: In most informal contexts, the use of can to express permission is generally accepted as standard usage. The children can have more pizza.
capital	*Capital* refers to uppercase letters, money, administrative cities, or crimes punishable by death. The first word should begin with a capital Q. [letters] The capital expenditures exceeded our budget. [money] Vilnius is the capital of Lithuania. [cities] Treason is a capital offense. [crimes]
capitol	*Capitol* refers only to a building that houses a legislature. The proper name *the Capitol* refers specifically to the building that houses the U.S. Congress in Washington, D.C. We met on the steps of the Virginia state capitol.
could have/ should have	*Could have* and *should have* are grammatically correct verb forms. I could have gone to Harvard.
could of/ should of	*Could of* and *should of* are meaningless forms that should never be used. They are mistakenly used because they sound like *could have* and *should have*.

CONFUSED TERMS	PROPER USAGE
elicit	*Elicit* is a verb meaning "draw out (a response, answer, or fact) from someone)."
	The police were unable to <u>elicit</u> a confession from the suspect.
illicit	*Illicit* is an adjective meaning "forbidden by law" or "improper."
	Ray's <u>illicit</u> use of the funds led to his dismissal.
emigrate	*Emigrate* means "move out of a country."
	Her grandfather <u>emigrated</u> from Poland in 1926.
immigrate	*Immigrate* means "move into a country."
	Gerda <u>immigrated</u> to Australia with her second husband.
good	*Good* is an adjective meaning "favorable" or "appropriate" or "pleasing."
	The dance performance was <u>good</u>.
well	*Well* is an adverb meaning "in a good or satisfactory way."
	She dances <u>well</u>.
lend	*Lend* is a verb meaning "grant the temporary use of." *Lend* is always a verb.
	I will <u>lend</u> my car to you.
loan	*Loan*, as a verb, means "grant the temporary use of." Hence, it can be a synonym of *lend*.
	I will <u>loan</u> my car to you.
	Loan, as a noun, means "a thing that is borrowed" or "an act of lending something."
	He thanked me for the <u>loan</u> of my car.
lay, laid	*Lay* is a verb meaning "put (something) down." The past tense of lay is *laid*.
	Let's <u>lay</u> our towels in a sunny spot.
	We are <u>laying</u> our towels in a sunny spot.
	We <u>laid</u> our towels in a sunny spot.

CONFUSED TERMS	PROPER USAGE
lie, lay	*Lie* is a verb meaning "assume a horizontal or resting position." The past tense of *lie* is *lay*. Let's <u>lie</u> on our towels. We are <u>lying</u> on our towels. Earlier today, we <u>lay</u> on our towels. Note: The base *lay* and the past tense *lay* are two different words with distinctly different usages.
personal	*Personal* is an adjective that refers to a person's private or individual affairs. I will give this matter my <u>personal</u> attention.
personnel	*Personnel* is a plural noun that refers to the people employed by an organization. All <u>personnel</u> are invited to attend the reception. *Personnel* is often used as a shortened form of *personnel department*. Ask someone in <u>personnel</u> for a copy of the form.
principal	*Principal,* as an adjective, means "most important." Our <u>principal</u> concerns are food and shelter. *Principal,* as a noun, refers to a person in charge or to a sum of money on which interest is paid. The <u>principal</u> of Franklin High School is Mr. Barnes. [person] I still owe most of the <u>principal</u> on my student loan. [money]
principle	*Principle* is a noun meaning "rule" or "basis for conduct." He strictly adhered to the <u>principles</u> of his faith.
real	*Real* is an adjective meaning "actual" or "genuine." Is that painting a <u>real</u> Picasso?
really	*Really* is an adverb used to mean "in actual fact" or as an emphasis to a statement. She and I are not <u>really</u> related. ["in actual fact"] Do you <u>really</u> want to go? [emphasis]

CONFUSED TERMS	PROPER USAGE
	Note: The word *real* is sometimes used adverbially for emphasis, in place of the adverb *really*. In informal contexts, such usage may be acceptable, but it should be strictly avoided in formal contexts. He is a <u>real</u> nice salesman. [informal] He is a <u>really</u> nice salesman.[formal]
than	*Than* is used in comparisons. The original movie was much better <u>than</u> the sequel.
then	*Then* is usually used to indicate a relative time. We saw the movie, and <u>then</u> we went home. *Then* sometimes means "also" or "in that case." The hours are great, and <u>then</u> there's the overtime. ["also"] You don't want salad? <u>Then</u> don't stop at the store. ["in that case"]
there	*There* is an adverb meaning "at that place." The tomatoes are over <u>there</u>.
their	*Their* is a possessive pronoun meaning "belonging to them." I wonder if they still have tomatoes in <u>their</u> garden.
they're	*They're* is the contracted form of "they are." I wonder if <u>they're</u> going to grow tomatoes this year.
to	*To* is a preposition that expresses motion in a particular direction or indicates a point reached. I've never been <u>to</u> Japan. *To* is also used as the mark of an infinitive. Would you like me <u>to</u> help?
too	*Too* is an adverb meaning "also" or "excessively." Is Arlene coming <u>too</u>? ["also"] He's driving <u>too</u> fast. ["excessively"]
two	*Two* is a number. There are <u>two</u> candles in the drawer.

CONFUSED TERMS	PROPER USAGE
waive	*Waive* is a verb meaning "give up (a right or claim)" or "refrain from enforcing." Sidney refused to <u>waive</u> his parental rights.
wave	*Wave*, as a verb, means "move one's hands to and fro, especially to signal a message such as a greeting." Sidney <u>waved</u> to reporters as he left the courthouse.
we	*We* is a subjective pronoun. It is used as a subject of a verb, either by itself or with a noun that expresses the category to which the *we* belongs. <u>We</u> received our schedules on Monday. <u>We</u> <u>teachers</u> received our schedules on Monday.
us	*Us* is an objective pronoun. It is used as an object of a verb. The schedules were distributed to us on Monday. Note: Especially in informal speech, the pronoun *us* is frequently used subjectively, but such usage is never correct. When Dr. Wilson retired, <u>us students</u> gave her a party. [incorrect] When Dr. Wilson retired, <u>we students</u> gave her a party. [correct]
who	*Who* is used as a subject. This is the woman <u>who</u> found your wallet.
whom	*Whom* is used as the object of a verb or preposition. For <u>whom</u> did you make the card?
whose	*Whose* is the possessive form of *who*. We're not sure <u>whose</u> money this is.
who's	*Who's* is the contracted form of *who is* and *who has*. <u>Who's</u> the new accountant? [*who is*] <u>Who's</u> got change for a ten? [*who has*]
your	*Your* is the possessive form of *you*. Why is Owen wearing <u>your</u> coat?
you're	*You're* is the contracted form of *you are*. If <u>you're</u> going home now, I'll lock up.

Clichés

A **cliché** is a worn-out expression. It was once fresh and meaningful, but it has lost its original impact through overuse. Numerous clichés have become so familiar that it would be virtually impossible to eradicate them from one's vocabulary. However, writers and speakers should make the effort to avoid using them, especially in formal material.

Common clichés to avoid:

above and beyond the call of
    duty
accident waiting to happen
acid test
add insult to injury
after all is said and done
all hands on deck
all in all
all wet
all's well that ends well
almighty dollar
along the same lines
A-OK
as luck would have it
at a loss for words
at arm's length
avoid like the plague
back in the saddle
back on track
backseat driver
ball is in your court
barking up the wrong tree
be your own worst enemy
beat a dead horse
beat around the bush

been there, done that
beggars can't be choosers
be an open book
believe me
better late than never
between a rock and hard place
between you, me, and the lamp-
    post
big picture
big spender
bigger fish to fry
bird's-eye view
bitter end
bone of contention
born and bred
both sides of the coin
brain trust
bring home the bacon
broad spectrum
broaden one's horizons
bundle of nerves
bury the hatchet
busy as a bee
buy into
by leaps and bounds

by the skin of one's teeth
call her bluff
can't judge a book by its cover
can't take a joke
cast the net
catbird seat
catch as catch can
center of attention
cheat death
chew the fat
clear as a bell
clear as mud
cloak and dagger
coast is clear
cold as ice
cold shoulder
come full circle
come to no good
come up for air
conspicuous by their absence
cool it
cop out
could eat a horse
counting on you
count your blessings
cover all the bases
crazy like a fox
cream of the crop
creature of habit
crossing the line
cut me some slack
cut to the chase
dead in the water
dead wrong
dog-eat-dog

done deal
done to death
don't know him from Adam
down and dirty
down and out
down in the dumps
down in the mouth
dressed to the nines
due in large measure to
duly noted
dumb luck
easier said than done
easy come, easy go
easy mark
easy target
eat crow
end of discussion
every fiber of my being
face the music
fair and square
fall from grace
fall through the cracks
far and away
feast or famine
few and far between
fighting the tide
fill the bill
find it in your heart
fit as a fiddle
fit to be tied
fits like an old shoe
flat as a pancake
fly in the ointment
fly off the handle
for all intents and purposes

for love or money
for your information
fork it over
free as a bird
from the frying pan into the fire
from time immemorial
game plan
get behind the eight ball
get down to brass tacks
get off scot-free
get our ducks in a row
get the lead out
get the show on the road
get to the bottom of it
give a damn
give rise to
go for the kill
go it alone
go the distance
go the extra mile
go to pieces
go with the flow
goes without saying
good for nothing
goodly number
grass is always greener
green with envy
grist for the mill
hammer out the details
handwriting on the wall
hang in there
has a screw loose
have your heart in your mouth
head over heels
heated argument

his bark is worse than his bite
hit or miss
hit the ceiling
hit the ground running
hit the nail on the head
hold that thought
holding back the tide
hook, line, and sinker
hour of need
I wasn't born yesterday
icing on the cake
if looks could kill
if the price is right
I'm all over it
I'm speechless
in a nutshell
in due course
in hot water
in layman's terms
in one fell swoop
in over their heads
in seventh heaven
in the bag
in the ballpark
in the driver's seat
in the event that
in the final analysis
in the groove
in the near future
in the neighborhood of
in the nick of time
in the same boat
in the zone
in this day and age
irons in the fire

it could be worse
it stands to reason
it takes all kinds
it takes guts
it's your baby
join the club
keep your fingers crossed
keep the home fires burning
keeping score
kill the fatted calf
kiss of death
knock on wood
knock the socks off of
know the ropes
last but not least
last straw
lay an egg
learning curve
leave no stone unturned
left to his own devices
lend me an ear
let the cat out of the bag
let your hair down
letter perfect
lie low
light of day
like a bull in a china shop
like a bump on a log
like greased lightning
like rolling off a log
little does he know
live it up
lock, stock, and barrel
look like a million bucks
low man on the totem pole

make ends meet
make tracks
makes her blood boil
method in (or to) my madness
millstone around your neck
mince words
misery loves company
moment of truth
Monday-morning quarterback
monkey on your back
more money than God
more than meets the eye
more than you could shake a
    stick at
nail to the wall
naked truth
nearing the finish line
needle in a haystack
needs no introduction
never a dull moment
nip and tuck
nip in the bud
no harm, no foul
no skin off my nose
no strings attached
no-brainer
none the worse for wear
nose to the grindstone
not one red cent
nothing new under the sun
off the cuff
old as the hills
old hat
old soldiers never die
older than dirt

on cloud nine
on the one hand/on the other
    hand
on the road
on the same page
on the same track
on the wagon
on top of the world
out of my league
out of the woods
over a barrel
pan out
par for the course
pass the buck
pay the piper
perish the thought
piece of cake
playing for keeps
powers that be
practice makes perfect
proud as a peacock
pulling my leg
pulling no punches
put faces to names
put on hold
put the bite on
put words in one's mouth
put your money where your
    mouth is
quick and dirty
rags to riches
rant and rave
reading me like a book
real McCoy

red as a beet
regret to inform you
reign supreme
rings a bell
ripe old age
rise and shine
rolling over in his grave
rub elbows
rule the roost
run circles around
run it up the flagpole
run off at the mouth
sadder but wiser
safe to say
salt of the earth
scarce as hen's teeth
sea of faces
see the forest for the trees
sell like hotcakes
set in stone
shake a leg
sharp as a tack
ships that pass in the night
shoot the breeze
shooting himself in the foot
shot in the arm
shot to hell
sight for sore eyes
sitting duck
skeleton in the closet
skin alive
sleep on it
smells fishy
smooth sailing

snake in the grass
spill the beans
stay in the loop
steal the limelight
stem the tide
stick to your guns
stick your neck out
straight from the horse's mouth
strange bedfellows
strike a balance
strong as an ox
stubborn as a mule
sturdy as an oak
suffice it to say
sweating bullets
take a breather
take into consideration
take on board
take one's word for
take pleasure in
take the bitter with the sweet
take the easy way out
take the liberty of
talk shop
talk the talk
talk through your hat
talk your ear off
that's all she wrote
the die is cast
they'll be sorry
thick as thieves
thin as a rail
think outside the box
think tank

those are the breaks
through thick and thin
throw caution to the wind
thrown to the wolves
tighten our belts
time is money
time marches on
time waits for no man
to each his own
to your heart's content
too funny for words
took the words right out of my
    mouth
touch base
turn the other cheek
turn up your nose
two peas in a pod
ugly as sin
under the wire
up a creek
upset the applecart
venture a guess
vicious circle
waiting for the other shoe to
    drop
walk the walk
walking encyclopedia
walking on air
welcome with open arms
when the cows come home
where angels fear to tread
where there's smoke, there's fire
whole nine yards
wild-goose chase

wipe the slate clean
wishful thinking
with bated breath
without further ado
without further delay
wonders never cease

words fail me
wreak havoc
yada, yada, yada
you said a mouthful
you'll never know if you don't try

Redundant Expressions

A redundant expression is a group of words (usually a pair) in which at least one word is superfluous—that is, unnecessary. The superfluous element can be removed without affecting the meaning of the expression. In formal speech or writing, redundant expressions should be strictly avoided.

In the following list of common redundant expressions, the superfluous elements have been crossed out.

~~absolute~~ guarantee
~~absolutely~~ certain
~~absolutely~~ essential
~~absolutely~~ necessary
AC ~~current~~
~~actual~~ fact
~~actual~~ truth
add ~~an additional~~
adding ~~together~~
~~advance~~ reservations
~~advance~~ warning
after ~~the end of~~
all meet ~~together~~
alongside ~~of~~
~~already~~ existing
~~and~~ moreover
~~annoying~~ pest
ATM ~~machine~~

~~awkward~~ predicament
bald-~~headed~~
~~basic~~ essentials
~~basic~~ fundamentals
blend ~~together~~
~~brief~~ moment
~~but~~ however
~~but~~ nevertheless
came ~~at a time~~ when
cancel ~~out~~
~~chief~~ protagonist
~~clearly~~ obvious
climb ~~up~~
~~close~~ proximity
~~close~~ scrutiny
collaborate ~~together~~
combine ~~into one~~
commute ~~back and forth~~

~~complete~~ monopoly

~~completely~~ destroyed

~~completely~~ eliminated

~~completely~~ empty

~~completely~~ filled

~~completely~~ random

consensus ~~of opinion~~

continue ~~on~~

~~continue to~~ remain

cooperate ~~together~~

currently ~~today~~

DC ~~current~~

~~decorative~~ garnish

~~deep~~ chasm

~~definitely~~ decided

descend ~~down~~

~~different~~ varieties

~~difficult~~ dilemma

~~direct~~ confrontation

drop ~~down~~

during ~~the course of~~

dwindled ~~down~~

each ~~and every~~

earlier ~~in time~~

~~empty~~ space

~~end~~ result

enter ~~in~~

equal ~~to one another~~

~~established~~ fact

estimated ~~at about~~

estimated ~~roughly at~~

~~every~~ now and then

~~evil~~ fiend

~~exact~~ duplicate

~~exact~~ opposites

~~fake~~ copy

~~false~~ pretenses

~~fellow~~ classmates

~~fellow~~ teammates

few ~~in number~~

filled ~~to capacity~~

~~final~~ conclusion

~~final~~ outcome

first ~~and foremost~~

~~first~~ began

~~first~~ introduction

first ~~of all~~

~~first~~ started

follow ~~after~~

for ~~a period of~~ six months

for ~~the purpose of~~

~~foreign~~ exports

~~foreign~~ imports

forever ~~and ever~~

foundered ~~and sank~~

~~free~~ gift

~~free~~ pass

~~future~~ prospects

gather ~~together~~

gave birth to a ~~baby~~ girl

~~glowing~~ ember

~~good~~ bargain

~~good~~ benefits

had done ~~previously~~

~~harmful~~ injury

HIV ~~virus~~

~~honest~~ truth

~~hopeful~~ optimism

~~hot~~ water heater

I ~~myself personally~~

if ~~and when~~

important ~~breakthrough~~ *(important is struck)* ~~important~~ breakthrough

in ~~close~~ proximity

~~intense~~ fury

introduced ~~for the first time~~

~~invited~~ guests

ISBN ~~number~~

joined ~~together~~

~~just~~ recently

kneel ~~down~~

last ~~of all~~

lift ~~up~~

look back ~~in retrospect~~

~~major~~ breakthrough

may ~~possibly~~

~~mental~~ telepathy

merged ~~together~~

meshed ~~together~~

~~midway~~ between

might ~~possibly~~

mix ~~together~~

~~mutual~~ cooperation

~~natural~~ instinct

never ~~at any time~~

~~new~~ beginning

~~new~~ bride

~~new~~ innovation

~~new~~ recruit

nine A.M. ~~in the morning~~

no trespassing ~~allowed~~

none ~~at all~~

~~now~~ pending

null ~~and void~~

~~old~~ cliché

~~old~~ proverb

~~opening~~ introduction

~~originally~~ created

over ~~and done with~~

~~over~~exaggerate

~~pair of~~ twins

parched ~~dry~~

~~passing~~ fad

~~past~~ experiences

~~past~~ history

~~past~~ memories

~~past~~ records

penetrate ~~into~~

~~perfect~~ ideal

permeate ~~throughout~~

~~personal~~ friend

~~personal~~ opinion

~~personally~~ believes

PIN ~~number~~

plan ~~in advance~~

~~poisonous~~ venom

~~positively~~ true

~~possibly~~ might

postponed ~~until a later time~~

~~pre~~recorded

~~present~~ incumbent

probed ~~into~~

proceed ~~ahead~~

protest ~~against~~

protrude ~~out~~

~~proven~~ facts

raise ~~up~~

reason ~~why~~

refer ~~back~~

reflect ~~back~~

repeat ~~again~~

reply ~~back~~
revert ~~back~~
Rio Grande ~~River~~
~~sad~~ tragedy
same ~~identical~~
seemed ~~to be~~
share ~~together~~
short ~~in length~~
since ~~the time when~~
~~sincerely~~ mean it
skipped ~~over~~
~~solemn~~ vow
spelled out ~~in detail~~
stacked ~~on top of each other~~
~~still~~ continues
~~still~~ persists
~~still~~ remains
strangled ~~to death~~
~~stupid~~ fool
~~suddenly~~ exploded
sufficient ~~enough~~
~~sum~~ total
summer ~~season~~
~~sworn~~ affidavit

~~temporary~~ recess
~~temporary~~ reprieve
~~terrible~~ tragedy
~~thoughtful~~ contemplation
~~thoughtful~~ deliberation
~~totally~~ eliminated
~~true~~ fact
~~twelve~~ midnight
~~twelve~~ noon
~~two~~ twins
~~ultimate~~ conclusion
~~unexpected~~ surprise
~~unintentional~~ mistake
~~uninvited~~ party crashers
UPC ~~code~~
~~usual~~ custom
~~utter~~ annihilation
~~very~~ unique
ways ~~and means~~
~~well-known old~~ adage
when ~~and if~~
whether ~~or not~~
widow ~~woman~~
written ~~down~~

CHAPTER 8

Correspondence

In business, there are many reasons for writing letters, even in the age of almost instantaneous communication. One of the important reasons for written communication is the need to have notifications, plans, contracts, and agreements in writing for legal purposes. How you present yourself through correspondence says much about you and your business, and people will often judge your ability on the basis of your presentation. Unlike a phone call, a letter gives you the opportunity to choose your words wisely, determining the intent of your message, and executing that intent at your own pace. Your tone, grammar, neatness, and layout play an important role in this process. While e-mails have offered the businessperson the opportunity to communicate on a more casual level, traditional forms of communication are not out of the picture and should be handled professionally. Taking the time to be concise, courteous, and neat can leave a lasting impression. In this case, your actions (choosing attractive stationery) and words (how you construct your correspondence) speak equally loudly.

STATIONERY

A business letter is typed on one side of white, unlined paper that measures 8½ x 11 inches. The letter should be mailed in a standard business envelope (usually about 4 x 10 inches) unless it is accompanied by documents (enclosures) that cannot or should not be folded. If your company has letterhead stationery and envelopes, of course that is what you should use. (In no case is it acceptable to send a hand-written business letter or to use lined paper.) It is important to keep in mind that most, if not all, letters are composed on a computer and, therefore, must be printed on the commonly used company ink-jet or laser printer. The standard copy paper used in most printers is 20-pound weight. Letterhead is usually slightly heavier and may even be textured, but printer requirements must be taken into account before choosing the stock. While textured or woven stock is more attractive and impressive, ask the paper supplier how characters will print on it. Bleeding or fuzzy letters will not convey the image you want to project on your letterhead. Crisp, clean print is the ideal. White and off-white stock is the preferred color choice, but very light pastels occasionally may be acceptable. Avoid dark paper. The print is diffi-cult to read and it is too showy in the business world.

COMMON FORMATS

Find out whether your company prefers a specific letter format. Some companies specify whether a full block, modified block, or simplified block format is to be used for your correspondence.

Block style features all elements of the letter keyed flush left. It has a neat and simple appearance. Paragraphs are separated by a double space.

Modified block is the more traditional style of letter formatting. It differs from block style in that the date, complimentary close, and signature lines begin at the center point of the line length. The beginning of each paragraph is indented five spaces, along with the subject line, if used. Depending on the length of the letter, paragraphs may be separated by a single or double space.

Simplified block is similar to block but has a more informal appearance. All elements are flush left, as in block, but the salutation and complimentary close are omitted. The addressee's name is usually mentioned in the beginning paragraph, as a way of personalizing the letter, but in keeping with a very informal style.

If you choose to use mixed punctuation, the salutation is followed by a colon and the complimentary close is followed by a comma. Or you may choose to have no punctuation after these two lines. But you must be consistent: either both lines receive punctuation, or both do not.

PARTS OF A LETTER

The basic components of a letter are:

- date
- inside address, including recipient's name, company name, street address, and city/state/ZIP code
- attention line
- salutation
- subject line
- body of the letter
- complimentary close
- signature, name, and title of sender
- closing notations such as keyer's initials, enclosure notation, copy notation, postscript, and file name notation (for computer filing reference)

Date

The date is keyed two or more lines below the letterhead, depending on the length of the letter, and includes the month, date, and year: March 19, 2002. Military (and European) style reverses the month and date and uses no punctuation: 19 March 2002. Do not abbreviate the month. Also, avoid using numerals only, as it can be confusing to some, especially if you're preparing an international letter. They are interpreted differently, depending on where the addressee is from. For example, 6/8/02 usually means June 8, 2002 in the United States, but it could also be read as August 6, 2002.

Inside Address

No matter what style of letter you use, the inside address is keyed flush left, three or more lines below the date, depending on the length of the letter. It includes the name of the addressee, title (if applicable), company name, street address (and suite number if applicable) or post office box, city, state, and ZIP or postal code. In the case of international mail, the country name is keyed in all caps on a separate line. If any particular line is too long and runs to the next line, indent the second line two or three spaces.

Name

Abbreviate Mr., Mrs., Ms., Messrs., and Dr., but spell out Miss, Professor, Father, Reverend, Captain, and so on. When addressing a letter to an individual using initials or a name common to both men and women (For example, L. M. Roberts or Robin Jackson.) and you're unsure of the addressee's sex, omit the gender reference (Mr., Ms., etc.). If you don't know the name of the person you are writing to, use a job title—for example, Managing Editor. In the case of a titled individual, such as a doctor, use only one title: Dr. Mary Evans, not Dr. Mary Evans, M.D. The same applies to an attorney: Ralph Stevens, Esq., not Mr. Ralph Stevens, Esq. If you are including a job title, it is keyed after the name, separated by a comma, or it goes on a separate line, flush left, for example,

D. G. Marshall, Managing Editor
   or
D. G. Marshall
Managing Editor

Company Name

The company name should be keyed as it appears on the company's letterhead, including all punctuation.

Street Address, Suite, or Post Office Box

Spell out numerical street and avenue names ten and under: Seventh Avenue; 42nd Street. Use numerals for house and building numbers but spell out number one: 301 Hubble Road; One Mulberry Street. Spell out *Street, Avenue, Boulevard, Circle, Road,* and so on. Room and suite numbers should be on the same line as the street address, separated by a comma. A post office box number is keyed on a separate line below the street address (use no punctuation for "PO"):

> 12 Main Street
> PO Box 1234

City, State, and ZIP

The city, state, and ZIP code should be keyed on one line. Do not abbreviate the city. Use the approved USPS two-letter abbreviation for the state or province. Always include a ZIP code + the 4-digit code after, if known. If correspondence is being mailed to another country, key the country name in all caps on a separate line, below the city and postal code:

> Oxford, OX2 6DP
> UNITED KINGDOM

Salutation

The salutation is keyed two lines below the inside address, flush left, in block and modified block style. It is omitted in the simplified block style. The salutation often begins with "Dear," followed by the formal address such as Mrs. Johnson, Dr. Hansen, Professor Michaels.

> Dear Mayor Jensen: Dear Dr. Lewis:
> Dear Ms. Hilliard: Dear Mr. Ngu:

Use a first name only if you are well acquainted with the recipient: "Dear Ann,". When addressing a woman, Ms. is acceptable if her marital status is not known, or if it is known to be the recipient's preference. The salutation is followed by a colon, if using mixed punctuation.

If you do not have a name to address your correspondence to, use a general salutation:

Dear Ladies and Gentlemen: Dear Human Resources Director:
Dear Board Members: Dear Sir or Madam:

If the name is available but the person's sex is unknown, you may address the individual using both first and last name:

Dear Robin Garvey: Dear A. S. Anderson:

While the very basic "To whom it may concern" is still acceptable, it is advantageous to take the time to research the name of the person to whom you should direct your letter. Often a single phone call will be sufficient to obtain such information. It avoids the probability that your letter will be passed from one in-box to another. If you are writing to someone in the U.S. government (a senator or representative, an officer in the military, etc.)

Subject

While a subject line is not necessary, it can be a welcome addition to a letter, especially when the recipient receives volumes of correspondence. It is eye-catching and spells out the purpose of the letter, eliminating the need to expound on the purpose of your letter in the first paragraph. It may be keyed as follows:

Block style: two lines below the salutation, flush left.
Modified block style: two lines below the salutation, indented.
Simplified block style: three lines below the inside address, no
   salutation.

The subject line may be preceded by the word *Subject*, followed by a colon. In the simplified block style, do not use the word *Subject*.

Body of the Letter

The body of the letter begins two lines below the salutation in block style and modified block style, and three lines below the subject line in simplified block style. The letter is single-spaced with a line space between paragraphs. Modified block style features indented paragraphs, about one-half inch (or five spaces) from the left margin.

Regardless of the specific purpose of a letter—whether it's a cover letter for a résumé or manuscript, a response to a customer's complaint or praise for an employee, or a request for payment—a business letter should seldom be longer than one page. The tone should be formal (without sounding too distant or patronizing), polite, and to the point. Avoid slang, clichés, colloquialisms, harsh or rude language, and repeating information that is contained in enclosures or attachments. It is appropriate, however, to provide a summary of the information available in additional documents, or to emphasize those points you regard as most important.

Always consider your audience when preparing a business letter. Do not say something in a letter that you would not say to the person in a face-to-face situation, and do not put in writing anything that might later embarrass you or your company, commit you or your company to something that you might not be able to fulfill, or be used against you (or your company) in the future. Explain technical terms and procedures that the recipient may not understand or know about, but provide only as much information as the individual will find useful. Whether you are writing to your immediate superior, an officer of the company you work for, or a disgruntled employee, be respectful and professional.

The content (body) of a business letter has five basic parts: (1) a reference, (2) the reason for writing, (3) a description of enclosed documents (if appropriate), (4) closing remarks, (5) and some reference to future contact. The first element tells the recipient what your letter refers to: "With reference to your classified advertisement in . . .," "your letter of June 19th . . .," "our phone conversation yesterday afternoon. . . ." This element is important as a beginning because several days (or weeks) may go by before your letter is delivered, and it provides the recipient with the context of your letter or refreshes his or her mind.

Next, state your reason for writing: "I am writing to apply for the position . . .," "to inquire about your offer . . .," "to confirm delivery of . . . ." If you want to ask for something, be specific and humble:

"Could you possibly extend my deadline . . .?" or "I would be grateful if you could send me a review copy of your new video." If you are agreeing to a request, be specific and gracious: "I would be delighted to speak to your organization about . . . ." If you must decline, be appreciative: "Thank you for the invitation to speak, but . . . ." "Bad news" letters are among the most difficult to write, and it is important that you use the right tone: "Unfortunately, I am the bearer of sad news . . ." or "I am afraid that my news isn't good." If you are writing to someone within your company, using the "Re:" line at the top of your letter is also appropriate.

Having given whatever information is required, state explicitly that you are enclosing documents (if you are), tell the recipient how many separate documents you are sending, explain what they are, and how they are relevant to the subject of your letter: "I am enclosing my résumé, which details . . ." or, more formally, "Please find enclosed a copy of your letter . . . ."

In your closing remarks, it is appropriate to thank the recipient in advance for help, offer to be of further service if it is necessary, or summarize the important points of your letter: "Thank you in advance for your help with . . ., "If I can provide additional information, please don't hesitate . . .," or "I hope this information will help you . . . ."

If you expect the recipient to initiate the next contact, say so: "I look forward to hearing from you soon," ". . . our meeting next week . . .," ". . . seeing you next Friday." At this point, if you expect the recipient to respond to you in a particular way (for example, if you are asking the person to fax you a document), specify in your letter how you expect him or her to respond. If you want the person to telephone you and are using company letterhead, the company telephone number will probably be on the stationery, but also provide your extension number or direct office number if you have one. If you want a document sent to you by fax, you should also provide that number. Both numbers, when necessary, should be part of the heading (as shown in the sample letter). If you definitely need an answer from the recipient, you might enclose a self-addressed, stamped envelope for his or her convenience and mention this fact. This shows both your consideration and your desire for a response.

Complimentary Close

In full-block style, your closing should be typed flush with the left-hand margin. If your company uses a modified block or indented format, the closing should be aligned with the heading on the right side of the letter. The closing consists of three or four elements: (1) a complimentary close, (2) your signature, (3) your typed name, and, if you are acting in an official capacity, (4) your title.

The complimentary close is typed two line spaces below the end of the body of the letter and must be followed by a comma. Several formal closes are acceptable, depending on the degree of formality:

Formal	Less Formal
Very truly yours,	Sincerely,
Sincerely yours,	Cordially,

Formal closings are formulaic and don't require any thought on the writer's part. When appropriate, friendlier, more informal closings may be used:

All best wishes,
With my best (*or* warmest) wishes,
Best wishes (for your future),
Warmest greetings,

Your recipient will notice whether you've taken the time to close your letter in an unusual way. (But don't end up saying something inappropriate. Use good judgment.)

Signature, Name, and Title of Sender

Leave three or four lines under the close for your signature, and type your name, aligned with the beginning of the close. If you are acting or responding in an official capacity, type your title, followed by a comma, and your department or committee, aligned with your typed name.

Cary D'Amato

Vice President, Sales

Closing Notations

Notations are the last elements of a business letter, and they should be typed flush with the left margin. There are three kinds of notation: (1) a reference to documents enclosed with or attached to the letter (enclosures/enc. or attachments/att.), (2) the names of people who are receiving copies of the letter (cc:), and, if someone else has typed the letter, (3) the initials of the writer and the typist—for example, KM/mds (KM is the writer; mds is the typist).

Reread your letter, checking for typographical errors, misspelled words, grammatical problems, and for elements or information you omitted. If you have typed the letter on a computer and have used the software's spell-checker (as you should), be sure to look for omitted words (especially grammatical elements) and typographical or spelling errors that have resulted in a legitimate, but wrong, word. English has numerous homonyms (words that sound alike but have different meanings or functions)—for example, *to, too, two*; *their, there, they're*; *its* (possessive), *it's* (contraction of *it is*); *your* (possessive), *you're* (contraction of *you are*). No software program can alert you to such problems, and inadvertently leaving them in a formal letter is sloppy. Many people believe they are experts on grammatical correctness and are critical of the writing of others. For such people, errors can raise questions about your ability. Once you are satisfied that your letter is clean in every respect, sign it, in ink.

SAMPLE BUSINESS LETTERS

Just as there is a standard form for business letters, which sets out the information that should be included in virtually every business letter, so there are also formulas that govern the content of specific business letters. Some types of business letter are more difficult to write than others, but as you gain experience in writing letters you'll find that knowing what to say and how to phrase it is largely a matter of common sense. To help you get started as a business correspondent, sample letters for some of the most commonly occurring situations are provided here.

Letter of Resignation

Writing a letter of resignation can be difficult, depending on the circumstances. For one thing, it's hard to strike just the right tone. Even if you're leaving a position because you're not happy or making enough money, you don't want to risk alienating your superiors or coworkers. You never know when you might want to ask one of them for a reference or recommendation.

The best tactic is to keep your resignation letter simple. Use company letterhead (this is an official act) and state only the barest facts and leave it at that. Date your letter, state the date on which your resignation is official and the position you're resigning, sign it, and hand (or send) it to the appropriate person.

February 3, 2003

Miriam Selznik, Personnel Manager
Acme Plumbing & Heating
12366 Industrial Parkway
Atlanta, GA 30094

Dear Ms. Selznik:

I am writing to let you know that I am resigning my position as Administrative Assistant to the Vice President for Marketing, effective February 17, 2003.

It's been a pleasure working for Acme.

Sincerely,
Joseph Clayhurst

[signature]

Administrative Assistant
Marketing

It is also appropriate for Ms. Selznik to acknowledge receipt of Mr. Clayhurst's letter of resignation.

February 5, 2003
Joseph Clayhurst, Administrative Assistant Marketing
Acme Plumbing & Heating
12366 Industrial Parkway
Atlanta, GA 30094

Dear Mr. Clayhurst:

It is with deep regret that I accept your resignation as Administrative Assistant to Acme's Vice President for Marketing, effective February 17th of this year.

We here at Acme are aware of the demands that this position has placed on you, and we appreciate the fine work you have done as an administrative assistant.

I wish you success in your new position.

Best wishes,

[signature]

Miriam Selznik
Personnel Manager

First Reminder of an Unpaid Invoice or Bill

Writing a dunning letter is never a pleasure, but it may become a necessary task. When a nonpayer forces you to resort to second and third requests for payment, you are losing valuable time as well as money in your efforts to collect the debt. You have to maintain a delicate balance between firmly stating your request and still retaining the recipient's goodwill. This is especially true for the first letter regarding an unpaid bill. The individual may have innocently forgotten to pay you, or the payment may be in the mail.

The letter can be brief without being rude. In a first notice, you should: (1) give a gentle reminder that payment is due; (2) state a relevant details regarding the invoice (invoice number, amount due, and due date); (3) make it clear to your customer that you assume this is a mistake or oversight; (4) affirm your confidence that nonpayment is a mistake or oversight and state that you look forward to receiving payment in a few days.

[Company letterhead]
[Date]
[Recipient's Name, Position]
[Company]
[Street Address]
[City, State ZIP code]

Dear [Name]:

I am writing to remind you that we have not yet received payment for invoice [number] for [amount], due on [date]. I am enclosing a full statement of your account as of [date] and a copy of the invoice.

We're sure that this is an oversight on your part, and would appreciate your prompt attention to this matter.

If your payment is already in the mail, please disregard this letter. Should you have any questions about your account, please do not hesitate to contact me.

Yours Sincerely,

[signature]

[Your name]
[Your title]
[ID initials: UC/lc]
Enclosures: 2

Introduction of New Colleague

If you have been asked to write a letter introducing a new colleague, your letter should be warm and friendly, at the same time maintaining a concise, businesslike tone. Be sure to include sufficient details so there is no confusion about who you're introducing, his or her last position and place of employment, and the details of the position for which he or she has been hired.

Start your letter by announcing the name of the new colleague and providing a few brief, relevant details of his or her previous position. Next, include a warm compliment that welcomes the new colleague and supply some initial details about his or her new role in the company. Finally, say that the new person is eager to meet all the members of the staff and looks forward to their help and assistance in carrying out the duties of his or her new position.

[Company letterhead]
[Date]

[Name]
[Address]

Dear [Name]:

I want to take this opportunity to inform you that [Name] will soon be joining us as the [Title] in the [Department]. [He or She] will be taking over from [Name] and will begin work on [Date].

[Name] has been the [Title] of the [Department] at [Company] for [number] years and we are delighted that [he or she] has decided to join our company at this stage of our development.

[He or She] is a person of [one or two qualities] and I have no doubt [he or she] will contribute significantly to all aspects of our work here.

I hope all of you will try to make [Name] feel welcome here as [he or she] becomes accustomed to [his or her] new position.

Yours Sincerely,

[signature]

[Your name]
[Your title]

Announcing or Acknowledging the Death of an Employee

Informing others of another person's death is not an easy task, but it is one you may be called on to perform at some point in your career. Keep your letter short and to the point. Express your sympathy for the individual's family, friends, and coworkers without exaggerated emotion. In this kind of letter, do not say more than is absolutely necessary. The fact that you have written it is the most genuine sign of your feelings.

[Company letterhead]
[Date]

[Name]
[Address]

Dear [Name],

I am writing to express the sadness all of us at [Company name] feel on hearing of [Name's] death.

[Name] was a much liked and respected employee. [He or She] will certainly be missed by everyone who worked with [him or her].
All of us send our deepest sympathies to you. If there is anything we can do, please do not hesitate to contact us.

Yours Sincerely,

[signature]

[Your name]
[Your title]

Apology for an Employee's Conduct

Having to apologize to a customer who was treated rudely by an employee is difficult, but it is among the most important communications you will ever undertake. An angry or offended customer is one who may never do business with your company again. Your goal is to convey a sincere apology to the customer. The more effectively you do this, the more inclined that individual may be to continue doing business with you.

This is a letter that must be written as soon as you have been informed that an employee has somehow alienated a customer. You cannot delay. First, assure the customer that your company does not tolerate such behavior from its employees and, second, that appropriate action will be taken. Finally, finish your letter with a full apology.

[Company letterhead]
[Date]

[Name]
[Address]

Dear [Name]:

Thank you for your [letter or call] of [date] detailing the offensive behavior of one of our employees. Please be assured that such conduct is not, and never will be, tolerated in this company.

After investigating your complaint, we severely reprimanded the individual involved. Please accept our sincere apology for any distress this situation may have caused you, and be assured that it will not happen again.

Thank you for bringing this matter to our attention. We place great importance on the conduct of our employees, and your complaint has given us the opportunity to remedy the problem.

Yours Sincerely,

[signature]

[Your Name]
[Your Title]

WRITING A MEMO

If you can write a good business letter, you can write a good memo (short for *memorandum,* 'a brief reminder'). In fact, many office memos are "brief reminders" about an upcoming meeting or taking up a collection to send a card to a colleague who's in the hospital, but the office setting also requires more complex memos. Think of a memo as an "in-house business letter," somewhere between a note and a brief report in length, to be read and passed on quickly. Now that most businesses of any size have individual computer work stations for employees, most memos are now sent as e-mail messages.

Like a business letter, memos provide needed information in an effective and efficient way without a time-consuming meeting and they are written in a somewhat formal style—no misspellings, slang, or sentence fragments. Because memos are written to be widely distributed and posted, they reach numerous people very quickly and the effects of careless errors multiply, resulting in more memos (requesting clarification or drawing attention to the errors).

There are three basic ways to organize office memos, each suited to providing information in the most effective format:

1. The *direct approach* states the most important information first and then goes on to supporting or supplementary information. This approach works well if you need to convey routine information or pass on organizational news.
2. The *indirect approach* first makes an appeal to the reader or points out the factual elements of a situation or issue and then states a conclusion based on the evidence provided. This approach is especially effective when you want to get the reader's attention before describing your proposed plan of action.
3. The *balanced approach* combines the direct and the indirect approaches, and is particularly effective when the information you are providing is "bad news."

Parts of a Memo

A good memo organizes the information to be conveyed both for the reader's convenience and ease of understanding and to achieve the writer's purpose in the most effective way.

HEADING.

The heading for every memo follows the same basic format:

> TO: [Reader's name and job title]
> cc: [List others who are receiving copies]
> FROM: [Your name and job title]
> DATE: [Month, day, and year, spelled out]
> SUBJECT: [Topic of the memo]

Some memo pads, in fact, already have this format printed at the top of each page. If your group or organization uses a slightly different format for the heading, use it. Be sure that you have the name of each recipient spelled correctly and his or her job title accurate. In general, some titles (for example, "Professor" or "Ms." are unnecessary), nor do you need the salutation required in a formal business letter. Next to your name, hand-write your initials (on a memo, a closing signature is not necessary).

Your subject line should be brief, no more than a few words, but explicit, so that there is no chance for misunderstanding. "Ordering Pizza" as a subject line, for example, might lead your readers to think that your memo will provide instructions on the correct procedure for ordering in pizza on late nights at the office when, in fact, you're passing on complaints from the cleaning staff about the tomato sauce on the carpet and the boxes strewn all over the floor. Something like, "Clean up your mess before leaving," announces the main point of the memo.

OPENING.

The opening sentences or paragraphs of a memo tell readers the context of the issue, the suggested assignment or task, and the purpose of the memo.

Context. The context you describe is the event, situation, or background of the problem or issue you are addressing. Whether it takes a sentence or a paragraph will depend on the complexity of the situation. For example, the context may begin with "The cleaning company has complained that it takes too long to clean our floors . . . ." Be clear and direct, providing only as much information as your readers need.

Task. Your task or assignment statement describes what you are doing to solve the problem, issue, or situation. If your reader asked that you act, you might say, "You asked me to look at . . . ." If you want to present alternatives for employees to consider, you might say, "We need to consider alternatives that will satisfy the cleaning company without . . . ."

Purpose. Your purpose statement explains why you are
writing the memo and leads in to the remainder of it. You
need to be direct, and avoid trying to downplay the
information. Your statement might begin with: "This memo
describes my understanding of the cleaning company's
complaint, proposes several ways of accommodating these
people, and my own recommendations for resolving the
problem." If the memo will be so long that adding section
headings will make it easier to follow the organization of
the information, by all means, do so.

When the purpose of a memo is to convince your readers that
there is a real problem, avoid going into more detail than the situation
requires. If you discover that you're having difficulty describing the
task, you may need to do more thinking before you write the memo. If
you decide to break your memo into segments, be sure that they the
most important points.

SUMMARY.

Wait until you've written the main body of your memo to write a summary section. If your memo is one page or less, a summary may not be
necessary. If, however, you've covered several important issues or
events, or your analysis is fairly detailed, a summary paragraph is
appropriate. If the memo is a short report on research you've done on
an issue or for a project, this is a good place to sum up methods and
sources you've used so far. Remember, though, that this is a summa-
tion. Keep it brief and don't needlessly repeat detailed information.

DISCUSSION PARAGRAPH(S).

After you've adequately covered the basic presentation of your topic,
here is where you lay out all the details—facts, statistics, hypothe-
ses—that support the ideas you've discussed. In this section you
demonstrate your ability to think creatively and critically by presenting your ideas.

Begin with the most important or most "telling" information, proceeding from your strongest fact to the weakest (or, if you're providing

historical background, from oldest to newest information). These paragraphs are also the place where you make your recommendations, acknowledge others' recommendations, and describe future problems that might occur and how your suggestions will ensure that such problems they simply don't happen. It often helps to put important facts or details into numbered or bulleted lists, again going from strongest point to weakest. (Caution: The items included in such lists must all be grammatically parallel. This means that each item must have the same grammatical form as all the others. That is, if your first list item is a noun phrase, every list item has to be a noun phrase; if one item begins with an –ing verb form, every item must begin with an –ing verb; if one item is a complete sentence, all the items must be complete sentences.)

YOUR CLOSING.

Once you've given your readers all the information relevant to the subject of your memo, use a courteous closing that describes the actions you want them to take, and point out how those actions will benefit everyone. This one-paragraph closing might begin with, "We can discuss my recommendations in greater detail at our next meeting . . . ." or "Should you need more information, I'll be glad to . . . ."

ATTACHMENTS.

Provide whatever documentation or additional information your readers will need to come to their own understanding of the event, issue, or problem you've described, and list such attachments at the end. For example, if there has been an exchange of letters regarding your subject, include copies of them (if doing so will not breach confidentiality or if they contain information that your readers need to know). If you've created graphs of facts or statistics or diagrams that illustrate physical relationships, attach those. You can also refer to such graphs, diagrams, or illustrations at appropriate points in your memo. Do not attach materials that do not bear directly on the subject of the memo.

CHAPTER 9

Making Speeches and Presentations

PUBLIC SPEAKING

There are many contexts in which public speaking is called for. One may think of a politician standing in front of hundreds of people and millions more on TV. Public speaking, of course, is not only a political speech; it is also the sales rep presenting a product to potential customers. It is the human relations manager explaining benefits to a group of new employees. It is the project manager discussing schedule changes with a project team. In everyday business, public speaking is an integral part of operations and effective communications.

Is Public Speaking Science or Art?

For some, public speaking is a science. It has forms and rules that must be followed and, as with most endeavors, practice makes perfect. For others, public speaking is an art that is guided more by inspiration than preparation. In reality, both views are correct. Public speaking has forms and rules that work best when coupled with inspiration and extemporaneous thought. We all know people who speak better "off the cuff," as well as those who require many hours of practice. Depending on the person, the topic, and/or the situation, a

236

speech or presentation might be best done with hours of preparation and several practice "run-throughs," or it may lose its freshness with too much rehearsal. Only the speaker knows how best to prepare.

This chapter enumerates the steps it takes to create an effective public speech, no matter the speaker, audience, or topic. It assumes a level of preparation that should go into any presentation or speech, but it does not assume the level of expertise, comfort, or extemporaneous speaking ability of the speaker. As with any recipe, you should adjust the ingredients to your taste.

Selecting a Topic

The most important part of public speaking is having a clear and concise topic. No matter your audience, people in business expect that you will respect their time. This is as true for a speaker in front of 300 people as it is for a presentation to three people in your department.

Selecting your topic may come easy, or it may take some thinking. It all depends on the event or assignment at hand. No matter how challenging, it is important that you answer the following questions as you consider your topic selection:

- To whom are you speaking?
- Can you speak confidently on the topic?
- Why were you asked to make the presentation?
- How much time is allotted for your speech?

Audience

Knowing the audience is the first step in planning a speech or presentation. Without an understanding of why people are there to hear you speak, it is impossible to plan for an effective presentation. Assess the audience to determine what they are expecting. An audience expecting to be sold a product has different assumptions than an audience expecting to learn how to use a software product. A management team learning about a quarterly sales performance requires a different approach than a group of interns learning the voice- and e-mail systems. By knowing your audience and their expectations, you can better plan your approach.

Knowledge

It is imperative that you feel comfortable discussing the topic you have chosen (or have had chosen for you). However, comfort isn't measured by how nervous you are, but by how much you know compared to what your audience knows. You may feel that you can easily demonstrate how to use a particular software program to anyone in your company but would not feel comfortable speaking about that same software to a group of programmers. Your level of comfort is in direct relation to the audience's expertise. Ask yourself if you can reasonably answer the needs of the audience at hand and try to determine why you were asked to make the presentation. If you feel that you can "fake your way through it," you probably can.

Goals

You are speaking or presenting for a reason. You know that your audience has expectations, but what about those who asked you to speak? Find out exactly what both the audience and those who asked you to present expect. Understanding what they want out of your presentation is a must because you can waste everyone's time if you do not satisfy the audience's expectations. By ignoring the goals of the audience, you may find that your presentation is either way over their heads or is too remedial to be useful to them. If you can find out what your audience expects and needs, you can better serve those needs.

Time

Not having enough or having too much time is one of the most common problems in public speaking; giving yourself enough time to present is not only important for you but also for your audience. Busy professionals will not sit idly by as you ramble on into their next appointment. Nor will people look too kindly on a fifteen-minute speech when they are expecting an hour's worth of your information. Make sure you know how much time you have and that you know exactly how much time you will need.

Preparation

Preparation for a presentation or speech is extremely important. Whether you are speaking on a topic that you are the world's foremost expert on or giving a presentation on something you have just learned, good preparation will make the difference between a fair and an outstanding performance.

WRITTEN OUTLINE.

Outlining what you will say in your speech is usually associated with presentation software. While it is important to have a clear outline to show your audience, charting the subtleties and nuances of your speech in notes to yourself is even more important. An outline that only you see (in note cards, on paper, or via a teleprompter) helps you prepare for and deliver your speech. Some people believe that you should write out everything that you will say in a speech. While this helps with judging time, there is a real danger that you will start reading off the page, and reading a prepared statement is usually stiff and unengaging.

An outline helps you formulate your thoughts, create clever asides, and embed the presentation plan in your head. Your outline should have one or two levels of detail more than what you hand out or show to your audience. If, for example, a slide shown while you are speaking says "Year-to-Date Sales $2.3 million," your outline may give you salient details to mention such as "Int'l $1.1mm, Domestic $1.8mm, Special Sales $400K."

Your outline, like a third-grade teacher during the class play, should feed you the first words of your lines, but not the entire script. Its function is both to help you prepare and to help you through the presentation in an ordered and logical fashion.

PRACTICE.

Practice may be in the form of actual run-throughs in real time or a mental walk through your written outline. The simple rule for most is that the more you practice, the better your speech or presentation.

Ideally, practicing should be done in the room or hall you will be using, so that you can learn the subtleties of the room. Think like a professional golfer and go out and learn the course.

If you cannot practice in the place where you will be presenting, try practicing in front of peers, friends, or family. Seeing how people react to what you are saying is important because you may learn that you need to stress certain words or concepts differently from what you had assumed.

Time your practice sessions and figure out how to stretch or cut your material if you need to. The more you practice, the more flexible you will become with your presentation. If something occurs that delays your speech (fire alarms, late attendees, etc.), all your practice will help you figure out the best way to edit on the spot and still get your point across.

SETTING UP: FACILITIES AND EQUIPMENT

Setting up the facility is the presenter's responsibility. That is how you must look at things because, when you go in to give a speech or presentation, you are the one everyone thinks poorly of when the presentation facilities are inadequate or the equipment does not work.

There are many memorable examples in the world of business presentations when equipment has sabotaged an otherwise excellent presentation and caused a speaker extreme embarrassment. A notable example happened to Bill Gates, CEO of Microsoft. While giving a speech demonstrating the latest and most stable version of the Microsoft Office Suite software, the PowerPoint presentation froze the PC he was using.

With this in mind, make sure that you arrive well in advance of the presentation time to check out the facilities. Here is a quick checklist to run through:

- Is there a podium, lectern, or special place for your notes?
- Is there a projector hooked up to a computer?
- Is your presentation loaded up and ready to go?

- Is there enough seating in the room?
- Will everyone be able to see and hear you?
- Is there a PA system and is it working?

Starting off with everything under control is the best way to start any presentation. By advance planning and preparation, your speech will stand on the merits of what you say, not how you say it. Planning and preparing reduces the risk of a harried or disjointed presentation.

GIVING A SPEECH AND MAKING A PRESENTATION

Most presentations and speeches should have the following structure:

- Introduction
- Warm Up
- Speech or Presentation
- Q & A
- Follow-Up/Action Items
- Thanks

Introduction

Whether you are being introduced to a room full of strangers, or you are standing in front of five peers, it is imperative that your audience knows exactly who you are and why you are there. Managing the expectations of the audience is your job. Make sure they are clear about what your goals are.

Warm-Up

Depending on the setting, the audience, and the topic, almost every presentation or speech is helped by some form of warm-up or decompression exercise. The setting dictates the kind of warm-up you select.

When speaking in front of a large group, again depending on the topic and audience, a joke or personal anecdote is often the perfect way to set up your talk. The context of the joke or anecdote should match your topic in some way. For a smaller, more intimate setting, a good exercise is to go around the room and let everyone introduce themselves and state what they hope to get out of the presentation. (This also helps you double-check the expectations of your audience.)

The warm-up should be designed to help both you and the audience focus on the topic at hand. Furthermore, the best warm-up sets up your presentation, so everyone is ready to listen and learn.

The Speech or Presentation

You have practiced, prepared, been introduced, warmed the audience up, and now you launch into the meat of your speech or presentation. Follow a few guidelines and you will be successful:

- Look around often, trying to make as much eye contact as possible. Don't stare at the PowerPoint slide or bury your face in your index cards. Smile!
- Use vocabulary you are comfortable with. Do not try to "sound smart." Be yourself!
- Breathe. The first few seconds can sometimes take your breath away. Breathe slowly and deeply and do not rush. Speak clearly!

Tips for the Nervous

Does speaking in front of people make you nervous? Relax; it makes everyone nervous. It's how individuals deal with it that makes some seem cooler and more collected than others. Here are some things you can do to quiet your nerves:

1. Drink plenty of fluids so you don't get dry-mouthed and mumble. Make sure there is water nearby while you speak.
2. Take deep, long breaths before speaking. Make your exhalation breaths last three times as long as your inhalation breaths.
3. Find a friendly face in the room and speak to that individual.
4. If you are speaking to a large group, pick a point in the middle of the audience and imagine your mom or your little brother sitting there. Talk directly to that person.

- Be aware of the time. Don't get so caught up in your topic or pace that you lose track of time. Wear a watch!
- If possible, walk around the room. If not, use your hands, your shoulders, and your face to show expression. Be engaging!
- Watch your audience. Make sure they are following what you say. Slow down if they look lost, speed up if they look bored. Be aware!

Q & A (Questions and Answers)

Depending on the time, the appropriateness, or the purpose of your presentation, you may need to offer a Q & A session following it. If so, consider the following:

- Make sure you understand the question by stating it back to the audience. You do not want to answer something that wasn't asked.
- Answer a question only if you feel you can or should.

Jokes

Relaxing yourself and your audience can make a big difference in a presentation, but one individual's humor may be another's insult. Making any assumptions about the people in your audience is always a bad idea. Humor is very much bound to ethnic and cultural experience, and you should avoid any jokes that rely on stereotypes of any group of people. A joke can be a great way to begin a speech if its humor does not come at someone else's expense. When choosing an appropriate joke to share with your audience, remember to keep the message lighthearted.

1. Never tell an ethnic, religious, or sexual joke. Your career may depend on someone's sensitivity to insult.
2. Try to find an amusing story or joke that you can connect to the speech or presentation in some way. The best speakers use jokes like the Bible uses parables (stories that illustrate deeper moral lessons).

- Guessing, speculating, and answering for others is generally bad form.
- If a question is posed that goes beyond your scope, write it down and offer to provide an answer later.
- Look at the person who asked the question when answering, but also look around at the rest of the audience.

(Note: Follow-up/Action Items and Thanks are discussed later in the chapter.)

Toastmasters International and Other Speakers' Organizations

If you're not comfortable speaking in front of a crowd, there are several organizations you can turn to for help and encouragement. One of the longest-established and best-known is Toastmasters International, which has clubs all over the world. Toastmasters International encourages leadership and speaking skills by providing a supportive environment in which to learn those skills. Members join small clubs where they learn to give both impromptu and prepared speeches and accept and give feedback and criticism. More information can be found at www.toastmasters.org.

If it's not just nervousness but an actual speech impediment that's holding you back, you might want to check out the National Stuttering Association (www.nsastutter.org) for more information and help. Another excellent organization is the Stuttering Foundation of America (www.stuttersfa.org). You can find information about and help for other speech disorders at the Web site of the American Speech-Language-Hearing Association (www.asha.org).

Once you're comfortable with public speaking, you might be ready to take the next step and become a professional. The National Speakers Association (www.nsaspeaker.org) is the leading organization for experts who speak professionally. Membership requirements are strict, but they provide certification and marketing help to professional speakers.

MAKING A MULTIMEDIA PRESENTATION

Good presentations have nothing to do with technical slickness. Remember those great IBM commercials from 1999 and 2000 in which executives are looking at Web-site designs and one asks, quizzically, "The logo, it's on fire?" The designer answers enthusiastically, "Yeah, it's on fire!" The commercial was illustrating the limitations of modern design software. You can do a lot of cool things, 99 percent of which are annoying.

Presentation software presents a similar challenge to the user. With all the bells and whistles that come with PowerPoint and other presentation software, it is easy to get carried away. So, before you go and set the corporate logo ablaze, read the rest of this chapter.

Do You Really Need a Multimedia Presentation?

With most presentation software programs such as PowerPoint you can animate letters and words, stream video, play background audio, and do many other things impossible with a paper presentation. Before you run off to get the digital camcorder, ask yourself this simple question: Do you really need a multimedia presentation?

Old-school thinking will say "no." The merits of what you present will stand on its own whether people are reading it on paper or as a projected image. However, there are many benefits, especially in a sales situation, to controlling the flow of information.

Multimedia presentations offer you the opportunity to control what people see and when they see it. By using presentation software and not giving out hard copies until the presentation is over, you have control over what the people in the room see.

If you decide that you need to do a multimedia presentation, here are a few things to consider:

- appropriateness
- facility capabilities
- creation time
- platform

- design rules
- plan B (*or* what if it doesn't work?)

APPROPRIATENESS.

The appropriateness of a multimedia presentation depends on the topic, the audience, and the facilities. You must ask yourself whether the topic is appropriate for a multimedia presentation. For example, a CPA wouldn't be wise to project a family's tax return on a conference room wall while reviewing it at a meeting. Nor would it be appropriate for a funeral director to show slides of other funerals to a grieving family there to bury a loved one. While both presentations would certainly make the process simpler, they lack tact and sensitivity.

FACILITY CAPABILITIES.

With your topic selected and deemed appropriate for a dazzling multimedia presentation, you work for hours finding video clips, editing background music, and animating the slides so they dramatically spell out the key points as you cue them. Then you find out that the conference room with all the technical gizmos is booked and you will be presenting in the reception waiting area. No computer, no network ports, no screen, no speakers . . . no presentation. This is why it is imperative that you first determine the capabilities of the facility where you will be working and, expecting the worst, always have a backup presentation in case there is a change of venue (more on that later).

CREATION TIME.

The last factor in determining whether to do a multimedia presentation is time. Typing up a list of key points in the form of an outline to hand out to an audience doesn't require much time or effort. However, taking that same outline, styling it, adding music, video, and animation is a sizable task.

Be sure that you have the time to create your presentation. Be wary if your plans include creating a presentation with elements that you have never used before. While software today makes an amazing amount of razzle-dazzle possible, you will often find yourself spending hours trying to figure out how to get an image to paste where you want it, as opposed to where it insists on being placed.

Staying up until 4 a.m. to finish a presentation that you will be making at 9 that morning is not the best use of your time, nor does it allow you to prepare properly. Do not underestimate the importance of creation time.

PLATFORM.

The most popular presentation software is PowerPoint, which is part of the Microsoft Office suite. However, PowerPoint is hardly the only player out there. For example, Mac users have their own presentation software, AppleWorks. Furthermore, depending on the topic, one might only require a spreadsheet program such as Excel or Lotus, a word-processing program such as Word or WordPerfect, or Web-presentation software such as Flash.

Whatever you choose to use, be sure that the computer you are using to present has the software installed and that it has the processing power to handle your presentation. Multimedia presentations have crashed more computers during key presentations due to lack of RAM or processing power than any other factor. Also be sure that you are platform conscious. Creating in a Mac environment may be easiest, but will you be able to run it on a PC?

DESIGN RULES.

It is likely that somewhere in your company is a document that outlines design rules. This document, perhaps called *design specs*, *design rules*, or *design bible*, is usually found in the marketing or advertising department and details the corporate color scheme, the rules of logo placement, and a list of approved fonts.

If you are making a presentation on behalf of your company, it is not acceptable to use random colors, a logo scanned off a catalog, and your sixteen favorite gothic fonts.

Before you begin building your presentation, find out if there is a PowerPoint (or other program) template already created. Chances are that many others in your organization have needed this before you. If there isn't such a template, ask for the design specs and an electronic copy of the corporate logo.

If your organization does not have either a template or a design spec, you are on your own . . . to a degree. Your company's Web site can provide you with the color scheme, the logo, and the corporate fonts. While this is hardly the best method, approximating by using the Web site is far better than making up your own design.

PLAN B (OR WHAT IF IT DOESN'T WORK?)

You have done everything right. You chose an appropriate topic. Your audience and facilities are perfect for a full-blown multimedia presentation. You and/or your design department have created a perfect presentation that runs perfectly during practice sessions. Then, as you turn down the lights and start up the projector, the bulb in the machine dies and your presentation is ruined.

Or is it? Being smart, you expect that technology will fail, and you have a backup plan. You ask that the lights be put back on and you reach into a box that you carried in with you and voilà! You hand out hard copies (preferably in color) of the presentation that you printed out the day before.

This kind of planning should be part of every presentation you make. Sure, you would rather control the pace of the show and not let attendees read ahead, but, all things considered, it is better to be able to go ahead with your presentation and have people follow in print. If you do not have copies, look for a white board or tear-away meeting note sheets and write the highlights of each PowerPoint slide as you speak. *Always have one hard copy of your speech with you.* Continue on as if your presentation hinged only on what you say, not how the message is delivered. Never let technology ruin what you have to say.

What Makes a Good Multimedia Presentation?

A good presentation is akin to telling a good story. There is a beginning, middle, and end. It needs to be clear. It needs to energize and excite the audience. It cannot be burdened with extraneous details, sounds, or visual effects.

A good presentation starts with a premise, describes the premise, and then reviews the premise. This elliptical approach is a proven pedagogy. Look at any textbook or learning aid you have ever used. They always outline the topic, then teach the topic, then review what was just taught. All presentations should be conceived with similar objectives and should have the following characteristics:

- clear topic
- repeated statement of ideas
- good information flow
- energizing style
- no gratuitous graphics, sounds, or animation
- follow-up/action items
- thanks

CLEAR TOPIC.

Without a clear topic, your presentation will not be successful. It will be difficult to create as you will find yourself looking to replace focus with fluff, substance with style. Most poor presentations are the result of a lack of clarity of topic. Example of a good topic: "Our Sales Goals and Selling Points for 2004"; bad topic: "Sales 2004."

REPEATED STATEMENT OF IDEAS.

Explain what you will be presenting. Clearly state the topic. Review what you just presented. Structure your presentation like a textbook chapter. You are teaching your audience.

GOOD INFORMATION FLOW.

Every presentation should have a logical flow of information. You must build an argument from the ground up. Make sure that you don't jump around haphazardly. Your audience must perceive a progression of thought. For example, if you were presenting the company benefits package to new employees, you wouldn't start with the 401K plan, then jump to the medical plan, then go on to discuss the profit-sharing plan, and finish with health-insurance payroll deductions. Though you may have covered all the broad topics, you didn't organize the process for your audience.

The more logical approach for such a presentation would be to start with Financial Benefits (401K, profit sharing) then move on to Health Benefits (medical plan, health-insurance payroll deductions). Information that is related works best together.

ENERGIZING STYLE.

Look around often, trying to make as much eye contact as possible (don't stare at the PowerPoint slide or bury your face in your index cards). If possible, walk around the room. If not, use your hands, your shoulders, and your face to show expression. Watch your audience. Make sure they are following you. Slow down if they look lost, speed up if they look bored.

NO GRATUITOUS GRAPHICS, SOUNDS, OR ANIMATION.

The importance of *substance over style* cannot be stressed too much. Just because you have the technical wherewithal to create elaborate effects does not mean you should go overboard. Don't create cartoon characters to dance across your slides. Don't program machine-gun sounds to accompany type as it flies onto a screen. Don't get "creative" with gaudy background colors or intrusive music.

Multimedia should be appropriate to the message. If you are presenting the new baby-care center to employees, you can get away with certain well-chosen cute graphics and sound effects. However, when presenting bad financial results or imminent layoffs, no sound or graphic effects are appropriate.

FOLLOW-UP/ACTION ITEMS.

Presentations, especially in sales situations, often have follow-up or action items. Before you end your presentation or speech, be sure to list aloud your follow-up or action items. It is always a good idea to bring hard copies of your presentation for those who wish to see it and for those who couldn't attend. Ask your host how many you should bring.

THANKS.

Thank your audience. Thank those who introduced you. Thank those who asked you to speak and present. No speech or presentation is complete without thanks to everyone who organized and participated in it.

Being Considerate of People with Disabilities

If you work with people who have readily apparent disabilities, you may already be sensitive to their needs and will have modified your presentations to make sure that they can get the most benefit from them. However, there are many 'silent' disabilities, including color-blindness and minor hearing loss, that you should take into consideration when planning a presentation. Here are some things to keep in mind:

Visual:
Is the room set up so that people can choose how close or far they sit from any screens?
Are you using readable type? Avoid light type on light backgrounds, or odd combinations of colors, especially red on green and vice-versa.
Avoid flashing animation and type set along curves.

Auditory:
Avoid background music.
Can you be heard clearly from every seat in the room? Is there noise from fans or vents that might interfere with hearing your talk? Arrange to have chairs moved away from them or have the vents shut during your presentation.
During Q&A sessions, repeat the question that was asked of you before answering it.

(continued)

Other:

Be aware of the length of your presentation. It's considerate to build in breaks for any presentation longer than an hour. Consider taking a five-minute break before taking questions if you've already spoken for an hour.

Have copies of your presentation available for people who may not have been able to get all the information they needed during the session.

Offer to answer questions by phone or e-mail as well. Some people may not feel comfortable asking questions in an open session.

One last thing: ask for feedback. If possible, ask your listeners to give you anonymous feedback about your style, your manner, and the presentation as a whole. Ask specifically about whether your listeners felt they comprehended what you had to say. It will help you, and your listeners, in future presentations.

Using Design Specs from the Corporate Web Site

Your corporate Web site can be a treasure trove of design elements if your marketing department cannot or will not give you assistance. There you will find the corporate logo as well as approved fonts and color schemes. Here is how to apply them to your presentation:

1. **Logo:** Go to the site and find your company logo. Using Windows, place the cursor or arrow on the logo and right-click your mouse. Select "Save Picture As" and save it to your computer's desktop. In your presentation, set up the page or slide and insert by using the Insert menu and selecting "Insert Picture." The logo will appear on the page where you can move it, resize it, or rotate it.

2. **Font:** This is a less scientific process. Here you must use your judgment as to what font will work best. Look at the company's Web site, note the font used there, and find a font on your computer that most closely matches it.

3. **Colors:** Look at the corporate site and figure out the colors used there. Go to your presentation software and go to Format, then Colors, and select "Custom Colors." From there you can play with the mix of colors to match your company's.

PowerPoint Mistakes to Avoid

1. Background music: Why would you ever need this?
2. Zooming type or other annoying effects: Business presentations rarely need this kind of effect.
3. Non-sanctioned colors and fonts: Make sure you represent your company appropriately.
4. Streaming video: This is rarely useful and very tough to pull off successfully.
5. Each slide having its own design: Every slide should have the identical background color, font, and logo placement. Create a template if there isn't one already, and work from that template.
6. Presenting in the edit mode: Make sure your slides are taking up the full screen (F5 in Windows).
7. Reading from the slide: Everyone in the room can read. Talk from the slide, don't read it.
8. Too much information on a slide: Slides should contain outline information, not your entire discussion.
9. Too little information on a slide: "Introduction" is not sufficient information for a slide.
10. Spelling: Make sure the spell-check in your word-processing program is on and that you triple-check your work!

CHAPTER 10

Managing Information

RECORDS MANAGEMENT

The managing of records, whether on paper, as microfilm, or as electronic files, entails the retention, protection, preservation, and organization of those records. Some records must be kept for legal purposes for a specified number of years, or even permanently, which may require considerable space for storage, depending on the size of the company.

Larger companies may have a centralized records department, with a full-time staff to handle the filing and maintaining of these records, along with handling retrieval or copy requests. Smaller companies would depend on the office professional for such a task. Records must be filed efficiently and concisely, whatever the size of the company. A misfiled record is as good as gone, and the consequences could be dire.

Consideration must also be placed on the type of storage units used for filing. If records are of a sensitive nature, is the storage adequately locked and secure? If records are valuable or irreplaceable, are they in a fireproof or waterproof cabinet?

Periodic disposal of outdated or unnecessary records is helpful in the maintenance of office files. Records that must be retained for legal or documentation purposes but are not necessary in the everyday workings of the business may be transferred to another location such as a warehouse or storage facility. The records must be labeled and dated for easy retrieval.

When more than one person works on a project, each participant may maintain a personal file for that project, adding to the accumulation of correspondence and records. It is advisable to maintain an official file for each project and keep it in the hands of one person. It should contain the original of every piece of correspondence and other documentation related to the project.

REMINDER AND FOLLOW-UP SYSTEMS

Organizational skills are best implemented with the help of daily reminder calendars and follow-up files. An efficiently run office depends on such tools to keep track of important meetings, appointments, and special occasions.

Calendar Management

It is imperative that the executive and assistant keep lines of communication open at all times regarding appointments. An appointment change written on the executive's calendar but not relayed to the assistant can result in embarrassment or even irate clients. It is a good idea for the assistant to check the executive's calendar each morning to be sure both calendars coincide.

CALENDAR ENTRIES.

Some activities require notation on only the office professional's calendar—those of a more personal nature or those that do not involve the executive in any way. Others require notation on both calendars, with possible reminders a few days in advance, such as special anniversaries, which would give the office professional time to send a letter or card for the occasion.

Some activities occur regularly, such as staff meetings. While it may seem unnecessary to mark such an item on the calendar, do it anyway. In the course of a busy day or week, it's easy to overlook something routine. Having it penciled in will avoid the need for changes in appointments later. Use the previous year's calendar to mark annually occurring events. If the exact date is unknown but the general time of year is always the same, make such a notation in pencil on the calendar, which can later be permanently noted when the exact date is known.

TYPES OF CALENDARS.

Calendars come in all shapes and sizes, from pocket to desk to wall. The traditional write-in types never go out of style and are a great visual reminder, and software programs are now available that give executives and office professionals the ability to schedule and keep track of appointments at the push of a button. Electronic schedulers may allow both the executive and the office professional to log into one calendar, so any additions or changes in appointments will be obvious at a glance, avoiding any confusion or missed dates.

Hand-held organizers, called personal digital assistants (PDAs) or personal information managers (PIMs), can store names, addresses, notes, and appointments, but it is important that any appointments made or cancelled be transferred to the office calendar as soon as possible. (See "Do You Need A PDA?" on pages 4–5.)

Follow-Up Files

A follow-up filing system may be as simple as an expandable letter file with pockets labeled Monday through Friday. Each transaction that requires some type of follow-up action should be placed in the corresponding day on which that action is supposed to take place. If an executive writes a memo stating that a client is requesting a phone call on Wednesday to confirm a luncheon meeting the following week, that memo is placed in the Wednesday pocket. On Wednesday, the memo will be acted upon when all the paperwork is pulled out of that day's pocket. Larger expanding files are also available, with such pocket designations as A to Z, January to December, and 1 to 31.

More complex versions of this system would require file cabinets or desk drawers. A common system uses twelve monthly files, with each month having numbered daily folders according to how many days there are in that month. As each day's follow-up transactions are taken care of, the reminders can be thrown away or correspondence can be filed in the appropriate regular file, such as a client's folder or a project folder.

A card file can also be set up in a similar way, taking up much less space. Notes may be written on cards, as reminders of actions to be taken on each day. Whatever system is chosen, it should be designed to give the office professional the means to handle each day in an organized, efficient manner.

CHAPTER 11

Meetings and Conferences

TYPES OF MEETINGS

Informal

Most in-house staff, departmental, or executive meetings are informal. An informal meeting is not firmly structured and can generate spontaneity and creativity. No matter the size or type, though, all meetings require planning. In larger companies, reservation of a meeting room may be called for, along with audiovisual equipment. Well in advance of the meeting, preferably at least a week before, all those expected to attend must be notified (usually by memo, phone, or e-mail). The notification should make clear the meeting time, place, and agenda. Whoever requests the meeting is considered the leader or facilitator. It is that person's responsibility not only to make up the agenda, but to keep the meeting on track and orderly. If minutes are not taken at a meeting, it is advisable that an appointed person jot down notes throughout the meeting. The leader can later have these notes summarized and sent to participants as a reminder of what was accomplished. The summary will be particularly useful should follow-up action be required. Whether the meeting is called to resolve a problem, discuss progress, or enact a plan, it must be conducted respectfully. It is important to listen to all ideas and agree or disagree on a professional level, not a personal one. All meetings should end with a sense of accomplishment or plans for a follow-up meeting.

Formal

A formal meeting may involve shareholders, board members, directors, or executives. Often there are bylaws, certain guidelines, or protocol to be followed, depending on the organization involved. The meetings are conducted usually by following parliamentary procedure, with officers assuming certain roles. For example, the meeting is announced formally, usually in an advanced mailing, and is headed by a chairperson or president. A secretary takes the minutes of the meeting, which will later be distributed to the appropriate people. Often, presentations are made by the officers or invited speakers. Formal meetings are structured and well-organized, offering few distractions. The agenda is detailed, listing allotted time frames for speakers and subject matter.

Off-Site

Off-site meetings require much advance planning that should be done in a number of steps: (1) reserve a hall or meeting room; (2) once you know the layout and size of the space, consider a seating plan; (3) notify participants of the meeting date and place and any aspects of the agenda they are responsible for; (4) make out the agenda; (5) book speakers; (6) secure transportation, accommodations, and meal plans; (7) plan before- or after-meeting entertainment; (8) find out if speakers will require special equipment for their presentations and secure it; (9) if audiovisual equipment will be used, be sure it is in good working order; (10) order necessary business supplies.

Whether using a formal or informal format, it is important to have a specific goal in mind. Individuals often invest much time, effort, and expense to attend an off-site meeting, so a purposeful experience is a prime objective. No one wants to walk away feeling nothing was gained or accomplished.

Tips for Better Videoconferencing

Telecommunications has made it possible to see and be seen while talking to others from a distance. As this technology becomes more common-place, it will be increasingly more important for users to follow certain rules of protocol and procedure.

1. Always identify yourself and your location when you begin speaking to another site.
2. The name on top of your video window should identify your site (its name and/or location) so that others can identify your image on their screens.
3. Do not use facial expressions and gestures that other participants might find inappropriate. Monitor the image you are showing to others.
4. If you don't know the person you are addressing in the video window, specify the individual's site (at the top of his or her window) before commenting or asking a question. Doing so also informs other participants to whom your comment or question is addressed.
5. Listen to verbal cues (falling intonation for a statement, followed by a pause) indicating that the person talking is finished before making a comment or asking a question. If someone has asked you a question, that person is usually waiting for your response.
6. If you must leave while actively involved in a conversation, inform the other participants before disconnecting. Indicate verbally (or by typing) that you must leave, just as you would when ending a telephone conversation.
7. If you join a reflector site where there is already an ongoing conversation, do not just start talking. Wait until someone speaks to you or there is a pause in the conversation. Respect the right of others to "hold the floor," just as you would in a face-to-face conversation.
8. If you plan to have a private conversation with a specific site or do not want to be interrupted by all participating sites, click on the necessary microphone or speaker buttons.
9. Conserving bandwidth is important, so check the area under your video window or your preferences menu for the

transmission send-and-receive rates to be sure that they conform to the reflector's standards.
10. For the same reason, do not leave a message moving across the screen.
11. Unless you have been asked to do so, do not remain connected for hours, especially if you will not be in front of the camera and participating in the conversation.
12. Above all, keep your questions and comments relevant and to the point.

PARLIAMENTARY PROCEDURE

When conducting a formal meeting, parliamentary procedure is usually followed. At such a meeting, each officer has specific tasks: The president (or chairperson) calls the meeting to order and follows the written agenda. Often, voting is required on certain issues, at which time "motions" will be called. The vice president acts as an assistant to the president but may also fill in as president at formal meetings if the president is unavailable. The secretary's most important task is the recording of the minutes, which become the official record of what occurred during the meeting. He or she may also be called on to fill in for an absent president or vice president by calling the meeting to order, at which time the assembled group elects a chair pro tem. The treasurer keeps the financial records and reports on them at certain meetings. He or she is also responsible for paying bills and making deposits.

Motions

When a topic is introduced for discussion, it is then opened up to the members of the meeting. The chairperson recognizes one of the members who then "moves" that the appointed topic be resolved. It might be stated as:

I move that we cancel all ties with XYZ Company and go with UVW Company.

The chairperson asks the members at the meeting for a second to the motion. Any member can answer by saying "I second the motion" or simply "Second." The chairperson then opens the meeting up for discussion on the topic by stating something like: "It has been moved by Li-yu Roberts and seconded by Brenton Josephs that we cancel all ties with XYZ Company and go with UVW Company. Is there any discussion?"

The floor is then opened for discussion. When all discussion is over, the chairperson calls for a vote on the matter. If discussion on a topic goes on and on, the chairperson (or someone else) may suggest that those in attendance agree on a time limit for discussion. Votes can be taken by voice ("aye" for yes and "nay" for no), a show of hands, ballot, or any method approved of in advance. The chairperson may say:

> Any further discussion on this matter? [*If all is quiet, chair proceeds.*] All those in favor of going with UVW Company, say "aye" [*waits for response*]; those opposed? [*waits for responses of "nay"*]. [*After tallying votes, chairperson responds:*] The "ayes" [*or "nays"*] have it.

The secretary is responsible for recording into the minutes every motion, who made it, who seconded it, and the outcome of the vote.

Minutes

The secretary is responsible for recording all minutes of the meeting, beginning with the time, place, and date, and listing all members present (even recording who came late and who left early) and those who are not present, and identifying the person chairing the meeting and what type of meeting it is (shareholders, executive, board members, etc.). The minutes are not a word-for-word accounting of the proceedings, but they must be accurate, concise, and unbiased. The minutes cover the agenda, point-by-point, recording who is responsible for each recorded statement. Sometimes minutes are used in legal proceedings, so accuracy and degree of detail can be critical. The time the meeting was adjourned must be recorded as well.

The minutes are typed, double-spaced to make corrections easier to mark, then checked for accuracy by the meeting secretary. The minutes are then typed in final draft form, single-spaced if company policy allows, following previous minutes format. The minutes are then distributed to the appropriate participants as soon as possible after the meeting. A master copy is always kept on file, along with copies of motions and resolutions and any reports or documents that were passed around during the meeting.

Note: The standard source for learning the basics and specifics of parliamentary procedure is *Robert's Rules of Order.* For information on the most recent version, visit www. robertsrules.com.

CHAPTER 12

International and Domestic Travel

GUIDE TO MAKING TRAVEL ARRANGEMENTS

Travel has been a necessity of "doing business" since our ancestors dropped out of trees and became bipedal. Even with telecommunications and videoconferencing, travel remains the only way of meeting your customers (and competitors) face-to-face. Now, however, instead of joining a caravan and riding a camel across Asia for a few months, it is possible to be anywhere in the world in a matter of hours. Domestic airplane travel carries us anywhere in the continental United States quickly. How long a trip will take, however, depends on how much you can spend and how well you plan ahead.

Planning the Trip

Before you make a reservation with an airline, you will need to know at least three things: your destination, the dates of your departure and return (assuming you're purchasing a round-trip ticket), and the preferred times of your departure and return. In addition, a good travel agent will also ask you whether you want a first-class, business, or coach ticket; your seating preference (aisle or window; over the wing or near the tail); whether you'll accept a flight with one or two inter-vening stops, how long you want layovers to be (if changing planes); whether you will require assistance boarding, leaving the plane, and changing flights; and, if a meal will be served, whether you have spe-cial dietary needs (diabetic, low-salt, vegetarian, kosher, etc.). If the agent fails to ask you any of these questions, you should make your needs and preferences known. Failing to do so may mean redoing your travel plans later, which translates into a loss of time and, per-haps, money. You may also choose to have your agent handle the reservations for hotel rooms and leased vehicles.

Making a Reservation

Most businesses, whatever their size, use a travel agency to book flights, and, regularly request the services of a specific travel agent who is familiar with the company and the travel requirements of its employees. An agent who has handled several travel arrangements for a company comes to know the company's preferred airlines, method of ticket and itinerary distribution, and various employee particulars, such as dietary restrictions and the need for handicapped access.

An agent who knows your company keeps reminders of special travel needs and preferences and will often see to such details auto-matically when making a reservation. But it is always the traveler's ultimate responsibility to confirm that all desired conditions have been satisfied.

Preparing to Fly

When you pack, you should be mindful of airport security precau-tions. Airlines recommend that passengers be at the airport two hours prior to takeoff to allow ample time for security searches (which may include the baggage you are checking through). Passengers are no longer allowed to have anything sharp in their carry-on baggage (only one carry-on bag is allowed) that might serve as a weapon, including nail files, razors (safety razors are allowed), box cutters, tweezers, scis-sors, plastic knives, and so forth. In order to avoid unnecessary prob-lems, be sure to call the airline about which items and materials could be problematic, especially if you must have them for your trip. Anything that might be perceived as strange or threatening could cost you valuable time.

You should also check to find out whether the airport you're using has curbside check-ins. If you will have to stand in line at the ticket counter to check your baggage, allow more time. Finally, if someone takes you to the airport and plans to park the vehicle, security guards, police officers, or a member of the National Guard may want to check the undercarriage of the vehicle and the trunk as well. Again, allow time for this procedure because you will probably have to wait in line to enter the parking area. Because no one is allowed beyond the security checkpoint, tearful goodbyes at the gate are a thing of the past. Take a taxi, drive yourself and use long-term parking, or use a limousine service (available at many hotels). Also, you may want to carry more than one form of picture ID.

Online Reservations

Many businesspeople use one of the many online travel services to book travel, instead of a traditional travel agent. If you do so, be sure to print out your receipts and itineraries, and make sure you have a toll-free number to call in case of problems with your tickets or reservations. If you are using an e-ticket, you must carry a copy of your printed itinerary.

TRIP FOLLOW-UP

When the executive has returned from a trip, it is important to get pertinent information right away, while details are fresh in mind and receipts are easily retrievable. Thank yous may have to be written for courtesies shown while traveling, and expenses will have to be accounted for.

Expense Reports

All receipts must be collected after a trip in order to make out the expense report. Many of the expenses are reimbursable and some are even tax deductible. Most companies have a specific form that must be filled out. It is a good idea to have the executive fill in pertinent information on receipts that are generic in nature—for example, writing on a restaurant receipt, telling who was present and what business was discussed.

If the trip involved dealing with foreign currency, the exchange rate will have to be figured into the expense. Tips, sometimes paid in cash, will have to be accounted for as well. Most expenses, though, are paid for with a credit card, so submitting a completed expense report will be delayed until the credit card bill is received. Having the report filled in up to that point will save time in the completion process later.

Correspondence

Collect any business cards accumulated during the trip and log them onto card or computer files. Any courtesies shown during the trip should be acknowledged with thank-you letters. Arranged business deals should also be acknowledged, and pertinent delivery dates for products or services sold should be confirmed in writing.

Reports

Any office communication received from the executive during the trip should be organized and typed in an outline form for the executive to use as a guide for writing a follow-up report. If you have no specific format for reports, you may choose to follow a chronological order when typing the final report, listing daily events from the trip. Or you may use a summary format, listing topics discussed and progress made. A single-spaced format is acceptable, with double spacing between paragraphs for easy reading.

COUNTRY PROFILES

Argentina
Best time to visit: Southern: November–February; Northern: May–September.
Times to avoid: Easter and Christmas; January–February (vacations).

Before you go: Start to adapt your body clock for long evening business engagements.

Etiquette tip: Leave the complex ritual of wine-pouring to your host.

Visa for U.S. citizens: No.

Australia

Best time to visit: Any, except as noted.

Times to avoid: December and January (vacations).

Before you go: Get permission for business samples in advance; they may be hard to bring in.

Etiquette tip: Men sit in the front with the taxi driver; women sit in the back on the passenger side.

Visa for U.S. citizens: Check with ticket vendor.

Belgium

Best time to visit: Late spring; early autumn.

Times to avoid: Midwinter (dismal weather); August (vacations).

Before you go: Pack an umbrella and something warm; leave room for chocolate!

Etiquette tip: Don't play divide and conquer with the Flemings and the Walloons.

Visa for U.S. citizens: No.

Brazil

Best time to visit: Any, except as noted.

Times to avoid: Carnival; December–February (vacations).

Before you go: Prepare high-quality, clear visual aids for your presentation.

Etiquette tip: Don't touch food with your hands; use utensils or napkins for everything.

Visa for US: Yes, if you will transact business.

Canada

Best time to visit: Any, except as noted.

Times to avoid: Weather can disrupt winter travel.

Before you go: Find out if a French interpreter is needed.

Etiquette tip: Modesty in Americans is unexpected and therefore appreciated.

Visa for U.S. citizens: No.

China

Best time to visit: Spring and autumn.

Times to avoid: Chinese New Year; July and August (very muggy).

Before you go: Get bilingual business cards printed with simplified PRC Chinese characters.

Etiquette tip: If you get applauded when introduced to a group, applaud back.

Visa for U.S. citizens: Yes.

Colombia

Best time to visit: December–March (dry season).

Times to avoid: December to mid-January (holidays and vacations).

Before you go: Pack cheap jewelry and accessories; leave the good stuff at home.

Etiquette tip: Don't neglect to shake everyone's hand when parting from them.

Visa for U.S. citizens: Yes.

France

Best time to visit: Any, except as noted.

Times to avoid: August (vacations); Christmas and Easter.

Before you go: Upgrade the wardrobe to the height of conservative fashion.

Etiquette tip: Learn and use peoples' titles, or use "Madame" and "Monsieur" at the very least.

Visa for US: No.

Germany

Best time to visit: Any, except as noted.

Times to avoid: July and August (vacations); May (five public holidays).

Before you go: Send your credentials and company information ahead if you want to be credible.

Etiquette tip: Use your sense of humor discreetly until you see if it works.

Visa for U.S. citizens: No.

Hong Kong

Best time to visit: November–April.

Times to avoid: Chinese New Year (late January).

Before you go: Pack a handful of hospitality gifts; they're useful everywhere.

Etiquette tip: Avoid physical contact except shaking hands.

Visa for U.S. citizens: No.

India

Best time to visit: November–March.

Times to avoid: June–August (monsoon season).

Before you go: Make sure you are carrying nothing made of gold.

Etiquette tip: Don't point at or touch anyone with your feet or shoes.

Visa for U.S. citizens: Yes.

Ireland

Best time to visit: Late spring; early autumn.

Times to avoid: July and August (vacations); Christmas through New Year's.

Before you go: Pack the golf clubs; they may be required for business success.

Etiquette tip: Buy a round of drinks if everyone else is doing this.

Visa for U.S. citizens: No.

Israel

Best time to visit: Spring and autumn.

Times to avoid: Major Jewish holidays.

Before you go: Print up engraved business cards; adding Hebrew is a plus.

Etiquette tip: Give and receive gifts with the right hand, not the left.

Visa for U.S. citizens: Yes, issued in-country.

Italy
Best time to visit: Any, except as noted.
Times to avoid: August; Christmas through New Year's.
Before you go: Have a designer go over your presentation materials to spruce them up.
Etiquette tip: Start out formally in business dealings and let the natives set the pace.
Visa for U.S. citizens: No.

Japan
Best time to visit: Spring and autumn.
Times to avoid: New Year's; Golden Week (late April–early May).
Before you go: Pack company-logo gifts to pass out liberally.
Etiquette tip: Bow frequently; don't blow your nose in public.
Visa for U.S. citizens: No.

Malaysia
Best time to visit: Any, except as noted.
Times to avoid: December–February (holidays); Chinese New Year; Ramadan.
Before you go: Send ahead an official-looking third-party letter of introduction.
Etiquette tip: Don't touch anyone on the head.
Visa for U.S. citizens: No.

Mexico
Best time to visit: Spring and late autumn.
Times to avoid: Holy Week and the Christmas season.
Before you go: Print up loads of bilingual business cards, and be generous with them.
Etiquette tip: All comparisons of Mexico with the United States are invidious.
Visa for US: No.

Netherlands
Best time to visit: Spring and summer.
Times to avoid: Easter and Christmas.

Before you go: Pack books and objets d'arts for business and hospitality gifts.

Etiquette tip: Repeat your last name while shaking hands with new acquaintances.

Visa for U.S. citizens: No.

Norway

Best time to visit: May–September.

Times to avoid: Easter; Christmas; winter holiday (February).

Before you go: Pack warm clothing; take simple and modest gifts.

Etiquette tip: Don't lump Norwegians with other Scandinavians.

Visa for U.S. citizens: No.

Philippines

Best time to visit: October–March.

Times to avoid: Christmas and Easter; midsummer (vacations).

Before you go: Make sure you have a dependable intermediary to make introductions.

Etiquette tip: Don't raise your voice in conversation; quiet repetition is better.

Visa for U.S. citizens: No.

Russia

Best time to visit: Mid-May–June; September–October.

Times to avoid: Early January; early May (many public holidays).

Before you go: Pack business and hospitality gifts that are not available in Russia.

Etiquette tip: Don't refer to a Russian as your "comrade," even jokingly.

Visa for U.S. citizens: Yes.

Saudi Arabia

Best time to visit: November–February.

Times to avoid: Ramadan and pilgrimage time.

Before you go: Forget travelers' checks, but take ATM cards.

Etiquette tip: Don't touch food or people with your left hand.

Visa for U.S. citizens: Yes.

Singapore
Best time to visit: Any, except as noted.
Times to avoid: Christmas; Easter; Chinese New Year.
Before you go: Divest yourself of all chewing gum.
Etiquette tip: Don't point, touch people on the head, or jaywalk.
Visa for U.S. citizens: Yes; issued on arrival.

South Korea
Best time to visit: Any, except as noted.
Times to avoid: New Year and Chusok (September).
Before you go: Tune up! Good karaoke may be your key to business success.
Etiquette tip: Always show deference and respect to senior citizens.
Visa for U.S. citizens: No, unless staying more than two weeks.

South Africa
Best time to visit: Spring and autumn (opposite times from N hemisphere).
Times to avoid: December and January (vacations).
Before you go: Brush up on cricket, soccer, and rugby; spectating is a common business entertainment.
Etiquette tip: Don't shrink from friendly physical contact.
Visa for U.S. citizens: No.

Spain
Best time to visit: Spring and autumn.
Times to avoid: Holy Week; Christmas; August (vacations).
Before you go: Pack American crafts, books, and CDs for gifts.
Etiquette tip: Let the natives set the pace for friendly physical contact.
Visa for U.S. citizens: No.

Sweden
Best time to visit: September–early December; spring.
Times to avoid: July and the long Christmas period (early December–early January).

Before you go: Prepare to deal with women on terms of 100% equality.

Etiquette tip: Avoid glib compliments; make only the ones you really mean.

Visa for U.S. citizens: No.

Switzerland
Best time to visit: April–May; September–October.

Times to avoid: Christmas week.

Before you go: Get plenty of business cards with your name, degrees, and founding date of your company.

Etiquette tip: Wait for someone to introduce you rather than introducing yourself.

Visa for U.S. citizens: No.

Taiwan
Best time to visit: April–September.

Times to avoid: Chinese New Year, late October (public holidays).

Before you go: Practice tiny sips in order to endure lengthy toasting sessions.

Etiquette tip: Save the handshake till you become friendly, then expect only a limp one.

Visa for U.S. citizens: No.

Thailand
Best time to visit: November–February.

Times to avoid: Christmas; April and May (vacations).

Before you go: Pack reading material to keep you amused in taxis during long traffic jams.

Etiquette tip: Your hands should be visible at all times in social situations.

Visa for U.S. citizens: No, unless staying longer than two weeks.

United Kingdom
Best time to visit: May–October.

Times to avoid: Easter; Christmas through New Year's; August (holidays).

Before you go: Work up your repertoire of droll and ironic jokes for use at business lunches.

Etiquette tip: Be sensitive to national divisions within the UK, especially between Scotland and England.

Visa for U.S. citizens: No.

Venezuela

Best time to visit: December–April (dry season)

Times to avoid: Holy Week; Christmas.

Before you go: Pick up some *New York Times* best-sellers as business gifts.

Etiquette tip: Don't back away from "in-your-face" conversations; this is the cultural norm.

Visa for U.S. citizens: No. (Tourist card issued en route.)

CHAPTER 13

Accounting Principles and Practices

BASIC ACCOUNTING PRINCIPLES

Understanding basic accounting principles still has a tremendous value in the modern, computerized office. Accounting is a quantitative, conceptual framework by which companies see where they have been and where they are going. Many call accounting the language of business.

Office professionals are often required to handle a variety of accounting tasks, often using modern software, tax preparation software, or spreadsheet programs. The first step in understanding the uses of accounting in the business world is learning the standard terms and underlying principles of accounting. These standard terms and principles make it possible for everyone (including managers, stockholders, creditors, government agencies, and customers) to understand the financial reports of any business. The ultimate goal of accounting is to provide information that will be useful in making decisions. This goal can be achieved through an understanding of accounting's terms and principles.

Assets and liabilities

All of business accounting revolves around two core concepts: **assets** and **liabilities**. Anything owned by the business, whether physical or intangible, and that is expected to bring future value, can be called an asset. A company's assets are recorded at their original or **historical cost** to the company, rather than any appraised or market value. This is consistent with the **cost principle** of accounting. Even though most items lose or gain value over time (computers, buildings, office furniture, patents), their historic cost is very rarely adjusted to its current value, in order to avoid having to recalculate a company's total assets to reflect these changes. Exceptions may be made for marketable securities or to reduce the value of an asset. The use of historical cost is consistent with the **objectivity principle** of accounting.

These and other items may be counted as part of a company's assets:

Cash

Money owed to the company (usually called *accounts receivable*)

Stocks, bonds, certificates of deposit (usually called *marketable securities*)

Credit with suppliers (especially prepaid rent or insurance payments)

Land, buildings, furniture, equipment

Raw materials, work in progress, and finished goods (inventory)

Liabilities can be viewed as debts. Creditors are the people who have either lent the business money, or extended credit to the business in order to sell goods or services. Creditors claim the amount lent or credited against the business. These claims are claims against the assets of a business. The claims of a creditor have a priority over the claims of the owners of the business. Creditors are entitled to be paid in full even when paying them would extinguish all the assets of the business and leave the owners with nothing.

Basic accounting equation

The basic accounting equation is this:

Assets = Liabilities + Owners' Equity

Owners' equity, often called stockholders' or shareholders' equity, is the value of the resources invested by the owner. Remember, an accounting system only deals with things that can be measured in dollars, such as the sale of land or the purchase of inventory.

Owners' equity represents a residual claim to the assets, because the claims of the creditors always come first. The amount of owners' equity may increase if the owners invest more money or if the operation of the business is profitable. Owners' equity may decrease if the owners withdraw cash and assets from the business or if the business operates at a loss. The total of all liabilities plus the owners' equity cannot exceed the amount of the assets of a business.

The business entity

Even if the business is owned by a particular person, the accounts are kept solely on behalf of the business, not for the owner. The records should only show the transactions of the business, and not the personal business of the owners. So if the owner buys a car for personal use, that transaction will not be recorded, since the owner and business are separate entities.

This is true regardless of whether the business is a corporation, a partnership, or a proprietorship.

The accrual principle

The net income of a business is not related to its cash flow but rather to the shifts in the owners' equity that come about through the operations of a business. Revenue increases the owners' equity, and expenses decrease it. This is the accrual principle. The difference between expenses and revenue is a company's *net income*.

The accrual basis of accounting is the most popular form of accounting, used by nearly all businesses that share their financial statements with shareholders, creditors, investors, and outside decision makers. The accrual basis simply recognizes revenue when it is earned and records expenses when related goods and services are used.

There are two related concepts that are important to understand:

The *realization concept* states that revenue is recognized when services are performed or goods are delivered, and not when the bill is paid or the cash is actually received.

The *matching concept* states that expenses related to obtaining revenue for a given period must be calculated and matched against the revenues to be recorded for that period, not when the expenses are actually paid. This allows the company to see the cause and effect of their operation.

Many small businesses do only *cash accounting*—that is, they account only for cash receipts and cash payments. This is simple accounting (it's essentially only what is involved in balancing a checkbook), but it does not allow the business to accurately measure the economic costs and benefits of their operations. In order to measure the income of a period, a business must use accrual accounting. This allocates income and expenses to the period for which they apply, not to the date when income is received or payment is made. Accrual accounting is necessary to accurately measure changes in owners' equity.

ACCOUNTING REPORTS

There are three main accounting reports that are used to give accounting information: the balance sheet, the income statement, and the statement of cash flows. Your employer will have a preferred format for each of these.

Balance sheet

People who are interested in the assets, liabilities, and owners' equity of a company will want to see that company's balance sheet. This is a document that shows the company's assets, owners' equity, and liabilities at a specific time. The balance sheet is, in effect, a snapshot of the business, which can be taken as often as needed: the end of the company's fiscal year, the end of each quarter, monthly, or weekly. It is the timeliness of the balance sheet that determines its usefulness.

The balance sheet is "balanced" because the total of the assets will always equal the total of the liabilities and the owners' equity (see accounting equation above). It represents the balance between what the business owns (assets) and who has claim to them (creditors and owners). Only analysis of the parts of a balance sheet will show whether the company is doing well or poorly.

BALANCE SHEET ACCOUNTS

A balance sheet is easier to read and more helpful when items are grouped into large categories instead of listed individually. For example, instead of listing

Don's computer	$750
Linda's computer	$1200
Rebecca's computer	$950

It would be easier to list them all, collectively, as "computers" or even more generally, "equipment."

These are some common headings used on balance sheets.

Current Assets: This includes cash and any other assets that are expected to be sold, consumed, or otherwise be capable of being converted to cash within a year without disrupting with business operations. They are often called "liquid" assets. Subheadings under current assets are usually

Cash: including all cash in savings and checking accounts as well as any petty cash. Under Cash, many companies also include "cash equivalents": securities held in money market funds and treasury bills maturing in three months or less. It's important that a company have a good reserve of cash in order to meet its obligations.

Marketable ecurities: If a company has a good reserve of cash, excess cash may be used to buy short-term investments, also known as "trading securities" and "securities available for sale". The investing company earns interest or dividends, but the investments can readily be turned back into cash if necessary. Only securities that the company plans to convert to cash within one year would be listed here.

Accounts receivable: This is money owed to the company by customers. This is generally money that can be collected within the next twelve months. This account is usually listed at its net value, which means that the company has reduced the amount due by subtracting its guess at the amount that will not be paid (bad debt). A company maintains subsidiary ledgers to keep track of accounts receivable. These ledgers show for each customer what has been sold and what has been paid. The totals from these ledgers are the total accounts receivable.

Inventories: Inventories are goods held for sale during the course of business and, in a manufacturing setting, may be sub-divided to include finished products, work in progress, and raw materials. They are listed at their cost or the current market value, whichever is lower. Inventory is often the largest part of a company's current assets. Inventory cannot usually be converted into cash as quickly as securities or receivables, as it takes time for the goods to be sold and the cash to be collected.

Credits (or Prepaid items): These are prepayments for rent, insurance, interest, and deposits that will be used in the next twelve months. Although the company has already paid them, they're still considered assets because they haven't yet been consumed. These are listed last under current assets because while they cannot be converted into cash, they do eliminate the need for future cash outlays.

Tangible fixed assets: This category can also be called *fixed assets*, *plant assets*, or *plant, property, and equipment*. These are assets that are held by the company for use in the production of goods or the sale of goods and services. They are long-lived; they're not acquired for resale and have a useful life of at least one year. The recorded value of tangible fixed assets is the *acquisition cost* or the *historical cost*, and it is based on the amount it cost the company to buy them. This can include land (with or without buildings), buildings, fixtures and furniture, and equipment.

Fixed assets other than land are called *depreciable assets*, because the have limited lives—they wear out or become obsolete and thus become less useful to the business. Depreciation is the process of allocating the proportion of the total cost of these items to the period in which they were used and benefitted the company, and then expensing it.

Depreciation expenses are listed as an expense on the income statement and are taken each accounting period. Depreciation attempts to allocate the acquisition cost of an item over that item's useful life. The depreciation from all previous periods is accumulated on the balance sheet as a reduction of the cost of the fixed asset account cost (also known as a *contra-asset account*). The fixed asset account cost minus the depreciation is called the *book value* of the fixed assets to the company on the date of the balance sheet.

The useful life of an asset is estimated and is subject to quite a few variables, including advances in technology, obsolescence, unexpected accidents, and wear and tear. Keep in mind that because of these variables, the balance sheet value of fixed assets may not be the value that the company would receive if the asset were sold on the date of the balance sheet.

Other assets are ones that are difficult to classify as current or fixed assets, such as *long-term receivables*, *investments*, and *goodwill*. These are usually assets that the company intends to hold for more than one year. Long-term investments, such as any securities that the company does not intend to convert to cash within one year, are listed here. Long-term investments could also include bonds held to maturity, notes receivable from other companies, investment in land and equipment held for future use, cash-value life insurance policies held by the business, as well as special funds to retire debt. Long-term receivables may be from the sale of items where the payments are spread out over several years. Goodwill is the difference between the net value of the assets acquired and the price paid when one company acquires another. This excess is what is called goodwill and it reflects the purchaser's valuation of the non-monetary assets of a company, such as an excellent workforce, great reputation, or large customer base.

Current liabilities: Claims against the assets of a business are called liabilities. Current liabilities are debts or obligations that must be paid or settled within a year (or within the company's normal business operating cycle). Current liabilities are the most pressing obligations, and usually require the use of cash or other current assets to pay (or liquidate) them. These claims are not usually against a specific asset of a business (like a plant or piece of equipment).

Included in current liabilities are:

Accounts payable: This is what is owed to ordinary creditors
  for the purchase of supplies or services. If the amount is
  backed up by a note or other written agreement, it is often
  listed separately as a note payable.
Bank loan payable: Money owed to a company's bank.
  Because it is listed under current liabilities, it is assumed
  that it is payable within the year.
Accrued wages and salaries payable: What is owed to
  employees of the company at the time the balance sheet
  is prepared.
Current portion of long-term debt: This amount represents the
  portion of the principal (but not the interest) of a long-term
  debt that is payable within a year of the balance sheet date.

Taxes payable: What is owed but has not yet been paid for income, payroll, or sales taxes. This includes federal, state, and local taxes.

Unearned revenues: Goods or services owed to customers who have made advance payments. Services due to customers who have bought long-term contracts, rent paid in advance to a landlord, and magazines outstanding on a subscription are types of unearned revenue.

Long-term liabilities: These are claims against the assets of a business that are due after the current year or are otherwise not expected to necessitate the use of current assets or the creation of a current liability within the next year. Unlike accounts payable, these liabilities tend to be supported by formal documents (like mortgages, bonds, or notes payable) that show a definite agreement to pay a certain amount at a specific future time. Some long-term liabilities are guaranteed claims against a specific asset (such as a building or piece of equipment) and are called *liens*. Any part of a long-term liability due in the next twelve months from the date of the balance sheet should be included under current liabilities.

Interest due on these kinds of payments is not recorded on a balance sheet, since interest is related to the use of money over time. Interest is not initially recorded until a business has had the use of the money for a certain period. Then the payment is recorded as a current liability and the expense is recorded on the income statement.

Owners' equity: The owners' equity is the residual portion of the company not claimed by anyone else. Per the accounting equation, owners' equity is the assets less the liabilities. How it is reported on the balance sheet depends on the type of business and how it is organized.

For a corporation, state and federal laws require that a distinction be made between the variation in owners' equity due to daily operations and the amount invested in the corporation by the original shareholders.

The amount invested, called *capital stock*, is listed on the balance sheet at its stated value, also called its par value. Any amounts paid for the stock above this par value is listed as *additional paid-in capital*. The total of these two amounts is called the *capital contribution*. This amount is not updated to reflect the market cost of the stock. There is no relationship between the market value of the stock and the recorded value. The *retained earnings* (the increase or decrease in owners' equity due to daily operations) are the earnings of the company from its operations in prior years that have not been paid out in the form of dividends. Retained earnings are a claim of the company's owners, and it is shown in the owners' equity section of the balance sheet after capital stock.

When a company is owned by one person, it is called a sole proprietorship, and the owner's equity may be recorded on the balance sheet in either of the following two ways:

1.	Joan Sanders, capital	$598,000
2.	Joan Sanders, capital,	
	January 1, 2002	$500,000
	Net income for the year ended	
	December 31, 2002	$327,000
	Withdrawals	229,000
	Excess of earnings over withdrawals	98,000
	Joan Sanders, capital,	
	December 31, 2002	$598,000

When two or more people are partners in a business, changes in their equity are shown in a separate statement of partners' equity. Only the totals from this sheet are shown on the balance sheet.

Joan Sanders, capital	$299,000
Jennifer Sanders, capital	$299,000

Owners' equity may include cash or assets contributed by the owners of a business.

BOBOCORP MANUFACTURING, INC.
Balance Sheet
December 31, 2001

Assets

Current Assets

Cash		$44,200	
Temporary investments in securities available for sale		58,300	
Accounts Receivable	$185,400		
Less: Allowance for Doubtful Accounts	22,600	162,800	
Inventories			
Raw Materials	36,800		
Goods in Process	72,900		
Finished Goods	14,500	124,200	
Prepaid expenses			
Rent	14,500		
Insurance	2,200	16,700	
Total Current Assets			$406,200

Long-term Investments

Investment in bonds held to maturity		$22,000	
Fund to retire bonds payable		32,500	
Total Long-term Investments			$54,500

Property, Plant, and Equipment

Land		$74,200	
Buildings	$764,300		
Less: Accumulated depreciation	87,600	676,700	
Equipment	243,700		
Less: Accumulated depreciation	121,900	121,800	
Total Property, Plant, and Equipment			$872,7000

Intangible Assets

Trademarks		$33,400	
Patents		69,000	
Total Intangible Assets			$102,400i
Total Assets			$1,435,800

Liabilities

Current Liabilities

Accounts Payable	$87,200		
Wages Payable	24,500		
Taxes Payable	23,000		
Customer Prepayments	8,500		
Total Current Liabilities		$143,200	

Long-term Liabilities

Bonds Payable	$185,400		
Mortgage Payable	325,600		
Total Long-term Liabilities		511,000	
Total Liabilities		$654,200	

Owners' Equity
Contributed Capital

Common Stock, $1 par (1,000,000 share authorized, 115,000 outstanding)		$115,000	
Additional paid-in capital on common stock		323,900	
Total Contributed Capital			$438,900
Retained Earnings, less Dividends			$342,700
Total Liabilities and Owners' Equity			$1,435,800

Income statement

A company's income statement (also called a *statement of revenues or expenses,* a *profit and loss report,* or *P&L*) shows the results of a company's operations for a definite period: a year, three months, or a month. The last day of that period will be the date of the balance sheet information that accompanies the income statement.

This statement shows sales, the costs of the goods or services sold, any other costs of selling the goods or services, and the resulting profit or loss. The income statement shows all revenue of a company as well as all expenses necessary to achieve that revenue.

Common accounting periods

Most companies use the calendar year as their official accounting period. Some companies end their year at the end of their busy season; called a *fiscal year end.* A *natural business year* is a year that ends a convenient time for a business—such as ending June 30 for a school or college, or ending at the end of the season for a sport. However, income statements are usually prepared for shorter periods—a month or a quarter, when they are called *interim statements.* Some information must be reported to government agencies or banks each month or quarter, so income statements are often prepared for them as well.

Very rarely, an accounting period may extend past one year, especially if the business has long-term contracts or a long production process, or is involved in a very drawn-out negotiation.

INCOME STATEMENT ACCOUNTS

Sales

Listed first on the income statement is sales for the period. Income statements usually show the gross sales revenue earned by the accrual method and then any deductions for returns, allowances (such as price reductions), or discounts. The difference between these two amounts is the net sales of a business. By showing these as two different numbers, it is easy to see any unusual increases or decreases in either.

BOBOCORP MANUFACTURING, INC.
Income Statement
For the Year Ending December 31, 2001

Sales		$985,600
Less: Returns & Allowances	$34,500	
Discounts Taken	12,800	(47,300)
Net Sales		$938,300
Cost of Goods Sold		(644,000)
Gross Profit		$294,300
Operating Expenses		
Sales Commissions	$18,500	
General & Administrative	29,700	
Depreciation	17,600	
Total Operating Expense		(65,800)
Operating Income		$228,500
Other Items		
Interest Revenue	$2,700	
Dividend Revenue	300	
Loss on Sale of Buidling	(16,800)	
Interest Expense	(3,900)	(17,700)
Pre-tax Income from Continuing Operations		$210,800
Income Tax Expense		(33,500)
Income from Continuing Operations		$177,300
Income from Discontinued Operations		
Income from Discontinued		
Widgecorp Segment (net tax)	$28,400	
Loss on disposal of Widgecorp Segment (net tax)	(55,300)	(26,900)
Income before extraordinary items		$150,400
Extraordinary loss from fire (net tax)		(14,600)
Net Income		$135,800

Components of Income	Earnings per Share (115,000 Shares)
Income from continuing operations	$1.54
Results from discontinued operations	(0.23)
Extraordinary loss from fire	(0.13)
Net Income	$1.18

Sales revenues are the cash or promises for cash as well as other assets received for goods or services performed. Non-sales revenues may also include rent, commissions, dividends, and interest.

Expenses are the cash and assets spent (or the debt incurred) during a specific period in order to produce revenue.

Cost of goods sold is the cost incurred in making products to sell, or in buying products to resell. This should include only the costs associated with what was sold in the current accounting period. These costs can include raw materials, labor, and manufacturing overhead. Manufacturing overhead includes all product-making costs except for the raw materials and the direct labor necessary to make the product, such as plant rent, employee benefits, insurance, utilities, shipping, etc. The cost of any product not sold at the end of the period is shown on the balance sheet as inventory, under current assets.

Gross profit, also called gross margin, is the amount of revenue over and above the cost of the goods sold. This must be larger than the amount of all other expenses in order for the company to be profitable.

Operating expenses are the expenses of running the business—not those involved in making a product. They are the costs for the period, and include things such as research and development, sales and distribution, and the expenses of administering the business (such as paying accountants).

Selling expenses are the costs of selling the product—paying salespeople, advertising costs, and rental of stores.

General and administrative expenses are the costs of running the business, including office supplies, management salaries, rental of office space, property taxes, legal fees, and depreciation of office equipment.

Research and development (R&D) expenses are those costs involved in improving a company's products or inventing new ones. This includes the salaries of R&D workers, research facilities and equipment, and other expenses.

Operating Income

Operating income (also called *net operating revenue* or *income from operations*) is the profit earned from the normal business operations of the company. It is the total of sales revenue minus the cost of goods sold and operating expenses.

Other items, or *non-operating sources of revenues or expenses* are expenses not related to the daily operations of the company. It includes such things as profit or loss from the sale of fixed assets, revenue from nonrelated business operations, interest expense on loans, or interest income from investments. These are listed separately to show that they are not related to the primary business of the company.

Pre-tax income, profit before taxes, or *income before taxes* is the difference between all expenses and the revenues of the business.

Income tax expense or *provision for corporate income taxes* is the amount set aside for federal taxes by a corporation. Local and state taxes may be included here as well or can be included under general and administrative expenses. If the company is a partnership or sole proprietorship, the business pays no taxes. Instead, the owners include their share of the profit or loss on their personal tax returns and pay their taxes there.

The bottom line, the *net profit* or *net income*, is the amount of profit the company has earned for the period covered by the income statement.

Statement of cash flows

The third kind of financial statement, also called *the source and application of funds statement* or the *"where got—where gone" statement* is the *statement of cash flows*. This statement shows the cash effects of the company's operating, investing, and financing activities for an accounting period. This information shows to interested parties events that may not be explicitly reflected in the balance statement or income statement.

BOBOCORP MANUFACTURING, INC.
Statement of Cash Flows
For the Year Ending December 31, 2001

Net Cash Flow from Operating Activities		
Net Income	$135,800	
Adjustments to reconcile net income to net cash from operating activities		
Add: Depreciation Expense	17,600	
Decrease in Accounts Receivable	34,500	
Decrease in Inventory	11,700	
Increase in Accounts Payable	14,600	
Increase in Taxes Payable	3,400	
Less: Increase in Prepaid Expenses	(11,600)	
Decrease in Salaries Payable	(14,800)	
Decrease in Customer Prepayments	(700)	
Net Cash provided by operating activities		$190,500
Cash Flows from Investing Activities		
Additions to Property, Plant, & Equipment	$(75,000)	
Payment for Bond Investment	(22,000)	
Net Cash used for investing activities		(97,000)
Cash Flows from Financing Activities		
Net Change in Debt	$(24,000)	
Mortgage Payments	(63,000)	
		(87,000)
Net Increase in Cash		$6,500
Cash January 1, 2001		37,700
Cash December 31, 2001		$44,200

Systems and procedures

Once you are familiar with the basic language of accounting, you will be better able to handle a great number of accounting-related duties, including recording receipts and payments, controlling petty cash, reconciling bank statements, recording investments, and keeping track of the acquisition of fixed assets.

Your company's accounting system includes all the business papers, records, reports, and procedures used in recording and reporting sales and expenses and other transactions. Most companies today use computers as the main part of their system. However, the bulk of the work must be done before the computer system is in place, in terms of envisioning what kinds of data will be important in the system and what information and reports will be required from it. For many systems, adding a new type of transaction or expense category is quite expensive and involved, so, for that reason, it is important to have allowed for all practical contingencies or possible business expansions when the system is installed or set up.

The accounting process

The basic accounting process is the same for all companies, and includes the same components, whether the company is large or small. The purpose of the process is to collect the data needed to make decisions and prepare the balance, income, and cash flow statements. The basic components are these:

> *General journals* and special journals are used formally to record the data received from analysis of individual transactions. As the journal is the where transactions are initially recorded, it is often called the book of original entry.
>
> *General ledgers* are used to summarize the data in the general and special journals in terms of the balance sheet and income statement accounts. There are separate sections for each general ledger account, including Accounts Payable, Accounts Receivable, and Cash.
>
> *Subsidiary ledgers* are used to give a detailed analysis of the pages in the general ledger.

Other special journals can be used to record large numbers of similar transactions efficiently. These journals can include purchases journals, cash disbursement journals, or sales journals.

A *cash receipts journal* is one kind of special journal. It is used to record all revenue received each day, including cash and credit sales and other revenue. These are totaled each month and the totals are recorded in the general ledger.

A *cash disbursements journal* is used to list all checks written. These are also totaled each month and recorded in the general ledger.

Petty cash fund

Most companies keep a *petty cash fund* (or *imprest fund*) for occasions when it is inconvenient to write a check or for when cash is needed immediately. This cash is often used to purchase small items such as stamps or office supplies, food for office parties, etc. The fund is usually large enough to cover two to four weeks of these minor expenses, usually $100 to $500. It is best to have only one employee be responsible for the fund, and of course it should be kept in a locked box in a secure place.

Only the employee in charge of the fund should have access to it, and that person should keep good records of what money has been spent. Preprinted petty cash vouchers can be purchased from any office supply store. Each voucher is sequentially numbered and shows the date, the nature of the expense, and the department or account charged, and is signed by both the person receiving the money and the person disbursing it. This information can also be kept in a list or in an account book, but this is not common.

When the fund runs low, the person in charge of it is often required to turn in a list of transactions (or the actual vouchers) before it can be replenished. This list or accounting should show the amount in the fund at the beginning of the period, an itemized list of each expense, and the balance in the fund at the end of the period.

It can be convenient to keep a list (either by hand or on the computer) of each payment from the fund as it occurs, in order to make preparing the petty cash report easier.

Investment transactions

Many companies purchase stocks and bonds with their excess funds in order to earn a return. It is important to record all the information about the purchase and sale of stocks and bonds carefully, not only for your own company's financial records but also to comply with government requirements.

Keep a separate record for each security owned, and keep the records in sequential order. Record all investment activity as it occurs, including sales, purchases, and payment of dividends. Keep a file of all the confirmation notices from brokers, and use these as the basis for recording information on the individual securities records. These notices should show the purchase or sale of a specific security, including the trade date, the settlement date, the price, and the broker's commission. If these notices are sent electronically, be sure to print them out and keep copies in a file, along with any paper copies sent by the broker. Keep a file of the monthly brokers' statements, and verify each individual transaction against the monthly statement. Keep a record of interest or dividend income received based on actual deposits into the cash account. Make a list of all securities owned, and update it on a regular basis (not less than monthly).

If the securities certificates are not held by the broker, it is important to keep securities certificates in a locked vault with limited

9. LIST OF SECURITIES OWED				
Security	No. of Shares or Bond Face Value	Cost	12/31/01 Fair Value	Cumulative Change in Fair Value
Stocks				
XYZZZ Corp	500	$129,375	$185,645	$56,270
PDQ, Inc	200	85,400	37,800	(47,600)
Bonds				
ABC Co 8.25% Bonds	$22,000	22,000	23,000	$1,000
Investment Funds				
Agape Index Fund	300	45,450	54,300	$8,850
Totals		$236,775	$246,445	$9,670

access. Access should only be permitted to two or more authorized persons accompanying each other.

Fixed asset record

It is important to keep records of all plant assets that have a productive life of more than a year. These records ensure that the company is keeping track of what it owns and is allocating the cost of the asset to the right accounting period that the asset is benefiting. This allocation is depreciation or depreciation expense.

The estimated life of a fixed asset is that time that the asset is used to produce or sell goods or services. This period is different for different assets (buildings, furniture, or equipment), but is usually set by company policy based on a combination of productive life and tax regulations. The part of the asset cost that can be recovered at the end of an asset's estimated useful life is the salvage value of that asset.

Determining the cost of an asset over its useful life, or depreciation, can be done by many different methods. The four methods traditionally used are the *straight line, declining balance, units of production,* and *sum of years digits* methods.

In the straight line method, the cost of the asset minus the asset's salvage value is divided by the asset's useful life in years or months. This allocates an equal share of the asset's cost to each accounting period.

In the declining balance method, depreciation of up to twice the straight line percentage rate may be applied to the declining book value of a new plant asset each year, as long as the asset has a estimated life of at least three years. If this method is used and twice the straight line percentage rate is applied, the amount charged as depreciation expense each year is calculated by doubling the straight line depreciation rate (100 percent divided by the asset's productive life in years), and applying that doubled rate to the asset's remaining book value at the end of each year of the asset's life.

With the units of production method, the cost of the asset after deducting the estimated salvage value is divided by the estimated units of goods that the asset will produce over its useful life. This gives depreciation per unit of goods produced. Depreciation for the period is calculated by multiplying the the number of units by unit depreciation produced in the period.

With the sum of years digits method, the years in an asset's useful life are added, and the sum is used as the denominator of a series of fractions used to allocate total depreciation to the periods in the asset's useful life. The numerators of the fraction are the years in the asset's life in reverse order. The following example shows the depreciation of an asset having a four-year life and a cost of $8000 (number of years for the denominator = $1 + 2 + 3 + 4 = 10$):

Year	Annual Depreciation Calculation	Annual Depreciation Expense
1	4/10 X $8,000	$3200
2	3/10 X $8,000	$2400
3	2/10 X $8,000	$1600
4	1/10 X $8,000	$800

Business and Finance Concepts and Equations

RATIO, ETC.	HOW DETERMINED	DEFINITION AND USE
accounts receivable days	(accounts receivable ÷ sales) × 365	average length of time between credit sales and payment receipts
accounts receivable turnover	net credit sales ÷ average accounts receivable	a short-term solvency ratio that measures how efficiently a company grants credit to produce revenue
acid test ratio	(current assets – inventories) ÷ current liabilities	a short-term solvency ratio that gives an indication of a company's liquidity and its ability to meet obligations. Also called **quick ratio** or **current ratio**.
asset/equity ratio	total assets ÷ stockholder equity	a ratio used to compare the revenue-producing abilities of companies within the same industry

Ratio, etc.	How determined	Definition and use
asset turnover	net sales ÷ total assets	a ratio that measures the efficiency of a company's use of its assets. It is typically inversely related to the profit margin.
average rate of return (ARR)	average net earnings ÷ average investment	a percentage figure used to compare different investment vehicles over the long term
bid-to-cover ratio	bids received ÷ bids accepted	a rough measure of the success of a treasury security auction
bond ratio	par value of bonds ÷ (this figure + all other equity)	a figure that represents the percentage of a company's capitalization in bonds
book-to-bill	orders taken ÷ orders filled (within the same period, e.g. one month)	a measure of supply and demand in a market or for a company's products, used especially in evaluating high-technology companies. Figures >1 indicate an expanding market.
cash flow coverage	EBITDA ÷ interest expense	a measure of a company's ability to service debt payments from operating cash flow
cash flow leverage	Total liabilities ÷ EBITDA	a measure of a company's ability to repay debt obligations from operating cash flow
debt/asset ratio	total liabilities ÷ total assets	a ratio used on companies within the same industry to compare their ability to manage their long-term debt
debt/equity ratio	long-term debt ÷ stockholder equity	a ratio that compares the assets of a company that are held by creditors to those held by owners. High ratios indicate aggressive use of debt to manage growth.

RATIO, ETC.	HOW DETERMINED	DEFINITION AND USE
debt-service coverage ratio	net operating income ÷ total debt service (in the same period, e.g. one year)	a ratio used to determine a company's or property's ability to remain viable.
earnings yield	yearly earnings per share ÷ share market price	a figure that essentially gives the percentage of earnings that one dollar of equity buys. It is the inverse of the price-earnings ratio.
EBITDA	revenues – expenses (excluding tax, interest, depreciation, and amortization)	earnings before interest, tax, depreciation, and amortization
fixed-charge coverage ratio	(net earnings + interest paid + lease expense) ÷ (interest paid + lease expense)	a measure of a company's ability to meet its fixed-charge obligations
inventory days	(inventory ÷ cost of goods sold) × 365	a measure of the value of inventory on hand, sometimes used as an indication of a company's ability to respond to market changes
inventory turnover	annual sales ÷ average inventory	a measure of the speed at which inventory is produced and sold. Higher figures normally indicate strong sales and good turnover.
loan-to-value (LTV) ratio	value of loan ÷ market value of property	a general indication of the risk involved in a mortgage. Banks usually require of ratio of at least 75%.
loss ratio	claims paid ÷ premiums collected (in a similar period, e.g. one year)	a factor in the profitability and efficiency of an insurance company or insurance market
management expense ratio (MRE)	total of all fees ÷ total value of portfolio	a percentage figure that expresses the amount of a mutual fund's value that is consumed by the expenses of managing it
member short sale ratio	total number of shares sold short ÷ total short sales	a tool used to anticipate bullish or bearish trends on the New York Stock Exchange

RATIO, ETC.	HOW DETERMINED	DEFINITION AND USE
Macaulay duration	weighted average term to maturity ÷ bond price	an indicator of the volatility of a bond's price to a change its yield
market to book ratio	share market price ÷ book value per share	a figure used in estimating the cost of capital of an enterprise
net operating margin	net operating income ÷ net sales	a performance indicator used on companies within the same industry or historically of the same company
operating cycle	accounts receivable days + inventory days	the time that elapses from when a product is added to inventory to receipt of the income from its sale
operating profit margin	operating profit ÷ net sales	a tool for measuring effective pricing strategy and operating efficiency
payout ratio	total dividend ÷ total earnings	a measure of how much profit a company is returning to stockholders in dividends, often used to mark historical trends
price-earnings (P/E) ratio	current share price ÷ earnings per share in the past 12 months	an often-quoted figure that is usually an indication of growth expectations. Useful only for comparisons within the same industry, or historically for the same company (also called **multiple**).
price-to-book ratio	current share price ÷ last quarter's book value per share	a tool used for speculating on the accuracy of the valuation of a company's stock. A low ratio could mean that the company is undervalued, or that there is something fundamentally wrong with it.
price-to-sales ratio	current share price ÷ revenue per share in the year to date	a tool for comparing a stock's valuation relative to its own history, to its industry peers, or to the market generally

RATIO, ETC.	HOW DETERMINED	DEFINITION AND USE
profit margin	net income ÷ revenue (in the same period)	a percentage that expresses profitability, most often used in comparisons within the same industry
prospective earnings growth (PEG) ratio	P/E ratio ÷ projected earnings growth rate	an indicator of a stock's potential value that is favored by some over the P/E ratio because it takes growth into account. Projected earnings growth rate is determined from proprietary sources.
Q ratio	market asset value ÷ asset replacement value	a figure used as an indication of the success of a company's investment strategy (also called **Tobin's Q ratio** after its inventor James Tobin)
receivables turnover ratio	total operating revenues ÷ average receivables	a figure that indicates efficiency in managing accounts receivable
retention rate	1 – payout ratio	the percentage of earnings retained by a company which may be a factor in its investment and growth strategy
return on assets (ROA)	net income ÷ total assets	a percentage figure that indicates how profitable a company is relative to its assets
return on equity (ROE)	net income ÷ stockholder equity	a comparative indicator of profitability within the same industry, expressed as a percentage
return on investment (ROI)	total income ÷ total capital	the percentage of income derived from the amount invested, used as a measure of a company's performance
return on net assets (RONA)	net income ÷ (fixed assets + net working capital)	a percentage figure used as a measure of the profitability of a company

RATIO, ETC.	HOW DETERMINED	DEFINITION AND USE
return on sales (ROS)	net profit ÷ net sales	a percentage figure widely used as an indicator of operational efficiency
risk-reward ratio	expected return on an investment ÷ standard deviation of an index	a figure that roughly indicates the amount of risk in an investment relative to comparable investments
relative strength	(current share price ÷ year-ago share price) ÷ (current S&P 500 ÷ year-ago S&P 500)	a measure of the strength of a stock relative to the market; values >1 show relative strength (does not take risk into account)
rule of 72	72 ÷ rate of interest	a figure that tells how many years it will take to double your money at a given rate of compound interest
Sharpe ratio	(ROI – T-bill rate) ÷ standard deviation of a portfolio	a measure of a portfolio's excess return relative to its total variability. It may indicate whether returns are due to wise investment or excess risk (see also **Treynor ratio**).
times-interest-earned ratio	earnings before interest and tax ÷ interest payments	a measure of a company's debt-servicing ability
total debt-service (TDS) ratio	total obligations ÷ gross income (calculated for the same period)	the percentage of gross income required to cover all payments for housing and all other debts such as car payments; used typically to calculate creditworthiness of a household borrower
Treynor ratio	excess return ÷ portfolio standard deviation	a measure of the return on an investment in excess of what could have been earned on a riskless investment (also called **reward-to-volatility ratio**)
working capital ratio	(current assets – current liabilities) ÷ total sales	a percentage figure used for comparing operating efficiency within the same industry

CHAPTER 14

Types of Business Organizations and Business Law

TYPES OF BUSINESS ORGANIZATIONS

In the United States individuals live under and all businesses operate under federal, state, and local laws and regulations, from birth or incorporation to death or dissolution. Office professionals are not expected to know details of the law affecting business, and it is illegal for those who are not lawyers to give legal advice, let alone practice law, but some understanding of the basic concepts of the types of business organizations, contract law, agency, and corporate law is useful for daily business operations and profitable for long-term career development. There are several kinds of business organizations briefly described below, going from the simplest to the most complicated.

1. **Individual or Sole Proprietorship.** This is the simplest kind of business: one person operates the business, owns all the assets, and is personally liable for all its debts. The business "lives and dies" with the sole proprietor.
2. **General partnership.** A general partnership is a partnership in which all the partners participate fully in running the business and share the profits and losses. In

most jurisdictions, general partnerships are not recognized as legal entities distinct from the individual partners; therefore, in filing a lawsuit each of the partners must be named. Because a general partnership usually conducts business under a trade name, the trade name is used in most agreements, especially when there are many general partners.

3. **Limited partnership (LP).** An LP consists of one or more individuals who contribute capital, share profits, have no managerial authority, and are liable *only* for the amount they have contributed. One or several general partners manage the business, have the authority to bind the partnership, and are *personally* liable for the partnership's debts. The name of the LP must be registered with the secretary of state, and it should be identified by its registered name and the state of its registration.

4. **Limited-liability partnership (LLP).** An LLP is a partnership in which one partner is not liable for the negligence of another partner or of an employee not under the partner's supervision. All states allow a business, typically a law or an accounting firm, to register as an LLP.

5. **Corporation.** A corporation is a legal person (as opposed to a human being, a "natural person") created under the laws of a state (and not under federal laws). The state treats a corporation as a single person that has rights and duties, can hold property, can transact business, and can sue and be sued. A corporation is distinct from its shareholders, who own it, has the right to issue stock, and, because a corporation survives the deaths of its investors, can transfer stock and exist indefinitely. The "personality" of a corporation and "what it does for a living" are determined by the articles of incorporation (informally called the "corporate charter") filed with the secretary of state.

CONTRACTS

All businesses depend on contracts of one kind or another: the negotiation, preparation, execution, and performance of contracts are fundamental to the ordinary conduct of business, and, therefore, the law of contracts is fundamental to business law. A contract is an agreement enforceable by law. A contract may be written or oral, or partly written and partly oral. (Note that a spoken contract is correctly called "oral," not "verbal" because "verbal" means "pertaining to words," and words may be spoken or written.)

Offer, Acceptance, and Consideration

A contract has three essentials: an offer (Jones offers to paint Smith's house for $1,500), an acceptance (Smith accepts Jones's offer), and a consideration. A consideration usually consists of a payment (Smith pays Jones the $1,500) or of a promise to do something (Smith promises to do $1,500 of body work on Jones's car) or not to do something ("forbear") (Smith will not sue Jones for breaking his ankle on Jones's steps). The consideration, except under certain circumstances, must be adequate (though not necessarily equal in value to the offer). If there is no consideration or if the consideration is not regarded as adequate, there is no contract: the law then considers the offer to be a gift, not a contract, and will not compel a party to make a gift.

Contract under Seal

A "contract under seal" is an exception because such a contract does not require a consideration. The contract under seal must be written or printed with the seal of the signer, and the contract must be delivered to become effective (this is the origin of the phrase "signed, sealed, and delivered"). The seal for the contract under seal may be an actual seal or an impress on the paper, or the contract may have on it the word *seal* or the abbreviation *L.S.* (for the Latin phrase *locus sigilli*, 'the place of the seal').

Intention, Legality, Competence, and Authority

One of the essentials of a contract is that the parties must intend to make a contract, and the parties must have a "meeting of minds" (also called "mutuality of assent")—that is, they must both or all agree or assent to a contract and its terms. The contract must comply with the laws and not be against public interest. An "illegal contract" is a contradiction.

The parties must have the capacity or competence to make a contract. If one of the parties has a legal disability, he or she cannot make a contract. For instance, a minor (someone under 18, also called an "infant") cannot enter upon a contract, nor can someone who is mentally ill or mentally incompetent, nor a person under the influence of drugs or alcohol.

A person must have authority to make a contract, which will depend on circumstances. If a legally competent person makes an agreement, he or she is bound by that agreement. Agreements made by corporations and other businesses are binding if the agreement was made by an officer, agent, or employee authorized to bind the company. Office professionals, therefore, especially those with some managerial and administrative responsibilities, must be careful of the potential consequences of their actions.

Terms of Agreement

There are no specific laws or rules about how the terms of agreement are to be expressed, but there must be enough evidence to establish that the parties have reached an agreement even if not all of the terms and conditions of the contract are clearly defined.

If the parties fail to express clearly the terms of their agreement, it is possible that a court may find that there is no contract; usually, however, a court will try to reconstruct what the intentions of the parties were when they made their contract, especially when one of the parties has fulfilled, or partially fulfilled, his or her part of the contract. The terms of a contract need not be complicated or elaborate: if a merchant offers a product or a service at a specified price and the customer accepts by paying for it or by submitting a purchase order, that is sufficient expression of the terms of agreement. Of course, for complicated contracts, more extensive terms and provisions are necessary.

Formalities of a Written Contract

A well-composed contract will follow certain forms, some of which are traditional in the practice of law or required by statute law, and some of which are simply common sense and good business practice.

INTRODUCTORY CLAUSE.

Clause here does not have its ordinary grammatical sense; in legal usage a clause is a paragraph or subdivision of a legal document. The introductory clause of a contract describes the agreement and identifies the parties, giving the full addresses of the parties and short descriptive terms such as *Seller* and *Buyer* for quick and easy reference in the contract. The date of the agreement may be given either in the introductory clause or in the testimonium clause (explained in a later section). The names of the parties signing the contract are not listed in the introductory clause but are given in the testimonium.

A corporation ought always to be identified by its registered name, the state of its incorporation, and its principal place of business, as in this example of an introductory clause between a corporation and an individual:

> This Agreement is made the seventeenth day of June 2002 between Margolin Incorporated, a Delaware corporation with a usual place of business in New Haven, Connecticut, hereinafter called the "Company," and Michael J. Wetlack, of 118 Boston Post Road, Eastbrook, Connecticut, hereinafter called the "Consultant."

A longer, slightly more formal identification of the corporation may be made:

> ... Margolin Incorporated, a corporation duly organized and validly existing under the General Corporation Law of the State of

Delaware and maintaining a usual place of business at 1115 Quin-
nipiac River Road, New Haven, Connecticut . . . .

A corporation may be organized under one name but doing business under another ("doing business as" is often abbreviated "d/b/a"
or "dba"). In such a case, the alternative name should be noted:

Margolin Incorporated, a Delaware corporation doing business in
New Jersey as Margolin Nonferrous Metals, Inc., and maintaining
a usual place of business at 1453 River Road, Hackensack, New
Jersey . . . .

If a contract is made with a *sole proprietor* of a business and the
agreement concerns the business, the business address is to be used:

This Agreement is made the nineteenth day of July 2002 between
Margate Incorporated, a Delaware corporation with a usual place of
business in Philadelphia, Pennsylvania, hereinafter called the
"Seller," and Joseph A. Arlen, of Arlen's Books and Records, 2020
Walnut Street Philadelphia, Pennsylvania, hereinafter called the
"Buyer."

If a contract is made with a general partnership, each of the general partners must be named. If the general partnership has many
general partners, the trade name is to be used:

This Agreement is made the twentieth day of August 2002 between
Hopwell Incorporated, a Delaware corporation with a usual place of
business in Philadelphia, Pennsylvania, hereinafter called the
"Seller," and Jacobsen & Crepps, attorneys at law, a general partnership engaged in the practice of law . . . .

If there are only a few general partners, it is also correct to identify each of them:

Edmund Jacobsen, Ruth Lee, and Mary Crepps, general partners
engaged in the practice of law under the name Jacobsen, Lee &
Crepps. . . .

Trustees and Other Fiduciaries

A trust is a property interest held by a person (the *trustee*) at the request of another (the *settlor*) for the benefit of a third (the *benefi-*

ciary). There are many kinds of trusts—accumulation, business, Clifford—and they generally do not have a separate legal identity; therefore, any agreement or contract involving a trust should be put in the name of the trustee:

> Olive Bela, as trustee of the Donna Gaffney Family Trust and not individually . . . .

A fiduciary in general is anyone who owes to another person the duties of good faith, candor, and confidence, such as a corporate officer to the shareholders or a trustee to a beneficiary (in a trust, *trustee* is equivalent to *fiduciary*). *Fiduciary* is commonly restricted to the guardian of a minor or infant, the conservator of an incompetent person, or the executor of a will. As with agreements and contracts made with trusts, the fiduciary should be clearly named as a party acting in the capacity of a fiduciary:

> . . . . Dennis Dillon, as fiduciary for James Farrell and not individually . . . .

RECITALS.

Recital in legal usage has an additional meaning as a preliminary statement in a deed or a contract giving the background of the transaction or agreement or showing particular facts.

Most people are familiar with the traditional style of a recital, which begins with WITNESSETH, each of the clauses beginning with WHEREAS, and the conclusion beginning with NOW, THEREFORE. The modern or contemporary style simply omits WITNESSETH, replaces the clauses beginning with WHEREAS with "a, b, c," and so forth, and simplifies NOW, THEREFORE to *Therefore*.

BODY.

The body of the contract contains all the provisions and terms of the agreement. There is no set style for the body of a contract; the rules and style of ordinary business documents apply.

TESTIMONIUM.

The testimonium is the clause or part of a contract following the body and preceding the signatures and affirming that the parties are aware that they are entering upon an agreement whose terms are legally binding. The following examples are typical of testimonia:

> IN WITNESS WHEREOF, the parties have hereunto set their hands and seals to this Agreement the date and year first set out above.

> IN WITNESS WHEREOF, the parties have executed this agreement in triplicate the 24th day of April 2002.

SIGNATURES.

If a business corporation or other legal person is entering upon a contract, the signature specifies which officer or other natural person is authorized to sign:

> IN WITNESS WHEREOF, the parties have caused this Agreement to be executed by their duly authorized officers on the 23rd day of March 2002.

> Joseph M. Bellantonio, as President of Bellantonio Clothing, Inc., and Joseph J. Bell, as President of Joseph J. Bell Associates, Inc., have signed this Agreement this 19th day of March 2002.

The testimonium will often state that the parties "have set their hands and seals," like a contract under seal, which eliminates the necessity of establishing a consideration to make a contract. The necessity and effect of a seal under current state laws depend on circumstances and jurisdiction. Many jurisdictions have provided statutes by which the mere statement that the document is sealed suffices to give the force of a contract under seal even if no seal is used.

Only someone who is a party or who is authorized to bind a party should sign a contract. The signer's name should appear below the signature line, and the authority of the signer should be indicated if the signer is not signing for him- or herself:

Harrison Incorporated
By_____
Daniel Walker, President

As a rule of thumb, a contract on behalf of any of the following entities should be signed by someone holding one of the positions indicated:

Entity	Signer's Position
corporation	corporate officer
LLC	officer
general partnership	general partner
limited partnership	general partner
trust	all trustees
estate	executor or administrator

If someone is a party to a contract in several capacities, he or she should sign the contract on separate lines for each capacity, and the description under each signature line will clarify the person's capacity.

ATTESTATIONS.

Witnesses often attest to the signatures of the contracting. This may be helpful if some doubt should later arise about who actually signed the document or about the circumstances of the signing. The attestation may consist of the signature of the witness, or there may be a clause of attestation such as:

> Signed, sealed, and delivered by the above-named Mary Anastasia Culhane, in my presence, at New York, New York, this 8th day of September 2002.

The corporate clerk or corporate secretary will often attest to the signatures of corporate officers to verify that the corporation has authorized the officer to sign the document. The corporate seal is then embossed over the attestation:

> Attest: [*corporate seal*]
>
> _____
> Clerk/Secretary

AGENCY

Agency is a legal relationship in which one person represents another and has the authority to act for that person. Most duties connected with running a business, such as administrative, clerical, or routine responsibilities, can be performed by an agent. Employees or independent contractors may or may not be agents.

Neither federal law nor the Uniform Commercial Code deals explicitly with the topic of agency, leaving the law regarding agency primarily to the states. Agency law is made up of all those rules recognized by society that enable one person to act on behalf of another. If there were no agency law, every individual would be required to act on his or her own behalf, and business enterprises would grind to a halt.

Agent and Principal

The *agent* is the person who acts on behalf of another; the *principal* is the individual for whom the agent acts. Most (but not all) agency relationships are created by contract. However, because consideration is not required, a contract is not a necessity. When an agent is appointed by contract, the contract determines the duties of both parties. The duties of the agent can, however, be changed by express agreement (oral or written) of both parties. An agency relationship is always created by the consent of both individuals, and either party—the agent or principal—can withdraw consent, ending the relationship. If there is a contract, withdrawing consent may be considered a breach.

In addition to *express agencies*, which are created by consent of both parties, there are three other main methods of creating agency relationships:

implied agency: this is created by the parties' conduct and
    governed by the same principles as implied contracts;
ratification: an unauthorized action is expressly or implicitly
    approved by the would-be principal after the action occurs;
estoppel: a third party assumes that someone else acted as an
    agent based on the supposed principal's actions or lack of
    action.

SCOPE OF AUTHORITY.

Because the agent represents the principal, principals are obligated to fulfill deals made by their agents acting within the bounds of the authority granted to them by the principals. Principals are bound contractually whether an agent has *actual authority* (express or implied) or *apparent authority* to make a contract for the principal. For example, if an agent can purchase supplies, manage rental property, or make financial decisions, then he or she has the *implied authority* to make contracts in order to perform these duties. Because virtually all business transactions involve contracts, it is understood that an agent with the authority to conduct a principal's business also has the authority to make contracts.

Unlike implied authority, apparent authority is created by the actions or behavior of a principal that causes a third party to assume that an agent has the authority to act on the behalf of the principal. For example, a person dealing with a salesperson behind the counter of a retail store has the right to believe that the salesperson has the authority to conduct normal business. If an agent has an office, a title, and subordinates, a third party can reasonably assume that the agent has the authority to make contracts on behalf of his or her employer (the principal). In fact, any indications or other signs of agency can create apparent authority (agency by estoppel).

DUTIES OF AN AGENT.

Because an agent acts in a fiduciary capacity, such agency entails three obligations: (1) accounting for all money collected for the principal; (2) meticulously keeping the principal's money separate from his or her own; (3) not using the principal's property with his or her property, which, beyond betraying the loyalty the agent owes to the principal, may also be a criminal act (embezzlement). In addition to these basic obligations to the principal, the agent has six additional duties (unless explicitly changed by contract):

1. *Obey instructions:* The agent must carry out the principal's instructions. Although this may seem so obvious as not to require statement, the agent is personally liable to the principal if he or she (1) makes the principal responsible for unauthorized contracts, (2) delegates his or her duties improperly to someone else, or (3) commits wrongful acts for which the principal may be responsible.
2. *Perform with skill:* All agents understand that they are expected to perform their duties with accuracy and skill. For this reason, a case against an agent for breach of contract requires proof of the standard of skill or care and evidence that the agent failed to meet that standard.
3. *Avoid conflict of interest:* Agents cannot act for themselves if they are also acting for a principal in the same matter. For example, agents cannot sell a principal's property to themselves (or to friends or relatives) at a special or lower price. Conflicts can be resolved by full disclosure of all the facts to the interested parties and the principal's informed consent to the action proposed or undertaken by the agent.
4. *Protect confidential information:* If an agent is to represent a principal well, that principal must be able to share all the relevant information with the agent (including trade secrets or proprietary information). If the principal is to feel confident in sharing such information, the agent must take responsibility for protecting such information from the public, third parties, and competitors. When the agency relationship is terminated, the agent must return such confidential information to the principal.
5. *Notify the principal of significant information:* Because an agent represents the interests of the principal, he or she is responsible for notifying the principal of all information

relevant to evaluation of a situation. This principle enables the principal to make informed decisions in connection with his or her business and to provide the agent with needed guidance.

6. *Make a full and accurate accounting:* Any contract regarding agency must specify the times and rules of accounting, and the agent is expected to maintain records of his or her work so that the principal can assess the agent's performance. When the agency relationship is ended, the agent must account for all of the principal's property and all income must be returned to the principal as stipulated in the agency contract.

PRINCIPAL'S DUTIES.

If there is a contract (express or implied) regarding the agency relationship, the duties of the principal are governed by it. The primary responsibility of a principal is to pay the agent for his or her services. In the event of an implied contract, the agent's compensation is the agent's fee as understood by both parties or whatever is reasonable compensation in that field. If there is no contract, and the agent has not agreed to work for free, then the agent's compensation should be figured at the reasonable value of the services performed.

In addition to the stipulations set forth in any contract, the principal has three additional responsibilities to the agent. The principal is obligated to:

1. pay whatever expenses are incurred by the agent in performing his or her duties;
2. tell the agent about any known risks;
3. (if the agent is also an employee) provide a workspace and access to the equipment, supplies, and other materials necessary for the agent's acceptable performance.

DEBTORS AND CREDITORS

A *debtor* is an individual or business that has borrowed money or bought something on credit (for example, tangible goods or services) and is obligated to repay the money or fulfill the credit agreement. A *creditor* is the entity, business, or bank that has loaned money to an individual or business or enabled either to use a line of credit to purchase goods or property. A *secured debt* is a loan that has been secured by collateral (usually tangible goods) in case the borrower fails to repay the loan. Should the debtor default on the obligation (that is, fail to honor the contract), the creditor has the right to sell the collateral in order to recover some portion of the amount owed. An *unsecured* loan is money or credit that has not been secured by collateral.

There are several federal statutes that protect consumers and apply to the debtor/creditor relationship, including the Truth-in-Lending Act (1968), the Fair Credit Billing Act (a 1974 amendment to the Truth-in-Lending Act), the Fair Debt Collection Practices Act (1977), the Fair Credit Reporting Act (a 1970 addition to the Truth-in-Lending Act), and the Equal Credit Opportunity Act (1976).

States have their own laws and regulations—for example, the Uniform Consumer Credit Code (UCCC), which has been adopted by ten states. It sets maximum interest rates that creditors can charge and requires full disclosure to those buying on credit. In addition, the UCCC provides criminal and civil penalties against creditors who fail to follow its rules.

Creditors' Rights

A creditor expects to be repaid and has the right to legal remedies should a debtor fail to fulfill his or her contract to repay the creditor. There are ten primary ways in which a creditor can collect a debt:

1. *Liens*. A lien is a burden on the title to a debtor's property or the property itself. A *mechanic's lien* allows the creditor to force a sale of the property to pay the debt. An

artisan's lien and a *hotel keeper's lien* allow the creditor to hold personal property until the debt for services, repairs, improvements, or care has been paid.

2. *Prejudgment attachment.* A prejudgment attachment is a court order that allows the debtor's property to be taken into custody before a judgment is entered, thereby protecting the creditor by protecting the property from damage or removal before the lawsuit is completed. (However, there are Fourteenth Amendment due process limits on such actions.)

3. *Security interest.* A creditor can take a security interest in a debtor's property, using the collateral as a substitute for all or part of the debt should the debtor default on the contract.

4. *Recovery of debt before a bulk transfer.* When a business sells its materials, supplies, merchandise or inventory outside the normal course of business, creditors are given notice at least ten days before the transfer so they can protect their interests. (Bulk transfers are governed by Article 6 of the Uniform Commercial Code.)

5. *Proceedings against fraudulent conveyance.* Creditors can begin proceedings if a debtor transfers property to a third party (fraudulent conveyance) in order to avoid paying off a debt.

6. *Payment from a guarantor or surety.* If a creditor is unable to collect a debt from the debtor, the creditor can seek payment from a surety or guarantor (someone who agreed to be liable for the debtors' unfulfilled obligations). A surety is primarily liable, which provides creditors with immediate remedy. A guarantor is secondarily liable, meaning that he or she is liable only if the creditor cannot collect the debt from the debtor. All guaranty agreements must be in written form; suretyships do not have to be in writing.

7. *Foreclosure.* A creditor can foreclose on real property held as security for a loan—for example, a mortgage. Some states allow a creditor to take possession of the property immediately, but most require a judicial sale. Proceeds of a judicial sale go first to pay for the cost of the sale, second to the creditor, and third, if any funds remain, to the debtor.

8. *Writ of execution or garnishment.* A writ of execution is a court order that allows a sheriff (or other court official) to seize a debtor's nonexempt property and sell it. A garnishment requires third parties that hold property or money owed to the debtor (for example, employers or banks) to send the property or money to the creditor. The federal Consumer Protection Act (Truth-in-Lending Act) regulates garnishments, and limits garnishments either to 25 percent of weekly disposable earnings or the amount by which a week's disposable earnings (net income after federal and state income taxes and social security tax) exceeds 30 times the hourly minimum wage, whichever is lower.)

9. *Composition or extension agreement.* In a composition agreement, each creditor agrees to accept a percentage of the actual sum owed. An extension agreement gives the debtor more to time to pay the debt. Under both of these arrangements, the debtor is released from the obligation (the debt is discharged).

10. *Assignment to a trustee.* An assignment to a trustee involves transferring some or all of the debtor's property to a trustee. The trustee sells the property for cash and distributes the proceeds to the creditors on a pro rata basis. Under this arrangement, the debt is also discharged.

Debtors' Rights

Debtors are protected by both state and federal laws such as exemption statutes, limits on garnishments, consumer protection statutes, and lender liability. State laws also exempt certain kinds of property from being seized and sold to satisfy a debt.

In some instances, consumers can sue lenders for damages that result from misconduct while extending or revoking credit, foreclosing on security, administering a loan, refusing to make a loan, or making a loan that the debtor now claims he or she should not have received. Furthermore, a lender may also be liable for breach of contract, excessive control (for example, interfering in a debtor's contracts with others), economic coercion, negligence, breach of fiduciary obligations, or fault based on consumer protection statutes, and securities or tax laws.

BANKRUPTCY AND REORGANIZATION

Should an individual or business become unable to pay its debts when they are due, one way of settling such obligations is *bankruptcy*. Federal law (as provided in the Bankruptcy Code and interpreted in federal court opinions) governs bankruptcy issues. Bankruptcy relieves (discharges) debtors for all or most of their debts after the bankruptcy proceeding has been completed. Such proceedings are governed by federal bankruptcy courts, and appeals are filed either in a U.S. District Court or with a bankruptcy appellate panel made up of bankruptcy judges from within that federal circuit.

Bankruptcy Code

There are three primary alternatives for seeking relief from debts:

Chapter 7 (Liquidation)
Chapter 11 (Business Reorganization)
Chapter 13 (Adjustment of an Individual's Debts)

A fourth type allows for the adjustment of a municipal corporation's debts (available under Chapter 9), and Chapter 12 of the Bankruptcy Code governs reorganization of family farms. Certain regulated businesses (railroads, banks, credit unions, insurance companies, and other financial institutions) cannot file bankruptcy. (Railroads, however, can file for reorganization under Chapter 11.) A filing of any kind of bankruptcy creates an estate that consists of all of the debtor's property. Only bankruptcies covered by Chapters 7, 11, and 13 will be discussed here.

CHAPTER 7.

Chapter 7 bankruptcies discharge all debts, including judgments, for individuals. Corporations and partnerships, however, remain liable for their debts should they acquire assets in the future, which prevents the entity from reforming after a Chapter 7 liquidation. The court appoints a trustee who takes charge of the debtor's estate, sells the debtor's nonexempt property, and distributes the proceeds to the creditors in order of their priorities under the law. (For example, taxes are usually paid before creditors' claims.)

CHAPTER 11.

A Chapter 11 proceeding allows an ongoing business to restructure its debts following a reorganization plan. The court appoints a trustee (or examiner) to conduct an investigation, file reports to the court, and submit a reorganization plan, including assets and debts, that covers all aspects of the entity's operation or recommend that the business instead file for liquidation under Chapter 7. The judge must accept the reorganization plan, and a portion of each class of creditor (for example, suppliers, employees, and lenders), representing at least two thirds of the dollar value for that class's total claims and more than one half of the total number of claimants, must accept the plan as well. Further, every creditor must receive at least as much as he or she would receive under a Chapter 7 liquidation.

CHAPTER 13.

This type of bankruptcy is available only to individuals who have regular sources of income, unsecured debts that do not exceed $100,000, and secured debts of $350,000 or less. Chapter 13 adjusts the debts of an individual by setting up a payment plan that allows the individual to pay about one fourth of his or her disposable income (depending both on the level of income and the extent of family responsibilities) to a court-appointed trustee. The trustee pays the creditors. Repayment must begin within 30 days after the petition is filed and can continue for up to five years. As with a Chapter 11 bankruptcy, creditors must receive at least the same amount they would receive under a Chapter 7 liquidation. Either the individual or the court can convert the case to a Chapter 7 proceeding at any time.

Property that may be exempt under bankruptcy proceedings includes equity in a home, interest in one motor vehicle, trade or business items, prescribed health aids, federal and state benefits, alimony and child support, and so forth. There is usually a cap on the amount allowed for such exemptions, but this differs from state to state.

PROPERTY

Property consists of both *rights* and *interests*. Central to the definition of both are the concepts of *ownership* and *use*. Broadly, property, conceived of as a "collection of rights," can be anything that can be owned individually, by a group, or for the benefit of others. The two principal kinds of property are: (1) *real property*, which is always *tangible property*—land and the other items attached to, grown on, or built on the land such as buildings and trees; and (2) *personal property*, essentially all property that is not real property.

Contract law strongly affects property law because, unless a contract involves only services, it is likely concerned with property (land, goods, etc.). A contract itself can also be a kind of property because whatever contractual rights the contracting parties own are usually transferable, and so a form of property.

Personal Property

There are two types of personal property: (1) *tangible personal property*, which consists of anything that can be physically owned and can include virtually anything that occupies space and can be moved (fixtures and real estate, for example, cannot be moved); and (2) *intangible personal property*, which consists primarily of rights in things that are not concrete, that do have physical substance (for example, contracts, stocks, software, utility services, and intellectual properties, including copyrights, patents, and trademarks). Documents or other materials concerned with intangible personal property (a written agreement, stock certificate, or copyright certificate) are *not* the property itself; they are only evidence of the property.

A *fixture* is personal property that has been attached to real property, and is usually treated under law as part of that real property. The more closely a fixture is connected to surrounding real property, the more likely it is that the item (for example, a porch swing or oven) is a fixture in the legal sense. If a business tenant has put *trade fixtures* on rented real estate for use in his or her business, however, those trade fixtures remain personal property unless removal causes damage. If the damage is slight, the tenant can reimburse the landlord. If removal would cause extensive or severe damage, however, the trade fixture will, in all likelihood, have to remain with the landlord.

Intellectual Property

Intellectual property is a special type of *created* property (acquiring title to something by invention, art, or another intellectual undertaking). What are owned are not the ideas themselves but the tangible *expressions* of those ideas—for example, patents, copyrights, trademarks, and brand names.

PATENTS.

A patent gives an inventor the exclusive right to make, use, and sell a process, machine, manufacture, or other composition for seventeen years. (A *design patent*, which is concerned with the appearance of a manufactured object, lasts fourteen years.) The invention has to be new, useful, and nonobvious. Someone can, however, combine or add to unpatented inventions or those whose patent has lapsed, thereby creating a new invention that can be patented. The U.S. Patent Office determines whether a requested patent is in conflict with a previously issued or pending patent. A patent cannot be renewed. After it lapses, the invention enters the public domain and anyone can make, use, or sell it without having a license from the inventor to do so.

COPYRIGHTS.

A copyright gives a creator the right to print, reproduce, sell, and exhibit creations in a tangible, preserved medium exclusively. Such creations include musical compositions, written works, artworks, photographs, movies, TV programs, data systems, and other creative objects. A copyright lasts for the life of the creator, plus fifty years, unless the copyright was obtained before the revised federal copyright became effective (January 1, 1978), in which case the copyright may last as long as seventy-five years.

Copyrights, unlike patents, are subject to a number of exceptions. *Fair use*, for example, allows limited reproduction of some creations for classroom use. Fair use is determined by the consideration of four factors: (1) the purpose and nature of the use (whether the use is nonprofit or educational, not commercial); (2) the proportion and significance of the part used in relation to the work as a whole; (3) the nature of the work; (4) the effect of such use on the value of the work, including its potential market. For example, if the use of some portion of a work might decrease its potential market, then it might not be fair use.

TRADEMARKS AND OTHER TRADE SYMBOLS.

A trademark is any symbol, word, letter, number, picture, or combination of these items adopted and used by a merchant or manufacturer to distinguish its products from those of similar products (or goods) available to consumers. Trademark laws are intended to keep competitors from cashing in on the reputation (or goodwill) of a merchant's or manufacturer's products or services and to prevent (or punish) the marketing of goods or services fraudulently. Both state and federal statutes and cases govern trademark law. If the U.S. Patent Office registers a trademark or trade symbol as belonging to a specific owner or user, that registration is effective for ten years after the first use and can be renewed for subsequent ten-year periods. Any other merchant or manufacturer who uses another's trademark fraudulently can be enjoined (ordered by a court to stop) and damages awarded. (Trade names cannot be registered with the U.S. Patent Office, but fraudulent use of them is still subject to injunction and award of damages.) In order to be protected, a trademark or trade symbol must not lapse as a result of disuse and must remain associated with the business or its goods and services. (Some former trade names have become generic terms used to refer to a class of similar products and so are no longer protected—for example, *aspirin* and *cellophane*.)

Other kinds of trade symbols include:

service marks—designate services rather than goods;
trade names—designate the business entity itself.

TRADE SECRETS.

A trade secret is any formula, process, list of customers, or method of operation used to produce goods or services needed by employees in the performance of their jobs and intended to be kept confidential by employees. Of course, employees can and do change jobs and go to work for competitors, but their obligation to hold the trade secrets of their former employer remains.

Real Property

The concept of real property is based on ownership, use, and possession. Ownership (title) is acquired in essentially two ways (although there are several types of deed with various warranties): (1) voluntary title transfer by deed (the grantor delivers a deed to the grantee), and (2) involuntary title transfer by law (either by *foreclosure*, because of unpaid mortgage payments or a mechanic's lien, or a *judgment sale*, because of an unpaid judgment). Two other ways in which title to real property can be obtained are: (1) *eminent domain,* which allows the federal, state, and some other government entities to take privately owned property *for the public benefit* (the U.S. Constitution does require that the government pay the owner the property's fair market value), and (2) *adverse possession,* continuous, exclusive, open occupation by a trespasser, without the owner's permission, for whatever period of time is required by the appropriate state statute (ranging from five to twenty years). Title to real property can also be transferred through a will or general state inheritance laws.

RIGHTS OF LAND OWNERSHIP.

Eight rights go along with land ownership:

1. *surface rights*—exclusive right to occupation of the land's surface
2. *subterranean rights*—exclusive right to oil, mineral, and other substances below the land's surface, including reasonable use of subsurface waters (sometimes treated as a *riparian right*)
3. *air rights*—exclusive right to the air space above the land, up to the height over which control is reasonable
4. *right to fixtures*—exclusive right to fixtures on the land, for example, a garage or deck)
5. *right to trees, crops, or other vegetation* on the land
6. *right to lateral and subjacent support*—other land owners adjacent to the land cannot change their land in any way that damages the owner's land or buildings
7. *right to be free of public or private nuisances*—right to enjoy use of the land without pollution, excessive noise, or other interference (if government actions make the land uninhabitable, the owner may seek *inverse condemnation,* an order requiring the government to take the land under eminent domain and compensate the owner fairly)

8. *riparian rights*—reasonable use of a natural waterway within the land's boundaries (these rights differ for navigable and nonnavigable streams)

RESTRICTIONS ON OWNERS' RIGHTS.

There are limits as well as rights to owners' use of their land. Various levels of government can control how owners use land. Local governments, usually at the city or county level, have zoning and building codes that owners must obey. Zoning laws regulate how property can be used, for example, by designating a specific area as "residential" or "commercial." Unlike eminent domain, owners are often not entitled to compensation as a result of zoning changes. In order to qualify for compensation, the owner must be able to show that some portion of the land must actually be taken as a consequence of land-use regulation; it is not enough that the property will be adversely affected.

Some private restrictions regarding land-use can be stated in deeds, subdivision plans, or other documents if they do not violate public policy and benefit all the landowners. Limits can be placed on the size, height, and design of buildings, for example.

Tenant/Landlord Relationship

The owner of a property, the *landlord,* may place possession of some or all of that property in the hands of a *tenant.* The *lease,* or rental agreement, sets forth the conditions of the relationship between the *lessor* (owner) and the *lessee* (tenant). In general, leases are contracts and should be in writing. However, as with contracts, some short-term lease agreements (usually less than one year) can be oral or implied. Federal, state, and local fair-housing laws forbid discrimination against potential tenants on the basis of race, color, religion, national origin, sex, handicap, age, or familial status. Increasingly, local governments also forbid discrimination on the basis of sexual preference.

A leasehold grants a nonownership, possessory interest in realty and generally has a set term. There are four primary kinds of leasehold:

1. *Estate for years.* The tenant can occupy the property for a specific period, which usually ends on or by a date stated in the lease. Termination can also occur by mutual agreement of the landlord and tenant, by a condition stated in the lease, by operation of law (for example, bankruptcy), or merger.
2. *Periodic tenancy.* The tenant can occupy the property for a definite period, often on a month-to-month basis, that renews automatically unless the tenant or landlord gives notice to the contrary. Such notice should usually be given one rental period in advance.
3. *Tenancy at will.* Either party can end the lease agreement at any time, although most states require advance notice of termination.
4. *Tenancy at sufferance.* The tenant continues to occupy the property even though the lease has expired. Most states hold that, in such a situation, the leasehold has implicitly become a periodic tenancy.

COVENANTS.

Most written leases contain *covenants*, explicit expressions of the landlord's and tenant's rights and duties under the agreement. Covenants usually deal with concerns such as security deposits, rent (how much, when due, and when considered late), subletting (whether, and in what circumstances, it is acceptable), and restrictions on the use of the property. In addition to explicit covenants, there are also often implicit covenants, for example, that:

1. the landlord has the right to transfer possession to the tenant;
2. the tenant will not cause damage to the property other than normal wear and tear;
3. the landlord will not disturb a tenant's use and enjoyment of the premises; and
4. the property is in habitable condition (*warrant of habitability*).

TERMINATION OF A LEASE.

A lease can be terminated before it is due to end in specific situations:

1. *Tenant's breach of covenant.* In order to evict a tenant who has breached covenants, the landlord must serve notice and obey whatever statutory provisions may apply.
2. *Constructive eviction.* Should a landlord disturb a tenant's "use and enjoyment" of the property, the tenant can terminate the agreement. Other breaches of covenant by a landlord may permit the tenant to collect damages, not end the lease.
3. *Frustration of the lease's purpose due to zoning changes, eminent domain, or similar events.*

A tenant who unilaterally abandons a leased property is still liable for the remaining rent because the lease has not been legally terminated. At the same time, it is also the landlord's duty to find a new tenant.

REGULATION OF BUSINESS

Securities, which include share certificates, bonds, debentures, and corporate notes, are *intangible personal property*. They are evidence of a right to property, not the property itself. Securities are either in *registered form*—registered in a specific name with the issuer (usually a corporation)—or in *blank*—payable to the holder.

A registered certificate can be transferred by delivery plus endorsement (signed by the holder of the certificate) or by delivery plus the execution of a *stock power* (or *assignment*). (Assignment transfers legal rights from one party to another.) A *street certificate* is a share certificate that has been transferred without a designated transferee, and can be further transferred by delivery only, without endorsement. Restrictions on transfer can be used to maintain voting control in a corporation, to preserve S corporation or close corporation status, and are exempt from federal or state laws that require registration of public offerings.

Securities Regulation

There are three sources of statutory securities regulation: the Securities Act of 1933, the Securities Exchange Act of 1934, and state regulations.

SECURITIES ACT OF 1933.

The Securities Act of 1933, and other federal securities laws as well, are administered by the Securities Exchange Commission (SEC). It is a "consumer protection law" for investors, and requires that the public be provided with full and complete disclosure regarding new securities offered for sale. Following the 1929 stock market crash, congressional investigations in the early 1930s revealed the necessity for federal regulation of securities. The act is intended to protect both investors, by ensuring that they can make informed decisions, and honest businesses seeking to raise funds through public investment.

In order to prevent circumvention of the law by the form of the document, the act broadly defines *security* not only as a stock, bond, debenture, note, or other evidence of indebtedness, but also as an investment contract, an undivided interest in oil, gas, or mineral rights, or any interest or instrument commonly referred to as a "security." Some securities—for example, those issued by the United States or any state, by not-for-profit organizations, or by a receiver or trustee in bankruptcy—are exempt from the regulatory provisions of the Securities Act.

The act also imposes *civil liability* on lawyers and accountants, acting as employees or consultants for a corporation, for misstatements or omissions of material fact in registration statements. A complaint against an accountant or financial officer is sufficient if it claims that the individual bought the security because of a registration statement that contained a materially defective statement certified by the accountant or financial officer, and that, as a direct consequence of that material defect, the person suffered damages. Finally, the act provides for *criminal liability*: an accountant participating in making materially defective statements can be punished by steep fines and imprisonment for a maximum of five years.

Securities Exchange Act of 1934.

This federal statute is concerned with *existing* (not *new*) securities in the marketplace. It has four primary aims: (1) to regulate the securities market and securities exchanges; (2) to provide investors with information about those who issue securities; (3) to prevent fraud in the trading of securities; and (4) to prevent the use of "insider information" for the gain of a privileged few and to the detriment of those outside the "charmed circle." All those who deal in the buying and selling of securities—stock exchanges, over-the-counter brokers, and dealers—must register with the SEC. In addition, any security to be traded on an exchange must be registered with the SEC and the exchange.

If an issuer of securities has gross assets in excess of $1 million, and at least 500 stockholders, the securities traded in the over-the-counter market must be registered with the SEC. Such registration requires full disclosure of all organizational and financial information about the business, the terms governing outstanding securities, and the names of underwriters and security holders with at least 10 percent of any class of registered security. In addition, a business offering securities must provide balance sheets and profit-and-loss statements covering the previous three fiscal years. A corporation is required to file three distinct reports with the SEC: an annual report, a quarterly report, and a monthly report that details significant changes in the corporation's financial or organizational structure.

State securities regulation.

Every state has what is known as a "blue sky law." Before the Securities Act of 1933, states understood the need to protect investors from unscrupulous salespeople who would sell them anything, even "the blue sky," so state statutes came to be known as "blue sky laws." State laws usually regulate only those securities issued at the state or local level.

Taxes

Governments at every level levy a variety of taxes. The federal government, for example, taxes transactions such as importing goods, and states and cities tax retail sales. The federal government and most states levy income taxes on personal income, the income of businesses, and, often, the income of estates and trusts. Other "special" taxes are also based on income: the social security contributions made by both employers and employees, and the payroll taxes levied against employers that fund unemployment compensation, workers' compensation, and other programs.

Antitrust Legislation

During the industrial revolution in the United States, big new business powers, such as trusts and monopolies, arose and attempted to control the marketplace in various ways. In order to control such powers and protect free competition, the federal government created *antitrust laws*. There are four major antitrust statutes: the Sherman Antitrust Act, the Clayton Act, the Robinson-Patman Act, and the Federal Trade Commission Act.

SHERMAN ACT.

The Sherman Act of 1890 forbids contracts and conspiracies intended to restrain trade and monopolization or attempted monopolization. Although the Sherman Act is relatively lenient, there are some automatic violations: price fixing, group boycotts, some territorial limitations, production quotas, and "tying arrangements"—requiring that a specific product be bought in return for a contract involving a different product. Monopolies that arise from sheer luck, extraordinary business skills, or patented products do not violate antitrust laws.

CLAYTON ACT.

The Clayton Act of 1914 requires only the *potential* for an adverse impact on competition, making it much stricter regarding possible monopolistic activities than the Sherman Act. The following activities are illegal under the Clayton Act and can be enjoined:

- making exclusive deals and tying arrangements when such contracts reduce competition or create monopolies;
- creating *interlocking directorships* whereby the same individual is the director of two or more companies that each have:
  1. capital, surplus, and undivided profits totaling more than $10 million, and
  2. competing activities that account for at least 4 percent of one company's total sales, and, for each company, more than $1 million in sales and 2 percent of its total revenue.

- mergers that create monopolies:
  1. *horizontal mergers:* mergers in which the merged entities ran the same kind of business at the same level (for example, both manufactured automobiles);
  2. *vertical mergers:* mergers in which the merged entities ran the same kind of business but at different levels (for example, a car manufacturer merges with a dealership);
  3. *conglomerate mergers:* mergers in which the merged entities are in different businesses, geographic regions, or both. This type of merger will likely be allowed.

ROBINSON-PATMAN ACT.

The Robinson-Patman Act (1936) makes it illegal for sellers engaged in interstate commerce to charge different prices for the same product if it significantly reduces competition or tends to create a monopoly. Charging different prices for the same goods is legal if it is the result of: (1) differences in costs; (2) an honest effort to compete in a specific region; or (3) different marketing conditions. Under the terms of this act, buyers can also be penalized if they request or knowingly accept an illegal price.

FEDERAL TRADE COMMISSION ACT.

The Federal Trade Commission Act (1914) forbids business practices or competitive methods that are unfair or deceptive. The Federal Trade Commission (FTC) looks into possible violations of the act and takes three aspects of the alleged violation into account: (1) Is it against public policy? (2) Is it immoral, unscrupulous, oppressive, or unethical? (3) Does it harm consumers in some way? The FTC has recourse to several methods of enforcing the act:

1. *seeking advisory opinions*—consulting experts regarding the legality of a proposed business undertaking;
2. *issuing consent decrees*—agreeing not to impose penalties if a business agrees to stop a specific activity;
3. *issuing cease-and-desist orders*—notifying businesses to stop engaging in illegal activities;
4. *resorting to extreme measures*—ordering that a business be dissolved or having its assets sold.

Both the Justice Department and the FTC are responsible for enforcing federal antitrust laws and both have published enforcement policy guidelines.

Certain groups have succeeded in placing themselves beyond the reach of the FTC—for example, fishermen, government officials, exporters, insurance companies, labor unions, and farm co-ops. Professional baseball has what is called an "overall exemption."

Environmental Law

In 1970, the Environmental Protection Agency (EPA) was created in response to increasing concern about the degree to which businesses, industries, and their manufacturing processes and products have polluted air, water, and land and contributed to the degradation of the planet's resources and the current health crisis. Before that, there had been some legislation (in 1963), preceded in 1962 by Rachel Carson's *Silent Spring* which exposed the health and environmental hazards of

DDT, causing its use to be banned in the United States. Since then, federal and state environmental statutes have provided a variety of penalties for environmental damage, including injunctions, fines, damage awards, and, in very rare cases, imprisonment. The EPA sets national pollution standards and enforces federal environmental laws. Some of the more significant federal statutes include:

- The National Environmental Policy Act of 1969 (NEPA), which created the Council of Environmental Quality, a group responsible for reporting annually on the state of the country's natural resources and studying plans and programs that will affect the environment. NEPA requires an *environmental impact statement* (EIS) on any activity that might affect environmental quality significantly and that involves federal funds, licensing, approval, or monitoring.
- The Clean Water Act of 1972 (CWA), which sets deadlines for cleaning up the country's waterways, and oversees a permit system that tells permit holders which pollutants they can discharge and in what quantities. Permit holders have to keep records of such discharges and provide summaries to authorities.
- The Clean Air Act of 1963 (CAA) makes the states responsible for controlling air pollution, although the EPA sets the standards and steps in when necessary.
- The Resource Conservation and Recovery Act of 1976 (RCRA) sets the standards that handlers of hazardous waste must meet.
- The Endangered Species Act of 1963 authorized the Secretary of the Interior to protect specific flora and fauna and their habitats from extinction.
- The Oil Pollution Act of 1990 increased the liability of entities responsible for oil spills and created a fund that pays for cleanup efforts when the guilty party is unknown or has already paid the maximum limit.

Employment Law

Employment legislation is enacted to protect the health and safety of workers, provide workers with a base level of economic support, and preserve workplaces in which discrimination and labor/management wars do not occur. There are many federal and state statutes that regulate employment, provide workers' compensation, and set minimum wage levels and maximum work hours.

HEALTH AND SAFETY LAWS.

The Occupational Safety and Health Act of 1970 is probably the most significant federal statute on health and safety in the workplace. It established a federal agency, the Occupational Safety and Health Administration (OSHA) to make certain that employers and employees observe health and safety standards. In addition, every state has workers' compensation statutes that require employees to give up the right to sue employers for accidental death, injury, or disease in exchange for which employers must pay financial benefits when employees are killed or injured on the job. A statutory schedule of benefits defines and limits the compensation.

FAIR LABOR STANDARDS ACT (FLSA).

Enacted in 1938, FLSA sets the minimum wage and a 40-hour work week, requires time and a half for overtime work, and limits the employment of minors. Groups that are not covered by FLSA include professionals (doctor, lawyers, teachers), executives (white-collar workers), and administrators.

WORKER ADJUSTMENT AND RETRAINING NOTIFICATION ACT (WARN).

WARN requires large businesses to notify workers at least 60 days prior to a plant closing or mass layoff. Also, there is a joint federal/state program of unemployment insurance pools supported by taxes paid in by employers. If workers in a protected group are fired through no fault of their own, they can collect unemployment benefits. In order to qualify, workers must have worked for a minimum time period or earned a minimum amount of wages. Another requirement is that the unemployed worker must be willing to accept a new job at any time.

Retired or Disabled Workers

The Federal Insurance Contributions Act (FICA) requires employers to withhold a specified sum from employees' wages, and contribute a matching sum. The Social Security Administration (SSA) compensates workers when job incomes decline or cease because of death, disability, or retirement from the pool of funds created by these contributions. The Employment Retirement Income Security Act of 1974 (ERISA) establishes standards for funding private pensions.

TITLE VII

Title VII, a provision of the Civil Rights Act of 1964, is the most significant statute on discriminatory practices in hiring, firing, promotion, compensation, or any other aspect of employment. It makes it illegal to discriminate in any aspect of employment on the basis of race, color, creed, sex, or national origin. Title VII does not apply to businesses with fewer than 15 employees,

Title VII is enforced by the Equal Employment Opportunity Commission (EEOC). In addition to forbidding discriminatory practices and actions, it also prohibits discrimination based on the judicially created doctrines of *disparate treatment*, *adverse impact*, and *pattern* or *practice*.

EQUAL PAY ACT.

An amendment to FLSA, the Equal Pay Act of 1963 forbids differences in pay based on sex for employees doing the same kind of work.

AGE DISCRIMINATION IN EMPLOYMENT ACT (ADEA).

Enacted in 1967, this Act outlaws job discrimination against people age 40 and over, but employers with fewer than twenty employees are not covered by ADEA.

AMERICANS WITH DISABILITIES ACT (ADA).

Passed in 1990, ADA outlaws job discrimination against qualified individuals who have mental or physical impairments if they can perform the job with "reasonable accommodation" on the part of the employer.

Most states have laws similar to Title VII, ADEA, and ADA, and some states and localities also prohibit employment discrimination on the basis of marital status or sexual preference. Such laws often apply to employers exempt from federal employment laws—for example, government bodies and small businesses.

Labor Relations Law

In the 1930s, a significant body of federal *labor relations law* emerged. The Norris-LaGuardia Act of 1932 created a federal policy that enabled workers to form unions. The National Labor Relations Act of 1935 (NLRA; also known as the Wagner Act) established the National Labor Relations Board (NLRB), announced that workers had a federally protected right to form unions and participate in collective bargaining, and outlawed unfair labor practices such as interference with workers' right to form unions and bargain collectively, attempts to control unions, discrimination against workers because of their union activities or for filing charges with or testifying before the NLRB, and refusal to negotiate in good faith with workers' elected representatives (unions).

The Taft-Hartley Act (1947), an amendment to the NLRA, forbids unions to engage in specific unfair practices:

- refusing to bargain collectively with an employer;
- requiring an employer to pay for work not performed;
- charging extreme or discriminatory fees or dues;
- creating obstacles to employees' choice of a union;
- discriminating against certain employees;
- engaging a secondary boycott of businesses besides the primary one in a labor dispute.

Another amendment to the NLRA outlaws "hot cargo" contracts—agreements in which an employer consents to not using or
purchasing goods from a certain business—and provides for federal
regulation of unions' internal activities.

U.S. labor law protects workers' right to strike with several noteworthy exceptions. Strikes cannot be violent; they cannot violate an
existing collective bargaining agreement; they must be called by the
representative union; they cannot involve occupation of an employer's
property; government employees cannot strike; and they cannot violate a court-ordered "cooling off" period of additional negotiation. It is
also legal for employers to use *lockouts* against strikes and, sometimes,
offensive lockouts in anticipation of a strikes are legitimate.

Business Terms in Other Languages

ENGLISH	GERMAN	FRENCH
100% location	1A Lage	situation exceptionelle
AAA rating	AAA rating	cotation AAA
ability to pay	Zahlungsfähigkeit	capacité contributive
accelerated purchase	vorgezogener Kauf	achat accéléré
acceptance credit	Akzeptkredit	crédit d'acceptation
account executive	Kontaktmann	chef de publicité
account number	Kontonummer	numéro de compte
accounting	Buchführung	comptabilité
accounting methods	Methoden der Rechnungslegung	méthodes comptables
accounting standards	Bilanzierungsrichtlinien	normes comptables
accounts payable	Verbindlichkeiten	montants à payer
accounts receivable	Außenstände	montants à recevoir
accrued income	antizipative Erträge	revenu gagné
accrued interest	Marchzins	intérêt couru
acid-test ratio	Liquidität ersten Grades	ration de liquidité immédiate
acquisition	Übernahme	acquisition
act of consent	Zustimmungserklärung	notification de l'acceptation
act of God	Naturkatastrophe	force majeure
active partner	geschäftsführender Gesellschafter	partenaire actif
actuary	Versicherungsstatistiker	actuaire
ad-hoc request	ad-hoc-Antrag	demande ad hoc
adjustment fatigue	Anpassungsmüdigkeit	fatigue de l'ajustement
administrative assistant	Verwaltungsangestellte	adjointe administrative
administrative law	Verwaltungsrecht	droit administratif
Administrative Officer	Mitarbeiter für Verwaltungsangelegenheiten	agent d'administration
adverse selection	Gegenauslese	sélection adverse
advertising	Werbung	publicité

SPANISH	RUSSIAN	JAPANESE
posición de la mejor calidad	privilegirovannoe polozhenie	basho ga daiichi
clasificación AAA	vysshiǐ reǐting	ichiryuu
capacidad contributiva	sposobnost' platit'	shiharai kanoo
compra acelerada	uskorennaia pokupka	kasoku koonyuu
crédito de aceptación	aktseptnyǐ kredit	hikiuke jooken tsuki shin'yoo
ejecutivo de cuentas	zaregistrirovannyǐ predstavitel'	akaunto eguzekutibu
número de cuenta	nomer scheta	kooza bangoo
contabilidad	bukhgalterskiǐ uchet	kaikeigaku
métodos contables	metody bukhgalterskogo ucheta	kaikei hoohoo
normas contables	normy ucheta	kaikei kijun
cuentas por pagar	scheta, podlezhashchie uplate	saimu kanjoo
cuentas por cobrar	ozhidaemye postupleniia	saiken kanjoo
ingreso acumulado	narosshiǐ dokhod	mishuu shuueki
interés acumulado	procentnyǐ dokhod	keika rishi
coeficiente de solvencia inmediata	otnoshenie tekushchikh aktivov k tekushchim passivam	tooza hiritsu
adquisición	priobretenie	shutoku
notificación de la aceptación	soglasie	dooi kooi
catástrofe natural	fors-mazhor	fuka kooryoku
socio activo	aktivnyǐ partner	gyoomu tantoo sha'in
actuario de seguros	aktuariǐ	hoken suu rishi
solicitud ad-hoc	khodataǐstvo dlia spetsial'noǐ tseli	tokubetsu na yookyuu
fatiga del ajuste	oslablenie stabilizatsii	okure no aru choosei
auxiliar administrativo	sekretar'-deloproizvoditel'	juuyaku
derecho administrativo	administrativnoe pravo	gyoosei hoo
Oficial administrativo	administrator	gyoosei shokuin
selección adversa	neblagopriiatnyǐ otbor	gyaku sentaku
publicidad	reklama	kookoku

ENGLISH	GERMAN	FRENCH
advertising agency	Werbeagentur	agence publicitaire
affiliate	Verbundunternehmen	entreprise affiliée
African Development Bank	Afrikanische Entwicklungsbank	Banque africaine de développement
after taxes	nach Steuern	après impôts
aftermarket	Nachbörse	après bourse
after-sales service	Kundendienst	services après-ventes
agency	Maklerbüro	agence
agribusiness	Agrarindustrie	agro-industries
allocation of resources	Ressourcenallokation	allocation des ressources
amortization	Amortisation	amortissement
annual percentage rate	jährliche Gesamtbelastung	taux d'intérêt annuel
annual report	Jahresbericht	rapport annuel
annuity	Annuität	annuité
anticipated growth rate	zu erwartende Wachstumsrate	taux de croissance prévu
antitrust law	Kartellgesetz	loi antitrust
appraisal	Bewertung	évaluation
arbitrator	Arbitrageur	arbitragiste
arbitration	Schiedsverfahren	arbitrage
arbitration clause	Schiedsgerichtsklausel	clause d'arbitrage
arrears (payments)	Rückstände	arriérés
articles of incorporation	Satzung	statuts d'une société
asking price	gefordeter Preis	prix demandé
assembly line	Montageband	chaîne de montage
assessor (of taxes)	Taxator	agent d'assiette
assets (accounting)	Aktiva	actifs
asset-stripping	Asset-Stripping	dépeçage
ATM (automated teller machine)	Bankautomat	guichet automatique
ATM card	Geldautomatenkarte	carte de retraite
attrition (of personnel)	natürliche Fluktuation	élimination naturelle

SPANISH	RUSSIAN	JAPANESE
agencia de publicidad	reklamnoe agentstvo	kookoku dairi ten
empresa afiliada	affilirovannaia kompaniia	gaishikei-kaisha
Banco Africano de Desarrollo	Afrikanskiĭ bank razvitiia	afurika kaihatsu ginkoo
deducidos de los impuestos	posle uplaty nalogov	tedori
mercado secundario	posle rynka	afutaa saabisu shijoo
servicio post-venta	garantiĭnoe obsluzhivanie	afutaa saabisu
agencia	agentstvo	dairi ten
agroindustria	agrobiznes	noogyoo ni kanren suru bijinesu
asignación de los recursos	raspredelenie resursov	shigen haibun
amortización	amortizatsiia	fusai shoo kyakugaku
tasa de interés anual	godovaia procentnaia stavka	nenri
Informe Anual	godovoĭ otchet	nenji hookoku sho
anualidad	renta	nenkin
tasa de crecimiento prevista	ozhidaemyĭ godovoĭ prirost	yosoo seichoo ritsu
ley antimonopólica	antitrestovskie zakony	dokusen kinshi hoo
evaluación	otsenka	kantei
arbitrajista	arbitr	chootei-nin
arbitraje	arbitrazh	chootei
cláusula de arbitraje	arbitrazhnaia ogovorka	saitei jookoo
atrasos	zadolzhennost'	tainoo kin
estatuos sociales	utverzhdaemyĭ vlastiami ustav korporatsii	kaisha teikan
precio de oferta	zaprashivaemaia tsena	teiji kakaku
cadena de montaje	sborochnaia liniia	nagare sagyoo
tasador	otsenshchik(nalogov)	kazei hyooka-nin
activo	aktivy	shisan kamoku
vaciamiento	raspodazha nepribyl'nykh aktivov	kaisha shisan no shuudatsu
cajero automático	bankomat	ei tii emu
tarjeta del cajero automático	bankomatnaia kartochka	ei tii emu no kaado
bajas vegetativas	estestvennyĭ iznos (rabocheĭ sily)	genshoo

ENGLISH	GERMAN	FRENCH
auction	Auktion	vente aux enchères
auction rate (of foreign exchange)	Auktionskurs	taux d'adjudication
audit	Rechnungsprüfung	inspection des comptes
audited statement	geprüfter Abschluß	état comptable vérifié
auditor	Rechnungsprüfer	vérificateur
authorized capital	autorisiertes Grundkapital	capital autorisé
automated clearing house	automatisches Zahlungssystem	chambre de compensation automatique
average daily balance	durchschnittlicher Tagesbestand	moyenne des soldes quotidiens
back office	Back Office	services d'exécution
backwardation	Terminabschlag	déport (à terme)
bad debt	uneinbringliche Forderung	créance irrécouvrable
bailout	Rettungsaktion	renflouement
balance due	zahlbar Betrag	solde dû
balance of trade	Handelsbilanz	balance commerciale
balance sheet	Bilanz	bilan
balancing item	Restposten	écriture de contrepartie
balloon loan	Anleihe mit hoher Restschuld	prêt ballon
bandwagon effect	Herdenverhalten	effet de panurge
bandwidth	Bandbreite	bande passante
bank check	Bankscheck	chèque de banque
bank of issue	Notenbank	banque d'émission
banker's acceptance	Bankwechsel	acceptation bancaire
bankruptcy	Konkurs	banqueroute
bargaining agent	Verhandlungsvertreter	agent négociateur
bargaining power	Verhandlungsmacht	pouvoir de négociation
bargaining unit	Verhandlungseinheit	unité de négociation
barrier to entry	Zugangsbeschränkung	barrière à l'entrée
barter	Tauschhandel	troc
basic rate	Grundzinssatz	taux be base
basis point	Basispunkt	point de base

SPANISH	RUSSIAN	JAPANESE
subasta	auktsion	kyoobai
tipo de cambio de adjudicación	aukcionnaia stavka	kyoobai sooba
verificación de cuentas	audit	kaikei kensa
estado verificado	odobrennyĭ auditorom otchet	kansa hookoku sho
auditor	auditor	kaikei kensain
capital autorizado	ustavnoĭ kapital	juken shihon
cámara de compensación automática	avtomatizirovannaia kliringovaia palata	ootomeishon tegata kookansho
saldo medio diario	sredniĭ dnevnoĭ balans	heikin zandaka
servicio de gestión	otdel konversionnykh i depozitnykh operatsiĭ	hieigyoo bumon
descuento a término	bekvardeishn (deport)	gyaku zaya
deuda incobrable	spisannyĭ dolg	furyoo saiken
operación de rescate	peredacha na poruki	kinkyuu enjo
saldo deudor	summa k uplate	fusoku gaku
balanza comercial	torgovyĭ balans	booeki shuushi
balance	svodnyĭ balans	baransu shiito
partida equilibradora	balansiruiushchaia stat'ia	gosa datsu roo
préstamo balón	bol'shoĭ edinovremennyĭ zaem	futoo tooki shita roon
efecto de manada	effekt azhiotazha	bandowagon kooka
ancho de banda	diapazon	tai'iki haba
cheque de gerencia	bankovskiĭ chek	ginkoo kogitte
banco de emisión	emissionnyĭ bank	hakken ginkoo
aceptación bancaria	bankovskiĭ akcept	ginkoo hikiuke tegata
bancarrota	bankrotstvo	hasan
agente de negociación	agent po sdelkam	kooshoo daihyoosha
poder de negociación	sil'naia pozitsiia	kooshoo ryoku
unidad de negociación	sil'nyĭ argument	kooshoo dantai
barrera a la entrada	bar'er k dostupu	sannyuu shooheki
trueque	barter	kookan
tasa básica	bazisnyĭ kurs	kijun kinri
punto básico	bazisnyĭ punkt	kiso tensuu

ENGLISH	GERMAN	FRENCH
basket of currencies	Währungskorb	panier de monnaies
bear market	Baissemarkt	marché baissier
bearer instrument	Inhaberpapier	instrument au porteur
bell curve (normal distribution)	Glockenkurve	courbe en cloche
benchmark	Referenzgröße	repère
benign neglect	wohlwollende Vernachlässigung	indifférence bienveillante
best-case scenario	Bestfall-Szenario	scénario optimiste
bid price	Geldkurs	cours demandé
bidder	Bieter	soumissionnaire
bill of exchange	Wechsel	lettre de change
bill of lading	Konnossement	commaisement
bill of sale	Verkaufsurkunde	acte de vente
black market	Schwarzmarkt	marché noir
blue chip	Blue Chip	valeurs de premier ordre
bond (security)	Anleihe	bon
bond market	Anleihemarkt	marché obligataire
bonded warehouse	öffentlich Zollgutlager	entrepôt sous douane
book loss	Buchverlust	perte comptable
book profit	Buchgewinn	bénéfice comptable
book value	Buchwert	valeur comptable
border trade	Grenzhandel	commerce frontalier
border worker	Grenzarbeiter	frontalier
borrowing capacity	Verschuldungskapazität	capacité d'endettement
borrowing requirement	Kreditbedarf	besoin d'emprunt
boycott	Boycott	boycottage
branch office	Zweigstelle	agence

SPANISH	RUSSIAN	JAPANESE
cesta de monedas	korzina valiut	basuketto hoo shiki hoo katsu suuka tan-i
mercado bajista	rynok "medvedeĭ"	kakoo sooba
instrumento al portador	finansovyĭ dokument na pred'iavitelia	mukimei shudan
curva campaniforme	kolokoloobraznaia krivaia	beru gata kyokusen
parámetro de referencia	standart	hyoojun
desatención benévola	politika nevmeshatel'stva	bookan suru koto
escenario optimista	naibolee blagopriiatnoe razvitie sobytiĭ	ichiban yoibaai no shinario
precio de compra	tsena pokupatelia	kai yobine
licitador	pokupatel'	nyuusatsusha
letra de cambio	perevodnyĭ veksel'	kawase tegata
conocimiento de embarque	konosament	funani shooken
contrato de compraventa	kupchaia	uriwatashi shooken
mercado negro	chernyĭ rynok	yami torihiki
acción de empresa de primera línea	pervoklassnyĭ	yuuryoo anzen kabu
bono	obligatsiia	saiken
mercado de bonos	rynok obligatsiĭ	saiken shijoo
almacén bajo control aduanero	tamozhennyĭ sklad	hozei sooko
pérdida contable	"bumazhnyĭ" ubytok	choobo funshitsu
beneficio contable	"bumazhnaia" pribyl'	choobo rieki
valor contable	balansovaia stoimost' aktivov	jika hyoo kagaku
comercio fronterizo	prigranichnaia torgovlia	kokkyoo booeki
trabajador fronterizo	pogranichnyĭ rabotnik	kokkyoo roodoosha
capacidad de endeudamiento	zaemnaia sila	kariire nooryoku
necesidad de financiamiento	potrebnost' v zaimstvovaniiakh	kariire hitsuyoo gaku
boicoteo	boĭkot	boikotto
sucursal	filial	shiten

ENGLISH	GERMAN	FRENCH
brand awareness	Markenbekanntheit	marque notoriété
brand image	Markenimage	image de marque
brand loyalty	Markentreue	fidélité (à une marque)
brand name (see trademark)		
break-even point	Gewinnschwelle	point mort
bridge loan	Überbrückungskredit	prêt-relais
brokerage (fee)	Maklergebühr	frais de courtage
budget	Budget	budget
budget deficit	Haushaltsdefizit	déficit budgétaire
budget surplus	Haushaltsüberschuß	excédent budgétaire
building and loan association	Bausparkasse	organisme de crédit mutuel immobilier
building permit	Baugenehmigung	permis de construire
bull market	Haußemarkt	marché haussier
business (buying and selling)	Geschäft	affaires
business (company or firm)	Unternehmen	compagnie
business administration	Geschäftsverwaltung	administration commerciale
business card	Geschäftskarte	carte de visite
business class	Geschäftsklasse	classe d'affaires
business cycle	Konjunkturzyklus	cycle économique
business ethics	Wirtschaftsethik	éthique économique
business expenses	Betriebsausgaben	frais de l'entreprise
business interruption insurance	Betriebsunterbrechg-ungsversicherun	assurance des pertes d'exploitation
business lease	gewerblicher Mietvertrag	bail commercial
business park	Gewerbepark	parc d'entreprise
business plan	Unternehmensplan	plan d'exploitation
business space	Gewerbefläche	locaux d'activité
business travel	Geschäftsreisen	voyages à titre professionnel
buyback agreement	Schuldenrückkaufs-vereinbarung	accord de rachat
buyer's market	Käufermarkt	marché d'acheteur
by-laws	Satzung	réglementation interne
by-product	Nebenprodukt	sous-produit

Spanish	Russian	Japanese
notoriedad de marca	znanie torgovoĭ marki	burando shikoo
imagen de marca	imidz torgovoĭ marki	burando imeeji
fidelidad a una marca	vernost' torgovoĭ marke	burando roiyarutii
		shoohyoo
punto muerto	tochka "pri svoikh"	shuushi bunki ten
préstamo puente	promezhutochnyĭ kredit	tsunagi yuushi
comisión de corretaje	brokerskaia komissiia	nakagai
presupuesto	biudzhet	yosan
déficit presupuestario	defitsit biudzheta	zaisei akaji
superávit presupuestario	aktiv biudzheta	zaisei kuroji
asociación de préstamo y construcción	ssudno-sberegatel'naia assotsiatsiia	chochiku kashitsuke kumiai
licencia de construcción	razreshenie na stroitel'stvo	kenchiku kyoka
mercado alcista	rynok "bykov"	jooshoo sooba
empresa	biznes	shoogyoo
negocio	biznes	kaisha
administración comercial	upravlenie biznesom	keiei gaku
tarjeta comercial	vizitnaia kartochka	meishi
clase preferente	biznes-klass	bijinesu kurasu
ciclo económico	delovoĭ tsikl	keiki hendoo
ética económica	delovaia etika	kigyoo rinri
gastos de empresa	delovye raskhody	eigyoo hi
seguro de interrupción de la empresa	strakhovanie na sluchaĭ pereryva iv delovoĭ aktivnost	jigyoo boogai hoken
arrendamiento comercial	arenda pod biznes	bijinesu riisu
centros de negocios	biznes-park	koogyoo danchi
plan de negocio	biznes-plan	keiei keikaku
sitio comercial	ploshchad' pod biznes	bijinesu kuukan
viajes de negocios	delovaia poezdka	bijinesu ryokoo
acuerdo de recompra	dogovor ob obratnoĭ pokupke	kaimodoshi kyootei
mercado de compradores	rynok pokupatelia	kaite shijoo
reglamento interno	vnutrennie pravila deiatel'nosti korporatsii	naiki
subproducto	pobochnyĭ produkt	fukusanbutsu

ENGLISH	GERMAN	FRENCH
cadastre (see land registry)		
calendar year	Kalenderjahr	année civile
call option	Kaufoption	option d'achat
capital	Kapital	capital
capital account	Kapitalkonto	compte capital
capital assets	Kapitalanlagen	immobilisations
capital expenditure	Investitionsausgaben	dépenses d'investissement
capital flight	Kapitalflucht	exode de capital
capital gain	Kapitalgewinn	gain de capital
capital gains tax	Kapitalertragssteuer	taxe sur les plus-values
capital good	Kapitalgut	bien d'équipement
capital investment	Anlageinvestition	investissement en capital
capital loss	Kapitalverlust	perte en capital
capitalization bond	Kapitalisierungsobligation	obligation de capitalisation
capitalization issue	Emission von Gratisaktien	émission de capitalisation
career change	Laufbahnänderung	changement de carrière
carrying cost (of inventory)	Lagerhaltungskosten	frais de détention
cartel	Kartelle	cartel
cash account	Kassenkonto	compte espèces
cash accounting (method)	Buchführung über Bargeschäfte	comptabilité base caisse
cash and carry	C&C Grosshandel	libre service de vente en gros
cash balance	Kassenguthaben	solde disponible
cash cow	Cash-Cow	vache à lait
cash crop	Marktfrüchte	culture commerciale
cash discount	Barzahlungsrabatt	remise pour paiement comptant
cash flow	Cash-flow	cash flow
cash management	Kassenhaltung	gestion de liquidité

SPANISH	RUSSIAN	JAPANESE
		tochi daichoo
ño natural	kalendarnyì god	rekinen
pción de compra	optsion "kol"	kooru opushon
apital	kapital	shihon kin
uenta de capital	balans dvizheniia kapitalov	shihon kanjoo
ctivos de capital	osnovnoì kapital	kotei shisan
esembolsos de capital	raskhody na priobretenie osnovnogo kapitala	shihon shishutsu
uga de capitales	begstvo kapitalov za granitsu	shihon toohi
lusvalía	prirost kapitala	shihon baikyaku shotoku
mpuesto sobre ganancias le capital	nalog na realizovannyì prirost kapitala	shihon ritoku zei
ien de capital	sredstva proizvodstva	shihon zai
nversión de capital	kapitalovlozhcnic	sctsubi tooshi
érdida de capital	kapital'nyì ubytok	shihon sonshitsu
ono de capitalización	bonusnaia aktsiia	shihon saiken
misión de capitalización	bonusnaia emissiia aktsiì	shihon kin kumi ire hakkoo
ambio de profesión	peremena kar'ery	keireki no henka
osto de mantener as existencias	stoimost' khraneniia tovarov	mochikoshi hiyoo
ártel	kartel'	karuteru
uenta de caja	nalichnyì schet	genkin kanjoo
ontabilidad base caja	uchet dvizheniia denezhnoì nalichnosti	genkin kaikeigaku
utoservicio mayorista	prodazha za nalichnye den'gi	genkin jikokusen shugi no
aldo de caja	balans nalichnosti	genkin zandaka
aca	biznes, daiushchiì pritok nalichnylkh deneg	mookaru shoohin
ultivo comercial	pribyl'nyì sel' skokhoziaìstvennyì produkt	kankin sakumotsu
escuento por pago en efectivo	skidka s tseny pri pokupke za nalichnye	genkin waribiki
lujo de caja	potok nalichnosti	shikinguri
estión de caja	upravlenie nalichnost'iu	genkin kanri

English	German	French
cash on delivery (COD)	Nachnahme	envoi contre remboursement
cash payment	Barzahlung	paiement au comptant
cash purchase	Barkauf	achat au comptant
cash register	Ladenkasse	caisse enregistreuse
cash reserves	Barbestand	trésorerie
casualty insurance	Unfallversicherung	assurance de dommages corporels
ceiling price	Preisobergrenze	prix plafond
central business district	Kerngebiet	quartier de commerces et de bureaux
certificate of deposit	Einlagenzertifikat	certificat de dépôt
certificate of origin	Ursprungsbescheinigung	certificat d'origine
certified public accountant	amtlich zugelassener Wirtschaftsprüfer	comptable diplômé
chamber of commerce	Handelskammern	chambre de commerce
change of ownership	Eigentumswechsel	transfert de propriété
charge account	Verbindlichkeitenkonto	compte-client
chief executive	Geschäftsführer	chef de la direction
clearing account	Verrechnungskonto	compte de compensation
clearing bank	Girobank	banque de virement
client	Mandant	client
collateral	Sicherheiten	nantissement
collective bargaining	Kollektivverhandlungen	négociation collective
comanager	Ko-Manager	cochef de file
command economy	Kommandowirtschaft	économie dirigée
commercial bank	Geschäftsbank	banque commerciale
commercial loan	Kredit zu Marktbedingungen	prêt bancaire
commercial paper	Wertpapier	papier commercial
commercial sample	kommerzielle Probe	échantillon commerciale
commission (on sales)	Provision	commission

SPANISH	RUSSIAN	JAPANESE
reembolso	oplata nalichnymi v moment postavki	genkin hikiwatashi barai
pago al contado	oplata nalichnymi	genkin barai
compra al contado	pokupka za nalichnye	genkin koonyuu
caja registradora	kniga ucheta nalichnosti	rejisutaa
reserva de caja	nalichnyĭ rezerv	genkin junbi
seguro daños personales	strakhovanie ot ubytkov v rezul'tate nepredvidennykh sobytiĭ	saigai hoken
precio máximo	predel'naia tsena	saikoo kakaku
distrito central de negocios	glavnyĭ delovoĭ raĭon	shuyoo sangyoo chi'iki
certificado de depósito	depozitnyj sertifikat	yokin shoosho
certificado de origen	sertifikat proiskhozhdeniia tovarov	gensanchi shoomei sho
contable revisor de cuentas	diplomirovannyĭ bukhgalter	koonin kaikeishi
cámara de comercio	torgovaia palata	shookoo kaigisho
traspaso de propiedad	peremena vladel'tsa	shoyuuken no henka
cuenta de cargo	credit po otkrytomu schetu	kakeuri
gerente general	glavnyĭ ispolnitel'nyĭ direktor	saikoo keiei sekininsha
cuenta de compensación	kliringovyĭ schet	kookan kanjoo
banco compensador	kliringovyĭ bank	tegata kookan kumiai ginkoo
cliente	klient	kuraianto
garantía real	obespechenie kredita	tanpo
negociación colectiva	kollektivnye peregovory	dantai kooshoo
codirector	sodirektor	kyoodoo keieisha
economía dirigida	komandnaia ekonomika	shirei keizai
banco comercial	kommercheskiĭ bank	shoogyoo ginkoo
préstamo comercial	kratkosrochnaia ssuda	shoogyoo kashitsuke
papel comercial	kommercheskie bumagi (vekseliia)	shoogyoo tegata
muestra comercial	kommercheskiĭ obrazets	komaasharu sanpuru
comisión	komissiia	inin

ENGLISH	GERMAN	FRENCH
committee	Ausschuß	comité
commodities	Rohstoffe	produits marchands
commodity exchange	Warenbörse	bourse de commerce
commodity market	Warenmarkt	marché des matières premières
common carrier	Transportunternehmen	transporteur public
common par value	einheitlicher Nominalwert	valeur nominale commune
common share	Stammaktie	action ordinaire
company	Gesellschaft	société
company brochure	Firmenbroschüre	brochures publicitaires d'entreprise
competitive advantage	Wettbewerbsvorteil	avantage compétitif
competitive disadvantage	Wettbewerbsnachteil	désavantage concurrentiel
competitiveness	Wettbewerbsfähigkeit	compétitivité
composite currency	Korbwährung	monnaie composite
compound rate (interest)	Zinseszins	taux composé
concessionaire	Konzessionär	concessionaire
conference call	Telekonferenz	téléconférence
confidence level	Konfidenzniveau	niveau de confiance
consortium	Konsortium	consortium
constructive discharge		démission forcée
consumer	Verbraucher	consommateur
consumer credit	Verbraucherkredit	crédit à la consommation
consumer durables	langlebige Konsumgüter	biens durables
consumer price index (CPI)	Verbraucherpreisindex	indice des prix à la consommateur
consumer protection	Verbraucherschutz	protection du consommateur
contingency clause	Eventualklausel	clause pour imprévus

Spanish	Russian	Japanese
comité	komitet	iinkai
mercancías	tovary	shoohin
bolsa de comercio	tovarnaia birzha	shoohin torihikisho
mercado de materias primas	tovarnyĭ rynok	shoohin shijoo
empresa de transporte	transportnaia kompaniia público	unsoo gyoosha
valor nominal común	obshchaia nominal'naia stoimost'	kyootsuu kawase heika
acción ordinaria	obyknovennaia aktsiia	kyooyuu kabu
empresa	kompaniia	kaisha
folleto publicitario de empresa	broshiura kompanii	kaisha annai
ventaja competitiva	preimushchestvo v konkurentsii	kyoosoo teki yuui
desventaja competitiva	nevygodnoe polozhenie v konkurentsii	kyoosoo teki furi
competitividad	konkurentosposobnost'	kyoosoo
moneda compuesta	sostavnaia valiuta	fukugoo tsuuka
tasa compuesta	slozhnaia protsentnay stavka	fukugoo reeto
concesionario	derzhatel' besplatnoĭ arendy	hoojin
teleconferencia	telekonferentsiia	denwa kaigi
nivel de confianza	uroven' uverennosti	shinrai reberu
consorcio	konsortsiyum	konsoochiamu
despido implícito	vynuzhdennyĭ ukhod s raboty	jun keiyaku tekina kaiko
consumidor	potrebitel'	shoohi sha
crédito al consumidor	potrebitel'skiĭ kredit	shoohi sha shin-yoo
bienes de consumo duraderos	dolgosrochnye potrebitel'skie tovary	shoohi zai
índice de precios al consumidor	indeks potrebitel'skikh tsen	shoohi sha bukka shisuu
protección del consumidor	zashchita potrebitelia	shoohi sha hogo hoo
cláusula para contingencias	stat'ia na sluchaĭ nepredvidennykh obstoiatel'stv	kiyakuno futai jikoo

ENGLISH	GERMAN	FRENCH
contingency fund	Sicherheitsreserve	fonds pour éventualités
contract	Vertrag	contrat
contract for sale	Kaufvertrag	contrat de vente
contract for services	Dienstvertrag	contrat de services
controller	Controller	contrôleur
controlled price	gesteuerter Preis	prix réglementé
conversion algorithm (of currency)	Umstellungsalgorithmus	règle de conversion
cooperative	Genossenschaft	coopérative
copyright	Urheberrecht	droits reservés
core inflation	Kerninflation	inflation de base
corporate body	Körperschaft	personne morale
corporate culture	Firmenkultur	culture d'entreprise
corporate discount	Unternehmensrabatten	escompte de corporation
corporate identity	Unternehmensidentität	image de l'entreprise
corporate image	Firmenimage	image de marque
corporation	Kapitalgesellschaft	société industrielle ou commerciale
cost minimization	Kostenminimierung	minimisation des coûts
cost of living	Lebenshaltungskosten	cout de la vie
"cost, insurance, and freight"	"Kosten, Versicherung und Fracht"	"coût, assurance et fret"
cost-benefit analysis	Kosten-Nutzen-Analyse	analyse coûts-avantages
cost-effectiveness	Preis-Leistungs-Verhältnis	rentabilité
cottage industry	Heimindustrie	industrie artisanale
counteroffer	Gegenangebot	contre-proposition
coupon bond	Schuldverschreibung mit Kupons	obligation à coupons
cover letter	Begleitschreiben	lettre explicative
coverage ratio	Deckungsgrad	rapport entre le sinistre et la protection
credit bureau	Kreditauskunftei	centrale des risques

Spanish	Russian	Japanese
fondo para contingencias	fond na sluchaĩ nepredvidennykh obstoiatel'stv	kinkyuu yoo tsumitate kin
contrato	kontrakt	keiyaku
contrato en venta	dogovor kupli-prodazhi	baikyaku keiyaku
contrato de servicios	kontrakt o predostavlenii uslug	teiki tenken keiyaku
interventor	glavnyĩ bukhgalter	kaikei kansa yaku
precio regulado	reguliruemaia tsena	toosei kakaku
algoritmo de conversión	formula konversii	kookan arugorizumu
cooperativa	kooperativ	kyoodoo kumiai
derecho de propriedad	kopiraĩt	chosaku ken
inflación básica	bazovaia infliatsiia	koa infureeshon
persona jurídica	korporativnaia organizatsiia	hoojin dantai
cultura de empresa	korporativnaia kul'tura	keiei hooshin
descuento corporativo	korporatsionnaia skidka	dantai waribiki
identidad corporativa	korporativnoe soznanie	kooporeeto aidentitii
imagen corporativa	korporativnyĩ imidzh	kigyoo imeeji
sociedad (anónima)	korporatsiia	hoojin
minimización de costos	minimalizatsiia izderzhek	hiyoo saishoogendo
costo de la vida	stoimost' zhizni	seikatsu hi
"costo, seguro y flete"	stoimost', strakhovanie, frakht	unchin, hoken, komi nedan
análisis de costo-beneficio	analiz izderzhek i pribyli	hiyoo ben-eki bunseki
relación costo-eficacia	ekonomichnost'	genka nooritsu
industria doméstica	kustarnaia promyshlennost'	reisai kigyoo
contraoferta	vstrechnoe predlozhenie	shuusei mooshikomi
bono con cupones	kuponnaia obligatsiia	kuupon tsuki saiken
carta adjunta	soprovoditel'noe pis'mo	soejoo
ratio de cobertura	koeffitsient pokrytiia obiazatel'stv	tekiyoo hani hiritsu
central de riesgo	kreditnoe biuro	shin-yoo choosa kikan

ENGLISH	GERMAN	FRENCH
credit card	Kreditkarte	carte de crédit
credit crunch	Kreditrestriktion	resserrement du crédit
credit entry	Gutschrift	inscription au crédit
credit limit	Kreditplafond	limite de crédit
credit note	Gutschriftsanzeige	note de crédit
credit rating	Kreditwürdikeit	cote de crédit
credit risk	Kreditrisiko	risque de contrepartie
credit union	Kreditgenossenschaft	coopérative d'épargne et de crédit
creditor	Gläubiger	créancier
creditor country	Gläubigerland	pays créancier
creditworthiness	Kreditwürdigkeit	solvabilité
crisis management	Krisenmanagement	gestion de crise
cross-border payment	grenzüberschreitende Zahlung	paiement transfrontalier
currency	Währung	devise
currency swap	Währungs-Swap	échange de devises
currency unit	Währungseinheit	unité monétaire
currency zone	Währungszone	zone monétaire
current account	Leistungsbilanz	compte courant
customs clearance	Zollabfertigung	dédouanement
customs duty	Zollgebühr	droit de douane
customs valuation	Zollwertermittlung	valeur en douane
data capture	Datenerfassung	saisie de données
data entry	Dateneingabe	introduction de données
data processing	Datenverarbeitung	traitement informatique
day laborer	Tagelöhner	journalier
day shift	Tagschicht	service de jour
daybook	Journal	livre de caisse
dealer	Händler	concessionnaire
debenture	Schuldverschreibung	obligation
debit card	Kontokarte	carte bancaire
debit entry	Lastschrift	inscription au débit

SPANISH	RUSSIAN	JAPANESE
tarjeta de crédito	kreditnaia kartochka	kurejitto kaado
escasez de crédito	szhatie kredita	shin-yoo kiki
asiento de crédito	zapis' v prikhodnoĭ chasti	saiken kisai jikoo
límite de crédito	kreditnyĭ limit	kashidashi gendo gaku
nota de abono	kreditnyĭ bilet	kashigata hyoo
calificación crediticia	pokazatel' kreditosposobnosti	shin-yoo tookyuu
riesgo de crédito	kreditnyĭ risk	shin-yoo risuku
cooperativa de crédito	kreditnyĭ soiuz	shin-yoo kumiai
acreedor	kreditor	saiken sha
país acreedor	strana-kreditor	saiken koku
solvencia	platezhesposobnost'	shin-yoo ryoku ga aru koto
gestión de crisis	razreshenie krizisa	kiki kanri
pago transfronterizo	mezhdunarodnaia oplata	toojitsu kei zaiken shiharai
moneda	valyuta	tsuuka
swap de monedas	valyutnyĭ svop	tsuuka suwappu
unidad monetaria	valiutnaia edinitsa	tsuuka tani
zona monetaria	valiutnaia zona	tsuuka ken
cuenta corriente	tekushchiĭ schet	tooza yokin
despacho de aduanas	tamozhennaia ochistka	tsuukan
derecho de aduanas	tamozhennaia poshlina	kanzei
aforo aduanero	tamozhennaia otsenka	kanzei kachi
toma de datos	sbor informatsii	deeta shuushuu
entrada de datos	vvod informatsii	deeta kinyuu
procesamiento de datos	obrabotka informatsii	deeta shori
jornalero	podennyĭ rabotnik	ichiji-teki roodoo sha
turno diurno	dnevnaia smena	hiruma no kinmu
libro diario	zhurnal	nikki choo
distribuidor	diler	diiraa
obligación	obrashchaiushchaiasia tsennaia bumaga	shasai
tarjeta de cobro automático	debetovaia kartochka	debitto kaado
asiento de débito	debetovaia zapis'	karigata kinyuu

ENGLISH	GERMAN	FRENCH
debt burden	Schuldenlast	poids de la dette
debt consolidation	Schuldenkonsolidierung	consolidation de la dette
debt management	Kreditaufnahmepolitik	gestion de dette
debt restructuring	Umschuldung	rééchelonnement de la dette
debt service	Schuldendienst	service de la dette
debtor	Schuldner	débiteur
default (on payment)	Zahlungsverzug	cessation de paiement
deficit spending	Defizitfinanzierung	financement par l'emprunt
deflation	Deflation	déflation
demand	Nachfrage	demande
demand deposit	Sichtguthaben	dépôt à vue
deposit account	Depositenkonto	comptes de dépôt
deposit insurance	Einlagenversicherung	garantie des dépôts
depreciation (of assets)	Abschreibung	dépréciation
depreciation (of currency)	Währungsabwertung	dépréciation
derivatives market	Derivatmarkt	marché des instruments dérivés
developer (property)	Bauträger	promotuer
development plan	Flächennutzungsplan	plan d'occupation des sols (POS)
direct debit	direkte Belastung	débit direct
direct marketing	Direktmarketing	vente directe
dirty float (of a currency)	schmutzig Floaten	flottement contrôlé
discount (in commerce)	Rabatt	rabais
discount store	Discountmarkt	solderie
distribution (of goods)	Vertrieb	distribution
distribution channel	Distributionskanal	réseau de distribution
distributor	Vertriebspartner	distributeur
divestment	Beraubung	dessaisissement
domain name	Domain Name	nom de domaine
domestic market	Binnenmarkt	marché intérieur

SPANISH	RUSSIAN	JAPANESE
carga de la deuda	dolgovoe bremia	saimu
consolidación de la deuda	nakoplenie dolgov	fusai gappei
gestión de la deuda	upravlenie dolgom	kokusai kanri
reprogramación de la deuda	restrukturizatsiia dolga	saimu kaikaku
servicio de la deuda	obsluzhivanie dolga	miharai kin
deudor	dolzhnik	kari nushi
mora	defolt	saimu fu rikoo
gasto financiado mediante déficit	defitsitnoe raskhodovanie	akaji shishutsu
deflación	defliatsiia	tsuka shuushuku
demanda	spros	juyoo
depósito a la vista	depozit do vostrebovaniia	yookyuu barai yokin
cuenta de ahorro	depozitnyi schet	teiki yokin kooza
garantía de depósitos	strakhovanie depozitnogo scheta	ginkoo yokin hoken
depreciación	snizhenie stoimosti aktivov	shisan no geraku
depreciación	deval'vatsiia	tsuuka teiraku
mercado de derivados	rynok derivativov	hasei shijoo
promotor	zastroishchik	fudoosan ya
plan de la promoción	plan razvitiia	kaihatsu keikaku
débito directo	priamoe debetovanie	kooza hikiotoshi
publicidad directa	priamoi marketing	dairekuto maaketingu
flotación sucia	"griaznoe" plavanie valiutnogo kursa	daatii furooto
descuento	skidka	waribiki
autoservicio descuento	diskontnyi magazin	disukaunto sutoa
distribución	raspredelenie	haitatsu
canal de distribución	kanaly raspredeleniia	ryuutsuu keiro
distribuidor	distrib'iutor	haitatsu sha
desinversión	lishenie prav	baikyaku
nombre de dominio	domennoe imia	shoyuu chimei
mercado interno	vnutrennii rynok	kokunai shijoo

ENGLISH	GERMAN	FRENCH
double taxation	Doppelbesteuerung	double imposition
down payment	Anzahlung	acompte
drawback (on imports)	Rückzug	rembours
drawing facility (on a bank)	Ziehungsfazilität	mécanisme de tirage
due date	Fälligkeitsdatum	échéance
Dutch auction	Auktion mit Abschlag	enchères au rabais
early retirement	Frühpensionierung	préretraite
earned income	Arbeitseinkommen	revenu du travail
earnings	Ertrag	profits
ECB (European Central Bank)	EZB	BCE
Economic and Monetary Union (EMU)	Wirtschafts und Währungsunion	Union économique et monétaire
economic performance	wirtschaftliche Entwicklung	résultats économiques
economies of scale	Größenvorteile	économies d'échelle
educated guess	wohlbegründete Vermutung	estimation raisonnée
electronic commerce	elektronischer Handel	commerce électronique
electronic funds transfer	elektronischer Geldtransfer	transfert électronique de fonds
electronic money	elektronisches Geld	monnaie électronique
emerging market	aufstrebender Markt	marché naissant
employee	Angestellte	employé
employment agency	Arbeitsvermittlungsstelle	agence pour l'emploi
employment growth	Beschäftigungswachstum	croissance de l'emploi
EMS (European Monetary System)	EWS	SME
encryption	Verschlüsselung	chiffrement
end consumer	Endverbraucher	consommateur final
end product	Endprodukt	produit fini
end user	Endverbraucher	utilisateur final
entrepôt (commercial center)	Umschlagplatz	entrepôt

SPANISH	RUSSIAN	JAPANESE
doble imposición	dvoìnoe nalogooblozhenie	nijuu kazei
entrada	vznos nalichnykh deneg	atamakin
reintegro	skidka s naloga	modoshi zei
servicio de giro	vypiska tratty	hikidashi setsubi
fecha de vencimiento	srok platezha vekselia	yoteibi
subasta a la baja	datskiî auktsion	gyakuseri
jubilación anticipada	ranniî ukhod na pensiiu	sooki taishoku
renta del trabajo	zarabotannyì dokhod	kinroo shotoku
ganancias	zarabotok	shuunyuu
BCE	Evropeìskiî Tsentral'nyì Bank	ooshuu chuuoo ginkoo
Unión económica y eonetaria	Ekonomicheskiî i Monetarnyì soiuz	keizai tsuuka dome
desempeño económico	ekonomicheskie pokazateli	keizai jisseki
economías de escala	snizhenie stoimosti za schet uvelicheniia ob'ema proizvodstva	kibo no keizai
estimación razonada	obosnovannoe predpolozhenie	keiken ni motozuku suisoku
comercio electrónico	elektronnaia kommertsiia	denshi shoogyoo
transferencia electrónica de fondos	sistema elektronnykh platezheì	furikae kessan shisutemu
dinero electrónico	elektronnye den'gi	erekutoronikku manei
mercado incipiente	novyì rynok	kore kara no shijoo
empleado	rabotnik	shain
agencia de empleo	agentstvo po trudoustroìstvu	shogyoo shookai jo
crecimiento del empleo	rost zaniatosti	shuusho kuritsu no jooshoo
SME	EVS	ooshuu tsuuka seido
cifrado	shifrovka	deita o koodo nichi kansuru koto
consumidor final	konechnyì potrebitel'	mattan shoohisha
producto final	konechnyì produkt	saishuu seisan butsu
usuario final	konechnyì pol'zovatel'	mattan shoohisha
centro de almacenaje y distribución	tsentr svobodnoì torgovli	hozei sooko

ENGLISH	GERMAN	FRENCH
entrepreneur	Unternehmer	entrepreneur
environmental accounting	ökologische Buchhaltung	comptabilité écologique
environmental impact	Folgen für die Umwelt	effet écologique
environmental tax	Ökosteuer	écotaxe
equities market	Aktienmarkt	marché des actions
equity financing	Aktienfinanzierung	financement par émission d'actions
ergonomics	Ergonomie	ergonomie
escalator clause	Gleitklausel	clause d'indexation
escape clause	Ausweichklausel	clause dérogatoire
escrow account	Anderkonto	compte-séquestre
euro area	Euro-Zone	zone euro
European Central Bank	Europäische Zentralbank	Banque centrale européenne
European Monetary System	Europäisches Währungssystem	système monétaire européen
excess profit	Übergewinn	superbénéfice
exchange control(s)	Devisenkontrolle	contrôle des changes
exchange rates	Wechselkurse	parités de change
exchange risk	Wechselkursrisiko	risque de change
excise tax	Verbrauchsteuer	excise
expense account	Spesenkonto	compte de dépenses
expense item	Ausgabenposten	poste de dépense
export credit	Exportkredit	crédit à l'exportation
export duty	Ausfuhrzoll	droit à l'exportation
export earnings	Exporterlöse	gains l'exportation
export license	Ausfuhrlizenz	licence d'exportation
face value	Nennvert	valeur nominale
facilities management	Immobilienmanagement	gestion d'immeubles

SPANISH	RUSSIAN	JAPANESE
empresario	predprinimatel'	kigyoo ka
contabilidad ambiental	uchet ekologicheskikh faktorov	kankyoo kanjoo
impacto medio ambiental	vliianie na ekologiiu	kankyoo eikyoo
impuesto ambiental	ekologicheskiĭ nalog	kankyoo zei
mercado de acciones	fondovyĭ rynok	kabushiki shijoo
financiamiento mediante emisión de acciones	mobilizatsiia kapitala s pomoshch'iu vypuska aktsiĭ	mochibun kinyuu
ergonomía	ergonomika	ningen koogaku
cláusula de escala móvil	uslovie kontrakta, pozvoliaiushchee uchityvat' rost izderzhek	esukareitaa jookoo
cláusula de evasión	punkt dogovora, osvobozhdaiushchiĭ ot otvetstvennosti	menseki jookoo
cuenta de depósito en garantía	kontrakt, deponirovannyĭ u tret'ego litsa	yotaku kooza
zona euro	evrozona	yuuroo tsukatte iru chiiki
Banco central europeo	Evropeĭskiĭ Tsentral'nyĭ Bank	ooshuu chuuoo ginkoo
sistema monetario europeo	Evropeĭskiĭ Valiutnyĭ Soiuz	ooshuu tsuuka seido
ganancias extraordinarias	sverkhpribyl'	chooka ritoku
control de cambios	kontrol' valiutnogo obmena	kawase kanri
paridades de cambio	valiutnyĭ kurs	kawase reito
riesgo de cambio	risk poter' v rezul'tate valiutnogo obmena	kawase risuku
impuesto interno	aktsiz	buppin zei
cuenta de gastos	schet podotchetnykh summ	settai hi
partida de gastos	stat'ia raskhoda	keihi
crédito de exportación	eksportnyĭ kredit	yushutsu shin-yoo joo
derecho de exportación	eksportnaia poshlina	yushutsu zei
ingresos de exportación	eksportnaia pribyl'	yushutsu shuunyuu
permiso de exportación	eksportnaia litsenziia	yushutsu kyoka
valor facial	nominal'naia stoimost'	gakumen kakaku
gerencia de las instalaciones	upravlenie kreditom	kanri setsubi

ENGLISH	GERMAN	FRENCH
factor (company)	Factoring-Unternehmen	facteur
factoring	Factoring	affacturage
factory (gate) price	Preis ab Werk	prix usine
fair market price	angemessener Marktpreis	prix équitable
feasibility study	Tauglichkeitsstudie	étude de faisabilité
fiat money	Papiergeld ohne Edelmetalldeckung	monnaie fiduciaire
field audit	Außenprüfung	audit sur place
finance company	Finanzierungsgesellschaft	société de financement
financial incentive	finanziell Anreize	stimulant financier
financial services	Finanzdienstleistungen	services financiers
financial statement	Finanzausweis	état financier
financial year	Geschäftsjahr	exercice
financing facility	Finanzierungsmechanismus	mécanisme de financement
financing package	Finanzpaket	montage financier
fine print	Kleingedrukte	petits caractères
firm offer	bindendes Angebot	offre ferme
fiscal policy	Finanzpolitik	politique budgétaire
fiscal year	Rechnungsjahr	exercice budgétaire
fixed assets	Anlagevermögen	immobilisations
fixed cost	Fixkosten	frais fixes
fixed rent	Festmiete	loyer ferme
flag of convenience	billige Flagge	pavillon de complaisance
flat rate	Einheitstarif	taux fixe
floating capital	frei verfügbare Kapital	capital disponible
floating currency	floatende Währung	devise flottante
floating rate	variabler Zinssatz	taux flottant
flotation (of securities)	Emission	lancement
foreign capital	Auslandskapital	capitaux étrangers
foreign currency	Fremdwährung	monnaie étrangère

SPANISH	RUSSIAN	JAPANESE
factor	faktoringovaia kompaniia	nakagainin
factoring	faktoring	fakutaringu
precio de fábrica	zavodskaia tsena	watashi nedan
precio justo	obosnovanaia rynochnaia tsena	tekisei kakaku
estudio de viabilidad	tekhniko-ekonomicheskoe obosnovanie	kanosei no kenkyuu
moneda fiduciaria	bumazhnye den'gi	fukan shihei
auditoría in situ	vyezdnaia proverka	sanchi kaikei kansa
financiera	finansovaia kompaniia	kin-yuu gaisha
incentivo financiero	finansovyì stimul	kin-yuu yuuin
servicios financieros	finansovye uslugi	kin-yuu saabisu
estado financiero	finansovyì otchet	zaimu shohyoo
ejercicio	finansovyì god	kaikei nendo
mecanismo de financiamiento	mekhanizm finansirovaniia	hosoku yuushi
paquete de financiamiento	finansovyì paket	kin-yuu pakkeeji
letra chica	melkiì shrift	saimoku
oferta en firme	tverdoe predlozhenie	faamu ofaa
política fiscal	biudzhetnaia i nalogovaia politika	zaisei seisaku
año fiscal	finansovyì god	kaikei nendo
activo fijo	kapital'nye aktivy	kotei shisan
costo fijo	fiksirovannye raskhody	kotei genka
arrendamiento fijo	fiksirovannaia arendnaia plata	kotei chidai
bandera de conveniencia	"udobnyì" flag	bengi senseki
tasa fija	edinoobraznaia stavka	kin-itsu kakaku
activo circulante	oborotnyì kapital	ryuudoo shihon
moneda flotante	plavaiushchaia valiuta	ryuudoo tsuuka
tasa variable	plavaiushchiì kurs	jiyuu hendoo sooba
emisión	vypusk aktsiì cherez birzhu	hakkoo
capital extranjero	inostrannyì kapital	gaikoku shihon
moneda extranjera	inostrannaia valiuta	gaikoku tsuuka

ENGLISH	GERMAN	FRENCH
foreign direct investment	Direktinvestitionen im Ausland	investissements étrangers directs
"foreign exchange, forex"	Devisenhandel	devises
foreign trade	Außenhandel	commerce extérieur
foreman	Vorarbeiter	contremaître
forward contract	Terminabschluss	contrat à terme
franchise agreement	Franchise-Vertrag	contrats de franchise
free market price	Freiverkehrskurs	prix du marché libre
free movement of capital	freier Kapitalverkehr	libre circulation des capitaux
free trade zone	Freihandelszone	zone de libre-échange
freehold (property)	Grundeigentum	propriété foncière perpetuelle et libre
freight rate	Frachtrate	tarifs de transport
fringe benefits	zusätzliche Leistungen	avantages sociaux
frontage	Straßenfront	façade
futures contract	Terminkontrakt	contrat à terme
garnishment	Verzierung	saisie-arrêt
GDP (gross domestic product)	BIP	PIB
general liability insurance	Haftpflicht-Versicherung	assurances responsabilité civile
global economy	Weltwirtschaft	économie globale
globalization	Globalisierung	mondialisation
GNP (gross national product)	BSP	PNB
going concern	gesunde Firma	entreprise viable
golden hello	Anwerbungsprämie	prime d'embauche
golden parachute	goldener Handschlag	parachute doré
goods on consignment	Konsignationswaren	biens en consignation

SPANISH	RUSSIAN	JAPANESE
inversión extranjera directa	priamoe investirovanie inostrannogo kapitala	gaikoku chokusetsu tooshi
divisas	inostrannaia valiuta	gaikoku kawase, forekkusu kurabu
comercio exterior	vneshniaia torgovlia	gaikoku booeki
capataz	brigadir	kantoku
contrato a término	forvardnyì kontrakt	nobe torihiki
contrato de franquicia	franshiznyì dogovor	tokkyo kyootei
precio de mercado libre	tsena na svobodnom rynke	jiyuu shijoo kakaku
circulación libre de capitales	svobodnoe dvizhenie kapitala	shihon no jiyuu hendoo
zona de comercio libre	svobodnaia torgovaia zona	jiyuu booeki chiiki
propiedad absoluta	polnoe pravo na vladenie	jiyuu hoyuu fudoosan ken
tarifa de flete	tarif za frakht	unchin ritsu
incentivos complementos	dopolnitel'nye l'goty	fuka kyuufu
fachada	fasad	shoomen
futuro	f'iucherskiì kontrakt	sakimono torihiki
orden de retención de pagos	sudebnyì prikaz ob uderzhanii chasti zarplaty sluzhashchego	saiken sashiosae
PIB	VVP	kokunai soo seisan
seguro de responsabilidad civil	strakhovanie otvetstvennosti	ippan songai baishoo hoken
economía global	global'naia ekonomika	sekai shijoo
globalización	globalizatsiia	guroo baru ka
PNB	VNP	kokumin soo seisan
empresa en marcha	deìstvuiushchee predpriiatie	keizoku kigyoo kachi
prima de enganche	krupnaia summa, poluchaemaia pri vstuplenii v dolzhnost'	koogaku no shitaku kin
paracaídas dorado	krupnaia summa, poluchaemaia pri uvol'nenii	gouruden parashuuto
bienes en consignación	partiia tovarov k otpravke	itaku seki shoohin

ENGLISH	GERMAN	FRENCH
goodwill	Goodwill	fonds commercial
government agency	Regierungsstelle	direction
government security	Staatspapier	titre d'état
grace period	tilgungsfreie Periode	délai de grâce
grandfather clause	Besitzstandsklausel	clause de non-rétroactivité
grievance procedure	Beschwerdeverfahren	procédure de réclamation
gross domestic product (GDP)	Bruttoinlandsprodukt	produit intérieur brut
gross national product (GNP)	Bruttosozialprodukt	produit national brut
gross rent	Bruttomiete	loyer brut
ground rent	Pacht	rente foncière
Group of Seven	Siebenergruppe	Groupe des Sept
guaranteed loan	verbürgter Kredit	prêt garanti
haircut (as collateral of securities)	Sicherheitsabschlag	marge de sécurité
hard currency	harte Währung	monnaie forte
headhunter	Kopfjäger	chasseur de têtes
headhunting	Rekrutierung durch Direktkontakt	recrutement par approche directe
headquarters	Zentrale	siège (social)
health insurance	Krankenversicherung	assurances-maladies
hedge fund	Hedge-Fonds	fonds de couverture
hidden reserves	stille Reserve	réserves cachés
historical cost	Anschaffungskosten	coût initial
holding company	Holdinggesellschaft	société de portefeuille

Spanish	Russian	Japanese
fondo de comercio	dobraia volia	eigyoo ken
organismo gubernamental	gosudarstvennoe uchrezhdenie	seifu kankei kikan
valor del estado	pravitel'stvennye tsennye bumagi	seifu shouken
período de gracia	l'gotnyǐ period	shiharai yuuyo kikan
cláusula de derechos adquiridos	uslovie dogovora, pri kotorom ego deǐstvie ne imeet obratnoǐ sily	sofu jooyaku
procedimiento de examen de reclamaciones	poriadok rassmotreniia zhalob	kujoo shori seido
producto interno bruto	valovoǐ vnutrenniǐ produkt	kokunai soo seisan
producto nacional bruto	valovoǐ natsional'nyǐ produkt	kokumin soo seisan
arrendamiento bruto	brutto-arendnaia plata	soo jidai
censo	zemel'naia renta	jidai
Grupo de los Siete	Bol'shaia Semerka	nana ka koku zooshoo kaigi
préstamo garantizado	garantirovannyǐ zaem	hoshoo tsuki no roon
recorte	faktor riska	heakatto
moneda dura	tverdaia valiuta	kooka
cazatalentos	agent po priamomu naǐmy vysokokvalifitsirovannykh rabotnikov	heddohantaa
reclutamiento directo	priamoǐ naǐm vysokokvalifitsirovannykh rabotnikov	heddohantingu
oficina central	glavnoe upravlenie	honbu
seguro de enfermedad	strakhovanie zdorov'ia	kenkoo hoken
fondo de inversión especulativo	khedzhevyǐ fond	kaketsunagi shikin
reserva oculta	skrytye rezervy	himitsu tsumitate kin
costo inicial	pervonachal'naia stoimost' aktiva	shutoku genka
compañía tenedora	kholdingovaia kompaniia	oya gaisha

ENGLISH	GERMAN	FRENCH
hostile takeover bid	feindliches Übernahmeangebot	offre d'une prise de contrôle hostile
hot money	Schwarzgeld	capitaux fébriles
house brand	Handelsmarke	marque de distributeur
human resources	Humanressourcen	ressources humaines
idle capacity	ungenutzte Kapazität	capacité inutilisée
import duty	Einfuhrzoll	taxe à l'importation
import license	Einfuhrerlaubnis	licence d'importation
imputed cost	kalkulatorische Kosten	coût imputé
incidentals	Nebenausgaben	faux-frais
income	Einkommen	revenu
income target	Einkommensziel	objectif de revenu
income tax	Einkommensteuer	impôt sur le revenu
incorporation	Eintragung	constitution
indebtedness	Verschuldung	endettement
indemnity	Schadensersatz	indemnité
indexation	Indexierung	indexation
indirect cost	indirekte Kosten	coût indirect
industrial accident insurance	betriebliche Unfallversicherung	assurances accidents du travail
industrial action	Arbeitskampf	action revendicative
industrial complex	Industriekomplex	complexe industriel
industrial espionage	Industriespionage	espionnage industriel
industrial park	Industriegebiet	zone industrielle
industrial safety	Betriebliches Sicherheitswesen	sécurité professionnelle
industrial waste	Industrieabfall	déchets industriels
industry	Industrie	industrie
infant industry	junger Wirtschaftszweig	industrie naissante
inflation	Inflation	inflation

SPANISH	RUSSIAN	JAPANESE
oferta pública de adquisición hostil (OPAH)	pogloshchenie kompanii putem skupki ee aktsiĭ na rynke	gooin na kabushiki kookai kaitsuke
capitales febriles	goriachie den'gi	tanki shi kin
marca blanca	firmennaia marka	juutaku meigara
recursos humanos	chelovecheskie resursy	jin-teki shigen
capacidad no utilizada	neispol'zovannyĭ potentsial	yuukyuu setsubi
derecho de importación	importnaia tamozhennaia poshlina	yunyuu zei
permiso de importación	importnaia litsenziia	yunyuu kyoka
costo implícito	otsenochnye izderzhki	kizoku hi
imprevistos	melkie raskhody	zappi
ingreso	dokhod	shuunyuu
meta de ingreso	planiruemyĭ dokhod	shuunyuu mokuhyoo
impuesto a los ingresos	podokhodnyĭ nalog	shotoku zei
constitución	inkorporatsiia	hoojin dantai
endeudamiento	zadolzhennost'	fusai
indemnización	garantiia vozmeshcheniia ubytka	songai baishoo kin
indexación	indeksatsiia	indekuseishon
coste indirecto	kosvennye izderzhki	kansetsu hi
seguro contra accidentes laborales	strakhovanie ot neschastnogo sluchaia na proizvodstve	roosai jiko hoken
acción sindical	zabastovka	koogyoo katsudoo
complejo industrial	industrial'nyĭ kompleks	koogyoo danchi
espionaje industrial	promyshlennyĭ shpionazh	sangyoo supai-katsudoo
zona industrial	zona promyshlennykh predpriiatiĭ	koogyoo danchi
seguridad industrial	tekhnika bezopasnosti na proizvodstve	sangyoo anzen
residuos industriales	promyshlennye otkhody	sangyoo haikibutsu
industria	industriia	sangyoo
industria naciente	molodaia industriia	yoochi sangyoo
inflatión	infliatsiia	infureishon

ENGLISH	GERMAN	FRENCH
information management	Informationsmanagement	gestion de l'information
information office	Auskunftsstelle	bureau des renseignements
information technology	Informationstechnik	informatique
initial margin	fester Abschlag	marge initiale
initial public offering (IPO)	Börsengang	premier appel public à l'épargne
in-service training	innerbetriebliche Schulung	formation en cours d'emploi
insider trading	Insiderhandel	délit d'initié
insolvency	Zahlungsunfähigkeit	insolvabilité
installment payment	Ratenzahlung	versement partiel
installment plan	Teilzahlung	contrat de vente à crédit
installment sale	Abzahlungskauf	vente à tempérament
institutional investor	institutioneller Anleger	investisseur institutionnel
insurance agent	Versicherungsvertreter	agent d'assurances
insurance company	Versicherungsgesellschaft	compagnie d'assurances
insurance policy	Versicherungspolice	police d'assurance
intangible assets	immaterielle Anlagwerte	immobilisations incorporelles
intellectual property	intellektuelles Eigentum	propriété intellectuelle
interactive marketing	interaktives Marketing	marketing interactif
interest payment	Zinszahlung	paiement d'intérêts
interest rate risk	Zinsrisiko	risque de taux d'intérêt
interest rate swap	Zinsswap	échange de taux d'intérêt
interest-free loan	zinsfreies Darlehen	prêt sans intérêts
interim balance	Zwischenbilanz	bilan provisoire
interim dividend	Vorschussdividende	acompte sur dividende
Internet billing	Online-Abrechnung	compte en ligne
Internet business	Internetunternehmen	entreprise internet

Spanish	Russian	Japanese
administración de información	upravlenie informatsieĭ	joohoo kanri
oficina de información	informatsionnyĭ otdel	infomeishon ofisu
tecnología de la información	informatsionnaia tekhnika	joohoo koogaku
margen inicial	pervonachal'naia marzha	shoki ri zaya
oferta pública inicial	pervonachal'noe publichnoe predlozhenie aktsiĭ	shoki koobo
capacitación interna	povyshenie kvalifikatsii bez otryva ot proizvodstva	genshokusha kenshuu
transacciones basadas en información privilegiada	nezakonnye operatsii s tsennymi bumagami litsami, imeiushchimi konfidentsial'nuiu informatsiiu	insaidaa torihiki
insolvencia	neplatezhesposobnost'	hensai funoo
cuota	oplata v rassrochku	bunkatsu barai no ikkai bun
compra a plazos	rassrochka	bunkatsu barai
venta a plazos	prodazha v rassrochku	fubarai hanbai
inversionista institucional	institutsional'nyĭ investor	kikan tooshi ka
agente de seguros	strakhovoĭ agent	hoken dairinin
compañía de seguros	strakhovaia kompaniia	hoken gaisha
póliza de seguros	strakhovoĭ polis	hoken keiyaku
activos intangibles	"neosiazaemye" aktivy	mukei shisan
propiedad intelectual	intellektual'naia sobstvennost'	chiteki zaisan
marketing interactivo	interaktivnyĭ marketing	soogo han'noo teki maaketingu
pago de intereses	oplata protsentov	rishi no shiharai
riesgo de interés	risk poter' v rezul'tate izmeneniia protsentnykh stavok	kinri kiken
swap de tipos de interés	obmen protsentnymi platezhami	kinri kookan
préstamo sin interés	besprotsentnyĭ zaem	muri shi roon
balance provisional	promezhutochnyĭ balans	chuukan zandaka
dividendo provisional	promezhutochnyĭ dividend	chuukan haitoo
factura en línea	vystavlenie scheta cherez Internet	intaanetto kanjoo
negocio internet	internet-biznes	intaanetto bijinesu

ENGLISH	GERMAN	FRENCH
Internet service provider	Internet-dienstanbieter	prestataire de services internet
Internet shopping	Einkaufen per Internet	achats par internet
inventory	Lagerbestand	stocks
inventory control	Bestandskontrolle	gestion des stocks
inventory valuation	Lagerbewertung	évaluation des biens
investment	Investition	investissement
investment income	Kapitalertrag	revenu de portefeuille de titres
investment portfolio	Portfolio im Investmentbereich	portefeuille d'investissement
invoice	Faktur	facture
isocost	Isokosten	isocoût
isoquant	Isoquante	isoquant
job creation	Arbeitsbeschaffung	création d'emplois
job description	Arbeitsplatzbeschreibung	description de poste
job offer	Stellenangebot	offre d'emploi
job opening	offene Stelle	emploi vacant
job rotation	Arbeitsplatzrotation	rotation de personnel
job seeker	Arbeitssuchender	demandeur d'emploi
job sharing	Job-sharing	partage de poste
job title	Stellenbezeichnung	titre de la fonction
joint ownership	Eignergemeinschaft	copropriété
joint stock company	Aktiengesellschaft	société par actions
joint tenancy	Miteigentum	co-location
joint venture	Zusammenarbeit	entreprise commune
junk bond	Junk Bond	obligation à haut rendement
labor contract	Flächentarifvertrag	convention collective
labor cost	Arbeitskosten	coût du travail
labor force	Erwerbsbevölkerung	population active
labor market	Arbeitsmarkt	marché du travail

Spanish	Russian	Japanese
proveedor de servicios de internet	provaîder na internete	intaanetto saabisu purobaidaa
compras por internet	internet-shoping	intaanetto shoppingu
inventario	tovarnye zapasy	zaiko
control de inventario	kontrol' tovarnykh zapasov	zaiko kanri
valoración de existencias	otsenka tovarnykh zapasov	zaiko hyooka
inversión	investirovanie	tooshi
rendimientos de capital mobilario	dokhod ot investitsiî	tooshi shotoku
cartera de inversión	investitsionnyî portfel'	tooshi mokuroku
factura	schet-faktura	okurijoo
isocosto	izokost	toohi yoo
isocuanta	izokvanta	toosei sanryoo kyoku sen
creación de nuevos puestos de trabajo	sozdanie rabochikh mest	shigoto o tsukuridasu koto
descripción del puesto	opisanie sluzhebnykh obiazannosteî	shokumu kijutsu sho
oferta de empleo	predlozhenie raboty	kyuujin
vacante	vakansiia	kyuujin
rotación de trabajo	rotatsiia rabochikh mest	shokuba no haichi tenkan
persona que busca empleo	ishchushchiî rabotu	kyuushoku sha
reparto del trabajo	raspredelenie rabochego mesta na dvoikh	jobu shearingu
nombre del cargo	naimenovanie sluzhebnogo polozheniia	jobu taitoru
copropiedad	sovmestnoe vladenie	kyooyuu ken
sociedad por acciones	aktsionernaia kompaniia	kabushiki gaisha
arrendamiento conjunto	sovmestnaia arenda	gooben
empresa en común	sovmestnoe predpriiatie	kyoodoo jigyootai
bono basero	brosovye obligatsii	janku bondo
convenio colectivo	trudovoî kontrakt	roodoo keiyaku
costo laboral	stoimost' rabocheî sulî	roodoo kosuto
fuerza de trabajo	rabochaia sila	roodoo ryoku jinkoo
mercado de trabajo	rynok truda	roodoo shijoo

ENGLISH	GERMAN	FRENCH
labor relations	Arbeitsbeziehungen	relations professionnelles
labor supply	Arbeitsangebot	offre de travail
labor union	Gewerkschaftsbund	syndicat
laborer	Hilfsarbeiter	travailleur
labor-saving	arbeitsparend	qui facilite le travail
land registry	Kataster	cadastre
late payment	verspätete Zahlung	paiement tardif
leading indicator	vorauseilender Indikator	indicateur avancé
leaseback	Verkauf mit Rückmietung	leaseback
leased line	Mietleitung	ligne privée
leasehold	Pacht	location à bail
least cost planning	Minimalkostenplanung	planification à moindre
legal fees	Anwaltsgebühren	honoraires de justice
legal services	juristische Dienstleistungen	services juridiques
legal tender	gesetzliches Zahlungsmittel	pouvoir libératoire
lender	Kreditgeber	prêteur
lending rate	Leihsatz	taux prêteur
lessee	Mieter	locataire à bail
letter of credit	Akkreditiv	lettre de crédit
letter of intent	Absichtserklärung	lettre d'intentions
leveraged buyout	Leveraged Buyout	rachat d'entreprise par endettement
liabilities	Verbindlichkeiten	passif(s)
lien	Pfandrecht	droit de rétention
limited liability company	Gesellschaft mit beschränkter Haftung	société à responsabilité limitée
limited partner	Kommanditist	commanditaire
limited partnership	Kommanditgesellschaft	société en commandité

Spanish	Russian	Japanese
relaciones de trabajo	trudovye otnosheniia	rooshi kankei
oferta de trabajo	nalichie rocheĭ sily	roodoo kyookyuu
sindicato	trudovoĭ soiuz	roodoo kumiai
trabajador	rabotnik	roodoo sha
que ahorra trabajo		roodoo setsuyaku teki
catastro	zemel'nyĭ registr	tochi toki
pago en mora	zaderzhka oplaty	kigen go shiharai
indicador anticipado	vedushchiĭ pokazatel'	senkoo shihyoo
compra y alquiler al vendedor	liz-bek	riisubakku
línea arrendada	arendovannaia telefonnaia liniia	riisudo rain
arrendamiento	arendovannaia sobstvennost'	tochi shoyuu ken
coût	planification à moindre coût	saishoo hiyoo keikaku
honorarios legales	sudebnye izderzhki	hootei no tesuuryoo
servicios legales	iuridicheskie uslugi	hootei no saabisu
curso legal	zakonnoe sredstvo platezha	hootei kahei
prestador	kreditor	kashite
tasa activa	ssudnyĭ protsent	kashidashi kinri
arrendatario lessor	Vermieter	karinushi
carta de crédito	akkreditiv	shin-yoo joo
carta de intención	pis'mo o namerenii sovershit' sdelku	kari keiyakusho
compra apalancada	pokupka kontrol'nogo paketa aktsiĭ	rebarejido baiauto
pasivos	obiazatel'stva	saimu
gravamen de retencíon	pravo aresta kreditorom imushchestva dolzhnika	sakidori tokken
sociedad de responsabilidad limitada	kompaniia s ogranichennoĭ otvetstvennost'iu	yuugen sekinin gaisha
comanditista	partner s ogranichennoĭ otvetstvennost'iu	yuugen sekinin shain
sociedad en comandita limitada	ogranichennoe tovarishchestvo	yuugen sekinin kumiai

ENGLISH	GERMAN	FRENCH
liquid assets	flüssige Mittel	liquidités
liquidation (of a company)	Liquidation	liquidation
liquidator	Liquidator	liquidateur
liquidity ratio	Liquiditätsquote	coefficient de liquidité
list price	Katalogpreis	prix au catalogue
local currency	Landeswährung	monnaie nationale
logo	Logo	logo
long-term trend	langfristiger Trend	tendance à longtemps
loss leader	Lockvogelangebot	article d'appel
lump sum	Pauschale	versement unique
mail order	Versandhandel	vente par correspondance
majority ownership	Mehrheitsbesitz	participation majoritaire
man-day	Manntag	homme-jour
man-hour	Arbeitsstunde	heure de main-d'oeuvre
manpower	Arbeitspotential	main-d'oeuvre
manpower shortage	Arbeitskräftemangel	pénurie de main-d'oeuvre
manufactured goods	Fertigprodukte	biens manufacturés
manufacturing industry	verarbeitendes Gewerbe	industrie manufacturière
man-year	Mannjahr	homme-année
marginal cost	Grenzkosten	coût marginal
margining agreement	Einschlußregelung	accord de garantie
markdown	Preissenkung	rabais
market access	Zugang zu den Märkten	accès aux marchés
market capitalization	Bewertung des Aktienkapitals	capitalisation boursière
market economy	Marktwirtschaft	économie de marché
market leader	Marktführer	chef de file
market price	Marktpreis	prix du marché
market rate (interest)	Marktzinssatz	taux du marché

SPANISH	RUSSIAN	JAPANESE
activo líquido	likvidnye aktivy	ryuudoo shisan
liquidación	likvidatsiia	seisan
liquidador	likvidator	seisan nin
coeficiente de líquidez	koeffitsient likvidnykh aktivov	ryuudoo hiritsu
precio de catálogo	katolozhnaia tsena	hyooji kakaku
moneda nacional	mestnia valiuta	kokunai tsuuka
logo	logotip	rogo
tendencia a largo plazo	dolgovremennaia tendentsia	chooki dookoo
artículo de reclamo	tovar, prodavaemyì v ubytok dlia privlecheniia pokupateleì	medama shoohin
cantidad global	paushal'naia summa	soogaku
venta por correo	torgovo-posylochnaia kompaniia	tsuushin hanbai
participación mayoritaria	vladenie kontrol'nym paketom aktsiì	kahansuu shoyuu
día-hombre	cheloveko-den'	nobe jitsu
hora-hombre	cheloveko-chas	nobe jikan
recursos humanos	rabochaia sila	jinteki shigen
carencia de personal	nekhvatka rabocheì sily	jinteki shigen fusoku
productos manufacturados	proizvedennye tovary	koogyoo seihin
industria manufacturera	proizvodstvennaia sfera	seizoo gyoo
año-hombre	cheloveko-god	ninnen
costo marginal	neznachitel'naia stoimost'	genkai genka
acuerdo de constitución de márgenes	soglashenie o pravilakh vedeniia marzhinal'nogo scheta	ri zaya kyootei
rebaja	snizhenie tseny	kakaku hiku sage
acceso a los mercados	dostup k rynku	maaketto akusesu
capitalización en el mercado	summarnaia rynochnaia stoimost' aktsiì kompanii	shijoo no shihon ka
economía de mercado	rynochnaia ekonomika	shijoo keizai
líder del mercado	vedushchiì igrok na rynke	shijoo sendoosha
precio de marcado	rynochnaia tsena	shijoo kakaku
tasa del mercado	rynochnaia stavka	shijoo kinri

ENGLISH	GERMAN	FRENCH
market research	Marktuntersuchung	étude de marché
market saturation	Marktschwemme	saturation du marché
market share	Marktanteil	part de marché
market value	Verkehrswert	valeur marchande
marketing	Marketing	mercatique
marketing mix	Marketing-Mix	marchéage
marketing strategy	Marketing-Strategie	stratégie de vente au marché
markup	Gewinnaufschlag	marge
mass consumption	Massenkonsum	consommation de masse
mass production	Massenproduktion	production en série
maturity (of an obligation)	Fälligkeit	échéance
mediation	Schlichtungsdienst	médiation
memorandum	Aktennotiz	note de service
merchant	Kaufmann	marchand
merchant marine	Handelsmarine	marine marchande
merger	Zusammenschluß	fusion d'entreprises
merit raise (in pay)	leistungsbezogene Gehaltserhöhung	augmentation au mérite
micropayment	Mikrozahlung	micropaiement
middle management	mittleres Management	cadres moyens
middleman	Zwischenhändler	intermédiaire
mission statement	Aufgaben	rapport de mission
mobile payment	mobile Bezahlung	paiement mobile
money laundering	Geldwäsche	blanchissement d'argent
money market	Geldmarkt	marché monétaire
money supply	Geldumlauf	masse monétaire
monopoly	Monopol	monopole
mortgage	Hypothek	hypothèque
mortgagee	Hypothekar	créancier hypothécaire
mortgagor	Hypothekenschuldner	débiteur hypothécaire

Spanish	Russian	Japanese
estudio de mercado	analiz rynka	shijoo choosa
saturación del mercado	perenasyshchenie rynka	shijoo hoowa
cuota de mercado	udel'nyì ves v oborote rynka	shijoo sen-yuu ritsu
valor de mercado	rynochnaia stoimost'	shijoo kachi
mercadotecnia	marketing	maaketingu
mezcla de marketing	nabor reklamnykh instrumentov	maaketingu mikkusu
estrategia de marketing	marketingovaya strategiia	maaketingu senryaku
margen de ganancia	nadbavka	neage
gran consumo	massovoe potreblenie	taishuushoohi
fabricación en serie	massovoe proizvodstvo	tairyoo seisan
vencimiento	srok pogasheniia	manki
mediación	posrednichestvo	chootei
memorándum	memorandum	memo
comerciante	torgovets	shoonin
marina mercante	rabotnik torgovogo flota	zenshoosen
fusion de empresas	sliianie	kyuushuu gappei
aumento por mérito	povyshenie zarplaty za khoroshuiu rabotu	zoogaku
micrópago	mikrooplata	bishoo shiharai
mandos intermedios	srednii upravlencheskii apparat	chookan kanri sha
intermediario	posrednik	naka gai nin
declaración de la misión	izlozhenie tselei	nin muichiran hyoo
pago móvil	podvizhnaia oplata	idooshiki shiharai
lavado de dinero	otmyvka deneg	fusei shi kin jooka
mercado monetario	denezhnyì rynok	kin-yuu shijoo
masa monetaria	denezhnaia massa v obrashchenii	kaihei kyookyuu ryoo
monopolio	monopoliia	dokusen
hipoteca	ipotechnyì kredit	teitoo
acreedor hipotecario	ipotechnyì kreditor	teitoo ken sha
deudor hipotecario	dolzhnik po ipotechnomu kreditu	teitoo ken settei sha

ENGLISH	GERMAN	FRENCH
most-favored nation	Meistbegünstigung	nation la plus favorisée
motor fleet	Fuhrpark	parc automobile
multinational corporation	multinationale Unternehmen	entreprise multinationale
mutual fund	offener Investmentfonds	fonds d'investissement
NAFTA	NAFTA	ALENA
negotiable instrument	übertragbares Handelspapier	titre négociable
negotiation	Verhandlung	négociation
negotiator	Unterhändler	négociateur
net income	Nettoeinkommen	revenue net
net present value	Zeitwert netto	valeur actualisée nette
net profit	Nettogewinn	profit net
net worth	Eigenkapital	fonds propres
network marketing	NetzMarketing	vente de réseau
nominal interest rate	nominaler Zinssatz	taux d'intérêt nominal
non-cash payment	bargeldlose Zahlung	paiement non comptant
nonprofit organization	eingetragener Verein	organisme à but non-lucratif
notary public	Notar	notaire
occupational safety and health	Arbeitsschutz	sécurité et santé au travail
office	Büro	bureau
office work	Büroarbeit	travail de bureau
offshore bank	exterritoriale Bank	banque extraterritorial
one-stop shop	One Stop Shop	guichet unique
online access	Online-Zugang	accès en ligne
online banking	Online Banking	banque online

Spanish	Russian	Japanese
nación más favorecida	naibolee blagopriiatstvuemaia v torgovle natsiia	saikei koku
parque móvil	avtomobil'nyì park	mootaa furiito
empresa multinacionale	mnogonatsional'naia korporatsiia	takokuseki kigyoo
fondo de inversión colectiva	paevoì investitsionnyì fond	myuuchuaru fando
TLCAN	Severo-Atlanticheskoe torgovoe soglashenie	kitatai seiyoo jiyuu booeki chiiki
instrumento negociable	oborotonye dokumenty	ryuutsuu shooken
negociación	peregovory	kooshoo
negociador	uchastnik peregovorov	kooshoo sha
ingreso neto	chistyì dokhod	jun shotoku
valor neto actualizado	tekushchaia stoimost' aktivov	jun genzaı kachı
beneficio neto	chistaia pribyl'	jun rieki
patrimonio neto	stoimost' aktivov kompanii	shoomi shisan
comercialización de la red	"tsepnoì" marketing, osushchestvliaemyì potrebiteliami	nettowaaku maaketingu
tasa de interés nominal	nominal'nye protsentnye stavki	hyoomen kinri
pago no efectivo	beznalichnaia oplata	higen kinbarai
institución sin ánimo de lucro (ISAL)	nekommercheskaia organizatsiia	hi eiri dantai
notario público	notarius	kooshoonin
seguridad y salud en el trabajo	tekhnika bezopasnosti na proizvodstve	shokugyoo joo no anzen tokenkoo
oficina	ofis	ofisu
trabajo de oficina	ofisnaia raborta	jimu
banco extraterritorial	offshornyì bank	ofushoa ginkoo
ventanilla única	spetsializirovannyì magazin	soko dake de kaimono ga sumu mise
acceso en línea	onlaìnovyì dostup	onrain akusesu
pagos en línea	vedenie bankovskikh del po Internetu	onrain bankingu

ENGLISH	GERMAN	FRENCH
online business	Internetgeschäfte	business en ligne
online payment	Zahlungsverkehr im Internet	paiement en ligne
on-the-job training	Ausbildung am Arbeitsstelle	formation en cours d'emploi
open economy	offene Volkswirtschaft	économie ouverte
open market	Offenmarkt	marché libre
open plan office	Großraumbüro	bureau paysager
operating costs	Betriebsausgaben	coûts de fonctionnement
operating income	Betriebseinnahmen	recettes d'exploitation
operating profit	Betriebsgewinn	bénéfice d'exploitation
opportunity cost	Opportunitätskosten	coût d'opportunité
order book	Auftragsbuch	carnet de commandes
order form	Auftragsformular	bon de commande
organization chart	Organigramm	organigramme
original equipment manufacturing	OEM—Produktion	fabrication de matériel original
outgoings	Ausgaben	sorties (de fonds)
outright purchase	Pauschalerwerb	achat direct
outsourcing	Fremdbeschaffung	sourçage
outstanding debt	ausstehende Schulden	dette non amortie
overcapacity	Überkapazität	surcapacité
overcapitalization	Überkapitalisierung	surcapitalisation
overdraft	Kontoüberziehung	découvert
overhead(s)	Gemeinkosten	frais généraux
overheating (in an economy)	konjunkturell Überhitzung	surchauffe
overindebtedness	übermäßige Verschuldung	surendettement
overpayment	Überbezahlung	trop-payé
overproduction	Überproduktion	surproduction
overstaffing	Überbesetzung	sureffectif
over-the-counter market	Freiverkehrsmarkt	marché hors côte

SPANISH	RUSSIAN	JAPANESE
comercio en línea	onlàinovyì biznes	onrain bijinesu
pago en línea	oplata po internetu	onrain peimento
capacitación práctica en el trabajo	obuchenie bez otryva ot proizvodstva	shokuba kunren
economía abierta	otkrytaia ekonomika	kaihoo keizai
mercado abierto	otkrytyì rynok	kookai shijoo
oficina sin particiones	ofis s otkrytoì planirovkoì	koukai hooshiki gaisha
costos de explotación	operatsionnye izderzhki	eigyoo hi
ingresos de explotación	operatsionnye dokhody	eigyoo shuueki
ganancia operativa	operatsionnaia pribyl'	eigyoo rieki
costo de oportunidad	izderzhki vybora investitsìi s bol'shim riskom	kikai hiyoo
libro de pedidos	kniga zakazov	chuumon choo
nota de pedido	blank zakaza	chuumon shoshiki
organigrama	strukturnaia skhema organizatsii	soshiki zu
fabricación de equipos originales	proizvodstvo komp'iuternykh komponentov	aite saki shoohyoo seihin seizoo gyoosha
gastos	raskhody	shuppi
compra directa	srochnaia pokupka	soo koonyuu kin gaku
tercerización	zakupka na storone	kumitate buhin no gaibu chootatsu
deuda viva	neoplachennyì dolg	miharai saimu
sobrecapacidad	izlishnìi potentsial	kajoo setsubi
sobrecapitalización	sverkhkapitalizatsiia	kadai shihon
descubierto	overdraft	tooza kashi koshi
gastos indirectos	nakladnye raskhody	kansetsu hi
recalentamiento	peregrev (ekonomiki)	keiki no kanetsu
sobreendeudamiento	bol'shaia zadolzhennost'	kajoo fusai
pago excesivo	pereoplata	shiharai chooka
sobreproducción	pereproizvodstvo	kajooseisan
exceso de personal	izlishek kadrov	kajoo jinin
mercado extrabursátil	vnebirzhevoì rynok	joogai shijoo

ENGLISH	GERMAN	FRENCH
ownership	Eigentum	propriété
packaging	Verpackung	conditionnement
packing slip	Lieferpapier	note de livraison
paper profit	schwebender Gewinn	bénéfices non matérialisés
paperwork	Schreibarbeit	paperasserie
par value	Parität	parité
parent company	Muttergesellschaft	organisation mère
partnership	Personengesellschaft	société en nom collectif
patent	Patent	brevet
pawn shop	Pfandhaus	mont-de-piété
pawnbroker	Pfanleiher	prêteur sur gages
payday	Zahltag	jour de paie
payment	. Zahlung	paiement
payment in kind	Sachleistung	paiement en nature
payroll (list of employees)	Gehaltsliste	ensemble du personnel
payroll (wages)	Lohnsumme	total des salaires
penny stock(s)	Billigaktie	actions cotées en cents
pension fund	Pensionsfonds	fonds d'assurance-viellesse
per capita	pro Kopf	par habitant
per diem	pro Tag	per diem
performance bond	Erfüllungsgarantie	garantie de bonne fin
performance evaluation	Leistungsbewertung	évaluation des performances
performing loan	produktives Darlehen	prêt productif
personal identification number (PIN)	persönliche Identifikationsnummer	numéro personnel d'identification
petty cash	Portokasse	petite caisse
picket	Streikposten	piquet de grève
pie chart	Kreisdiagramm	diagramme circulaire
piece rate	Stücklohn	tarif à la pièce
piecework	Akkordarbeit	travail à la pièce
PIN (personal identification number)	PIN	NIP
piracy (of intellectual property)	Raubkopie	piraterie

SPANISH	RUSSIAN	JAPANESE
propiedad	vladenie	shoyuu ken
embalaje	upakovka	hoosoo
albarán	upakovochnyì blank	hoosoo meisai sho
beneficio en el papel	bymazhnaia pribyl'	mikomi rieki
papeleo	(kantseliarskoe) oformlenie	kijoojimu
paridad	nominal'naia stoimost'	gakumen kakaku
empresa matriz	materinskaia kompaniia	oya gaisha
sociedad (colectiva)	tovarishchestvo	kyoo ryoku
patente	patent	tokkyo
casa de empeño	lombard	shichiya
prestamista	vladelets lombarda	shichiya sha
día de pago	den' zarplaty	kyuuryoo bi
pago	oplata	shiharai
pago en especie	oplata v nature	genbutsu barai
nómina de sueldos	shtat	juugyoo no soosuu
gasto en remuneraciones	shtatnoe raspisanie	shiharai daichoo
chicharro	aktsiia tsenoì men'she dollara	penii kabu
fondo de pensiones	pensionnyì fond	nenkin kikin
per cápita	na dushu (naseleniia)	hitori atari
dietas	za den'	ichinichi atari
garantía de cumplimiento	kontraktnaia garantiia	keiyaku hoshoo
evaluación del desempeño	otsenka effektivnosti	gyooseki hyooka
préstamo productivo	pribyl'nyì zaem	pafoomingu roon
número de identificación personal	personal'nyì identifikatsionnyì nomer	anshoo bangoo
caja chica	nebol'shaia nalichnost'	koguchi genkin
piquete de huelga	piket	piketto
gráfico circular	sektornaia diagramma	en gurafu
referido al trabajo a destajo	sdel'nyì tarif	tanka
trabajo a destajo	sdel'naia rabota	chin shigoto
NIP	PIN	anshoo bangoo
piratería	piratstvo	choosa kuken shuugai

ENGLISH	GERMAN	FRENCH
planned economy	Planwirtschaft	économie planifiée
plant capacity	Betriebskapazität	capacité installée
point of sale	Verkaufsstelle	point de vente
policy statement	Grundsatzerklärung	déclaration de politique générale
preferred stock	Vorzugsaktien	actions privilégiées
premium	Aufgeld	agio
premium rent	beste Miete	surloyer
prepayment	Vorauszahlung	prépaiement
press conference	Pressekonferenz	conférence de presse
price control	Preiskontrolle	contrôle des prix
price discrimination	Preisunterscheidung	différenciation des prix
price fixing	Preisabsprache	fixation du prix
price freeze	Preisstop	blocage des prix
price list	Preisliste	liste de prix
price range	Preisspanne	fourchette
price stability	Preisstabilität	stabilité des prix
price tag	Preisschild	étiquette
price war	Preiskrieg	guerre de prix
price-earnings ratio	Kurs-Gewinn-Verhältnis	ratio cours
prime property	Beste Immobilie	propriété exceptionelle
prime rate	Primarate	taux d'escompte bancaire
private company	Personengesellschaft	société privée
private investment	Privatinvestment	investissements privés
private investor	Privatinvestor	investisseur privé
private sector	Privatsektor	secteur privé
privatization	Privatisierung	privatisation
proceeds	Erlöse	produit
product development	Produktentwicklung	développement des produits
product feature	Produkteigenschaft	caractéristique produit
product launch	Neueinführung	lancement de produit

SPANISH	RUSSIAN	JAPANESE
economía planificada	planovaia ekonomika	keikaku keizai
capacidad productiva	proizvodstvennaia moshchnost' predpriiatiia	setsubin o ryoku
punto de venta	torgovaia tochka	hanbai jiten
declaración de política	izlozhenie politiki	shisei hooshin hookoku sho
acciónes preferentes	privilegirovannaia aktsiia	yuusen kabu
premio	marzha	puremiamu
alquiler excesivo	naivysshaia stavka	puremiamu rento
pago anticipado	predoplata	maebarai
conferencia de prensa	press-konferentsiia	kisha kaiken
control de precios	kontrol' tsen	kakaku toosei
discriminación de precios	diskriminatsiia tsen	kakaku sabetsu
fijación de precios	fiksirovanie tsen	kakaku soosa
congelación de precios	zamorazhivanie tsen	kakaku tooketsu
tarifa de precios	preìskurant	kakaku hyoo
gama de precios	diapazon tsen	kakaku tai
estabilidad de los precios	stabil'nost' tsen	kakaku antei
etiqueta de precio	tsennik	ne fuda
guerra de precios	voìna tsen	ne biki kyoosoo
bénéfices	relación precio-ganancia	kabuka shuueki ritsu
propiedad principal	prestizhnaia sobstvennost'	yuuryoo fudoosan
tipo de interés preferencial	stavka po kreditam dlia pervoklassnykh zaemshchikov	puraimu reito
sociedad personalista	chastnaia kompaniia	yuugen gaisha
inversiones privadas	chastnoe investirovanie	minkan tooshi
inversor privado	chastnyì investor	kojin tooshi ka
sector privado	chastnyì sektor	minkan bumon
privatización	privatizatsiia	min'ei ka
producto	postupleniia	uriage daka
desarrollo de productos	razrabotka produkta	seihin kaihatsu
caracteristica del producto	parametry produkta	seihin no tokuchoo
lanzameinto de producto	zapusk produkta	shi seihin no uri dashi

ENGLISH	GERMAN	FRENCH
product liability insurance	Produkthaftpflicht-Versicherung	assurances responsabilité produit
product life cycle	Produktlebenszyklus	cycle de vie de produit
product line	Produktlinie	ligne de produits
product placement	Produktpositionierung	mise en rayon
product range	Produktpalette	gamme de produits
product safety	Produktsicherheit	sécurité des produits
production capacity	Produktionskapazität	capacité de production
production time	Produktionszeit	temps de production
professional staff	Fachpersonal	cadre
professional worker	Geistesarbeiter	travailleur intellectuel
profit	Gewinn	bénéfice
profit center	Profit center	centre de profit
profit margin	Gewinnspanne	marge bénéficiaire
profit sharing	Gewinnbeteiligung	intéressement des salariés aux bénéfices
profitability	Rentabilität	rentabilité
progress report	Lagebericht	rapport d'avancement
project management	Projektmanagement	gestion de projets
promissory note	Schuldschein	billet à ordre
property insurance	Sachschaden-Versicherung	assurances dommages matériels
proprietary name	Markenname	appellation exclusive
public holiday	Feiertag	jour férié
public offering	öffentliches Verkaufsangebot	appel public
public relations	Öffentlichkeitsarbeit	relations publiques
public sector	öffentlicher Sektor	secteur public
public service corporation	öffentlicher Versorgungsbetrieb	service d'utilité publique

Spanish	Russian	Japanese
seguro de responsabilidad sobre el producto	strakhovanie na sluchaĭ otvetstvennosti za kachestvo produkta	seihin sekinin hoken
ciclo de vida de un producto	dlitel'nost' prebyvaniia tovara na rynke	seihin jumyoo
gama de productos	liniia tovarov	purodakuto rain
estantería	pozitsionirovanie tovara	seihin no haichi
gama de producto	assortiment tovarov	seisan haba
seguridad de un producto	bezopasnost' tovarov	seihin no anzen sei
capacidad productiva	proizvodstvennaia moshchnost'	seisan ryoku
período de producción	vremia, zatrachivaemoe na vypusk produkta	seisan jikan
personal profesional	kvalifitsirovannyĭ shtat	senmon ka shokuin
trabajador intelectual	kvalifitsirovannyĭ rabotnik	jukuren roodoo sha
ganancias	pribyl'	rieki
centro de beneficios	podrazdelenie kompanii, kotoroe poluchaet pribyl' samostoiatel'no	purofitto sentaa
margen de ganancia	marzha pribyli	rizaya
participación en las ganancias	uchastie v pribyliakh	rijun bunpai
rentabilidad	pribyl'nost'	shuueki sei
informe de avance	otchet o khode vypolneniia rabot	keika hookoku sho
gerencia de proyectos	rukovodstvo proekta	keikaku kanri
pagaré	prostoĭ veksel'	yakusoku tegata
seguros de daños materiales	strakhovanie sobstvennosti	songai hoken
nombre registrado	firmennoe naimenovanie	tokkyo shoohin mei
día de fiesta	prazdnichnyĭ den'	kookyuu bi
oferta pública de venta (OPV)	vypusk novykh aktsiĭ dlia prodazhi shirokoĭ publike	kooboo
relaciones públicas	sviazi s obshchestvennost'iu	pii aaru
sector público	gosudarstvennyĭ sektor	kookyoo bumon
empresa de servicios públicos	kompaniia po obshchestvennomu obsluzhivaniiu	kookyoo kigyoo tai

ENGLISH	GERMAN	FRENCH
purchase contract	Kaufvertrag	contrat d´acquisition
put option	Verkaufsoption	option de vente
quality control	Qualitätskontrolle	contrôles de qualité
quota (in trade)	Kontingent	quota
racketeering	Schwindel	racket
real estate agency	Immobilienbüro	agence immobilière
real estate investment	Immobilieninvestitionen	investissements immobiliers
recession	Rezession	récession
reconciliation (of accounts)	Kontenabstimmung	concordance
redemption (of securities)	Ablösung	remboursement
redevelopment	Sanierung	réaménagement
refinancing	Refinanzierung	refinancement
registered share	Namenaktie	action nominative
reinsurance	Rückversicherung	réassurance
remuneration	Bezahlung	rémunération
rental income	Mieteinkommen	revenu locatif
rental value	Mietwert	valeur locative
rent-free period	mietfreie Zeit	franchise de loyer
repayment schedule	Tilgungsplan	calendrier d'échéances
replacement cost	Wiederbeschaffungskosten	coût de remplacement
repo market (in securities)	Repo-Markt	marché des prises en pension
repossession	Wiederbeschaffung	reprise de possession
repurchase agreement	Rückkaufsvereinbarung	prise en pension
request for proposal (RFP)	Ausschreibung	demande de propositions
research and development (R&D)	Forschung und Entwicklung	recherche-développement
reseller	Wiederverkäufer	revendeur

SPANISH	RUSSIAN	JAPANESE
contrato de compra	dogovor na pokupku	shi'ire keiyaku
opción de venta	pravo prodazhi aktsii v techenie opredelennogo vremeni	uri opushon
control de calidad	kontrol' kachestva	hinshitsu kanri
cuota	kvota	wariate gaku
bandolerismo	reket	yusuri
agencia inmobiliaria	rielterskoe agentstvo	fudoosan gyoosha
inversiones inmobiliarias	investirovanie v nedvizhimost'	fudoosan tooshi
recesión	spad	keiki kootai
conciliación	privedenie klientom ucheta svoikh operatsïî v sootvetstvie s uchetom banka	wakai
amortización	pogashenie	shookan
reorganización	reorganizatsiia	sai kaihatsu
refinanciación	perefinansirovanie	rifainansu
acción nominativa	zaregistrirovannaia (imennaia) aktsiay	kimei kabu
reaseguro	perestrakhovanie	sai hoken
remuneración	voznagrazhdenie	hooshuu
ingresos por alquiler	dokhod s arendnoï platy	chintai ryoo shotoku
valor en alquiler	stoimost' arendy	chintai kachi
período de carencia	period svobodnyì ot uplaty arendy	shiyoo ryoo tada de no kikan
calendario de vencimientos	raspisanie vyplat	hensai yotei
costo de reposición	stoimist' zameshcheniia (vykupa)	shinpin torikae hi
mercado de repos	rynok REPO	kaishuu shijoo
recuperación	vosstanovlenie vo vladenii	saisho yuu
pacto de recompra	obratnaia sdelka	kai modo shi yakudoo
solicitud de propuestas	vystavlenie na tender	tei'an no irai
investigación y desarrollo	nauchno-issledovatel'skie i opytno-konstruktorskie raboty	kenkyuu kaihatsu
reuendedor	perekupshchik	tenbai sha

ENGLISH	GERMAN	FRENCH
reserve price (at auction)	Mindestgebot	prix minimum
restraint of trade	Handelsbeschränkung	entrave au commerce
retail	Einzelhandel	vente au détail
retail price index	Einzelhandelspreisindex	indice des prix de détail
retailer	Einzelhändler	detaillent
retirement plan	betriebliche Pensionskasse	plan de retraite
return (on investment)	Rendite	rendement
revaluation	Neubewertung	réévaluation
reverse mortgage	Hypothek mit Leibrente	prêt hypothécaire inversé
reverse repo	Rückkaufgeschäft	contrat de report inversé
revolving credit	Revolvingkredit	crédit permanent
right of first refusal	Vorkaufsrecht	droit de premier refus
rights issue	Bezugsrechtsemission	émission de droits de souscription
risk management	Risikosteuerung	gestion des risques
rounding error	Rundungsfehler	erreur d'arrondi
rounding-down	Abrundung	arrondi vers le bas
royalty (payment)	Lizenzgebühr	redevances
salary	Gehalt	salaire
salary scale	Gehaltsskala	barème des salaires
sale price (amount paid)	Sonderangebotspreis	prix de vente
sale price (reduced)	Ausverkaufspreis	prix de liquidation
sales	Umsatz	ventes
sales clerk	Verkäufer	vendeur
sales force	Außendienst	force de vente
sales office	Handelsniederlassung	bureau des ventes
sales promotion	Verkaufsförderung	promotion des ventes
sales tax	Umsatzsteuer	tax à l'achat
sales volume	Absatzmenge	volume des ventes
saturated market	gesättigter Markt	marché saturé

Spanish	Russian	Japanese
precio mínimo	rezervirovannaia tsena	saitei kyoobai kakaku
limitación al libre comercio	ogranicheniia na torgovliu	torihiki seigen
comercio al por menor	roznichnaia torgovlia	kouri
índice de precios minoristas	indeks potrebitel'skikh tsen	kouri bukka shisuu
detallista	roznichnyì torgovets	kouri gyoosha
plan de pensiones	pensionnyì plan	taishoku kinseido
ganancia	dokhod	rimawari
revaluación	pereotsenka	sai hyooka
hipoteca inversa con renta vitalicia	obratnaia ipoteka	gyaku teitoo
operación de dobles	obratnyì REPO	gyaku kaimodoshi
crédito rotatorio	avtomaticheski vozobnovliaemyì kredit	kaiten shin-yoo
primera opción (de compra)	preimushchestvennoe pravo na pokupku	koonyuu ken
emisión de derechos preferentes	vypusk obyknovennykh aktsiì dlia prodazhi sushchestvuiushchim aktsioneram	shasai hakkoo ken
gestión de riesgos	upravlenie riskom	risuku maneejimento
error de redondeo	oshibka okrugleniia	keisan gosa
redondeo hacia abajo	okruglenie v men'shuiu storonu	kirisage
regalías	gonorar	inzei
sueldo	oklad	kyuuryoo
escala de sueldos	shkala okladov	kyuuryoo shisuu
precio de oferta	prodazhnaia tsena	hanbai kakaku
precio de saldo	tsena na rasprodazhe	waribiki hanbai kakaku
ventas	prodazhi (sbyt)	hanbai
vendedor	prodavets	tenin
servicio externo	sbytchiki	hanbai in
delegación comercial	otdel sbyta	eigyoo sho
promoción de venta	reklama prodazhi	hanbai sokushin
impuesto sobre las ventas	nalog na prodazhi	buppin zei
volumen de ventas	ob'em prodazh	uriage daka
mercado saturado	perenasyshchennyì rynok	hoowa shijoo

ENGLISH	GERMAN	FRENCH
savings	Ersparnis	épargne
savings account	Sparkonto	compte d'épargne
savings bank	Sparkasse	caisse d'épargne
savings bond	Sparbond	bon de caisse
scab (in labor disputes)	Streikbrecher	jaune
seasonal labor	Saisonarbeiterschaft	travailleurs saisonniers
second mortgage	zweitrangige Hypothek	deuxième hypothèque
secondary market (in securities)	Sekundärmarkt	marché secondaire
sector	Sektor	secteur
securities	Wertpapiere	valeurs boursières
self-financing	Eigenfinanzierung	autofinancement
seller	Verkäufer	vendeur
seller's market	Verkäufermarkt	marché à la hausse
selling point	Verkaufsargument	argument de vente
selling price	Verkaufspreis	prix de vente
semipublic enterprise	halbstaatliches Unternehmen	entreprise semi-publique
semiskilled labor	angelernte Arbeiterschaft	ouvrier spécialisé
senior debt	vorrangige Schulden	créance de premier rang
service charge (banks)	Bearbeitungsgebühr	gestion de compte
service charge (other institutions)	Nebenkosten	charges particulières
service economy	Dienstleistungswirtschaft	économie de services
service industry	Dienstleistungsbetrieb	secteur tertiaire
service(s) contract	Dienstleistungsvertrag	contrat de louage de services
services for businesses	unternehmensbezogene Dienstleistungen	services d'entreprises
settlement currency	Verrechnungswährung	monnaie de règlement
settlement of accounts	Abrechnung der Konten	règlement des comptes
severance pay	Abfindung	indemnité de licenciement
sexual harassment	sexuelle Belästigung	harcèlement sexuel
share capital	Aktienkapital	capital-actions

Spanish	Russian	Japanese
ahorro	sberezheniia	chochiku
cuenta de ahorro	sberegatel'nyì schet	yokin kooza
caja de ahorros	sberegatel'nyì bank	chochiku ginkoo
bono de ahorro	sberegatel'naia obligatsiia	chochiku saiken
esquirol	shtreìkbrekher	suto yaburi
trabajadores de temporada	sezonnyì trud	kisetsu roodoosha
segunda hipoteca	vtoraia ipoteka	niban teitoo
mercado secundario	vtorichnyì rynok	ryuutsuu shijoo
sector	sektor	sekutaa
valores bursatiles	tsennye bumagi	yuuka shooken
autofinanciamiento	samofinansirovanie	jiko kinyuu
vendedor	prodavets	urite
mercado favorable a los vendedores	rynok prodavtsa	urite shijoo
argumento de venta	naibolee privlekatel'nyì aspekt tovara	seringu pointo
precio de venta	realizatsionnaia tsena	hanbai kakaku
empresa mixta	polu-gosudarstvennoe predpriiatie	hankookyoo kigyoo
trabajador semicalificado	nizkokvalifitsirovannyì trud	hanjukuren roodoo
crédito de rango superior	"starshiì" dolg	yuusen saiken
comisión de giro	bankovskaia komissiia	tesuuryoo
servicio	komissiia za uslugi	tesuuryoo
economía de servicios	ekonomika, orientirovannaia na servis	saabisu keizai
sector servicios	industriia servisa	saabisu sangyoo
contrato de servicios	kontrakt na obsluzhivanie	yakumu keiyaku
servicios para negocios	obsluzhivanie biznesa	bijinesu no tame no saabisu
moneda de pago	raschetnaia valiuta	kessan tsuuka
liquidación de cuentas	pogashenie schetov	seisan kanjoo
indemnización por cese	vyplata pri uvol'nenii	taishoku kin
hostigamiento sexual	seksual'noe presledovanie	sekusharu harasumento
capital accionario	aktsionernyì kapital	kabishiki shihon

ENGLISH	GERMAN	FRENCH
shelf life	Haltbarkeitsdauer	durée de conservation
shell company	Firmenmantel	coquille vide
shift differential	Schichtzuschlag	rémunération supplémentaire
shipment	Verschiffung	expédition
shortfall	Fehlmenge	manque
short-term interest rate	kurzfristiger Zinssatz	taux d'intérêt à court terme
showroom	Ausstellungsraum	salle d'exposition
sick pay	Krankengeld	prestations maladies
signature loan	Personalkredit	prêt personnel
silent partner	stiller Gesellschafter	commanditaire
single currency	einheitliche Währung	monnaie unique
Single Market (in the EU)	Binnenmarkt	Marché unique
sinking fund	Tilgungsfonds	fonds d'amortissement
sitdown strike	Sitzstreik	grève sur le tas
site (of a property)	Grundstück	terrain
site plan	Grundstücksplan	plan de masse
skilled labor	gelernte Arbeiter	main-d'oeuvre qualifiée
social cost	Sozialkosten	coût social
social security	Sozialversicherung	sécurité sociale
soft currency	weiche Währung	monnaie faible
solvency	Solvenz	solvabilité
split shift	Teilschicht	poste fractionné
spot market (commodities)	Kassamarkt	marché au comptant
spot price (commodities)	Kassapreis	cours du disponible
spot price (foreign exchange)	Kassakurs	cours du comptant
spreadsheet	Arbeitsblatt	tableur
staff development	Personalentwicklung	valorisation du personnel
stagflation	Stagflation	stagflation

SPANISH	RUSSIAN	JAPANESE
caducidad	srok godnosti	chozoo jumyoo
empresa fantasma	zaregistrirovannaia kompaniia, ne imeiushchaia bol'shikh aktivov	peepaa kanpanii
compensación por trabajo en turnos	tarif za smennuiu rabotu	shifuto jikan ni yoru chigai
embarque	otgruzka	shukka
deficiencia	defitsit	fusoku
tasa de interés a corto plazo	kratkosrochnaia protsentnaia stavka	tanki kinri
salón de demostraciones	ekspozitsionnyĭ zal	shooruumu
subsidios de enfermedad	bol'nichnye	byooki teate
préstamo sin garantía real	personal'nyĭ kredit	shinyoo gashi
socio comanditario	passivnyĭ chlen tovarıshchestva	tokumei shain
moneda única	edinaia valiuta	tanitsu tsuuka
Mercado único	Obshchiĭ Rynok	tanitsu shijoo
fondo de amortización	fond pogasheniia	gensai kikin
sentada	sidiachaia zabastovka	suwarikomi suto
terreno	mestopolozhenie	shikichi
plano del terreno	situatsionnyĭ plan	shikichi keikaku
mano de obra calificada	kvalifitsirovannaia rabochaia sila	jukuren roodoosha
costo social	sotsial'nye izderzhki	shakai hiyoo
seguridad social	sotsial'nay zashchita	shakai hoshoo
moneda débil	slabaia valiuta	nan ka
solvencia	platezhesposobnost'	shiharai nooryoku
jornada partida	razdelennaia smena	bunkatsu kinmu
mercado de entrega inmediata	nalichnyĭ rynok	genkin torihiki shijoo
precio de entrega inmediata	nalichnaia tsena	genbutsu kakaku
tipo al contado	nalichnyĭ kurs	supotto puraisu
hoja de cálculo	svodnaia vedomost'	supureddo shiito
perfeccionamiento del personal	povyshenie kvalifikatsii sluzhashchikh	shain kaihatsu
estanflación	stagfliatsiia	sutagufureeshon

ENGLISH	GERMAN	FRENCH
stamp duty	Stempelsteuer	droit de timbre
standing order (for goods)	Abonnement	commande permanente
start-up capital	Gründungskapital	capital initial
start-up cost	Anlaufkosten	frais d'établissement
statement of account	Rechnungsabschluss	relevé de compte
state-owned enterprise	staatliches Unternehmen	enterprise étatique
statutory power	gesetzliche Befugnis	pouvoir statutaire
stock certificate	Besitzurkunde	certificat d'actions
stock company	Aktiensgesellschaft	société anonyme
stock corporation	Aktiengesellschaften	sociétés anonymes par actions
stock dividend	Stockdividende	dividende actions
stock exchange	Börse	bourse
stock market	Aktienmarkt	marché des valeurs
stock market index	Aktienmarktindex	indice de marché boursier
stock option plan	Aktienbezugsrecht	plan d'option sur titres
storefront	Schaufensterfront	devanture
strike (labor)	streik	grève
strike pay	Streikgeld	indemnité de grève
strikebreaker	Streikbrecher	briseur de grève
structural unemployment	strukturelle Arbeitslosigkeit	chômage structurel
subcontracting	Zulieferaufträge	sous-traitance
sublease	Untermietvertrag	sous-location
subletter	Untermieter	sous-locataire
subletting	Untervermietung	sous-location
subordinated debt	nachgeordnete Verbindlichkeit	créances subordonnées
subsidiary	Tochtergesellschaft	filiale

Spanish	Russian	Japanese
impuesto de timbre	gerbovyì sbor	inshi zei
orden de pedido permanente	postoiannoe poruchenie	joorei chuumon
capital generador	startovyì kapital	shinki shihon
costos de puesta en marcha	stoimost' pervonachal'nogo vlozheniia	shinjigyoo kaisetsu hi
estado de cuenta	vypiska s bankovskogo scheta	kanjoo sho
empresa estatal	gosudarstvennoe predpriiatie	kokuyuu kigyoo
poder legal	pravomochie po zakonu	hooteki chikara
póliza de compra	sertifikat deponirovniia aktsiì	kabu ken
sociedad anónima		kabu shiki gaisha
sociedades anónimas	aktsionernaia kompaniia	kabu shiki gaisha
dividendo en acciones	vyplata dividenda tsennymi bumagami	kabu ken haitoo
bolsa de valores	fondovaia birzha	shooken torihiki jo
mercado de valores	fondovyì rynok	kabu shiki shijoo
índice de bolsa de valores	indeks fondovogo rynka	kabu shiki shijoo shisuu
plan de opción de compra de acciones	plan fondovogo optsiona	jisha kabu koonyuu ken keikaku
fachada	magazinnaia vitrina	tentoo
"huelga, paro"	zabastovka	sutoraiki
subsidio de paro	posobie zabastovshchikam	sutorai kiteate
rompehuelgas	shtreìkbrekher	suto yaburi
desempleo estructural	bezrabotitsa v rezul'tate strukturnykh izmeneniì v ekonomike	koozoo teki shitsugyoo
subcontratación	podriad	shitauke
subarrendamiento	subarenda	matagashi
subarrendatario	subarendator	matagashi suru hito
subalquiler	subarenda	matagashi
deuda subordinada	subordinirovannyì dolg	retsui bensai saimu
filial	docherniaia kompaniia	ko gaisha

ENGLISH	GERMAN	FRENCH
subsidy	filial	subvention
successful bidder	erfolgreicher Bieter	adjudicataire
summary statement (of accounts)	zusammengefaßte Übersicht	état récapitulatif
sunrise industry	Zukunftindustrie	industrie en expansion
superannuation fund	Rentenfonds	caisse de retraite
supplier	Lieferant	fournisseur
supply (economics)	Angebot	approvisionnement
support price	Stützungspreis	prix de soutien
surplus (accounting)	Aktivsaldo	excédent
surplus (economics)	Überschuss	surplus
suspense account	Zwischenkonto	compte d'attente
swap (currency)	Swap	échange
swap market	Markt für Swapgeschäfte	marché des échanges financiers
sweatshop	Ausbeutungsbetrieb	atelier de misère
syndicated loan	syndizierte Anleihe	crédit syndiqué
takeover	Übernahme	prise de contrôle
takeover bid	Tender-Offerte	offre publique d'achat
tangible assets	materielle Vermögenswerte	avoirs corporels
tariff	Zoll	tarif douanier
tariff barrier	Zollschranke	barrière tarifaire
tax avoidance	Steuervermeidung	évasion fiscale
tax bracket	Steuerstufe	tranche d'imposition
tax break	Steuererleichterung	allégement fiscal
tax burden	Steuerbelastung	charge fiscale
tax credit	Steuerfreibetrag	crédit d'impôt
tax evasion	Steuerhinterziehung	fraude fiscale
tax haven	Steueroase	paradis fiscal
tax incentive	Steueranreiz	incitation fiscale
tax loophole	Steuerschlupfloch	échappatoire fiscale
tax revenues	Steueraufkommen	rentrées fiscales
tax shelter	Steuerbegünstigung	refuge fiscal
tax write-off	Steuerabschreibung	déduction fiscale

SPANISH	RUSSIAN	JAPANESE
subvención	subsidiia	hojo kin
adjudicatario	uspeshnyì uchastnik torga	raku satsu sha
estado resumido	summarnaia vypiska s bankovskogo scheta	gaiyoo hookokusho
industria del porvenir	novaia otrasl' ekonomiki	shinkoo sangyoo
fondo de pensiones	pensionnyì fond	taishoku sha nenkin kikin
proveedor	postavshchik	kyookyuu sha
oferta	predlozhenie	kyookyuu
precio sostén	interventsionnaia tsena	shiji kakaku
superávit	aktivnoe sal'do	choo kagaku
excedente	izbytok	fuka shihon
cuenta de suspensión	promezhutochnyì schet	kari kanjoo
permuta financiera	svop	suwappu
mercado de swaps	obmennyì rynok	suwappu shijoo
fábrica donde se explota al obrero	potogonnoe predpriiatie	sakushu koojoo
crédito de consórcio	konsortsial'nyì kredit	shinjikeeto roon
adquisición	pogloshchenie	nottori
oferta pública de adquisición de acciones	popytka pogloshcheniia	kabushiki kookai kaitsuke
activos tangibles	real'nye aktivy	yuukei shisan
arancel aduanero	tarif	kanzei
barrera arancelaria	tarifnyì bar'er	kanzei shooheki
evasión de impuestos	izbezhanie nalogov	datsu zei
banda impositiva	mesto v nalogovoì shkale	zei ritsu tookyuu
reducción impositiva	nalogovaia l'gota	zei seijoo no yuuguu sochi
carga impositiva	nalogovoe bremia	sozei futan
descuento impositivo	nalogovyì kredit	zeigaku koojo
evasión ilegal de impuestos	uklonenie ot nalogov	datsu zei
paraíso fiscal	nalogovoe ubezhishche	zeikin toohichi
incentivo fiscal	nalogovoe stimulirovanie	sozei yuuhin
escapatoria fiscal	nalogovaia lazeìka	sozei no nuke ana
ingresos fiscales	dokhod s nalogov	zei shuu
refugio tributario	nalogovaia zashchita	zeikin hinan chi
deducción fiscal	spisanie nalogov	zeikin hikisage

ENGLISH	GERMAN	FRENCH
taxable income	steuerpflichtiges Einkommen	revenu imposable
taxation	Besteuerung	taxation
technology transfer	Technologietransfer	transfert de technologie
telecommuting	Telearbeit	télétravail
telemarketing	Telemarketing	télémarketing
tenant	Mieter	locataire
tender	Ausschreibung	soumission
terms and conditions	Bedingungen	modalités
tick size (minimum price fluctuation)	Tickgröße	échelon de cotation
time deposit	Termineinlage	dépôt à terme
time management	Zeitmanagement	gestion du temps
trade agreement	Handelsabkommen	accord commercial
trade association	Handelsverband	association commerciale
trade discount	Handelsrabatt	remise professionnelle
trade embargo	Handelsembargo	embargo commercial
trade gap	Handelslücke	déficit commercial
trade liberalizataion	Handelsliberalisierung	libéralisation des échanges
trade policy	Handelspolitik	politique du commerce
trade relations	Wirtschaftsbeziehungen	relations économiques
trade sanctions	Handelssanktionen	sanctions commerciales
trade secret	Geschäftsgeheimnis	secret de fabrication
trade show	Messe	salon
trade surplus	Handelsüberschuss	excédent commercial
trade war	Handelskrieg	guerre commerciale
trademark	Warenzeichen	marque déposée
trading partner	Handelspartner	partenaire commercial
trading volume	Handelsvolumen	volume de transactions
transaction	Transaktion	transaction
transfer payment	Transferzahlung	paiement de transfert
transportation services	Transportdienstleistungen	services de transport
treasury bill	Schatzwechsel	bon du Trésor

SPANISH	RUSSIAN	JAPANESE
renta imponible	dokhod, podlezhashchiĭ nalogooblozheniiu	kazei shotoku
impuestos	nalogooblozhenie	kazei
transferencia de tecnología	peredacha tekhnologii	gijutsu te ni
teletrabajo	rabota na domu cherez komp'iuternuiu sviaz'	terecomyuutingu
telemarketing	telemarketing	teremaaketingu
inquilino	(kvartiro)s'emshchik	tenanto
oferta	tender	nyuusatsu
términos y condiciones	postanovleniia i usloviia	sho jooken
escala de magnitudes de variación mínima	minimal'no dopustimoe izmenenie tseny	saishoo kakaku hendoo
depósito a plazo fijo	srochnyĭ depozit	teiki yokin
administración del tiempo	ratsional'noe ispol'zovanie vremeni	taimu maneejimento
convenio comercial	torgovyĭ dogovor	booeki kyootei
asociacion comercial	torgovaia assotsiatsiia	jigyoo sha dantai
descuento comercial	torgovaia skidka	torihiki waribiki
embargo comercial	torgovoe embargo	torihiki seigen
déficit comercial	torgovyĭ defitsit	booeki kesson
liberalización del comercio	liberalizatsiia torgovli	booeki jiyuuka
política comercial	torgovaia politika	booeki seisaku
relaciones económicas	torgovye otnosheniia	torihiki kankei
sanciones comerciales	torgovye sanktsii	booeki seisan
secreto comercial	kommercheskiĭ sekret	eigyoo himitsu
feria comercial	torgovaia iarmarka	tenji
superávit comercial	aktivnoe sal'do	booeki shuushi no kuroji
guerra comercial	torgovaia voĭna	booeki sensoo
marca comercial	torgovaia marka	tooroku shoohyoo
socio comercial	torgovyĭ partner	booeki aite koku
volumen de contratación	ob'em torgovli	deki daka
transacción	operatsiia	torihiki
pago de transferencia	perevodnyĭ platezh	iten shishutsu
servicios de transporte	transportnye uslugi	yusoo saabisu
letra del Tesoro	kaznacheĭskiĭ veksel'	ookurashoo shooken

ENGLISH	GERMAN	FRENCH
treasury bond	Schatzobligation	obligation du Trésor
trend analysis	Trendanalyse	analyse de la tendance
trigger price	Mindestpreis	prix d'intervention
turnover	Umsatz	chiffre d'affaires
uncommitted resources	frei verfügbare Mittel	ressources non-engagées
underemployment	Unterbeschäftigung	sous-emploi
underground economy	Schattenwirtschaft	économie souterraine
underinvestment	unzureichende Investitionen	sous-investissement
underwriters (of a security issue)	Emissionskonsortium	syndicat de placement
unemployment	Arbeitslosigkeit	chômage
unemployment compensation	Arbeitslosenunterstützung	indemnisation du chômage
unemployment insurance	Arbeitslosenversicherung	assurance chômage
unfair competition	unlauterer Wettbewerb	concurrence déloiale
unfair labor practices	unlautere Arbeitspraktiken	pratiques déloiales en matière de travail
unincorporated business	Einzelunternehmen	entreprise individuelle
unique selling point (USP)	Alleinstellungsmerkmal	choix et valorisation d'un argument publicataire
unit labor cost	Lohnstückkosten	coût unitaire du travail
unit price	Stückpreis	prix unitaire
unsecured loan	ungesichertes Darlehen	prêt non-gagé
upset price (see reserve price)		
upstream industry	Zulieferindustrie	industrie d'amont
usance	Wechselfrist	usance
usury	Wucher	usure
valuation basis	Bewertungsgrundlage	base d'évaluation
value analysis	Wertanalyse	analyse des valeurs
value at risk	Risikoposition	valeur à risque
value-added tax (VAT)	Mehrwertsteuer	taxe à la valeur ajoutée

Spanish	Russian	Japanese
bono del Tesoro	kaznacheìskaia obligatsiia	ookurashoo saiken
análisis de tendencia	analiz tendentsii	jikei retsu bunseki
precio de intervención	trigger-tsena	torigaa kakaku
facturación	oborot	deki daka
recursos no comprometidos	svobodnye resursy	chuuritsu shisan
subempleo	nepolnaia zaniatost'	kashoo koyoo
economía subterránea	tenevaia ekonmika	chika keizai
subinversión	nedoinivestirovanie	kashoo tooshi
sindicato de emisión	garant razmeshcheniia tsennykh bumag	hoken gyoosha
desempleo	bezrabotitsa	shitsugyoo
indemnización de desempleo	posobie po bezrabotitse	shitsugyoo teate
seguro de desempleo	strakhovanie na sluchai bezrabotitsy	shitsugyoo hoken
competencia desleal	nechestnaia konkurentsiia	fusei kyoosoo
prácticas laborales indebidas	nechestnyì rezhim truda	futoo roodoo kooi
empresa no constituida en sociedad	individual'noe predpriiatie	hi hoojin kigyoo
argumento de venta único (AVU)	unikal'naia kharakteristika tovara	yuniiku seirusu pointo
costo unitario del trabajo	stoimost' rabocheì sily na edinitsu produktsii	tan-i roodoo kosuto
precio unitario	stoimost' edinitsy produktsii	tanka
préstamo no garantizado	neobespechennyì zaem	shin-yoo gashi
		kyoobai kaishi nedan
industria abastecedora	bazovaia industriia	jooshoo sangyoo
usanza	srok perevodnogo vekselia	tegata kigen
usura valoración	Bewertung	koori kashi
base de valoración	osnova otsenki stoimosti	hyooka kijun
análisis del valor	analiz tsennosti	kachi bunseki
valor en riesgo	stoimost' riska	kiken ni sara sareta kachi
impuesto al valor agregado	Nalog na dobavlennuiu stoimost'	fuka kachi zei

ENGLISH	GERMAN	FRENCH
variation margin	Nachschuß	marge de variation
VAT (value-added tax)	MWS	TVA
vending machine	Verkaufsautomat	machine distributrice
venture capital	Risikokapital	capital-risque
vertical integration	vertikale Integration	intégration verticale
videoconference	Videokonferenz	vidéoconférence
wage agreement	Lohnabkommen	convention collective
wage earner	Lohnempfänger	travailleur salarié
wage freeze	Lohnstopp	gel salarial
wage settlement	Tarifvertrag	convention collective
wage-price spiral	Lohn-Preis-Spirale	course des salaires et des prix
waste management	Abfallmanagement	gestion des déchets
waybill	Konossement	lettre de voiture
wellhead price	Bohrturm-Preis	prix en tête de puits
wholesale price	Selbstkostenpreis	prix de revient
wholesale price index	Großhandelspreisindex	indice des prix de gros
wholesaler	Großhändler	grossiste
wholly owned subsidiary	hundertprozentige Tochtergesellschaft	filiale en propriété exclusive
wildcat strike	wilder Streik	grève sauvage
windfall profit	unerwartete Gewinne	gain fortuit
wire transfer	telegrafische Überweisung	virement télégraphique
withholding tax	Quellensteuer	précompte
work permit	Arbeitserlaubnis	permis de travail
working capital	Betriebskapital	fonds de roulement
working conditions	Arbeitsbedingungen	conditions de travail
workplace	Arbeitsplatz	lieu de travail
World Bank	Weltbank	Banque mondiale
world market price	Weltmarktpreis	cours mondial

SPANISH	RUSSIAN	JAPANESE
margen de variación	variatsionnaia marzha	hendoo maajin
IVA	NDS	fuka kachi zei
máquina de ventas		jidoo han baiki
capital de riesgo	riskovyĭ kapital	tooki shihon
concentración vertical	vertikal'naia integratsiia	suichoku toogoo
videoconferencias	telekonferentsiia	terebi kaigi
convenio colectivo	dogovor o zarplate	chingin kyootei
asalariado	poluchaiushchiĭ zarplatu	chingin seikatsu sha
congelación salarial	zamorazhivanie zarplaty	chingin tooketsu
convenio colectivo	ustanovka razmera zarplaty	chingin kettei
espiral salarios-precios	spiral' sootnosheniia zarplat i tsen	chingin bukka no aku junkan
gestión de residuos	utulizatsiia otkhodov	gomi shori
orden de embarque	putevoĭ list	kamotsu hiki kaeshoo
precio en la cabeza de pozo	tsena v moment dobychi	kookoo kakaku
precio de costo	optovaia tsena	oroshiuri kakaku
índice de precios al por mayor	indeks optovykh tsen	oroshiuri bukka shisuu
mayorista	optovik	oroshiuri gyoosha
filial de propiedad exclusiva	docherniaia kompaniia, nakhodiashchaiiasia v individual'nom vladenii	kanzen shoyuu ko gaisha
huelga salvaje	stikhiĭnaia zabastovka	yamaneko suto
ganancias inesperadas	nepredvidennaia krupnaia pribyl'	guuhatsu rieki
giro telegráfico	elektronnaia sviaz' dlia soversheniia platezheĭ	denshin gawase
impuesto retenido en la fuente	nalog putem vychetov	gensen choosuu
permiso de trabajo	razreshenie na rabotu	roodoo kyo kashoo
capital de explotación	oborotnyĭ kapital	unten shikin
condiciones laborales	usloviia truda	roodoo jooken
lugar de trabajo	rabochee mesto	roodoo basho
Banco Mundial	Mirovoĭ bank	sekai ginkoo
precio mundial	tsena na mirovom rynke	kokusai shijoo kakaku

English	German	French
World Trade Organization (WTO)	Welthandelsorganisation	Organisation mondiale du commerce
worst-case scenario	Szenario bei ungünstigster Entwicklung	scénario pessimiste
WTO (World Trade Organization)	WTO	OMC
yield to maturity	Ertrag bis Fälligkeit	rendement à l'échéance
zero-coupon bond	Nullkuponanleihe	obligation sans coupon
zero growth	Nullwachstum	croissance nulle
zero-base budget	Null-Basis-Budget	budget base-zéro

Spanish	Russian	Japanese
Organización Mundial del Comercio	Mezhdunarodnaia organizatsiia torgovli	sekai booeki kikan
escenario pesimista	naimenee blagopriiatnoe razvitie sobytiĭ	sai aku no ba'ai
OMC		sekai booeki kikan
rendimiento al vencimiento	dokhod pri pogashenii	saishuu rimawari
bono cero-cupón	obligatsiia s nulevymi kuponami	rifuda tsuki saiken
crecimiento nulo	nulevoĭ rost	zero seichoo
presupuesto cero-base	biudzhet s nulevoĭ bazoĭ	zero beisu yosan

Glossary of Business and Finance Terms

ab•so•lute ad•van•tage ▸ n. the ability of an individual or group to carry out a particular economic activity more efficiently than another individual or group.

ab•sorp•tion cost•ing ▸ n. [mass noun] a method of calculating the cost of a product or enterprise by taking into account indirect expenses (overheads) as well as direct costs.

ac•cept ▸ v. agree to meet (a draft or bill of exchange) by signing it.

ac•cept•ance ▸ n. agreement to meet a draft or bill of exchange, effected by signing it.
■ a draft or bill so accepted.

ac•cep•tor ▸ n. a person or bank that accepts a draft or bill of exchange.

ac•count ▸ n. (abbr.: **acct.**) a record or statement of financial expenditure or receipts relating to a particular period or purpose. ■ an arrangement by which a body holds funds on behalf of a client or supplies goods or services to the client on credit: *a bank account | I began buying things on account.*
■ the balance of funds held under such an arrangement. ■ a client having such an arrangement with a supplier. ■ a contract to do work periodically for a client.

ac•count•ant (abbr.: **acct.**) ▸ n. a person whose job is to keep or inspect financial accounts.

ac•count ex•ec•u•tive ▸ n. a business executive who manages the interests of a particular client, typically in advertising.

ac•count•ing ▸ n. the action or process of keeping financial accounts.

ac•counts pay•a•ble ▸ plural n. money owed by a company to its creditors.

ac•counts re•ceiv•a•ble ▸ plural n. money owed to a company by its debtors.

ac•crue ▸ v. (**accrues, accrued, accruing**) (of sums of money or benefits) be received by someone in regular or increasing amounts over time.
■ accumulate or receive (such payments or benefits). ■ make provision for (a charge) at the end of a financial period for work that has been done but not yet invoiced.

ac•cu•mu•la•tion ▸ n. the growth of a sum of money by the regular addition of interest.

ac•quire ▸ v. buy or obtain (an asset or object) for oneself.

ac•qui•si•tion ▸ n. an act of purchase of one company by another.
■ buying or obtaining an asset or object.

ac•qui•si•tion ac•count•ing ▸ n. a procedure in accounting in which the value of the assets of a company is changed from book to fair market level, after a takeover.

ac•tu•ar•y ▸ n. (pl. **-ies**) a person who compiles and analyzes statistics and uses them to calculate insurance risks and premiums.

ADR ▸ abbr. American depositary receipt.

ad va•lo•rem ▸ adv. & adj. (of the levying of tax or customs duties) in proportion to the estimated value of the goods or transaction concerned.

ad•vice ▸ n. a formal notice of a financial transaction: *remittance advices.*

af•fin•i•ty card ▸ n. a credit card carrying the name of an organization to which a portion of the money spent using the card is paid.

af•ter•mar•ket ▸ n. the market for shares and bonds after their original issue.

a•gainst ▸ prep. in relation to (an amount of money owed or due) so as to reduce or cancel it.

A•mer•i•can de•pos•i•tar•y re•ceipt (also **American depositary share**) ▸ n. (in the US) a negotiable certificate of title to a number of shares in a non-US company that are deposited in an overseas bank.

Amex ▸ abbr. American Stock Exchange.

am•or•tize ▸ v. reduce or extinguish (a debt) by money regularly put aside: *loan fees can be amortized over the life of the mortgage.*
- gradually write off the initial cost of (an asset).

AMT ▸ abbr. alternative minimum tax, introduced to prevent companies and individuals using deductions and credits to pay no tax.

an•nu•al•ized ▸ adj. (of a rate of interest, inflation, or return on an investment) recalculated as an annual rate: *an annualized yield of about 11.5%.*

an•nu•i•tant ▸ n. formal a person who receives an annuity.

an•nu•i•ty ▸ n. (pl. **-ies**) a fixed sum of money paid to someone each year, typically for the rest of their life.
- a form of insurance or investment entitling the investor to a series of annual sums.

an•swer•ing serv•ice ▸ n. a business that receives and answers telephone calls for its clients.

an•ti•trust ▸ adj. of or relating to legislation preventing or controlling trusts or other monopolies, with the intention of promoting competition in business.

APR ▸ abbr. annual or annualized percentage rate, typically of interest on loans or credit.

ar•bi•trage ▸ n. the simultaneous buying and selling of securities, currency, or commodities in different markets or in derivative forms in order to take advantage of differing prices for the same asset.

ar•bi•tra•geur (also **arbitrager**) ▸ n. a person who engages in arbitrage.

ask ▸ v. request (a specified amount) as a price for selling something.
▸ n. the price at which an item, esp. a financial security, is offered for sale.

ask•ing price ▸ n. the price at which something is offered for sale.

as•sess ▸ v. (usu. **be assessed**) calculate or estimate the price or value of.
- (often **be assessed**) set the value of a tax, fine, etc., for (a person or property) at a specified level.

as•ses•sor ▸ n. a person who calculates or estimates the value of something or an amount to be paid, chiefly for tax or insurance purposes.

as•set ▸ n. (usu. **assets**) property owned by a person or company, regarded as having value and available to meet debts, commitments, or legacies: *growth in net assets.*

as•set-backed ▸ adj. denoting securities having as collateral the return on a series of mortgages, credit agreements, or other forms of lending.

as•set-strip•ping ▸ n. the practice of taking over a company in financial difficulties and selling each of its assets separately at a profit without regard for the company's future.

ATM ▸ abbr. automated (or automatic) teller machine.

au•dit ▸ n. an official inspection of an individual's or organization's accounts, typically by an independent body.
▸ v. (**audited, auditing**) conduct an official financial examination of (an individual's or organization's accounts): *companies must have their accounts audited.*

au•di•tor ▸ n. a person who conducts an audit.

aus•ter•i•ty ▸ n. (pl. **-ies**)
- difficult economic conditions created by government measures to reduce a budget deficit, esp. by reducing public expenditure.

av•er•age (abbr.: **avg.**) ▸ n. the apportionment of financial liability resulting from loss of or damage to a ship or its cargo.
- reduction in the amount payable under an insurance policy, e.g., in respect of partial loss.

back end ▸ adj. relating to the end or outcome of a project, process, or investment: *many annuities have back-end surrender charges.*

back•load ▸ v. (usu. **be backloaded**) place more charges at the later stages of (a financial agreement) than at the earlier stages.

bad debt ▸ n. a debt that cannot be recovered.

bail•out ▸ n. informal an act of giving financial assistance to a failing business or economy to save it from collapse.

bait-and-switch ▸ n. the action (generally illegal) of advertising goods that are an apparent bargain, with the intention of substituting inferior or more expensive goods.

bal•ance ▸ n. a figure representing the difference between credits and debits in an account; the amount of money held in an account.
- the difference between an amount due and an amount paid: *unpaid credit-card balances.* ■ an amount left over.
▸ v. compare debits and credits in (an account), typically to ensure that they are equal.
- (of an account) have credits and debits equal.
– PHRASES **balance of payments** the difference in total value between payments into and out of a country over a period. **balance of trade** the difference in value between a country's imports and exports.

bal•ance sheet ▸ n. a statement of the assets, liabilities, and capital of a business or other organization at a particular point in time, detailing the balance of income and expenditure over the preceding period.

bal•loon pay•ment ▸ n. a repayment of the outstanding principal sum made at the end of a loan period, interest only having been paid hitherto.

bank draft ▸ n. a check drawn by a bank on its own funds in another bank.

bank•note (also **bank note**) ▸ n. a piece of paper money, constituting a central bank's promissory note to pay a stated sum to the bearer on demand.

bank•rupt ▸ adj. (of a person or organization) declared in law unable to pay outstanding debts: *the company was declared bankrupt | he committed suicide after* **going bankrupt.**
▸ n. a person judged by a court to be insolvent, whose property is taken and disposed of for the benefit of creditors.
▸ v. reduce (a person or organization) to bankruptcy: *the strike nearly bankrupted the union.*

ba•sis point ▸ n. one hundredth of one percent, used chiefly in expressing differences of interest rates.

bas•ket ▸ n. a group or range of currencies or investments: *the European currency unit is made up of a basket of ten currencies.*

bean count•er ▸ n. informal, derogatory a person, typically an accountant or bureaucrat, perceived as placing excessive emphasis on controlling expenditure and budgets.

bear ▸ n. a person who forecasts that prices of stocks or commodities will fall, esp. a person who sells shares hoping to buy them back later at a lower price.

bear•er ▸ n. a person who presents a check or other order to pay money.
■ payable to the possessor: *bearer bonds.*

bear•ish ▸ adj. characterized by falling share prices.
■ (of a dealer) inclined to sell because of an anticipated fall in prices.

bear mar•ket ▸ n. a market in which prices are falling, encouraging selling.

bid price ▸ n. the price that a dealer or other prospective buyer is prepared to pay for securities or other assets.

Big Board n. informal term for the New York Stock Exchange.

bill•ing ▸ n. the process of making out or sending invoices.
■ the total amount of business conducted in a given time, esp. that of an advertising agency.

bill of ex•change ▸ n. a written order to a person requiring the person to make a specified payment to the signatory or to a named payee; a promissory note.

bill of goods ▸ n. a consignment of merchandise.

bill of sale ▸ n. a certificate of transfer of personal property.

black mon•ey ▸ n. income illegally obtained or not declared for tax purposes.

blank check ▸ n. a bank check with the amount left for the payee to fill in.

block ▸ v. restrict the use or conversion of (currency or any other asset).

blue-chip ▸ adj. denoting companies or their shares considered to be a reliable investment, though less secure than gilt-edged stock.

Board of Trade ▸ n. (also **Chicago Board of Trade**) the Chicago futures exchange.

boil•er room ▸ n.
■ a room used for intensive telephone selling.

bond ▸ n. a certificate issued by a government or a public company promising to repay borrowed money at a fixed rate of interest at a specified time. ■ (of dutiable goods) a state of storage in a bonded warehouse until the importer pays the duty owing. ■ an insurance policy held by a company, which protects against losses resulting from circumstances such as bankruptcy or misconduct by employees.

bond•ed ▸ adj. (of a person or company) bound by a legal agreement, in particular:
■ (of a debt) secured by bonds. ■ (of dutiable goods) placed in bond.

bond•ed ware•house ▸ n. a customs-controlled warehouse for the retention of imported goods until the duty owed is paid.

bo•nus is•sue ▸ n. an issue of additional shares to shareholders instead of a dividend, in proportion to the shares already held.

book•keep•ing ▸ n. the activity or occupation of keeping records of the financial affairs of a business.

book val•ue ▸ n. the value of a security or asset as entered in a company's books.

bounce ▸ v. informal (of a check) be returned by a bank when there are insufficient funds to meet it.
■ informal write (a check) on insufficient funds: *I've never bounced a check.*

bourse ▸ n. a stock market in a non-English-speaking country, esp. France.
■ (**Bourse**) the Paris stock exchange.

bp ▸ abbr. basis point(s).

BPR ▸ abbr. business process reengineering.

brand a•ware•ness ▸ n. the extent to which consumers are familiar with the distinctive qualities or image of a particular brand of goods or services.

brand ex•ten•sion ▸ n. an instance of using an established brand name or trademark on new products, so as to increase sales.

brand im•age ▸ n. the impression of a product held by real or potential consumers.

brand lead•er ▸ n. the best-selling or most highly regarded product or brand of its type.

brand loy•al•ty ▸ n. the tendency of some consumers to continue buying the same brand of goods despite the availability of competing brands.

brand man•age•ment ▸ n. the activity of supervising the promotion of a particular brand of goods.

brand name ▸ n. a name given by the maker to a product or range of products, esp. a trademark.

Brand X ▸ n. a name used for an unidentified brand contrasted unfavorably with a product of the same type being promoted.

break ▸ v. (past **broke**; past part. **broken**) (of prices on the stock exchange) fall sharply.

break-e•ven ▸ n. the point or state at which a person or company breaks even.

bridge loan ▸ n. a sum of money lent by a bank to cover an interval between two transactions, typically the buying of one house and the selling of another.

bro•ker ▸ n. a person who buys and sells goods or assets for others.
▸ v. arrange or negotiate (a settlement, deal, or plan): *fighting continued despite attempts to broker a cease-fire.*

bro•ker•age ▸ n. the business or service of acting as a broker.
■ a fee or commission charged by a broker: *a revenue of $1,400 less a sales brokerage of $12.50.* ■ a company that buys or sells goods or assets for clients.

bro•ker-deal•er ▸ n. a brokerage firm that buys

and sells securities on its own account as a principal before selling the securities to customers.

BS ▸ abbr. balance sheet.

bub•ble e•con•o•my ▸ n. an unstable expanding economy; in particular, a period of heightened prosperity and increased commercial activity in Japan in the late 1980s brought about by artificially adjusted interest rates.

buck•et shop ▸ n. informal, derogatory an unauthorized office for speculating in stocks or currency using the funds of unwitting investors.

budg•et ▸ n. an estimate of income and expenditure for a set period of time.
■ an annual or other regular estimate of national revenue and expenditure put forward by the government, often including details of changes in taxation.

bulk buy•ing ▸ n. the purchase of goods in large amounts, typically at a discount.

bull ▸ n. a person who buys shares hoping to sell them at a higher price later.

bull•ish ▸ adj. characterized by rising share prices.
■ (of a dealer) inclined to buy because of an anticipated rise in prices.

bull mar•ket ▸ n. a market in which share prices are rising, encouraging buying.

buoy•an•cy ▸ n. figurative a high level of activity in an economy or stock market.

busi•ness cy•cle ▸ n. a cycle or series of cycles of economic expansion and contraction.

busi•ness proc•ess re•en•gi•neer•ing (abbr.: **BPR**) ▸ n. the process or activity of restructuring a company's organization and methods, esp. to exploit the capabilities of computers.

busi•ness stud•ies ▸ plural n. [treated as sing.] the study of economics and management, esp. as an educational topic.

buy-back ▸ n. the buying back of goods by the original seller.
■ the buying back by a company of its own shares. ■ a form of borrowing in which shares or bonds are sold with an agreement to repurchase them at a later date.

buy•er ▸ n. a person who makes a purchase.
■ a person employed to select and purchase stock or materials for a large retail or manufacturing business, etc.
–PHRASES **a buyer's market** an economic situation in which goods or shares are plentiful and buyers can keep prices down.

buy-in ▸ n. a purchase of shares by a broker after a seller has failed to deliver similar shares, the original seller being charged any difference in cost.

buy•out ▸ n. the purchase of a controlling share in a company, esp. by its own managers.

ca•das•tral ▸ adj. (of a map or survey) showing the extent, value, and ownership of land, esp. for taxation.

ca•das•tre ▸ n. a register of property showing the extent, value, and ownership of land for taxation.

CAF ▸ abbr. cost and freight.

call ▸ n. a demand for payment of lent or unpaid capital. ■ short for CALL OPTION.

call mon•ey ▸ n. money lent by a bank or other institutions that is repayable on demand.

call op•tion ▸ n. an option to buy assets at an agreed price on or before a particular date.

cap ▸ n. an upper limit imposed on spending or other activities.
▸ v. (**capped, capping**) (often **be capped**) place a limit or restriction on (prices, expenditure, or other activity): *council budgets will be capped.*

cap•i•tal ▸ n. wealth in the form of money or other assets owned by a person or organization or available or contributed for a particular purpose such as starting a company or investing.
■ the excess of a company's assets over its liabilities.

cap•i•tal ad•e•qua•cy ▸ n. the statutory minimum reserves of capital that a bank or other financial institution must have available.

cap•i•tal gain ▸ n. (often **capital gains**) a profit from the sale of property or of an investment.

cap•i•tal gains tax ▸ n. a tax levied on profit from the sale of property or of an investment.

cap•i•tal goods ▸ plural n. goods that are used in producing other goods, rather than being bought by consumers.

cap•i•tal-in•ten•sive ▸ adj. (of a business or industrial process) requiring the investment of large sums of money.

cap•i•tal•ize ▸ v. provide (a company or industry) with capital. realize (the present value of an income); convert into capital.
■ reckon (the value of an asset) by setting future benefits against the cost of maintenance.

cap•i•tal mar•ket ▸ n. the part of a financial system concerned with raising capital by dealing in shares, bonds, and other long-term investments.

cap•i•tal sum ▸ n. a lump sum of money payable to an insured person or paid as an initial fee or investment.

cap•i•ta•tion ▸ n. the payment of a fee or grant to a doctor, school, or other person or body providing services to a number of people, such that the amount paid is determined by the number of patients, pupils, or customers.

cap•tive ▸ adj. (of a facility or service) controlled by, and typically for the sole use of, an establishment or company: *a captive power plant.*

car•bon tax ▸ n. a tax on fossil fuels, esp. those used by motor vehicles, intended to reduce the emission of carbon dioxide.

card•hold•er ▸ n. a person who has a credit card or debit card.

car•ry ▸ n. (pl. **-ies**) [usu. in sing.] the maintenance of an investment position in a securities market, esp. with regard to the costs or profits accruing.

car•ry•ing charge ▸ n. an expense or effective cost arising from unproductive assets such as stored goods or unoccupied premises. a sum payable for the conveying of goods.

car•tel ▸ n. an association of manufacturers or suppliers with the purpose of maintaining prices at a high level and restricting competition.

car•tel•ize ▸ v. (of manufacturers or suppliers) form a cartel in (an industry or trade).

cash and car•ry ▶ n. a system of wholesale trading whereby goods are paid for in full at the time of purchase and taken away by the purchaser.
■ a wholesale store operating this system.

cash cow ▶ n. informal a business, investment, or product that provides a steady income or profit.

cash flow ▶ n. the total amount of money being transferred into and out of a business, esp. as affecting liquidity.

cash•ier ▶ n. a person handling payments and receipts in a store, bank, or other business.

cash nex•us ▶ n. the relationship constituted by monetary transactions.

cash on de•liv•er•y (abbr.: COD) ▶ n. the system of paying for goods when they are delivered.

cash reg•is•ter ▶ n. a machine used in places of business for regulating money transactions with customers. It typically has a compartmental drawer for cash and totals, displays, and records the amount of each sale.

cen•tral bank ▶ n. a national bank that provides financial and banking services for its country's government and commercial banking system, as well as implementing the government's monetary policy and issuing currency.

cer•tif•i•cate of de•pos•it (abbr.: CD) ▶ n. a certificate issued by a bank to a person depositing money for a specified length of time.

cer•ti•fied check ▶ n. a check that is guaranteed by a bank.

cer•ti•fied pub•lic ac•count•ant (abbr.: CPA) ▶ n. a member of an officially accredited professional body of accountants.

c.f. ▶ abbr. carried forward (used to refer to figures transferred to a new page or account).

CGT ▶ abbr. capital gains tax.

chae•bol ▶ n. (pl. same or **chaebols**) (in South Korea) a large business conglomerate, typically a family-owned one.

cham•ber of com•merce (abbr.: C. of C.) ▶ n. a local association to promote and protect the interests of the business community in a particular place.

change man•age•ment ▶ n. the management of change and development within a business or similar organization, esp. the personal management of those having to adapt to new conditions.

Chap•ter 11 ▶ n. protection from creditors given to a company in financial difficulties for a limited period to allow it to reorganize.

charge ▶ n. a price asked for goods or services: *an admission charge.*
■ a financial liability or commitment: *an asset of $550,000 should have been taken as a charge on earnings.*

charge ac•count ▶ n. an account to which goods and services may be charged on credit.

charge card ▶ n. a credit card for use with an account that must be paid when a statement is issued.

char•tist ▶ n. a person who uses charts of financial data to predict future trends and to guide investment strategies.

churn ▶ v. (of a broker) encourage frequent turno-ver of (investments) in order to generate commission.

cir•cu•la•tion (abbr.: cir. or circ.) ▶ n. the movement, exchange, or availability of money in a country: *the new coins go into circulation today.*

claim ▶ n. an application for compensation under the terms of an insurance policy: ■ a right or title to something: *they have first claim on the assets of the trust.*

clear ▶ adj. (of a sum of money) net: *a clear profit of $1,100.*
▶ v. pass (a check) through a clearinghouse so that the money goes into the payee's account. ■ (of a check) pass through a clearinghouse in such a way. ■ earn or gain (an amount of money) as a net profit.

clear•ing•house (also **clearing house**) (abbr.: c.h. or C.H.) ▶ n. a bankers' establishment where checks and bills from member banks are exchanged, so that only the balances need be paid in cash.

closed-end ▶ adj. denoting an investment trust or company that issues a fixed number of shares.

closed shop ▶ n. a place of work where membership in a union is a condition for being hired and for continued employment.
■ [in sing.] a system whereby such an arrangement applies: *the outlawing of the closed shop.*

clos•ing price ▶ n. the price of a security at the end of the day's business in a financial market.

Co. ▶ abbr. company: *the Consett Iron Co.*
–PHRASES **and Co.** used as part of the titles of commercial businesses to designate the partner or partners not named.

co•de•ter•mi•na•tion ▶ n. cooperation between management and workers in decision-making, esp. by the representation of workers on management boards.

COLA ▶ abbr. cost-of-living adjustment, an increase made to wages or Social Security benefits to keep them in line with inflation.

col•lat•er•al•ize ▶ v. provide something as collateral for (a loan).

col•lec•tive a•gree•ment ▶ n. an agreement about pay and working conditions reached collectively by management and the workforce.

col•lec•tive own•er•ship ▶ n. ownership of something, typically land or industrial assets, by all members of a group for the mutual benefit of all.

com•mand e•con•o•my ▶ n. an economy in which production, investment, prices, and incomes are determined centrally by a government.

com•mer•cial bank ▶ n. a bank that offers services to the general public and to companies.

com•mer•cial pa•per ▶ n. short-term unsecured promissory notes issued by companies.

com•mod•i•ty ▶ n. (pl. -ies) a raw material or primary agricultural product that can be bought and sold, such as copper or coffee.

com•mon car•ri•er ▶ n. a person or company that transports goods or passengers on regular routes at rates made available to the public.
■ a company providing public telecommunications facilities.

com•mon mar•ket ▸ n. a group of countries imposing few or no duties on trade with one another and a common tariff on trade with other countries.

com•mon stock ▸ plural n. (also **common stocks**) shares entitling their holder to dividends that vary in amount and may even be missed, depending on the fortunes of the company.

com•mu•ta•tion ▸ n. the conversion of a legal obligation or entitlement into another form, e.g., the replacement of an annuity or series of payments by a single payment.

com•mute ▸ v. (**commute something for/into**) change one kind of payment or obligation for (another). ▪ replace (an annuity or other series of payments) with a single payment: *he commuted his pension and got $50,000.*

com•par•a•tive ad•van•tage ▸ n. the ability of an individual or group to carry out a particular economic activity (such as making a specific product) more efficiently than another activity.

com•pound ▸ adj. (of interest) payable on both capital and the accumulated interest.
▸ v. calculate (interest) on previously accumulated interest: *the yield at which the interest is compounded.* ▪ (of a sum of money invested) increase by compound interest.

comp•trol•ler ▸ n. a controller (used in the title of some financial officers).

con•ces•sion ▸ n. the right to use land or other property for a specified purpose, granted by a government, company, or other controlling body. *new logging concessions.* ▪ a commercial operation within the premises of a larger concern, typically selling refreshments.

con•ces•sion•aire (also **concessioner**) ▸ n. the holder of a concession or grant, esp. for the use of land or commercial premises.

con•glom•er•ate ▸ n. a large corporation formed by the merging of separate and diverse firms.
▸ adj. of or relating to a conglomerate, esp. a large corporation: *conglomerate businesses.*
▸ v. form a conglomerate by merging diverse businesses.

con•sign•ment ▸ n. a batch of goods destined for or delivered to someone: *a consignment of beef.* ▪ agreement to pay a supplier of goods after the goods are sold: *new and used children's clothing on consignment.*

con•sol•i•date ▸ v. combine (a number of financial accounts or funds) into a single overall account or set of accounts.

con•sor•ti•um ▸ n. (pl. **consortia** or **consortiums**) an association, typically of several business companies.

con•sum•er ▸ n. a person who purchases goods and services for personal use.

con•sum•er dur•a•ble ▸ n. (usu. **consumer durables**) a manufactured item, typically a car or household appliance, that is expected to have a relatively long useful life after purchase.

con•sum•er goods ▸ plural n. goods bought and used by consumers, rather than by manufacturers for producing other goods.

con•sum•er•ism ▸ n. the protection or promotion of the interests of consumers. ▪ *often derogatory* the preoccupation of society with the acquisition of consumer goods.

con•sum•er price in•dex (abbr.: **CPI**) ▸ n. an index of the variation in prices paid by typical consumers for retail goods and other items.

con•sum•er re•search ▸ n. the investigation of the needs and opinions of consumers, esp. with regard to a particular product or service.

con•sum•er so•ci•e•ty ▸ n. *chiefly derogatory* a society in which the buying and selling of goods and services is the most important social and economic activity.

con•sum•er sov•er•eign•ty ▸ n. the situation in an economy where the desires and needs of consumers control the output of producers.

con•sump•tion ▸ n. the purchase and use of goods and services by the public.

con•tin•gen•cy fund ▸ n. a reserve of money set aside to cover possible unforeseen future expenses.

con•tin•gent ▸ adj. (of losses, liabilities, etc.) that can be anticipated to arise if a particular event occurs.

con•trar•i•an ▸ n. a person who opposes or rejects popular opinion, esp. in stock exchange dealing.

con•trol ac•count ▸ n. an account used to record the balances on a number of subsidiary accounts and to provide a cross-check on them.

con•trol•ling in•ter•est ▸ n. the holding by one person or group of a majority of the stock of a business, giving the holder a means of exercising control.

con•ver•sion fac•tor ▸ n. the manufacturing cost of a product relative to the cost of raw materials.

con•vert ▸ v. change (money, stocks, or units in which a quantity is expressed) into others of a different kind.

con•vert•i•ble ▸ adj. (of currency) able to be converted into other forms, esp. into gold or US dollars. ▪ (of a bond or stock) able to be converted into ordinary or preference shares.
▸ n. (usu. **convertibles**) a convertible security.

co-op ▸ n. *informal* a cooperative society, business, or enterprise.

co•op•er•a•tion (also **co-operation**) ▸ n. the formation and operation of cooperatives.

co•op•er•a•tive (also **co-operative**) ▸ adj. ▪ (of a farm, business, etc.) owned and run jointly by its members, with profits or benefits shared among them.
▸ n. a farm, business, or other organization that is owned and run jointly by its members, who share the profits or benefits.

cor•ner ▸ n. a position in which one dominates the supply of a particular commodity.
▸ v. control (a market) by dominating the supply of a particular commodity. ▪ establish a corner in (a commodity).

Corp. ▸ abbr. corporation: *IBM Corp.*

cor•po•rate ▸ adj. of or relating to a corporation, esp. a large company or group: *airlines are very keen on their corporate identity.*

■ (of a company or group of people) authorized to act as a single entity and recognized as such in law.

▸n. a corporate company or group.

cor•po•rate raid•er ▸ n. a financier who makes a practice of making hostile takeover bids for companies, either to control their policies or to resell them for a profit.

cor•po•ra•tion ▸ n. a company or group of people authorized to act as a single entity (legally a person) and recognized as such in law.

cor•po•ra•tize ▸ v. convert (a state organization) into an independent commercial company.

cor•rec•tion ▸ n. a temporary reversal in an overall trend of stock market prices, esp. a brief fall during an overall increase.

cost ac•count•ing ▸ n. the recording of all the costs incurred in a business in a way that can be used to improve its management.

cost-ben•e•fit ▸ adj. relating to or denoting a process that assesses the relation between the cost of an undertaking and the value of the resulting benefits: *a cost-benefit analysis.*

cost-ef•fec•tive ▸ adj. effective or productive in relation to its cost.

cost of liv•ing ▸ n. the level of prices relating to a range of everyday items.

cost-of-liv•ing in•dex (abbr.: CLI) ▸ n. former term for CONSUMER PRICE INDEX.

cost-plus ▸ adj. relating to or denoting a method of pricing a service or product in which a fixed profit factor is added to the costs.

cot•tage in•dus•try ▸ n. a business or manufacturing activity carried on in a person's home.

coun•ter•of•fer ▸ n. an offer made in response to another.

coun•ter•trade ▸ n. international trade by exchange of goods rather than by currency purchase.

coun•ter•vail•ing du•ty ▸ n. an import tax imposed on certain goods in order to prevent dumping or counter export subsidies.

cou•pon ▸ n. a voucher entitling the holder to a discount off a particular product.
■ a detachable portion of a bond that is given up in return for a payment of interest.

cou•pon bond ▸ n. an investment bond on which interest is paid by coupons.

cov•er•age ▸ n. the amount of protection given by an insurance policy.

CP ▸ abbr. commercial paper.

CPA ▸ abbr. certified public accountant.

cr ▸ abbr. credit. ■ creditor.

cre•a•tive ac•count•an•cy (also creative accounting) ▸ n. informal the exploitation of loopholes in financial regulation in order to gain advantage or present figures in a misleadingly favorable light.

cred•it ▸ n. the ability of a customer to obtain goods or services before payment, based on the trust that payment will be made in the future.
■ the money lent or made available under such an arrangement: *the bank refused to extend their credit.* ■ an entry recording a sum received, listed on the right-hand side or column of an account. The opposite of DEBIT.
■ a payment received.

▸v. (credited, crediting) (often be credited) add (an amount of money) to an account: *this deferred tax can be credited to the profit and loss account.*

cred•it an•a•lyst ▸ n. a person employed to assess the credit rating of people or companies.

cred•it bu•reau ▸ n. a company that collects information relating to the credit ratings of individuals and makes it available to credit card companies, financial institutions, etc.

cred•it card ▸ n. a small plastic card issued by a bank, business, etc., allowing the holder to purchase goods or services on credit.

cred•i•tor ▸ n. a person or company to whom money is owed.

cred•it rat•ing ▸ n. an estimate of the ability of a person or organization to fulfill their financial commitments, based on previous dealings.
■ the process of assessing this.

cred•it un•ion ▸ n. a nonprofit-making money cooperative whose members can borrow from pooled deposits at low interest rates.

cred•it•worth•y ▸ adj. (of a person or company) considered suitable to receive credit, esp. because of being reliable in paying money back in the past.

cross own•er•ship ▸ n. the ownership by one corporation of different companies with related interests or commercial aims.

cross-rate ▸ n. an exchange rate between two currencies computed by reference to a third currency, usually the US dollar.

cross-sell ▸ v. sell (a different product or service) to an existing customer: *their database is used to cross-sell financial services.*

cross-sub•si•dize ▸ v. subsidize (a business or activity) out of the profits of another business or activity.

cru•el•ty-free ▸ adj. (of cosmetics or other commercial products) manufactured or developed by methods that do not involve experimentation on animals.

crunch ▸ n. a severe shortage of money or credit.

ct. ▸ abbr. cent.

CTT ▸ abbr. capital transfer tax.

cum div•i•dend ▸ adv. (of share purchases) with a dividend about to be paid.

cu•mu•la•tive pre•ferred stock ▸ n. a preferred stock whose annual fixed-rate dividend, if it cannot be paid in any year, accrues until it can and is paid before common dividends.

curb mar•ket ▸ n. a market for selling shares not dealt with on the normal stock exchange.

cur•rent as•sets ▸ plural n. cash and other assets that are expected to be converted to cash within a year.

cur•rent cost ac•count•ing ▸ n. a method of accounting in which assets are valued on the basis of their current replacement cost, and increases in their value as a result of inflation are excluded from calculations of profit.

cur•rent li•a•bil•i•ties ▸ plural n. amounts due to be paid to creditors within twelve months.

cut•back ▸ n. an act or instance of reducing something, typically expenditures.

cut•o•ver ▸ n. a rapid transition from one phase of a business enterprise or project to another.

c.w.o. ▸ abbr. cash with order.

day•book ▸ n. an account book in which a day's transactions are entered for later transfer to a ledger.

day shift ▸ n. a period of time worked during the daylight hours in a hospital, factory, etc., as opposed to the night shift.
■ [treated as sing. or pl.] the employees who work during this period.

day•work ▸ n. casual work paid for on a daily basis.

dead ▸ adj. (of money) not financially productive.

dead cat bounce ▸ n. a temporary recovery in share prices after a substantial fall, caused by speculators buying in order to cover their positions.

dead weight (also **deadweight**) ▸ n. losses incurred because of the inefficient allocation of resources, esp. through taxation or restriction.

deal•er ▸ n. a person or business that buys and sells goods: *a car dealer.*
■ a person who buys and sells shares, securities, or other financial assets as a principal (rather than as a broker or agent).

dear ▸ adj. (of money) available as a loan only at a high rate of interest.

death tax ▸ n. another term for ESTATE TAX.

de•ben•ture ▸ n. (also **debenture bond**) an unsecured loan certificate issued by a company, backed by general credit rather than by speciifed assets.

deb•it ▸ n. an entry recording an amount owed, listed on the left-hand side or column of an account. The opposite of CREDIT.
■ a payment made or owed.
▸ v. (**debited, debiting**) (usu. **be debited**) (of a bank or other financial organization) remove (an amount of money) from a customer's account, typically as payment for services or goods: *$10,000 was debited from their account.*
■ remove an amount of money from (a bank account).

deb•it card ▸ n. a card issued by a bank allowing the holder to transfer money electronically to another bank account when making a purchase.

debt coun•se•lor ▸ n. a person who offers professional advice on methods of debt repayment.

debt•or ▸ n. a person or institution that owes a sum of money.

debt se•cu•ri•ty ▸ n. a negotiable or tradable liability or loan.

debt swap (also **debt-for-na•ture swap**) ▸ n. a transaction in which a foreign exchange debt owed by a developing country is transferred to another organization on the condition that the country use local currency for a designated purpose, usually environmental protection.

dec•i•mal•ize ▸ v. convert (a system of coinage or weights and measures) to a decimal system.

dec•la•ra•tion ▸ n. a listing of goods, property, income, etc., subject to duty or tax.

de•con•trol ▸ v. (**decontrolled, decontrolling**) release (a commodity, market, etc.) from controls or restrictions.

de•duct•i•ble ▸ adj. able to be deducted, esp. from taxable income or tax to be paid: *child-care vouchers will be deductible expenses for employers.*
▸ n. (in an insurance policy) a specified amount of money that the insured must pay before an insurance company will pay a claim: *a traditional insurance policy with a low deductible.*

de•duc•tion ▸ n. the action of deducting or subtracting something.
■ an amount that is or may be deducted from something, esp. from taxable income or tax to be paid: *tax deductions.*

deep-dis•count ▸ adj. denoting financial securities carrying a low rate of interest relative to prevailing market rates and issued at a discount to their redemption value, thus mainly providing capital gain rather than income.
■ heavily discounted; greatly reduced in price.

de•ferred an•nu•i•ty ▸ n. an annuity that commences only after a lapse of some specified time after the final purchase premium has been paid.

de•fi•cien•cy pay•ment ▸ n. a payment made, typically by a government body, to cover a financial deficit incurred in the course of an activity such as farming or education.

def•i•cit ▸ n. the amount by which something, esp. a sum of money, is too small.
■ an excess of expenditure or liabilities over income or assets in a given period.

def•i•cit fi•nanc•ing ▸ n. government funding of spending by borrowing.

def•i•cit spend•ing ▸ n. government spending, in excess of revenue, of funds raised by borrowing rather than from taxation.

de•flate ▸ v. bring about a general reduction of price levels in (an economy).

de•fla•tion ▸ n. reduction of the general level of prices in an economy.

de•fla•tion•ar•y ▸ adj. of, characterized by, or tending to cause economic deflation.

de•gres•sive ▸ adj. (of taxation) at successively lower rates on lower amounts.

de-in•dex ▸ v. end the indexation to inflation of (pensions or other benefits).

de•in•dus•tri•al•i•za•tion ▸ n. decline in industrial activity in a region or economy: *severe deindustrialization with substantial job losses.*

de•lin•quen•cy ▸ n. (pl. **-ies**) a failure to pay an outstanding debt.

de•lin•quent ▸ adj. in arrears: *delinquent accounts.*

de•list ▸ v. remove (a security) from the official register of a stock exchange: *the stock collapsed and was delisted.* ■ remove (a product) from the list of those sold by a particular retailer.

de•liv•er•a•ble ▸ n. (usu. **deliverables**) a thing able to be provided, esp. as a product of a development process.

de•mand ▸ n. the desire of purchasers, consumers, clients, employers, etc., for a particular commodity, service, or other item: *a recent slump in demand.*

de•mand curve ▸ n. a graph showing how the demand for a commodity or service varies with changes in its price.

de•mand de•pos•it ▸ n. a deposit of money that can be withdrawn without prior notice.

de•mand draft ▸ n. a financial draft payable on demand.

de•mand-led (also **demand-driven**) ▸ adj. caused or determined by demand from consumers or clients.

de•mand note ▸ n. a formal request for payment.
■ another term for DEMAND DRAFT.

de•mand pull ▸ adj. relating to or denoting inflation caused by an excess of demand over supply.

de•ma•te•ri•al•ize ▸ v. (**dematerialized**) replace (physical records or certificates) with a paperless computerized system.

dem•o•graph•ics ▸ plural n. statistical data relating to the population and particular groups within it: *the demographics of book buyers.*

de•mon•e•tize ▸ v. (usu. **be demonetized**) deprive (a coin or precious metal) of its status as money.

de•mo•nop•o•lize ▸ v. introduce competition into (a market or economy) by privatizing previously nationalized assets.

de•mu•tu•al•ize ▸ v. change (a mutual organization such as a savings and loan association) to one of a different kind.

de•nom•i•nate ▸ v. (**be denominated**) (of sums of money) be expressed in a specified monetary unit.

de•ple•tion al•low•ance ▸ n. a tax concession allowable to a company whose normal business activities (in particular oil extraction) reduce the value of its own assets.

de•pos•it ▸ n. a sum of money placed or kept in a bank account, usually to gain interest.
■ an act of placing money in a bank account: *I'd like to make a deposit.* ■ a sum payable as a first installment on the purchase of something or as a pledge for a contract, the balance being payable later.
■ a returnable sum payable on the rental of something, to cover any possible loss or damage.
▸ v. (**deposited, depositing**) pay (a sum of money) into a bank account: *the money is deposited with a bank.* ■ pay (a sum) as a first installment or as a pledge for a contract.

de•pos•i•tar•y (also **depository**) ▸ adj. (of a share or receipt) representing a share in a foreign company. The depositary share or receipt is traded on the stock exchange of the investor's country rather than the actual share, which is deposited in a foreign bank.

de•pos•i•tor ▸ n. a person who keeps money in a bank account.

de•pre•ci•ate ▸ v. diminish in value over a period of time: *the pound is expected to depreciate against the dollar.*
■ reduce the recorded value in a company's books of (an asset) each year over a predetermined period.

de•pre•ci•a•tion ▸ n. a reduction in the value of an asset with the passage of time, due in particular to wear and tear.
■ decrease in the value of a currency relative to other currencies.

de•press ▸ v. reduce the level or strength of activity in (something, esp. an economic or biological system): *fear of inflation in America depressed bond markets*

de•pres•sant ▸ n. an influence that depresses economic or other activity.

de•pres•sion ▸ n. a long and severe recession in an economy or market: *the depression in the housing market.* ■ (**the Depression** or **the Great Depression**) the financial and industrial slump of 1929 and subsequent years.

de•riv•a•tive ▸ adj. (of a financial product) having a value deriving from an underlying variable asset: *equity-based derivative products.*
▸ n. (often **derivatives**) an arrangement or instrument (such as a future, option, or warrant) whose value derives from and is dependent on the value of an underlying asset.

de•rived de•mand ▸ n. a demand for a commodity, service, etc., that is a consequence of the demand for something else.

de•skill ▸ v. reduce the level of skill required to carry out (a job).
■ make the skills of (a worker) obsolete.

de•val•ue ▸ v. (**devalues, devalued, devaluing**) (often **be devalued**) reduce the official value of (a currency) in relation to other currencies.

de•vel•op•ing coun•try ▸ n. a poor agricultural country that is seeking to become more advanced economically and socially.

dig•it•al cash (also **digital money**) ▸ n. money that may be transferred electronically from one party to another during a transaction.

di•lute ▸ v. (often **be diluted**) reduce the value of (a shareholding) by issuing more shares in a company without increasing the values of its assets.

di•lu•tion ▸ n. a reduction in the value of a shareholding due to the issue of additional shares in a company without an increase in assets.

di•rect la•bor ▸ n. labor involved in production rather than administration, maintenance, and other support services. labor employed by the authority commissioning the work, not by a contractor.

di•rect mail ▸ n. unsolicited advertising sent to prospective customers through the mail.

di•rect mar•ket•ing ▸ n. the business of selling products or services directly to the public, e.g., by mail order or telephone selling, rather than through retailers.

di•rec•tor (abbr.: **dir.**) ▸ n. a member of the board of people that manages or oversees the affairs of a business.

di•rec•to•rate ▸ n. [treated as sing. or pl.] the board of directors of a company.

di•rect tax ▸ n. a tax, such as income tax, that is levied on the income or profits of the person who pays it, rather than on goods or services.

dirt•y mon•ey ▸ n. money obtained unlawfully or immorally.

dis•count ▸ n. a deduction from the usual cost of something, typically given for prompt or advance payment or to a special category of buyers: *many stores will offer a discount on bulk purchases.*
■ a percentage deducted from the face value of a

bill of exchange or promissory note when it changes hands before the due date.

▸v. deduct an amount from (the usual price of something).
■ reduce (a product or service) in price. ■ buy or sell (a bill of exchange) before its due date at less than its maturity value.

▸adj. (of a store or business) offering goods for sale at discounted prices: *a discount drugstore chain.*
■ at a price lower than the usual one.

–PHRASES **at a discount** below the nominal or usual price.

dis•count•ed cash flow ▸n. a method of assessing investments taking into account the expected accumulation of interest.

dis•count house ▸n. another term for DISCOUNT STORE.

dis•count rate ▸n. the minimum interest rate set by the Federal Reserve for lending to other banks. a rate used for discounting bills of exchange.

dis•count store ▸n. a store that sells goods at less than the normal retail price.

dis•cre•tion•ar•y ▸adj. denoting or relating to investment funds placed with a broker or manager who has discretion to invest them on the client's behalf: *discretionary portfolios.*

dis•cre•tion•ar•y in•come ▸n. income remaining after deduction of taxes, other mandatory charges, and expenditure on necessary items.

dis•e•con•o•my ▸n. (pl. -ies) an economic disadvantage such as an increase in cost arising from an increase in the size of an organization: *in an ideal world, these **diseconomies of scale** would be minimized.*

dis•e•qui•lib•ri•um ▸n. a loss or lack of equilibrium in relation to supply, demand, and prices.

dis•hon•or ▸v. refuse to accept or pay (a check or a promissory note).

dis•in•cor•po•rate ▸v. dissolve (a corporate body).

dis•in•fla•tion ▸n. reduction in the rate of inflation.

dis•in•ter•me•di•a•tion ▸n. reduction in the use of banks and savings institutions as intermediaries in the borrowing and investment of money, in favor of direct involvement in the securities market.

dis•in•vest ▸v. withdraw or reduce an investment.

dis•pos•a•ble ▸adj. (chiefly of financial assets) readily available for the owner's use as required.

dis•pos•a•ble in•come ▸n. income remaining after deduction of taxes and other mandatory charges, available to be spent or saved as one wishes.

dis•sav•ing ▸n. the action of spending more than one has earned in a given period.
■ (**dissavings**) the excess amount spent.

dis•tressed ▸adj. ■ (of property) for sale, esp. below market value, due to mortgage foreclosure or because it is part of an insolvent estate. ■ (of goods) for sale at unusually low prices or at a loss because of damage or previous use.

dis•tri•bu•tion (abbr.: **distr.**) ▸n. the action or process of supplying goods to stores and other

businesses that sell to consumers: *a manager has the choice of four types of distribution.*

dis•tri•bu•tive ▸adj. concerned with the supply of goods to stores and other businesses that sell to consumers: *transportation and distributive industries.*

dis•trib•u•tor (abbr.: **distr.**) ▸n. an agent who supplies goods to stores and other businesses that sell to consumers: *a wholesale liquor distributor | the movie's distributor booked the film into theaters.*

dis•u•til•i•ty ▸n. the adverse or harmful effects associated with a particular activity or process, esp. when carried out over a long period.

di•ver•si•fy ▸v. (-ies, -ied) (of a company) enlarge or vary its range of products or field of operation.
■ (**diversified**) enlarge or vary the range of products or the field of operation of (a company): *the rise of the diversified corporation.* ■ spread (investment) over several enterprises or products in order to reduce the risk of loss.

di•vest ▸v. rid oneself of something that one no longer wants or requires, such as a business interest or investment: *it appears easier to carry on in the business than to divest | the government's policy of **divesting itself of** state holdings.*

di•vest•i•ture (also **divesture**) ▸n. the action or process of selling off subsidiary business interests or investments: *the divestiture of state-owned assets.*

di•vest•ment ▸n. another term for DIVESTITURE.

div•i•dend ▸n. a sum of money paid regularly (typically quarterly) by a company to its shareholders out of its profits (or reserves).
■ a payment divided among a number of people, e.g., members of a cooperative or creditors of an insolvent estate. ■ an individual's share of a dividend.

div•i•dend cov•er•age ▸n. the ratio of a company's dividends to its net income.

div•i•dend yield ▸n. a dividend expressed as a percentage of a current share price.

di•vi•sion•al•ize ▸v. subdivide (a company or other organization) into a number of separate divisions: *a large divisionalized Western corporation.*
■ undergo this process.

dock•et ▸n. a document or label listing the contents of a package or delivery.

▸v. (**docketed, docketing**) (usu. **be docketed**) mark (goods or a package) with a document or label listing the contents.

dol•lar ▸n. the basic monetary unit of the US, Canada, Australia, and certain countries in the Pacific, Caribbean, Southeast Asia, Africa, and South America.

dol•lar ar•e•a ▸n. the area of the world in which currency is linked to the US dollar.

dol•lar gap ▸n. the amount by which a country's import trade with the dollar area exceeds the corresponding export trade.

dol•lar•i•za•tion (also **-sation**) ▸n. the process of aligning a country's currency with the US dollar.

dom•i•cile (also **domicil**) ▸n. formal or Law the place at which a company or other body is registered, esp. for tax purposes.

dou•ble-en•try ▸ adj. denoting a system of book-keeping in which each transaction is entered as a debit in one account and a credit in another.

dou•ble in•dem•ni•ty ▸ n. provision for payment of double the face amount of an insurance policy under certain conditions, e.g., when death occurs as a result of an accident.

dou•ble time ▸ n. a rate of pay equal to double the standard rate, sometimes paid for working on holidays or outside normal working hours.

Dow short for **Dow Jones Industrial Average**.

Dow Jones In•dus•tri•al Av•er•age (also **Dow Jones Average**) an index of figures indicating the relative price of shares on the New York Stock Exchange, based on the average price of selected stocks.

down pay•ment ▸ n. an initial payment made when something is bought on credit.

down•side ▸ n. a downward movement of share prices.

down•swing ▸ n. another term for **DOWNTURN**.

down•turn ▸ n. a decline in economic, business, or other activity: *a downturn in the housing market.*

dr. ▸ abbr. debit.

draft ▸ n. a written order to pay a specified sum; a check.

draw•back ▸ n. an amount of excise or import duty remitted on imported goods that the importer reexports rather than sell domestically.

draw•down ▸ n. a withdrawal of oil or other commodity from stocks.

draw•ee ▸ n. the person or organization, typically a bank, who must pay a draft or bill.

draw•er ▸ n. a person who writes a check.

due date ▸ n. the date on which something falls due, esp. the payment of a bill or the expected birth of a baby.

dump ▸ v. send (goods unsalable in the home market) to a foreign market for sale at a low price. ■ informal sell off (assets) rapidly.

du•op•o•ly ▸ n. (pl. **-ies**) a situation in which two suppliers dominate the market for a commodity or service.

Dutch auc•tion ▸ n. a method of selling in which the price is reduced until a buyer is found.

du•ti•a•ble ▸ adj. liable to customs or other duties.

du•ty ▸ n. (pl. **-ies**) a payment due and enforced by law or custom, in particular: ■ a payment levied on the import, export, manufacture, or sale of goods.

ear•ly re•tire•ment ▸ n. the practice of leaving employment before the statutory age, esp. on favorable financial terms.

earn ▸ v. (of a person) obtain (money) in return for labor or services: *they earn $35 per hour | he now earns his living as a truck driver.* ■ (of capital invested) gain (money) as interest or profit.

earned in•come ▸ n. money derived from paid work.

ease ▸ v. (of share prices, interest rates, etc.) decrease in value or amount.

eas•y mon•ey ▸ n. money available at relatively low interest.

e-cash ▸ n. electronic financial transactions conducted in cyberspace via computer networks.

e•con•o•met•rics ▸ plural n. [treated as sing.] the branch of economics concerned with the use of mathematical methods (esp. statistics) in describing economic systems.

ec•o•nom•ic ▸ adj. of or relating to economics or the economy: *the government's economic policy.* ■ justified in terms of profitability: *many organizations must become larger if they are to remain economic.* ■ requiring fewer resources or costing less money: *solar power may provide a more economic solution.* ■ (of a subject) considered in relation to trade, industry, and the creation of wealth: *economic history.*

ec•o•nom•i•cal•ly ▸ adv. in a way that involves careful use of money or resources: *the new building was erected as economically as possible.*

ec•o•nom•ic good ▸ n. a product or service that can command a price when sold.

ec•o•nom•ic rent ▸ n. the extra amount earned by a resource (e.g., land, capital, or labor) by virtue of its present use.

ec•o•nom•ics ▸ plural n. [often treated as sing.] the branch of knowledge concerned with the production, consumption, and transfer of wealth. ■ the condition of a region or group as regards material prosperity.

e•con•o•mist ▸ n. an expert in economics.

e•con•o•my ▸ n. (pl. **-ies**) the wealth and resources of a country or region, esp. in terms of the production and consumption of goods and services. ■ a particular system or stage of an economy. ▸ adj. (of a product) offering the best value for the money: [in comb.] *an economy pack.* ■ designed to be economical to use: *an economy car.*

–PHRASES **economy of scale** a proportionate saving in costs gained by an increased level of production. **economy of scope** a proportionate saving gained by producing two or more distinct goods, when the cost of doing so is less than that of producing each separately.

ef•fec•tive ▸ adj. assessed according to actual rather than face value: *an effective price of $176 million.*

ef•fec•tive de•mand ▸ n. the level of demand that represents a real intention to purchase by people with the means to pay.

EFTPOS ▸ abbr. electronic funds transfer at point of sale.

e•las•tic ▸ adj. (of demand or supply) sensitive to changes in price or income.

em•bar•go ▸ n. (pl. **-oes**) an official ban on trade or other commercial activity with a particular country: *an embargo on grain sales.* ▸ v. (**-oes, -oed**) (usu. **be embargoed**) impose an official ban on (trade or a country or commodity): *the country has been virtually embargoed by most of the noncommunist world.*

e•mol•u•ment ▸ n. (usu. **emoluments**) formal a salary, fee, or profit from employment or office: *the directors' emoluments.*

en•dorse ▸ v. sign (a check or bill of exchange) on the back to make it payable to someone other than the stated payee or to accept responsibility for paying it.

en•dorse•ment ▸ n. a clause in an insurance policy detailing an exemption from or change in coverage. the action of endorsing a check or bill of exchange.

en•dow•ment ▸ n. an income or form of property given or bequeathed to someone.
■ a form of life insurance involving payment of a fixed sum to the insured person on a specified date, or to their estate should they die before this date: *an endowment policy.*

end us•er (also **end-user**) ▸ n. the person who actually uses a particular product.

en•ter•prise zone ▸ n. an impoverished area in which incentives such as tax concessions are offered to encourage business investment and provide jobs for the residents.

en•tre•pre•neur ▸ n. a person who organizes and operates a business or businesses, taking on greater than normal financial risks in order to do so.

en•try-lev•el ▸ adj. at the lowest level in an employment hierarchy.

EPOS ▸ abbr. electronic point of sale (used to describe retail outlets that record information electronically).

eps ▸ abbr. earnings per share.

e•qui•lib•ri•um ▸ n. (pl. **equilibria**) a situation in which supply and demand are matched and prices stable.

eq•ui•ty ▸ n. (pl. **-ies**) the value of the shares issued by a company: *he owns 62% of the group's equity.*
■ (**equities**) stocks and shares that carry no fixed interest. the value of a mortgaged property after deduction of charges against it.

es•ca•la•tor clause ▸ n. a clause in a contract that allows for an increase or a decrease in wages or prices under certain conditions.

es•crow ▸ n. a bond, deed, or other document kept in the custody of a third party, taking effect only when a specified condition has been fulfilled.
■ a deposit or fund held in trust or as a security. ■ the state of being kept in custody or trust in this way: *the board holds funds in escrow.*
▸ v. place in custody or trust in this way.

es•tate tax ▸ n. a tax levied on the net value of the estate of a deceased person before distribution to the heirs.

eu•ro ▸ n. (also **Euro**) the single European currency introduced into some of the states of the European Union countries in 1999 as an alternative currency in noncash transactions and scheduled to replace national currencies in 2002.

Eu•ro•bond ▸ n. an international bond issued in Europe or elsewhere outside the country in whose currency its value is stated (usually the US or Japan).

Eu•ro•cheque ▸ n. a check issued under an arrangement between European banks that enables account-holders from one country to use their checks in another.

Eu•ro•cur•ren•cy ▸ n. a form of money held or traded outside the country in whose currency its value is stated (originally US dollars held in Europe).

Eu•ro•dol•lar ▸ n. a US dollar deposit held in Europe or elsewhere outside the US.

Eu•ro•mar•ket ▸ n. a financial market that deals with Eurocurrencies. ■ the European Union regarded as a single commercial or financial market.

ex an•te ▸ adj. & adv. based on forecasts rather than actual results.

ex•change ▸ n. the giving of money for its equivalent in the money of another country.
■ the fee or percentage charged for converting the currency of one country into that of another. ■ a system or market in which commercial transactions involving currency, shares, commodities, etc., can be carried out within or between countries. ■ a building or institution used for the trading of a particular commodity or commodities: *the New York Stock Exchange.*

ex•change con•trol ▸ n. a governmental restriction on the movement of currency between countries.

ex•change rate ▸ n. (also **rate of exchange**) the value of one currency for the purpose of conversion to another.

ex•cise ▸ n. a tax levied on certain goods and commodities produced or sold within a country and on licenses granted for certain activities.

ex•clu•sive ec•o•nom•ic zone ▸ n. an area of coastal water and seabed within a certain distance of a country's coastline, to which the country claims exclusive rights for fishing, drilling, and other economic activities.

ex div. ▸ abbr. ex dividend.

ex div•i•dend ▸ adj. & adv. (of stocks or shares) not including the next dividend.

ex•ec ▸ n. informal an executive: *top execs.*

ex•ec•u•tive ▸ n. a person with senior managerial responsibility in a business organization.
■ an executive committee or other body within an organization: *the union executive.*

ex•emp•tion ▸ n. (also **personal exemption**) the process of exempting a person from paying taxes on a specified amount of income for themselves and their dependents.
■ a dependent exempted in this way.

ex•er•cise price ▸ n. the price per share at which the owner of a traded option is entitled to buy or sell the underlying security.

ex•pense ▸ n. the cost required for something; the money spent on something.
■ (**expenses**) the costs incurred in the performance of one's job or a specific task, esp. one undertaken for another person.
▸ v. (usu. **be expensed**) offset (an item of expenditure) as an expense against taxable income.

ex•pense ac•count ▸ n. an arrangement under which sums of money spent in the course of business by an employee are later reimbursed by their employer.

ex•pi•ra•tion ▸ n. the ending of the fixed period for which a contract is valid.

ex•po•nen•tial growth ▸ n. growth whose rate becomes ever more rapid in proportion to the growing total number or size.

ex•port ▸ v. send (goods or services) to another country for sale: *we exported $16 million worth of mussels to Japan.*
▸n. (usu. **exports**) a commodity, article, or service sold abroad.
  ■ (**exports**) sales of goods or services to other countries, or the revenue from such sales: *meat exports.* ■ the selling and sending out of goods or services to other countries: *the export of Western technology.* ■ of a high standard suitable for export: *high-grade export coal.*
ex•port sur•plus ▸ n. the amount by which the value of a country's exports exceeds that of its imports.
ex post ▸ adj. & adv. based on actual results rather than forecasts.
ex•po•sure ▸ n. the action of placing oneself at risk of financial losses, e.g., through making loans, granting credit, or underwriting insurance.
ex•ter•nal•i•ty ▸ n. (pl. **-ies**) a side effect or consequence of an industrial or commercial activity that affects other parties without this being reflected in the cost of the goods or services involved, such as the pollination of surrounding crops by bees kept for honey.
ex•tinc•tion ▸ n. the wiping out of a debt.
ex•tin•guish ▸ v. (often **be extinguished**) cancel (a debt) by full payment.
ex•traor•di•nar•y ▸ n. (usu. **extraordinaries**) an item in a company's accounts not arising from its normal activities.
face val•ue ▸ n. the value printed or depicted on a coin, banknote, postage stamp, ticket, etc., esp. when less than the actual or intrinsic value.
fac•tor ▸ n. a business agent; a merchant buying and selling on commission.
  ■ a company that buys a manufacturer's invoices at a discount and takes responsibility for collecting the payments due on them.
▸v. sell (one's receivable debts) to a factor.
fac•tor•age ▸ n. the commission or charges payable to a factor.
fac•tor cost ▸ n. the cost of an item or a service in terms of the various factors that have played a part in its production or availability, and exclusive of tax costs.
Fan•nie Mae ▸ n. informal the Federal National Mortgage Association, a corporation (now privately owned) that trades in mortgages.
farm ▸ n. an area of land and its buildings used for growing crops and rearing animals, typically under the control of one owner or manager.
  ■ an establishment at which something is produced or processed: *an energy farm.*
▸v. (**farm someone/something out**) send out or subcontract work to others.
FDIC ▸ abbr. Federal Deposit Insurance Corporation, a body that underwrites most private bank deposits.
feath•er•bed ▸ v. (also **feather-bed**) provide (someone) with advantageous economic or working conditions.

  ■ (**featherbedding**) deliberately limit production or retain excess staff in (a business) in order to create jobs or prevent unemployment, typically as a result of a union contract.
Fed•er•al Re•serve the federal banking authority in the US that performs the functions of a central bank and is used to implement the country's monetary policy, providing a national system of reserve cash available to banks. Created in 1913, the Federal Reserve System consists of twelve Federal Reserve Districts, each having a Federal Reserve Bank. These are controlled from Washington, DC by the Federal Reserve Board consisting of governors appointed by the US president with Senate approval.
fi•at mon•ey ▸ n. inconvertible paper money made legal tender by a government decree.
fi•du•ci•ar•y ▸ adj. involving trust, esp. with regard to the relationship between a trustee and a beneficiary.
  ■ (of a paper currency) depending for its value on securities (as opposed to gold) or the reputation of the issuer.
▸n. (pl. **-ies**) a trustee.
FIFO ▸ abbr. first in, first out (chiefly with reference to methods of stock valuation and data storage).
fi•nance ▸ n. the management of large amounts of money, esp. by governments or large companies.
  ■ monetary support for an enterprise: *housing finance.* ■ (**finances**) the monetary resources and affairs of a country, organization, or person.
▸v. provide funding for (a person or enterprise).
fi•nance com•pa•ny ▸ n. a company concerned primarily with providing money, e.g., for short-term loans.
fi•nan•cial ▸ adj. of or relating to finance: *an independent financial adviser.*
Fi•nan•cial Times in•dex another term for **FTSE** INDEX.
fin•an•cier ▸ n. a person concerned with the management of large amounts of money on behalf of governments or other large organizations.
firm¹ ▸ adj. (of a currency, a commodity, or shares) having a steady value or price that is more likely to rise than fall: *the dollar was firm against the yen.*
▸v. (of a price) rise slightly to reach a level considered secure: *he believed house prices would firm by the end of the year.*
firm² ▸ n. a business concern, esp. one involving a partnership of two or more people: *a law firm.*
fis•cal ▸ adj. of or relating to government revenue, esp. taxes: *monetary and fiscal policy.*
  ■ of or relating to financial matters: *the domestic fiscal crisis.* ■ used to denote a fiscal year: *the budget deficit for fiscal 1996.*
fis•cal year ▸ n. a year as reckoned for taxing or accounting purposes.
fixed as•sets ▸ plural n. assets that are purchased for long-term use and are not likely to be converted quickly into cash, such as land, buildings, and equipment.
fixed cap•i•tal ▸ n. capital invested in fixed assets.
fixed charge ▸ n. a liability to a creditor that relates to specific assets of a company.

fixed costs ▸ plural n. business costs, such as rent, that are constant whatever the amount of goods produced.

flat ▸ adj. (**flatter, flattest**) (of a market, prices, etc.) not showing much activity; sluggish: *cash flow was flat at $214 million | flat sales in the drinks industry.* (of a fee, wage, or price) the same in all cases, not varying with changed conditions or in particular cases: *a $30 flat fare.*

fli•er (also **flyer**) ▸ n. a small handbill advertising an event or product. a speculative investment.

flight cap•i•tal ▸ n. money transferred abroad to avoid taxes or inflation, achieve better investment returns, or to provide for possible emigration.

float ▸ v. offer the shares of (a company) for sale on the stock market for the first time. ■ (of a currency) fluctuate freely in value in accordance with supply and demand in the financial markets. ■ allow (a currency) to fluctuate in such a way.

float•er ▸ n. a worker who is required to do a variety of tasks as the need for each arises. an insurance policy covering loss of articles without specifying a location.

float•ing debt ▸ n. a debt that is repayable in the short term.

floor ▸ n. figurative the minimum level of prices or wages: *the dollar's floor against the yen.* ■ (of the stock exchange) the large central hall where trading takes place.

flo•ta•tion (also **floatation**) ▸ n. the process of offering a company's shares for sale on the stock market for the first time.

f.o.b. ▸ abbr. free on board.

Foot•sie ▸ n. Brit. informal term for **FTSE INDEX**.

f.o.r. ▸ abbr. free on rail.

fore•clo•sure ▸ n. the process of taking possession of a mortgaged property as a result of someone's failure to keep up mortgage payments.

for•eign ex•change ▸ n. the currency of other countries. ■ an institution or system for dealing in such currency.

fran•chise ▸ n. an authorization granted by a government or company to an individual or group enabling them to carry out specified commercial activities, e.g., providing a broadcasting service or acting as an agent for a company's products. ■ a business or service given such authorization to operate. ■ an authorization given by a league to own a sports team. ▸ v. grant a franchise to (an individual or group). ■ grant a franchise for the sale of (goods) or the operation of (a service).

free ▸ adj. (**freer, freest**) given or available without charge: *free health care.* ▸ adv. without cost or payment. –PHRASES **for free** informal without cost or payment: *these professionals were giving their time for free.* **free on board** (abbr.: **f.o.b.**) including or assuming delivery without charge to the buyer's named destination.

free en•ter•prise ▸ n. an economic system in which private business operates in competition and largely free of state control.

free mar•ket ▸ n. an economic system in which prices are determined by unrestricted competition between privately owned businesses.

free trade ▸ n. international trade left to its natural course without tariffs, quotas, or other restrictions.

freeze ▸ v. (past **froze**; past part. **frozen**) prevent (assets) from being used for a period of time: *the charity's bank account has been frozen.* ▸ n. an act of holding or being held at a fixed level or in a fixed state: *workers faced a pay freeze.*

fric•tion•al un•em•ploy•ment ▸ n. the unemployment which exists in any economy due to people being in the process of moving from one job to another.

fringe ben•e•fit ▸ n. an extra benefit supplementing an employee's salary, for example, a company car, subsidized meals, health insurance, etc.

front-run•ning ▸ n. the practice by market makers of dealing on advance information provided by their brokers and investment analysts, before their clients have been given the information.

FRS ▸ abbr. ■ Federal Reserve System.

FTA ▸ abbr. Free Trade Agreement, used to refer to that signed in 1988 between the US and Canada.

FTC ▸ abbr. Federal Trade Commission.

FT in•dex ▸ another term for **FTSE INDEX**.

FTSE in•dex a figure (published by the *Financial Times*) indicating the relative prices of shares on the London Stock Exchange, esp. (also **FTSE 100 index**) one calculated on the basis of Britain's one hundred largest public companies.

fund ▸ n. a sum of money saved or made available for a particular purpose. ■ (**funds**) financial resources: *the misuse of public funds.* ■ an organization set up for the administration and management of a monetary fund. ▸ v. provide with money for a particular purpose.

fund•ed debt ▸ n. debt in the form of securities with long-term or indefinite redemption.

fund man•ag•er ▸ n. an employee of a large institution (such as a pension fund or an insurance company) who manages the investment of money on its behalf.

fun•gi•ble ▸ adj. (of goods contracted for without an individual specimen being specified) able to replace or be replaced by another identical item; mutually interchangeable.

fu•ture ▸ n. (**futures**) short for **FUTURES CONTRACT**.

FY ▸ abbr. fiscal year.

GDP ▸ abbr. gross domestic product.

gilt-edged ▸ adj. relating to or denoting stocks or securities that are regarded as extremely reliable investments.

GNP ▸ abbr. gross national product.

gold card ▸ n. a charge card or credit card issued to people with a high credit rating and giving benefits not available with the standard card.

gold•en par•a•chute ▸ n. informal a large payment or other financial compensation guaranteed to a company executive should the executive be dismissed as a result of a merger or takeover.

gold re•serve ▸ n. a quantity of gold held by a central bank to support the issue of currency.

good•will (also **good will**) ▸ n. the established reputation of a business regarded as a quantifiable asset, e.g., as represented by the excess of the price paid at a takeover for a company over its fair market value.

gov•ern•ment se•cu•ri•ties ▸ plural n. bonds or other promissory certificates issued by the government.

gray mar•ket ▸ n. an unofficial market or trade in something, esp. unissued shares or controlled or scarce goods.

green•field ▸ adj. relating to or denoting previously undeveloped sites for commercial development or exploitation.

▸ n. an undeveloped site, esp. one being evaluated and considered for commercial development or exploitation.

green•mail ▸ n. the practice of buying enough shares in a company to threaten a takeover, forcing the owners to buy them back at a higher price in order to retain control.

Gresh•am's law the tendency for money of lower intrinsic value to circulate more freely than money of higher intrinsic and equal nominal value (often expressed as "Bad money drives out good").

gross ▸ adj. (of income, profit, or interest) without deduction of tax or other contributions; total. Often contrasted with NET.

▸ adv. without tax or other contributions having been deducted.

▸ v. produce or earn (an amount of money) as gross profit or income.

▸ n. (pl. **grosses**) a gross profit or income.

gross do•mes•tic prod•uct (abbr.: GDP) ▸ n. the total value of goods produced and services provided in a country during one year. Compare with GROSS NATIONAL PRODUCT.

gross na•tion•al prod•uct (abbr.: GNP) ▸ n. the total value of goods produced and services provided by a country during one year, equal to the gross domestic product plus the net income from foreign investments.

group ▸ n. a commercial organization consisting of several companies under common ownership.

growth in•dus•try ▸ n. an industry that is developing particularly rapidly.

growth stock ▸ n. a company stock that tends to increase in capital value rather than yield high income.

guar•an•tee fund ▸ n. a sum of money pledged as a contingent indemnity for loss.

guar•an•ty (also **guarantee**) ▸ n. (pl. **-ies**) a formal pledge to pay another person's debt or to perform another person's obligation in the case of default.

■ a thing serving as security for a such a pledge.

han•dler ▸ n. Informal a publicity agent.

Hang Seng in•dex a figure indicating the relative price of shares on the Hong Kong Stock Exchange.

hard ▸ adj. (of prices of stock, commodities, etc.) stable or firm in value.

hard cash ▸ n. negotiable coins and paper money as opposed to other forms of payment.

hard cur•ren•cy ▸ n. currency that is not likely to depreciate suddenly or to fluctuate greatly in value.

hard•en ▸ v. (of prices of stocks, commodities, etc.) rise and remain steady at a higher level.

hard sell ▸ n. a policy or technique of aggressive salesmanship or advertising.

haul•age ▸ n. the commercial transport of goods. ■ a charge for such transport.

head count ▸ n. a total number of people, esp. the number of people employed in a particular organization.

head•hunt•er ▸ n. a person who identifies and approaches suitable candidates employed elsewhere to fill business positions.

heav•y in•dus•try ▸ n. the manufacture of large, heavy articles and materials in bulk.

hedge ▸ n. a contract entered into or asset held as a protection against possible financial loss.

▸ v. protect (one's investment or an investor) against loss by making balancing or compensating contracts or transactions.

hid•den re•serves ▸ plural n. a company's funds that are not declared on its balance sheet.

high-end ▸ adj. denoting the most expensive of a range of products.

high fi•nance ▸ n. financial transactions involving large amounts of money.

hire ▸ v. employ (someone) for wages.

■ employ for a short time to do a particular job. ■ (**hire oneself out**) make oneself available for temporary employment.

▸ n. the action of hiring someone or something. a recently recruited employee.

hold•back ▸ n. a sum of money withheld under certain conditions.

hold•ing ▸ n. (**holdings**) stocks, property, and other financial assets in someone's possession.

hold•ing com•pa•ny ▸ n. a company created to buy and possess the shares of other companies, which it then controls.

hon•or ▸ v. accept (a bill) or pay (a check) when due.

hon•o•rar•i•um ▸ n. (pl. **honorariums** or **honoraria**) a payment given for professional services that are rendered nominally without charge.

hos•tile ▸ adj. (of a takeover bid) opposed by the company to be bought.

hot-desk•ing ▸ n. the practice in an office of allocating desks to workers when they are required or on a rotating system, rather than giving each worker their own desk.

hot mon•ey ▸ n. capital that is frequently transferred between financial institutions in an attempt to maximize interest or capital gain.

house ▸ n. a business or institution.

hu•man cap•i•tal ▸ n. the skills, knowledge, and experience possessed by an individual or population, viewed in terms of their value or cost to an organization or country.

hy•poth•e•cate ▸ v. pledge (money) by law to a specific purpose.

i•dle ▸ adj. (**idler, idlest**) (esp. of a machine or factory) not active or in use.

■ (of a person) not working; unemployed. ■ (of

money) held in cash or in accounts paying no interest.

▸v. take out of use or employment: *he will close the newspaper, idling 2,200 workers.*

il•liq•uid ▸ adj. (of assets) not easily converted into cash: *illiquid assets.*

■ (of a market) with few participants and a low volume of activity.

im•age-mak•er ▸ n. a person employed to identify and create a favorable public image for a person, organization, or product.

IMF ▸ abbr. International Monetary Fund.

im•per•fect com•pe•ti•tion ▸ n. the situation prevailing in a market in which elements of monopoly allow individual producers or consumers to exercise some control over market prices.

im•port ▸ v. bring (goods or services) into a country from abroad for sale.

▸n. (usu. **imports**) a commodity, article, or service brought in from abroad for sale.

■ (**imports**) sales of goods or services brought in from abroad, or the revenue from such sales: *this surplus pushes up the yen, which ought to boost imports.* ■ the action or process of importing goods or services.

im•po•si•tion ▸ n. a thing that is imposed, especially a tax or duty.

im•post ▸ n. a tax or similar compulsory payment.

im•prest ▸ n. a fund used by a business for small items of expenditure and restored to a fixed amount periodically.

■ an advance of money made to someone engaged in some business with the state, enabling them to carry out the business. ■ a sum of money advanced to a person for a particular purpose.

im•pute ▸ v. assign (a value) to something by inference from the value of the products or processes to which it contributes.

Inc. ▸ abbr. incorporated.

in•come ▸ n. money received, esp. on a regular basis, for work or through investments.

in•come tax ▸ n. tax levied directly on personal income.

in•con•vert•i•ble ▸ adj. (of currency) not able to be converted into another form on demand.

in•cor•po•rate ▸ v. (often **be incorporated**) constitute (a company, city, or other organization) as a legal corporation.

in•cor•po•rat•ed ▸ adj. (of a company or other organization) formed into a legal corporation.

in•dem•ni•ty ▸ n. (pl. **-ies**) security or protection against a loss or other financial burden.

in•dex ▸ n. (pl. **indexes** or esp. in technical use **indices**) a figure in a system or scale representing the average value of specified prices, shares, or other items as compared with some reference figure.

▸v. link the value of (prices, wages, or other payments) automatically to the value of a price index.

in•dif•fer•ence curve ▸ n. a curve on a graph (the axes of which represent quantities of two commodities) linking those combinations of quantities that the consumer regards as of equal value.

in•di•rect ▸ adj. (of costs) deriving from overhead charges or subsidiary work.

■ (of taxation) levied on goods and services rather than income or profits.

in•di•rect tax ▸ n. a tax levied on goods and services and not on income or profits.

in•dul•gence ▸ n. an extension of the time in which a bill or debt has to be paid.

in•dus•tri•al ▸ n. (**industrials**) shares in industrial companies.

in•dus•tri•al es•pi•o•nage ▸ n. spying directed toward discovering the secrets of a rival manufacturer or other industrial company.

in•fla•tion ▸ n. a general increase in prices and fall in the purchasing value of money.

in•fla•tion•ar•y ▸ adj. of, characterized by, or tending to cause monetary inflation.

in•fo•mer•cial ▸ n. a television program that promotes a product in an informative and supposedly objective way.

in•i•tial pub•lic of•fer•ing ▸ n. a company's flotation on the stock exchange.

in-serv•ice ▸ adj. (of training) intended for those actively engaged in the profession or activity concerned.

in•sid•er trad•ing ▸ n. the illegal practice of trading on the stock exchange to one's own advantage through having access to confidential information.

in•sol•vent ▸ adj. unable to pay debts owed.

in•stall•ment ▸ n. a sum of money due as one of several equal payments for something, spread over an agreed period of time.

in•stall•ment plan ▸ n. an arrangement for payment by installments.

in•sti•tu•tion•al ▸ adj. (of advertising) intended to create prestige rather than immediate sales.

in•sti•tu•tion•al in•ves•tor ▸ n. a large organization such as a bank, pension fund, labor union, or insurance company, that makes substantial investments on the stock exchange.

in•sur•ance ▸ n. a practice or arrangement by which a company or government agency provides a guarantee of compensation for specified loss, damage, illness, or death in return for payment of a premium.

in•sur•ance a•gent ▸ n. a person employed to sell insurance policies.

in•sur•ance car•ri•er ▸ n. an insurer; an insurance company.

in•sur•ance pol•i•cy ▸ n. a document detailing the terms and conditions of a contract of insurance.

in•sure ▸ v. arrange for compensation in the event of damage to or loss of (property), or injury to or the death of (someone), in exchange for regular advance payments to a company or government agency.

■ provide insurance coverage with respect to.

in•sured ▸ adj. covered by insurance.

▸n. (**the insured**) (pl. same) a person or organization covered by insurance.

in•sur•er ▸ n. a person or company that underwrites an insurance risk; the party in an insurance contract undertaking to pay compensation.

in•tan•gi•ble ▸ adj. (of an asset or benefit) not constituting or represented by a physical object and of a value not precisely measurable.

in•ter•bank ▸ adj. agreed, arranged, or operating between banks.

in•ter•est ▸ n. money paid regularly at a particular rate for the use of money lent, or for delaying the repayment of a debt. a stake, share, or involvement in an undertaking, esp. a financial one.

–PHRASES **declare an (or one's) interest** make known one's financial interests in an undertaking before it is discussed. **with interest** with interest charged or paid.

in•tra•pre•neur ▸ n. a manager within a company who promotes innovative product development and marketing.

in•ven•to•ry ▸ n. (pl. -**ies**) a complete list of items such as property, goods in stock, or the contents of a building.
 ■ a quantity of goods held in stock. ■ (in accounting) the entire stock of a business, including materials, components, work in progress, and finished products.

in•vest ▸ v. expend money with the expectation of achieving a profit or material result by putting it into financial schemes, shares, or property, or by using it to develop a commercial venture.

in•vest•ment ▸ n. the action or process of investing money for profit or material result.
 ■ a thing that is worth buying because it may be profitable or useful in the future.

in•vest•ment bank ▸ n. a bank that purchases large holdings of newly issued shares and resells them to investors.

in•vest•ment grade ▸ n. a level of credit rating for stocks regarded as carrying a minimal risk to investors.

in•vest•ment trust ▸ n. a limited company whose business is the investment of shareholders' funds, the shares being traded like those of any other public company.

in•voice ▸ n. a list of goods sent or services provided, with a statement of the sum due for these; a bill.
 ▸ v. send an invoice to (someone).
 ■ send an invoice for (goods or services provided).

IPO ▸ abbr. initial public offering.

IRA ▸ abbr. individual retirement account.

ir•re•deem•a•ble ▸ adj. (of paper currency) for which the issuing authority does not undertake ever to pay coin.

Jay•cee ▸ n. a member of a Junior Chamber of Commerce, a civic organization for business and community leaders.

JIT ▸ abbr. (of manufacturing systems) just-in-time.

job ▸ n. a paid position of regular employment. a task or piece of work, esp. one that is paid.
 ▸ v. (**jobbed, jobbing**) buy and sell (stocks) as a broker-dealer, esp. on a small scale.
 –PHRASES **on the job** while working; at work. **out of a job** unemployed.

job an•a•lyst ▸ n. a person employed to assess the essential factors of particular jobs and the qualifications needed to carry them out.

job•ber ▸ n. a wholesaler. ■ a person who does casual or occasional work.

job ro•ta•tion ▸ n. the practice of moving employees between different tasks to promote experience and variety.

joint ac•count ▸ n. a bank account held by more than one person, each individual having the right to deposit and withdraw funds.

joint stock ▸ n. a portion of capital held jointly; a common fund.

joint-stock com•pa•ny ▸ n. a company whose stock is owned jointly by the shareholders.

joint ven•ture ▸ n. a commercial enterprise undertaken jointly by two or more parties that otherwise retain their distinct identities.

jour•nal ▸ n. (in bookkeeping) a daily record of business transactions with a statement of the accounts to which each is to be debited and credited.

junk bond ▸ n. a high-yield, high-risk security, typically issued by a company seeking to raise capital quickly in order to finance a takeover.

just-in-time ▸ adj. denoting a manufacturing system in which materials or components are delivered immediately before they are required in order to minimize inventory costs.

kai•zen ▸ n. a Japanese business philosophy of continuous improvement of working practices, personal efficiency, etc.

kan•ban ▸ n. (also **kanban system**) a Japanese manufacturing system in which the supply of components is regulated through the use of a card displaying a sequence of specifications and instructions, sent along the production line.
 ■ a card of this type.

kei•ret•su ▸ n. (pl. same) (in Japan) a conglomeration of businesses linked together by cross-shareholdings to form a robust corporate structure.

la•bor mar•ket ▸ n. the supply of available workers with reference to the demand for them.

Laf•fer curve ▸ n. a supposed relationship between economic activity and the rate of taxation that suggests the existence of an optimum tax rate that maximizes tax revenue.

lais•sez-faire ▸ n. abstention by governments from interfering in the workings of the free market.

land bank ▸ n. a bank whose main function is to provide loans for land purchase, esp. by farmers.

laun•der ▸ v. conceal the origins of (money obtained illegally) by transfers involving foreign banks or legitimate businesses.

lay•off ▸ n. a discharge, esp. temporary, of a worker or workers.
 ■ a period when this is in force.

LBO ▸ abbr. leveraged buyout.

l.c. ▸ abbr. letter of credit.

lead time ▸ n. the time between the initiation and completion of a production process.

leak•age ▸ n. deliberate disclosure of confidential information.

ledg•er ▸ n. a book or other collection of financial accounts of a particular type.

lend ▸ v. (past and past part. **lent**) allow (a person or organization) the use of (a sum of money) under an agreement to pay it back later, typically with interest.

lend•er ▸ n. an organization or person that lends money.

let•ter of cred•it ▸ n. a letter issued by a bank to another bank (typically in a different country) to serve as a guarantee for payments made to a specified person under specified conditions.

lev•er•age ▸ n. the ratio of a company's loan capital (debt) to the value of its ordinary shares (equity).
▸ v. (**leveraged**) use borrowed capital for (an investment), expecting the profits made to be greater than the interest payable.

lev•er•aged buy•out ▸ n. the purchase of a controlling share in a company by its management, using outside capital.

li•a•bil•i•ty ▸ n. (pl. **-ies**) (usu. **liabilities**) a thing for which someone is responsible, esp. a debt or financial obligation.

life in•sur•ance ▸ n. insurance that pays out a sum of money either on the death of the insured person or after a set period.

life ta•ble ▸ n. a table of statistics relating to life expectancy and mortality for a given category of people.

LIFO ▸ abbr. last in, first out (chiefly with reference to methods of stock valuation and data storage). Compare with **FIFO**.

light in•dus•try ▸ n. the manufacture of small or light articles.

lim•it•ed ▸ adj. (**Limited**) Brit. denoting a company whose owners are legally responsible for its debts only to the extent of the amount of capital they invested (used after a company name).

lim•it•ed part•ner ▸ n. a partner in a company or venture who receives limited profits from the business and whose liability toward its debts is legally limited to the extent of his or her investment.

line ▸ n. a company that provides ships, aircraft, or buses on particular routes on a regular basis. a range of commercial goods.
–PHRASES **above the line** denoting or relating to money spent on items of current expenditure. **below the line** denoting or relating to money spent on items of capital expenditure. **line of credit** an amount of credit extended to a borrower.

liq•uid ▸ adj. (of assets) held in cash or easily converted into cash.
■ having ready cash or liquid assets. ■ (of a market) having a high volume of activity.

liq•ui•date ▸ v. wind up the affairs of (a company or firm) by ascertaining liabilities and apportioning assets.
■ (of a company) undergo such a process. ■ convert (assets) into cash. ■ pay off (a debt).

liq•ui•da•tion ▸ n. the process of liquidating a company or firm.
■ the conversion of assets into cash (i.e., by selling them). ■ the clearing of a debt.
–PHRASES **go into liquidation** (of a company or firm) be closed and have its assets apportioned.

liq•ui•da•tor ▸ n. a person appointed to wind up the affairs of a company or firm.

liq•uid•i•ty ▸ n. the availability of liquid assets to a market or company.
■ liquid assets; cash. ■ a high volume of activity in a market.

li•quid•i•ty ra•tio ▸ n. the ratio between the liquid assets and the liabilities of a bank or other institution.

list•ed ▸ adj. admitted for trading on a stock exchange.

list price ▸ n. the price of an article as shown in a list issued by the manufacturer or by the general body of manufacturers of the particular class of goods.

liv•er•y ▸ n. (pl. **-ies**) a special design and color scheme used on the vehicles, aircraft, or products of a particular company.

liv•ing wage ▸ n. [in sing.] a wage that is high enough to maintain a normal standard of living.

load ▸ v. add an extra charge to (an insurance premium) in the case of a poorer risk.

load•ing ▸ n. an increase in an insurance premium due to a factor increasing the risk involved.

loan ▸ n. a thing that is borrowed, esp. a sum of money that is expected to be paid back with interest.
■ an act of lending something to someone.
▸ v. (often **be loaned**) borrow (a sum of money or item of property).

lock-in ▸ n. an arrangement according to which a person or company is obliged to negotiate or trade only with a specific company.

lock•up ▸ n. an investment in assets that cannot readily be realized or sold on in the short term.

lodg•ment (also **lodgement**) ▸ n. the depositing of money in a particular bank, account, etc.

lo•go ▸ n. (pl. **-os**) a symbol or other small design adopted by an organization to identify its products, uniform, vehicles, etc.

long ▸ adj. (**longer, longest**) (of shares, bonds, or other assets) bought in advance, with the expectation of a rise in price.
■ (of a broker or their position in the market) buying or based on long stocks. ■ (of a security) maturing at a distant date.
▸ n. (**longs**) long-dated securities, esp. gilt-edged securities.
■ assets held in a long position.

loss-lead•er ▸ n. a product sold at a loss to attract customers.

loss-mak•ing ▸ adj. (esp. of a business) losing money, rather than making a profit.

low•ball ▸ adj. informal (of an estimate, bid, etc.) deceptively or unrealistically low.
▸ v. offer a deceptively or unrealistically low estimate, bid, etc.

Ltd. Brit. ▸ abbr. (after a company name) Limited.

lump sum ▸ n. a single payment made at a particular time, as opposed to a number of smaller payments or installments.

mac•ro•ec•o•nom•ics ▸ plural n. [treated as sing.] the part of economics concerned with large-scale or general economic factors, such as interest rates and national productivity.

mac•ro•e•con•o•my ▸ n. a large-scale economic system.

mail or•der ▸ n. the selling of goods to customers by mail, generally involving selection from a special catalog.

mall ▸ n. (also **shopping mall**) a large building or series of connected buildings containing a variety of retail stores and typically also restaurants.

man•aged cur•ren•cy ▸ n. a currency whose exchange rate is regulated or controlled by the government.

man•aged fund ▸ n. an investment fund run on behalf of an investor by an agent (typically an insurance company).

man•age•ment ac•count•ing ▸ n. the provision of financial data and advice to a company for use in the organization and development of its business.

man•age•ment com•pa•ny ▸ n. a company that is set up to manage a group of properties, a mutual fund, an investment fund, etc.

mar•gin ▸ n. a profit margin.
■ a sum deposited with a broker to cover the risk of loss on a transaction or account.
▸ v. (**margined, margining**) deposit an amount of money with a broker as security for (an account or transaction).

mar•gin•al ▸ adj. (chiefly of costs or benefits) relating to or resulting from small or unit changes.
■ (of taxation) relating to increases in income.
■ close to the limit of profitability, esp. through difficulty of exploitation.

mar•gin•al cost ▸ n. the cost added by producing one extra item of a product.

mar•gin call ▸ n. a demand by a broker that an investor deposit further cash or securities to cover possible losses.

mark•down ▸ n. a reduction in price.

mar•ket ▸ n. an area or arena in which commercial dealings are conducted: *the labor market.*
■ a demand for a particular commodity or service. ■ the state of trade at a particular time or in a particular context. ■ the free market; the operation of supply and demand. ■ a stock market.
▸ v. (**marketed, marketing**) advertise or promote (something).
■ offer for sale. ■ buy or sell provisions in a market.
–PHRASES **make a market** take part in active dealing in particular shares or other assets.

mar•ket forc•es ▸ plural n. the economic factors affecting the price, demand, and availability of a commodity.

mar•ket•ing ▸ n. the action or business of promoting and selling products or services, including market research and advertising.

mar•ket•ing mix ▸ n. a combination of factors that can be controlled by a company to influence consumers to purchase its products.

mar•ket•i•za•tion ▸ n. the exposure of an industry or service to market forces.
■ the conversion of a national economy from a planned to a market economy.

mar•ket mak•er (also **market-maker**) ▸ n. a dealer in securities or other assets who undertakes to buy or sell at specified prices at all times.

mar•ket pen•e•tra•tion ▸ n. the action of entering a market with a new product or brand.

■ a measure of the success with which a product or brand has entered a market.

mar•ket price ▸ n. the price of a commodity when sold in a given market.

mar•ket re•search ▸ n. the action or activity of gathering information about consumers' needs and preferences.

mar•ket share ▸ n. the portion of a market controlled by a particular company or product.

mar•ket val•ue ▸ n. the amount for which something can be sold on a given market.

mark-to-mar•ket ▸ adj. denoting or relating to a system of valuing assets by the most recent market price.

mark•up ▸ n. the amount added to the cost price of goods to cover overhead and profit.

mart ▸ n. a trade center or market.

mass mar•ket ▸ n. the market for goods that are produced in large quantities.
▸ v. (**mass-market**) market (a product) on a large scale.

ma•trix ▸ n. (pl. **matrices** or **matrixes**) an organizational structure in which two or more lines of command, responsibility, or communication may run through the same individual.

ma•ture ▸ adj. (**maturer, maturest**) denoting an economy, industry, or market that has developed to a point where substantial expansion and investment no longer takes place. ■ (of a bill) due for payment.
▸ v. (of an insurance policy, security, etc.) reach the end of its term and hence become payable.

ma•tu•ri•ty ▸ n. the time when an insurance policy, security, etc., matures.

MBA ▸ abbr. Master of Business Administration.

meg•a•store ▸ n. a very large store, typically one specializing in a particular type of product.

mel•on ▸ n. figurative a large profit, esp. a stock dividend, to be divided among a number of people.

melt•down ▸ n. figurative a disastrous event, esp. a rapid fall in share prices.

merg•er ▸ n. a combination of two things, esp. companies, into one.

met•age ▸ n. the official weighing of loads of coal, grain, or other material.
■ the duty paid for this.

mez•za•nine ▸ adj. relating to or denoting unsecured, higher-yielding loans that are subordinate to bank loans and secured loans but rank above equity.

MFN ▸ abbr. most favored nation.

mi•cro•ec•o•nom•ics ▸ plural n. [treated as sing.] the part of economics concerned with single factors and the effects of individual decisions.

mid•dle•man ▸ n. (pl. **-men**) a person who buys goods from producers and sells them to retailers or consumers.
■ a person who arranges business or political deals between other people.

mid•dle man•age•ment ▸ n. the level in an organization just below that of senior administrators.
■ the managers at this level regarded collectively.

mid•dling ▸ n. (**middlings**) bulk goods of medium grade, esp. flour of medium fineness.

mill ▸ n. a monetary unit used only in calculations, worth one thousandth of a dollar.

min•i-mall ▸ n. a shopping mall containing a relatively small number of retail outlets and with access to each shop from the outside rather than from an interior hallway.

mint par (also **mint parity**) ▸ n. the ratio between the gold equivalents of currency in two countries. ■ their rate of exchange based on such a ratio.

mixed e•con•o•my ▸ n. an economic system combining private and public enterprise.

MLR ▸ abbr. minimum lending rate.

mon•e•ta•rism ▸ n. the theory or practice of controlling the supply of money as the chief method of stabilizing the economy.

mon•e•tar•y ▸ adj. of or relating to money or currency.

mon•e•tize ▸ v. convert into or express in the form of currency.

mon•ey•chang•er (also **money-changer**) ▸ n. a person whose business is the exchanging of one currency for another.

mon•ey•lend•er (also **money-lender**) ▸ n. a person whose business is lending money to others who pay interest.

mon•ey mar•ket ▸ n. the trade in short-term loans between banks and other financial institutions.

mon•ey of ac•count ▸ n. a denomination of money used in reckoning, but not issued as actual coins or paper money.

mon•ey or•der ▸ n. a printed order for payment of a specified sum, issued by a bank or post office.

mon•ey sup•ply ▸ n. the total amount of money in circulation or in existence in a country.

mon•ey wag•es ▸ plural n. income expressed in terms of its monetary value, with no account taken of its purchasing power.

mo•nop•o•list ▸ n. a person or business that has a monopoly.

mo•nop•o•ly ▸ n. (pl. **-ies**) the exclusive possession or control of the supply or trade in a commodity or service. ■ a company or group having exclusive control over a commodity or service. ■ a commodity or service controlled in this way: *electricity, gas, and water were considered to be natural monopolies.*

mo•nop•so•ny ▸ n. (pl. **-ies**) a market situation in which there is only one buyer.

mort•gage ▸ n. the charging of real (or personal) property by a debtor to a creditor as security for a debt (esp. one incurred by the purchase of the property), on the condition that it shall be returned on payment of the debt within a certain period. ■ a deed effecting such a transaction. ■ a loan obtained through the conveyance of property as security. ▸ v. (often **be mortgaged**) convey (a property) to a creditor as security on a loan.

mort•ga•gee ▸ n. the lender in a mortgage, typically a bank.

mort•gage rate ▸ n. the rate of interest charged by a mortgage lender.

mort•ga•gor ▸ n. the borrower in a mortgage, typically a homeowner.

most fa•vored na•tion ▸ n. a country that has been granted the most favorable trading terms available by another country.

moun•tain ▸ n. a large surplus stock of a commodity.

move ▸ v. (of merchandise) be sold: *despite the high prices, goods are moving.* ■ sell (merchandise). ▸ n. a change of job, career, or business direction.

mul•ti•pli•er ▸ n. ■ a factor by which an increment of income exceeds the resulting increment of savings or investment.

mu•ni ▸ n. (pl. **munis**) short for MUNICIPAL BOND.

mu•nic•i•pal bond ▸ n. a security issued by or on behalf of a local authority.

mu•tu•al ▸ adj. denoting an insurance company or other corporate organization owned by its members and dividing some or all of its profits between them.

mu•tu•al fund ▸ n. an investment program funded by shareholders that trades in diversified holdings and is professionally managed.

mu•tu•al in•sur•ance ▸ n. insurance in which some or all of the profits are divided among the policyholders.

mu•tu•al•ize ▸ v. organize (a company or business) on mutual principles. ■ divide (something, esp. insurance losses) between involved parties.

nar•row mon•ey ▸ n. money in forms that can be used as a medium of exchange, generally banknotes, coins, and certain balances held by banks.

NASDAQ ▸ abbr. National Association of Securities Dealers Automated Quotations, a computerized system for trading in securities.

na•tion•al bank ▸ n. a commercial bank that is chartered under the federal government and is a member of the Federal Reserve System.

na•tion•al debt ▸ n. the total amount of money that a country's government has borrowed, by various means.

na•tion•al in•come ▸ n. the total amount of money earned within a country.

NAV ▸ abbr. net asset value.

near mon•ey ▸ n. assets that can readily be converted into cash, such as government bonds.

neg•a•tive eq•ui•ty ▸ n. potential indebtedness arising when the market value of a property falls below the outstanding amount of a mortgage secured on it.

neg•a•tive in•come tax ▸ n. money credited as allowances to a taxed income, and paid as a benefit when it exceeds debited tax.

ne•go•ti•ate ▸ v. transfer (a check, bill, or other document) to the legal ownership of another person. ■ convert (a check) into cash.

ne•go•ti•a•tion ▸ n. (also **negotiations**) the action or process of transferring ownership of a document.

net ▸ adj. (of an amount, value, or price) remaining after a deduction, such as tax or a discount, has been made: *net earnings per share rose.* Often contrasted with GROSS.

■ (of a price) to be paid in full; not reducible.

▸v. (netted, netting) acquire or obtain (a sum of money) as clear profit.

■ return (profit or income) for (someone). ■ (net something down/off/out) exclude a nonnet amount, such as tax, when making a calculation, in order to reduce the amount left to a net sum.

net book val•ue ▸ n. the value of an asset as recorded in the accounts of its owner.

net na•tion•al prod•uct (abbr.: NNP) ▸ n. the total value of goods produced and services provided in a country during one year, after depreciation of capital goods has been allowed for.

net prof•it ▸ n. the actual profit after working expenses not included in the calculation of gross profit have been paid.

NIC ▸ abbr. newly industrialized country.

niche ▸ n. a specialized but profitable corner of the market.

Nik•kei in•dex a figure indicating the relative price of representative shares on the Tokyo Stock Exchange. Also called Nikkei average.

NNP ▸ abbr. net national product.

no-fault ▸ adj. denoting an insurance policy that is valid regardless of whether the policyholder was at fault.

no-load ▸ adj. (of shares in a mutual fund) sold without a commission being charged at the time of sale.

nom•i•nal ▸ adj. (of a price or amount of money) very small; far below the real value or cost: some firms charge only a nominal fee for the service. ■ (of a quantity or dimension, esp. of manufactured articles) stated or expressed but not necessarily corresponding exactly to the real value.

■ (of a rate or other figure) expressed in terms of a certain amount, without making allowance for changes in real value over time: the nominal exchange rate.

nom•i•nal ac•count ▸ n. an account recording the financial transactions of a business in a particular category, rather than with a person or other organization.

nom•i•nal ledg•er ▸ n. a ledger containing nominal accounts, or one containing both nominal and real accounts.

nom•i•nal val•ue ▸ n. the value that is stated on currency; face value.

■ the price of a share, bond, or security when it was issued, rather than its current market value.

nom•i•nee ▸ n. a person or company whose name is given as having title to a stock, real estate, etc., but who is not the actual owner.

non•con•trib•u•to•ry ▸ adj. (of a pension or pension plan) funded by regular payments by the employer, not the employee.

non•earn•ing ▸ adj. (esp. of a person or an investment) not earning a regular income.

non•ne•go•ti•a•ble ▸ adj. (of a document) not able to be transferred or assigned to the legal ownership of another person.

non•par•tic•i•pat•ing ▸ adj. (of an insurance policy) not allowing the holder a share of the profits, typically in the form of a bonus, made by the company.

non•pay•ment ▸ n. failure to pay an amount of money that is owed.

North A•mer•i•can Free Trade A•gree•ment (abbr.: NAFTA) an agreement that came into effect in January 1994 between the US, Canada, and Mexico to remove barriers to trade between the three countries over a ten-year period.

NPV ▸ abbr. net present value. See PRESENT VALUE.

num•bered ac•count ▸ n. a bank account, esp. in a Swiss bank, identified only by a number and not bearing the owner's name.

nu•me•raire ▸ n. an item or commodity acting as a measure of value or as a standard for currency exchange.

NYSE ▸ abbr. New York Stock Exchange.

oc•troi ▸ n. a tax levied in some countries on various goods entering a town or city.

odd lot ▸ n. a transaction involving less than the usual round number of shares.

OECD ▸ abbr. Organization for Economic Cooperation and Development.

OEM ▸ abbr. original equipment manufacturer (an organization that makes devices from component parts bought from other organizations).

off-brand ▸ adj. denoting or relating to an item of retail goods of an unknown, unpopular, or inferior brand.

▸n. an unknown, unpopular, or inferior brand.

of•fer ▸ v. (usu. be offered) make available for sale: the product is offered at a very competitive price.

▸n. an amount of money that someone is willing to pay for something: the prospective purchaser who made the highest offer.

■ a specially reduced price or terms for something on sale: the offer runs right up until Christmas Eve.

–PHRASES on offer available: the number of permanent jobs on offer is relatively small. open to offers willing to sell something or do a job for a reasonable price.

of•fer doc•u•ment ▸ n. a document containing details of a takeover bid that is sent to the shareholders of the target company.

of•fer•ing price ▸ n. the price at which a dealer or institution is prepared to sell securities or other assets.

of•fice ▸ n. a room, set of rooms, or building used as a place for commercial, professional, or bureaucratic work.

■ the local center of a large business. ■ a room, department, or building used to provide a particular service: a ticket office | a post office. ■ the consulting room of a professional person.

of•fi•cer ▸ n. a holder of a post in a society, company, or other organization, esp. one who is involved at a senior level in its management: a chief executive officer.

off-price ▸ n. a method of retailing in which brand-name goods (esp. clothing) are sold for less than the usual retail price.

▸adv. using this method: selling goods off-price.

off•set ▸ n. a consideration or amount that diminishes or balances the effect of a contrary one: an offset against taxable profits.

off•shore ▸ adj. & adv. of or relating to the business of extracting oil or gas from the seabed: offshore *drilling.* ■ made, situated, or conducting business abroad, esp. in order to take advantage of lower costs or less stringent regulation: *deposits in off-shore accounts.*

ol•i•gop•o•ly ▶ n. (pl. **-ies**) a state of limited competition, in which a market is shared by a small number of producers or sellers.

ol•i•gop•so•ny ▶ n. (pl. **-ies**) a state of the market in which only a small number of buyers exists for a product.

OPEC ▶ abbr. Organization of the Petroleum Exporting Countries.

o•pen ▶ adj. (of a store, place of entertainment, etc.) officially admitting customers or visitors; available for business.
■ (of a bank account) available for transactions.

o•pen en•roll•ment ▶ n. a period during which employees may change, add, or drop benefits coverage.

o•pen in•ter•est ▶ n. the number of contracts or commitments outstanding in futures and options that are trading on an official exchange at any one time.

o•pen mar•ket ▶ n. (often **the open market**) an unrestricted market with free access by and competition of buyers and sellers.

o•pen out•cry ▶ n. a system of financial trading in which dealers shout their bids and contracts aloud.

op•er•at•ing prof•it ▶ n. profit from business operations (gross profit less operating expenses) before deduction of fixed costs.

op•er•a•tions re•search ▶ n. the application of scientific principles to business management, providing a quantitative basis for complex decisions.

op•por•tu•ni•ty cost ▶ n. the loss of potential gain from other alternatives when one alternative is chosen: *idle cash balances represent an opportunity cost in terms of lost interest.*

op•tion ▶ n. a right to buy or sell a particular thing at a specified price within a set time: *Columbia Pictures **has an option on** the script.*
▶ v. buy or sell an option on (something): *his script will have been optioned by the time you read this.*

Or•gan•i•za•tion of the Pe•tro•le•um Ex•port•ing Coun•tries (abbr.: **OPEC**) an association of eleven major oil-producing countries, founded in 1960 to coordinate policies and prices and headquartered in Vienna. Members are Algeria, Gabon, Indonesia, Iran, Iraq, Kuwait, Libya, Nigeria, Qatar, Saudi Arabia, the United Arab Emirates, and Venezuela.

o•rig•i•na•tion fee ▶ n. a fee charged by a lender on entering into a loan agreement to cover the cost of processing the loan.

out•let ▶ n. a place from which goods are sold or distributed.
■ a retail store that sells the goods of a specific manufacturer or brand. ■ a retail store offering discounted merchandise, esp. overstocked or irregular items. ■ a market for goods.

out•place•ment ▶ n. the provision of assistance to laid-off employees in finding new employment, either as a benefit provided by the employer directly, or through a specialist service.

out•sert ▶ n. a piece of promotional material that is placed on the outside of a package, publication, or other product.

out•side ▶ adj. (of an estimate) the greatest or highest possible: *new monthly charges that, according to outside estimates, may total $8 per line.*

out•side di•rec•tor ▶ n. a director of a company who is not employed by that company, typically an employee of an associated company.

out•side mon•ey ▶ n. money held in a form such as gold that is an asset for the holder and does not represent a corresponding liability for someone else.
■ money or investment from an independent source.

out•source ▶ v. obtain (goods or a service) from an outside supplier, esp. in place of an internal source.
■ contract (work) out: *you may choose to **outsource** this function to another company or do it yourself.*

out•turn ▶ n. the amount of something produced, esp. money; output: *the financial outturn.*

o•ver•age ▶ n. an excess or surplus, esp. the amount by which a sum of money is greater than a previous estimate.

o•ver•buy ▶ v. (past and past part. **-bought**) buy more of (something) than one needs.

o•ver•ca•pac•i•ty ▶ n. the situation in which an industry or factory cannot sell as much as it can produce.

o•ver•cap•i•tal•ize ▶ v. (**overcapitalized**) provide (a company) with more capital than is advisable or necessary.
■ estimate or set the capital value of (a company) at too high an amount.

o•ver•draft ▶ n. a deficit in a bank account caused by drawing more money than the account holds.

o•ver•draw ▶ v. (past **-drew**; past part. **-drawn**) (usu. **be overdrawn**) draw money from (one's bank account) in excess of what the account holds: *you only pay interest if your account is overdrawn.*
■ (**be overdrawn**) (of a person) have taken money out of an account in excess of what it holds.

o•ver•ful•fill (Brit. **-fulfil**) ▶ v. (**-fulfilled, -fulfilling**) fulfill (a contract or quota) earlier or in greater quantity than required: *he overfulfilled the quota by forty percent.*

o•ver•head ▶ adj. (of a cost or expense) incurred in the general upkeep or running of a plant, premises, or business, and not attributable to specific products or items.
▶ n. overhead cost or expense.

o•ver•heat ▶ v. (of a country's economy) show marked inflation when increased demand results in rising prices rather than increased output.

o•ver•in•sured ▶ adj. having insurance coverage beyond what is necessary.

o•ver•is•sue ▶ v. (**-issues, -issued, -issuing**) issue (bonds, shares of stock, etc.) beyond the authorized amount or the issuer's ability to pay them on demand.
▶ n. the action of overissuing bonds, shares of stock, etc.

o•ver•pro•duce ▸ v. produce more of (a product or commodity) than is wanted or needed.

o•ver•sell ▸ v. (past and past part. -sold) sell more of (something) than exists or can be delivered: *a surge in airlines overselling flights.*

o•ver•stock ▸ n. (esp. in a manufacturing or retailing context) a supply or quantity in excess of demand or requirements: *factory overstock | publishers' overstocks and remainders.*

o•ver•sub•scribed ▸ adj. applied for in greater quantities than are available or expected: *those bonds were said to be 12 to 14 times oversubscribed.*

o•ver•trade ▸ v. engage in more business than can be supported by the market or by the funds or resources available.

o•ver•val•ue ▸ v. (-values, -valued, -valuing) fix the value of (something, esp. a currency) at too high a level.

pack•ag•ing ▸ n. materials used to wrap or protect goods.
■ the business or process of packing goods.

pack•er ▸ n. a person or machine that packs something, esp. someone who prepares and packs food for transportation and sale.

paid-up ▸ adj. denoting the part of the subscribed capital of an undertaking that has actually been paid: *paid-up capital.*
■ denoting an endowment policy in which the policyholder has stopped paying premiums, resulting in the surrender value being used to purchase single-premium whole-life insurance.

P & L ▸ abbr. profit and loss account.

par ▸ n. the face value of a stock or other security, as distinct from its market value.
■ (also par of exchange) the recognized value of one country's currency in terms of another's.

par•cel ▸ n. a quantity or amount of something, in particular:
■ a piece of land, esp. one considered as part of an estate. ■ a quantity dealt with in one commercial transaction: *a parcel of shares.*

par•i•ty ▸ n. the value of one currency in terms of another at an established exchange rate.

part•ner ▸ n. a person who takes part in an undertaking with another or others, esp. in a business or company with shared risks and profits.

part•ner•ship ▸ n. the state of being a partner or partners: *we should go on working together in partnership.*
■ an association of two or more people as partners: *an increase in partnerships with housing associations.* ■ a business or firm owned and run by two or more partners. ■ a position as one of the partners in a business or firm.

pass ▸ v. (of a company) not declare or pay (a dividend).

pass•book ▸ n. a booklet issued by a bank to an account holder for recording sums deposited and withdrawn.

pat•ent ▸ n. a government authority to an individual or organization conferring a right or title, esp. the sole right to make, use, or sell some invention: *he took out a patent for an improved steam hammer.*
▸ adj. made and marketed under a patent; proprietary: *patent milk powder.*
▸ v. obtain a patent for (an invention).

pat•ent•ee ▸ n. a person or organization that obtains or holds a patent for something.

pay•a•ble ▸ adj. (of money) required to be paid; due: *interest is payable on the money owing.* ■ able to be paid: *it costs just $195, payable in five monthly installments.*
▸ n. (payables) debts owed by a business; liabilities.

pay-as-you-go ▸ adj. relating to a system of paying debts or meeting costs as they arise.

pay•back ▸ n. financial return or reward, esp. profit equal to the initial outlay of an investment: *a long time lag between investment and payback.*

pay•back pe•ri•od ▸ n. the length of time required for an investment to recover its initial outlay in terms of profits or savings.

pay•ee ▸ n. a person to whom money is paid or is to be paid, esp. the person to whom a check is made payable.

pay•roll ▸ n. a list of a company's employees and the amount of money they are to be paid: *there are just three employees on the payroll.*
■ the total amount of wages and salaries paid by a company to its employees: *small employers with a payroll of less than $45,000.*

peg ▸ n. a point or limit on a scale, esp. of exchange rates. informal a strong throw, esp. in baseball.
▸ v. (pegged, pegging) fix (a price, rate, or amount) at a particular level.

pen•e•tra•tion ▸ n. the successful selling of a company's or country's products in a particular market or area: *Japanese import penetration.* ■ the extent to which a product is recognized and bought by customers in a particular market.

pen•ny stock ▸ n. a common stock valued at less than one dollar, and therefore highly speculative.

pen•sion ▸ n. a regular payment made during a person's retirement from an investment fund to which that person or their employer has contributed during their working life.
■ a regular payment made by the government to people of or above the official retirement age and to some widows and disabled people.
▸ v. (pension someone off) dismiss someone from employment, typically because of age or ill health, and pay them a pension.

pen•sion•a•ble ▸ adj. entitling to or qualifying for a pension.

pen•sion•ar•y ▸ adj. of or concerning a pension.

pen•sion fund ▸ n. a fund from which pensions are paid, accumulated from contributions from employers, employees, or both.

per an•num ▸ adv. for each year (used in financial contexts): *an average growth rate of around 2 percent per annum.*

p/e ra•tio ▸ abbr. price–earnings ratio.

per con•tra ▸ n. the opposite side of an account or an assessment.

per di•em ▸ adv. & adj. for each day (used in financial contexts).
▸ n. an allowance or payment made for each day.

per•fect com•pe•ti•tion ▸ n. the situation prevailing in a market in which buyers and sellers are so numerous and well informed that all elements of monopoly are absent and the market price of a commodity is beyond the control of individual buyers and sellers.

per•form ▸ v. (of an investment) yield a profitable return.

per•for•mance ▸ n. the extent to which an investment is profitable, esp. in relation to other investments.

per•for•mance bond ▸ n. a bond issued by a bank or other financial institution, guaranteeing the fulfillment of a particular contract.

per•pet•u•al ▸ adj. (of an investment) having no fixed maturity date; irredeemable.

per•pe•tu•i•ty ▸ n. (pl. -ies) a bond or other security with no fixed maturity date.

per•son•al i•den•ti•fi•ca•tion num•ber (abbr.: **PIN**) ▸ n. a number allocated to an individual and used to validate electronic transactions.

per•son•al shop•per ▸ n. an individual who is paid to help another to purchase goods, either by accompanying them while shopping or by shopping on their behalf.

per•son•nel de•part•ment ▸ n. the part of an organization concerned with the appointment, training, and welfare of employees.

pet•ro•dol•lar ▸ n. a notional unit of currency earned by a country from the export of petroleum: *petrodollars were pouring into the kingdom.*

pet•ty cash ▸ n. an accessible store of money kept by an organization for expenditure on small items.

phan•tom ▸ n. denoting a financial arrangement or transaction that has been invented for fraudulent purposes but that does not really exist.

phar•ma•ceu•ti•cal ▸ n. (usu. **pharmaceuticals**) (**pharmaceuticals**) companies manufacturing medicinal drugs.

Phil•lips curve ▸ n. a supposed inverse relationship between the level of unemployment and the rate of inflation.

piece rate ▸ n. a rate of payment for piecework.

piece•work ▸ n. work paid for according to the amount produced.

PIN (also **PIN number**) ▸ abbr. personal identification number.

pi•rate ▸ n. a person who appropriates or reproduces the work of another for profit without permission, usually in contravention of patent or copyright.
▸ v. (**pirated**) use or reproduce (another's work) for profit without permission, usually in contravention of patent or copyright: *he sold pirated tapes of Hollywood blockbusters.*

pit ▸ n. an area reserved or enclosed for a specific activity, in particular:
■ a part of the floor of an exchange in which a particular stock or commodity is traded, typically by open outcry.

place ▸ v. dispose of (something, esp. shares) by selling to a customer.

planned ob•so•les•cence ▸ n. a policy of producing consumer goods that rapidly become obsolete and so require replacing, achieved by frequent changes in design, termination of the

supply of spare parts, and the use of nondurable materials.

plas•tic ▸ n. informal credit cards or other types of plastic card that can be used as money: *he pays with cash instead of with plastic.*

plc (also **PLC**) Brit. ▸ abbr. public limited company.

PO ▸ abbr. purchase order.

point ▸ n. a percentage of the profits from a movie or recording offered to certain people involved in its production.
■ a unit of varying value, used in quoting the price of stocks, bonds, or futures.

point of sale (abbr.: **POS**) ▸ n. the place at which goods are retailed.

poi•son pill ▸ n. a tactic used by a company threatened with an unwelcome takeover bid to make itself unattractive to the bidder.

pol•i•cy ▸ n. (pl. -ies) a contract of insurance: *they took out a joint policy.*

pool ▸ n. a group of people available for work when required: *the typing pool.*
■ a group of people considered as a resource: *a nationwide pool of promising high-school students.*
■ an arrangement, illegal in many countries, between competing parties to fix prices or rates and share business in order to eliminate competition. ■ a common fund into which all contributors pay and from which financial backing is provided: *big public investment pools.* ■ a source of common funding for speculative operations on financial markets.
▸ v. (of two or more people or organizations) put (money or other assets) into a common fund.

port•fo•li•o ▸ n. (pl. -os) a range of investments held by a person or organization: *better returns on its investment portfolio.*
■ a range of products or services offered by an organization, esp. when considered as a business asset: *an unrivaled portfolio of quality brands.*

POS ▸ abbr. point of sale.

po•si•tion ▸ n. an investor's net holdings in one or more markets at a particular time; the status of an individual or institutional trader's open contracts: *traders were covering short positions.*
▸ v. promote (a product, service, or business) within a particular sector of a market, or as the fulfillment of that sector's specific requirements.

post[1] ▸ v. (often **be posted**) announce or publish (something, esp. a financial result): *the company posted a $460,000 loss.*

post[2] ▸ v. (in bookkeeping) enter (an item) in a ledger: *post the transaction in the second column.*
■ complete (a ledger) in this way.

post[3] ▸ n. a position of paid employment; a job.

post•in•dus•tri•al ▸ adj. of or relating to an economy that no longer relies on heavy industry.

post-tax ▸ adj. (of income or profits) remaining after the deduction of taxes.

pov•er•ty line ▸ n. the estimated minimum level of income needed to secure the necessities of life.

PPP ▸ abbr. purchasing power parity (a way of measuring what an amount of money will buy in different countries).

PR ▸ abbr. press release.
■ public relations.

pred•a•to•ry pric•ing ▸ n. the pricing of goods or services at such a low level that other suppliers cannot compete and are forced to leave the market.

pre•emp•tive ▸ adj. relating to the purchase of goods or shares by one person or party before the opportunity is offered to others: *preemptive rights.*

pref. ▸ abbr. preference (with reference to preference shares).
■ preferred (with reference to a preferred stock).

pref•er•en•tial ▸ adj. (of a union shop) giving employment preference to union members.
■ (of a creditor) having a claim on the receipt of payment from a debtor that will be met before those of other creditors.

pre•ferred stock ▸ n. stock that entitles the holder to a fixed dividend, whose payment takes priority over that of common-stock dividends.

pre•mi•um ▸ n. (pl. **premiums**) an amount to be paid for an insurance policy. a sum added to an ordinary price or charge.
■ a sum added to interest or wages; a bonus. ■ relating to or denoting a commodity or product of superior quality and therefore a higher price: *premium beers.* ■ the amount by which the price of a share or other security exceeds its issue price, its nominal value, or the value of the assets it represents: *the fund has traded at a premium of 12%.*

pre-need ▸ adj. denoting a scheme in which one pays in advance for a service or facility: *preneed funeral sales.*

pres•ent val•ue (also **net present value**) ▸ n. the value in the present of a sum of money, in contrast to some future value it will have when it has been invested at compound interest.

pres•tige pric•ing ▸ n. the practice of pricing goods at a high level in order to give the appearance of quality.

pre•tax ▸ adj. (of income or profits) considered or calculated before the deduction of taxes.

price con•trol ▸ n. a government regulation establishing a maximum price to be charged for specified goods and services, esp. during periods of war or inflation.

price dis•crim•i•na•tion ▸ n. the action of selling the same product at different prices to different buyers, in order to maximize sales and profits.

price-earn•ings ra•tio (also **price-earnings multiple**) ▸ n. the current market price of a company share divided by the earnings per share of the company.

price-fix•ing (also **price fixing**) ▸ n. the maintaining of prices at a certain level by agreement between competing sellers.

price list ▸ n. a list of current prices of items on sale.

price point ▸ n. a point on a scale of possible prices at which something might be marketed.

price-sen•si•tive ▸ adj. denoting a product whose sales are greatly influenced by the price.
■ (of information) likely to affect share prices if it were made public.

price sup•port ▸ n. government assistance in maintaining the levels of market prices regardless of supply or demand.

price tag ▸ n. the label on an item for sale, showing its price.
■ figurative the cost of a company, enterprise, or undertaking: *a $400 billion price tag was put on the venture.*

price-tak•er ▸ n. a company that must accept the prevailing prices in the market of its products, its own transactions being unable to affect the market price.

price war ▸ n. a fierce competition in which retailers cut prices in an attempt to increase their share of the market.

pri•ma•ry in•dus•try ▸ n. industry, such as mining, agriculture, or forestry, that is concerned with obtaining or providing natural raw materials for conversion into commodities and products for the consumer.

prime ▸ n. short for PRIME RATE.

prime cost ▸ n. the direct cost of a commodity in terms of the materials and labor involved in its production, excluding fixed costs.

prime rate ▸ n. the lowest rate of interest at which money may be borrowed commercially.

prin•ci•pal ▸ adj. (of money) denoting an original sum invested or lent.
▸ n. a sum of money lent or invested on which interest is paid: *the winners are paid from the interest without even touching the principal.* ■ a person for whom another acts as an agent or representative: *stockbrokers in Tokyo act as agents rather than as principals.*

pri•vate en•ter•prise ▸ n. business or industry that is managed by independent companies or private individuals rather than by the state.

pri•vate sec•tor ▸ n. the part of the national economy that is not under direct government control.

pri•vate trea•ty ▸ n. the agreement for the sale of a property at a price negotiated directly between the vendor and purchaser or their agents.

pri•va•tize ▸ v. transfer (a business, industry, or service) from public to private ownership and control: *a plan for privatizing education.*

pro•duc•er ▸ n. a person, company, or country that makes, grows, or supplies goods or commodities for sale: *an oil producer.* ■ a person responsible for the financial and managerial aspects of making of a movie or broadcast or for staging a play, opera, etc.
■ a person who supervises the making of a musical recording, esp. by determining the overall sound.

pro•duc•tion line ▸ n. an arrangement in a factory in which a thing being manufactured is passed through a set linear sequence of mechanical or manual operations.

pro•duc•tiv•i•ty ▸ n. the state or quality of producing something, esp. crops: *the long-term productivity of land | agricultural productivity.*
■ the effectiveness of productive effort, esp. in industry, as measured in terms of the rate of output per unit of input.

prod•uct li•a•bil•i•ty ▸ n. the legal liability a manufacturer or trader incurs for producing or selling a faulty product.

prod•uct life-cy•cle ▸ n. the series of four stages (introduction, growth, maturity, and decline) through which the levels of sales of a product pass during its market life.

prod•uct mix ▸ n. the total range of products offered by a company.

prof•it ▸ n. a financial gain, esp. the difference between the amount earned and the amount spent in buying, operating, or producing something.
▸ v. (**profited, profiting**) obtain a financial advantage or benefit, esp. from an investment.
–PHRASES **at a profit** making more money than is spent buying, operating, or producing something: *fixing up houses and selling them at a profit.*

prof•it•a•ble ▸ adj. (of a business or activity) yielding profit or financial gain.

prof•it and loss ac•count (abbr.: **P & L**) ▸ n. an account in the books of an organization to which incomes and gains are credited and expenses and losses debited, so as to show the net profit or loss over a given period.
■ a financial statement showing a company's net profit or loss in a given period.

prof•it cen•ter ▸ n. a part of an organization with assignable revenues and costs and hence ascertainable profitability.

prof•it mar•gin ▸ n. the amount by which revenue from sales exceeds costs in a business.

prof•it-tak•ing (also **profit taking**) ▸ n. the sale of securities that have risen in price.

pro for•ma ▸ adj. denoting a standard document or form, esp. an invoice sent in advance of or with goods supplied.
■ (of a financial statement) showing potential or expected income, costs, assets, or liabilities, esp. in relation to some planned or expected act or situation.
▸ n. a standard document or form or financial statement of such a type.

pro•gram trad•ing ▸ n. the simultaneous purchase and sale of many different stocks, or of stocks and related futures contracts, with the use of a computer program to exploit price differences in different markets.

prom•is•so•ry note ▸ n. a signed document containing a written promise to pay a stated sum to a specified person or the bearer at a specified date or on demand.

pro•mote ▸ v. give publicity to (a product, organization, or venture) so as to increase sales or public awareness: *they are using famous personalities to promote the library nationally.* ■ (often **be promoted**) advance or raise (someone) to a higher position or rank: *she was promoted to general manager.*

pro•mot•er ▸ n. a person or thing that promotes something, in particular:
■ a person or company that finances or organizes a sporting event or theatrical production: *a boxing promoter.* ■ a person involved in setting up and funding a new company.

pro•mo•tion ▸ n. the publicization of a product, organization, or venture so as to increase sales or public awareness.

■ a publicity campaign for a particular product, organization, or venture: *the paper is reaping the rewards of a series of promotions.* ■ (**promotions**) the activity or business of organizing such publicity or campaigns: *she's the promotions manager for the museum.* ■ the action of raising someone to a higher position or rank or the fact of being so raised: *a promotion to divisional sales director.*

prop. ▸ abbr. proprietor.

prop•er•ty ▸ n. (pl. **-ies**) a building or buildings and the land belonging to it or them.

pro•pri•e•tar•y ▸ adj. of or relating to an owner or ownership: *the company has a proprietary right to the property.*
■ (of a product) marketed under and protected by a registered trade name.

pro•pri•e•tar•y name ▸ n. a name of a product or service registered by its owner as a trademark and not usable by others without permission.

pro•pri•e•tor ▸ n. the owner of a business.

pro•tect ▸ v. (often **be protected**) (of an insurance policy) promise to pay (someone) an agreed amount in the event of loss, injury, fire, theft, or other misfortune.
■ shield (a domestic industry) from competition by imposing import duties on foreign goods.
■ provide funds to meet (a bill of exchange or commercial draft).

pro•tec•tion•ism ▸ n. the theory or practice of shielding a country's domestic industries from foreign competition by taxing imports.

pro•tec•tive ▸ adj. of or relating to the protection of domestic industries from foreign competition: *protective tariffs.*

pro•vi•sion ▸ n. (**provision for/against**) financial or other arrangements for future eventualities or requirements: *farmers have been slow to make provision for their retirement.*
■ an amount set aside out of profits in the accounts of an organization for a known liability, esp. a bad debt or the diminution in value of an asset.
▸ v. set aside an amount in an organization's accounts for a known liability.

psy•chic in•come ▸ n. the nonmonetary or nonmaterial satisfactions that accompany an occupation or economic activity.

pub•lic ▸ adj. of or provided by the government rather than an independent, commercial company: *public spending.*
–PHRASES **go public** become a public company.

pub•lic com•pa•ny ▸ n. a company whose shares are traded freely on a stock exchange.

pub•lic good ▸ n. a commodity or service that is provided without profit to all members of a society, either by the government or a private individual or organization: *a conviction that library informational services are a public good, not a commercial commodity.*

pub•lic•i•ty ▸ n. the giving out of information about a product, person, or company for advertising or promotional purposes.
■ material or information used for such a purpose.

pub•lic re•la•tions ▸ plural n. [also treated as sing.] the professional maintenance of a favorable public image by a company or other organization or a famous person.
■ the state of the relationship between the public and a company or other organization or a famous person.

pub•lic sec•tor ▸ n. the part of an economy that is controlled by the government.

pull•back ▸ n. a reduction in price or demand: *there is no sign of a consumer pullback.*

pump-prim•ing ▸ n. the stimulation of economic activity by investment.

pur•chase ▸ v. acquire (something) by paying for it; buy.
▸ n. the action of buying something.
■ a thing that has been bought.

put ▸ n. short for PUT OPTION.

put op•tion ▸ n. an option to sell assets at an agreed price on or before a particular date.

Pvt. (also PVT) ▸ abbr. (in company names) private.

pyr•a•mid ▸ n. a system of financial growth achieved by a small initial investment, with subsequent investments being funded by using unrealized profits as collateral.
▸ v. achieve a substantial return on (money or property) after making a small initial investment.

pyr•a•mid scheme ▸ n. a system of selling goods in which agency rights are sold to an increasing number of distributors at successively lower levels.

Q ▸ abbr. quarter (used to refer to a specified quarter of the fiscal year): *we expect to have an exceptional Q4.*

qual•i•ty as•sur•ance ▸ n. the maintenance of a desired level of quality in a service or product, esp. by means of attention to every stage of the process of delivery or production.

qual•i•ty cir•cle ▸ n. a group of employees that meets regularly to consider ways of resolving problems and improving production in their organization.

quant ▸ n. informal a quantity analyst.

quan•ti•ty the•o•ry (also **the quantity theory of money**) ▸ n. the hypothesis that changes in prices correspond to changes in the monetary supply.

quo•ta ▸ n. a limited quantity of a particular product that under official controls can be produced, exported, or imported.

quo•ta•tion ▸ n. a price offered by a broker for the sale or purchase of a stock or other security.
■ a registration granted to a company enabling their shares to be officially listed and traded.

quote ▸ v. give someone (the estimated price of a job or service).
■ (usu. **be quoted**) give (a company) a quotation or listing on a stock exchange.
▸ n. a price offered by a broker for the sale or purchase of a stock or other security.
■ a quotation or listing of a company on a stock exchange.

R ▸ abbr. (also ®) registered as a trademark.

rack rent ▸ n. an extortionate or very high rent, esp. an annual rent equivalent to the full value of the property to which it relates.

▸ v. (**rack-rent**) exact an excessive or extortionate rent from (a tenant) or for (a property).

raid ▸ n. a hostile attempt to buy a major or controlling interest in the shares of a company.

raise ▸ n. an increase in salary: *he wants a raise and some perks.*

ral•ly ▸ v. (**-ies**, **-ied**) (of share, currency, or commodity prices) increase after a fall: *prices of metals such as aluminum and copper have rallied.*

rate ▸ n. a fixed price paid or charged for something, esp. goods or services: *the basic rate of pay.*
■ the amount of a charge or payment expressed as a percentage of some other amount, or as a basis of calculation.

rate of ex•change ▸ n. another term for EX-CHANGE RATE.

rate of re•turn ▸ n. the annual income from an investment expressed as a proportion (usually a percentage) of the original investment.

rat•ing ▸ n. a classification or ranking of someone or something based on a comparative assessment of their quality, standard, or performance: *the hotel regained its five-star rating.*
■ (**ratings**) the estimated audience size of a particular television or radio program: *the soap's ratings have recently picked up.* ■ the value of a property or condition that is claimed to be standard, optimal, or limiting for a substance, material, or item of equipment: *fuel with a low octane rating.*

ra•tio ▸ n. (pl. **-os**) the relative value of silver and gold in a bimetallic system of currency.

ra•tion•al ex•pec•ta•tions hy•poth•e•sis ▸ n. the hypothesis that an economic agent will make full use of all available information when forming expectations, esp. with regard to inflation, and not just past values of a particular variable.

re•act ▸ v. (of stock prices) fall after rising.

read•y mon•ey (also **ready cash**) ▸ n. money in the form of cash that is immediately available.

re•al ▸ adj. adjusted for changes in the value of money; assessed by purchasing power.

real es•tate a•gent ▸ n. a person who sells and rents out buildings and land for clients.

re•al•i•za•ble ▸ adj. in or able to be converted into cash: *10 percent of realizable assets.*

re•al•i•za•tion ▸ n. the action of converting an asset into cash.
■ a sale of goods: *auction realizations.*

re•al•ize ▸ v. make (money or a profit) from a transaction: *she realized a profit of $100,000.*
■ (of goods) be sold for (a specified price); fetch.
■ convert (an asset) into cash.

re•al•tor ▸ n. a person who acts as an agent for the sale and purchase of buildings and land; a real estate agent.

re•badge ▸ v. relaunch (a product) under a new name or logo.

re•base ▸ v. establish a new base level for (a tax level, price index, etc.).

re•bate ▸ n. a partial refund to someone who has paid too much money for tax, rent, or a utility.
■ a deduction or discount on a sum of money due.
▸ v. pay back (such a sum of money).

re•brand ▸ v. change the corporate image of (a company or organization).

re•cap•i•tal•ize ▸ v. provide (a business) with more capital, esp. by replacing debt with stock.

re•ceipt ▸ n. a written or printed statement acknowledging that something has been paid for or that goods have been received.
  ■ (**receipts**) an amount of money received during a particular period by an organization or business: *box-office receipts.*
▸v. mark (a bill) as paid: *the receipted hotel bill.*
  ■ write a receipt for (goods or money).

re•ceiv•a•ble ▸ plural n. (**receivables**) amounts owed to a business, regarded as assets.

re•ceiv•er ▸ n. a person or company appointed by a court to manage the financial affairs of a business or person that has gone bankrupt.

re•ceiv•er•ship ▸ n. the state of being dealt with by an official receiver.

re•ces•sion ▸ n. a period of temporary economic decline during which trade and industrial activity are reduced, generally identified by a fall in GDP in two successive quarters.

re•ces•sive ▸ adj. undergoing an economic recession: *the recessive housing market.*

rec•on•cile ▸ v. (often **be reconciled**) make (one account) consistent with another, esp. by allowing for transactions begun but not yet completed.

rec•on•cil•i•a•tion state•ment ▸ n. a statement of account in which discrepancies are adjusted so that different accounts balance.

re•coup ▸ v. regain (money spent or lost), esp. through subsequent profits: *oil companies are keen to recoup their investment.*
  ■ reimburse or compensate (someone) for money spent or lost. ■ deduct or keep back (part of a sum due).

re•course ▸ n. [in sing.] the legal right to demand compensation or payment.
–PHRASES **without recourse** a formula used to disclaim responsibility for future nonpayment, esp. of a negotiable financial instrument.

re•cov•er•y stock ▸ n. a stock that has fallen in price but is thought to have the potential of climbing back to its original level.

re•deem ▸ v. gain or regain possession of (something) in exchange for payment.
  ■ repay (a stock, bond, or other instrument) at the maturity date. ■ exchange (a coupon, voucher, or trading stamp) for merchandise, a discount, or money. ■ pay the necessary money to clear (a debt): *owners were unable to redeem their mortgages.* ■ exchange (paper money) for gold or silver.

re•demp•tion ▸ n. the action of regaining or gaining possession of something in exchange for payment, or clearing a debt.

re•demp•tion yield ▸ n. the yield of a stock calculated as a percentage of the redemption price with an adjustment made for any capital gain or loss the price represents relative to the current price.

re•dis•count ▸ v. (of a central bank) discount (a bill of exchange or similar instrument) that has already been discounted by a commercial bank.

re•em•ploy ▸ v. employ (someone, typically a former employee) again.

re•en•gi•neer ▸ v. restructure (a company or part of its operations), esp. by exploiting information technology.

re•ex•port ▸ v. export (imported goods), typically after they have undergone further processing or manufacture.

re•fi•nance ▸ v. finance (something) again, typically with a new loan at a lower rate of interest.

re•flate ▸ v. expand the level of output of (an economy) by government stimulus, using either fiscal or monetary policy.

reg•u•late ▸ v. control or supervise (something, esp. a company or business activity) by means of rules and regulations.

reg•u•la•tor ▸ n. a person or body that supervises a particular industry or business activity.

re•im•port ▸ v. import (goods processed or made from exported materials).

re•in•sure ▸ v. (of an insurer) transfer (all or part of a risk) to another insurer to provide protection against the risk of the first insurance.

re•in•vest ▸ v. put (the profit on a previous investment) back into the same place.

re•mit ▸ v. (**remitted, remitting**) send (money) in payment or as a gift.

re•mort•gage ▸ v. take out another or a different kind of mortgage on (a property).
▸n. a different or additional mortgage.

re•mu•ner•ate ▸ v. pay (someone) for services rendered or work done.

re•na•tion•al•ize ▸ v. transfer (a privatized industry) back into state ownership or control.

rent ▸ n. a tenant's regular payment to a landlord for the use of property or land.
  ■ a sum paid for the hire of equipment.
▸v. pay someone for the use of (something, typically property, land, or a car).
  ■ (of an owner) let someone use (something) in return for payment: *he purchased a large tract of land and rented out most of it to local farmers.*
  ■ be let or hired out at a specified rate: *skis or snowboards rent for $60–80 for six days.*
–PHRASES **for rent** available to be rented.

rent•a•ble ▸ adj. available or suitable for renting.

ren•tal ▸ n. an amount paid or received as rent.
  ■ the action of renting something: *the office was on weekly rental.* ■ a rented house or car.
▸adj. of, relating to, or available for rent: *rental properties.*

re•or•der ▸ n. a renewed or repeated order for goods.

rep informal ▸ n. a representative: *a union rep.*
  ■ a sales representative.
▸v. (**repped, repping**) act as a sales representative for a company or product: *at eighteen she was working for her dad, repping on the road.*

re•pa•tri•ate ▸ v. send or bring (money) back to one's own country: *foreign firms would be permitted to repatriate all profits.*

re•po informal ▸ n. (pl. **-os**) a car or other item that has been repossessed.
▸v. (**repo's, repo'd**) repossess (a car or other item) when a buyer defaults on payments.

re•pos•sess ▸ v. retake possession of (something) when a buyer defaults on payments.

re•pos•ses•sor ▸ n. a person hired by a credit company to repossess an item when the buyer defaults on payments.

re-pre•sent ▸ v. present (a check or bill) again for payment.

re•price ▸ v. put a different price on (a product or commodity).

re•pur•chase ▸ v. buy (something) back.
▸n. the action of buying something back.

re•pur•chase a•gree•ment ▸ n. a contract in which the vendor of a security agrees to repurchase it from the buyer at an agreed price.

re•sale ▸ n. the sale of a thing previously bought.

re•sell ▸ v. (past and past part. **resold**) sell (something one has bought) to someone else.

re•serve ▸ n. (often **reserves**) a supply of a commodity not needed for immediate use but available if required.
■ funds kept available by a bank, company, or government: *the foreign exchange reserves.* ■ a part of a company's profits added to capital rather than paid as a dividend. ■ short for RE-SERVE PRICE.

re•serve bank ▸ n. a regional bank operating under and implementing the policies of the US Federal Reserve.

re•serve price ▸ n. the price stipulated as the lowest acceptable by the seller for an item sold at auction.

re•sid•u•al ▸ n. a royalty paid to a performer, writer, etc., for a repeat of a play, television show, etc. the resale value of a new car or other item at a specified time after purchase, expressed as a percentage of its purchase price.

re•source ▸ n. (usu. **resources**) a stock or supply of money, materials, staff, and other assets that can be drawn on by a person or organization in order to function effectively.
■ (**resources**) a country's collective means of supporting itself or becoming wealthier, as represented by its reserves of minerals, land, and other assets. ■ (**resources**) available assets.
▸v. provide (a person or organization) with materials, money, staff, and other assets necessary for effective operation.

re•stock ▸ v. replenish (a store) with fresh stock or supplies.

re•straint of trade ▸ n. action that interferes with free competition in a market.

re•struc•ture ▸ v. convert (the debt of a business in difficulty) into another kind of debt, typically one that is repayable at a later time.

re•tail ▸ n. the sale of goods to the public in relatively small quantities for use or consumption rather than for resale.
▸adv. being sold in such a way: *it is not yet available retail.*
▸v. sell (goods) to the public in such a way: *the difficulties in retailing the new products.*
■ (**retail at/for**) (of goods) be sold in this way for (a specified price): *the product retails for around $20.*

re•tire ▸ v. leave one's job and cease to work, typically upon reaching the normal age for leaving employment: *he retired from the navy in 1966.*
■ withdraw (a bill or note) from circulation or currency. ■ pay off or cancel (a debt).

re•trench ▸ v. (of a company, government, or individual) reduce costs or spending in response to economic difficulty: *as a result of the recession the company retrenched.*

re•turn ▸ v. yield or make (a profit).
▸n. (often **returns**) a profit from an investment.
■ a good rate of return.

re•val•ue ▸ v. (**revalues, revalued, revaluing**) assess the value of (something) again.
■ adjust the value of (a currency) in relation to other currencies.

rev•e•nue ▸ n. income, esp. when of a company or organization and of a substantial nature.

rev•e•nue tar•iff ▸ n. a tariff imposed principally to raise government revenue rather than to protect domestic industries.

re•verse en•gi•neer•ing ▸ n. the reproduction of another manufacturer's product following detailed examination of its construction or composition.

re•verse take•o•ver ▸ n. a takeover of a public company by a smaller company.

re•volv•ing cred•it ▸ n. credit that is automatically renewed as debts are paid off.

re•volv•ing fund ▸ n. a fund that is continually replenished as withdrawals are made.

RFP ▸ abbr. request for proposal, a detailed specification of goods or services required by an organization, sent to potential contractors or suppliers.

rig ▸ v. (**rigged, rigging**) cause an artificial rise or fall in prices in (a market, esp. the stock market) with a view to personal profit.

rights is•sue ▸ n. an issue of shares offered at a special price by a company to its existing shareholders in proportion to their holding of old shares.

risk ▸ n. the possibility of financial loss.

risk cap•i•tal ▸ n. another term for VENTURE CAPITAL.

ROCE ▸ abbr. return on capital employed.

ROI ▸ abbr. return on investment.

roll•out (also **roll-out**) ▸ n. the official launch of a new product or service.

roll•o•ver ▸ n. the extension or transfer of a debt or other financial arrangement.

run ▸ n. (**a run on**) a widespread and sudden or continuous demand for (a particular currency or commodity): *there's been a big run on nostalgia toys this year.*
■ a sudden demand for repayment from a bank made by a large number of lenders.

run-up ▸ n. a marked rise in the value or level of something.

sales tax ▸ n. a tax on sales or on the receipts from sales.

sat•u•rate ▸ v. (usu. **be saturated**) supply (a market) beyond the point at which the demand for a product is satisfied.

sav•ings ac•count ▸ n. a bank account that earns interest.

sav•ings and loan (also **savings and loan asso-ciation**) ▸ n. an institution that accepts savings at interest and lends money to savers chiefly for home mortgage loans and may offer checking accounts and other services.

sav•ings bank ▸ n. a financial institution that receives savings accounts and pays interest to depositors.

sav•ings bond ▸ n. a bond issued by the government and sold to the general public.

Say's law a law stating that supply creates its own demand.

SBA ▸ abbr. (in the US) Small Business Administration.

sci•en•tif•ic man•age•ment ▸ n. management of a business, industry, or economy, according to principles of efficiency derived from experiments in methods of work and production, esp. from time-and-motion studies.

scrip ▸ n. a provisional certificate of money subscribed to a bank or company, entitling the holder to a formal certificate and dividends.
■ such certificates collectively. ■ (also **scrip issue** or **dividend**) an issue of additional shares to shareholders in proportion to the shares already held. ■ (also **land scrip**) a certificate entitling the holder to acquire possession of certain portions of public land.

SDR ▸ abbr. special drawing right (from the International Monetary Fund).

SEAQ ▸ abbr. (in the UK) Stock Exchange Automated Quotations (the computer system on which dealers trade shares and seek or provide price quotations on the London Stock Exchange).

SEC ▸ abbr. Securities and Exchange Commission, a US governmental agency that monitors trading in securities and company takeovers.

sec•ond mort•gage ▸ n. a mortgage taken out on a property that is already mortgaged.

se•cure ▸ v. seek to guarantee repayment of (a loan) by having a right to take possession of an asset in the event of nonpayment.

se•cu•ri•tize ▸ v. convert (an asset, esp. a loan) into marketable securities, typically for the purpose of raising cash by selling them to other investors.

se•cu•ri•ty ▸ n. (pl. **-ies**) (often **securities**) a certificate attesting credit, the ownership of stocks or bonds, or the right to ownership connected with tradable derivatives.

seign•ior•age (also **seignorage**) ▸ n. profit made by a government by issuing currency, esp. the difference between the face value of coins and their production costs.

self-as•sess•ment ▸ n. assessment or evaluation of oneself or one's actions and attitudes, in particular, of one's performance at a job or learning task considered in relation to an objective standard.

self-fi•nanc•ing ▸ adj. (of an organization or enterprise) having or generating enough income to finance itself.

self-in•sur•ance ▸ n. insurance of oneself or one's interests by maintaining a fund to cover possible losses rather than by purchasing an insurance policy.

self-liq•ui•dat•ing ▸ adj. denoting an asset that earns back its original cost out of income over a fixed period.
■ denoting a loan used to finance a project that will bring a sufficient return to pay back the loan and its interest and leave a profit. ■ denoting a sales promotion offer that pays for itself by generating increased sales.

sell ▸ v. (past and past part. **sold**) give or hand over (something) in exchange for money.
■ have a stock of (something) available for sale: *the store sells hi-fis, TVs, videos, and other electrical goods.* ■ (of a thing) be purchased: *this magazine of yours won't sell.* ■ (of a publication or recording) attain sales of (a specified number of copies): *the album sold 6 million copies in the United States.* ■ (**sell for/at**) be available for sale at (a specified price): *these antiques sell for about $375.* ■ (**sell out**) sell all of one's stock of something: *they had nearly sold out of the initial run of 75,000 copies.* ■ (**sell out**) be all sold: *it was clear that the performances would not sell out.* ■ (**sell through**) (of a product) be purchased by a customer from a retail outlet. ■ (**sell up**) sell all of one's property, possessions, or assets.

sell•er ▸ n. a person who sells something.
■ (**the seller**) the party in a legal transaction who is selling: *the seller may accept the buyer's offer.* ■ a product that sells in some specified way: *the game will undoubtedly be the biggest seller of the year.*
–PHRASES **seller's (or sellers') market** an economic situation in which goods or shares are scarce and sellers can keep prices high.

sell-in ▸ n. the sale of goods to retail traders prior to public retailing.

sell•ing point ▸ n. a feature of a product for sale that makes it attractive to customers.

sell-off ▸ n. a sale of assets, typically at a low price, carried out in order to dispose of them rather than as normal trade.
■ a sale of shares, bonds, or commodities, esp. one that causes a fall in price.

sell•out ▸ n. the selling of an entire stock of something, esp. tickets for an entertainment or sports event.
■ an event for which all tickets are sold. ■ a sale of a business or company.

sell-through ▸ n. the ratio of the quantity of goods sold by a retail outlet to the quantity distributed to it wholesale.
■ the retail sale of something, typically a prerecorded videocassette, as opposed to its rental.

sen•si•tive ▸ adj. (of a market) unstable and liable to quick changes of price because of outside influences.

serv•ice ▸ n. assistance or advice given to customers during and after the sale of goods.
■ short for SERVICE INDUSTRY: *a private security service.* ■ work done for a customer other than manufacturing. ■ the action or process of serving food and drinks to customers: *they complained of poor bar service.* ■ short for SERVICE

CHARGE: *service is included in the final bill.* ■ a period of employment with a company or organization: *he retired after 40 years' service.* ■ employment as a servant.

■ pay interest on (a debt): *taxpayers are paying $250 million just to service that debt.*

serv•ice charge (also **service fee**) ▸ n. an extra charge assessed for a service.

serv•ice con•tract ▸ n. a business agreement between a contractor and customer covering the maintenance and servicing of equipment over a specified period.

serv•ice in•dus•try ▸ n. a business that does work for a customer, and occasionally provides goods, but is not involved in manufacturing.

serv•ice mark ▸ n. a legally registered name or designation used in the manner of a trademark to distinguish an organization's services from those of its competitors.

set-off ▸ n. an item or amount that is or may be set off against another in the settlement of accounts.

set•tle•ment ▸ n. the action or process of settling an account.

sev•er•ance ▸ n. dismissal or discharge from employment.

■ short for SEVERANCE PAY.

sev•er•ance pay ▸ n. an amount paid to an employee upon dismissal or discharge from employment.

shade ▸ v. make a slight reduction in the amount, rate, or price of: *banks may shade the margin over base rate they charge customers.*

shad•ow price ▸ n. the estimated price of a good or service for which no market price exists.

share ▸ n. a part or portion of a larger amount that is divided among a number of people, or to which a number of people contribute.

■ one of the equal parts into which a company's capital is divided, entitling the holder to a proportion of the profits: *bought 33 shares of American Standard.* ■ part proprietorship of property held by joint owners.

share•hold•er ▸ n. an owner of shares in a company.

shelf life ▸ n. the length of time for which an item remains usable, fit for consumption, or saleable.

shell com•pa•ny ▸ n. an inactive company used as a vehicle for various financial maneuvers or kept dormant for future use in some other capacity.

shel•ter ▸ v. protect (income) from taxation.

shift ▸ n. one of two or more recurring periods in which different groups of workers do the same jobs in relay: *the night shift.*

■ a group of workers who work in this way.

shift work ▸ n. work comprising recurring periods in which different groups of workers do the same jobs in rotation.

ship ▸ v. (**shipped, shipping**) (often **be shipped**) transport (goods or people) on a ship.

■ transport by some other means: *the freight would be shipped by rail.* ■ send (a package) somewhere via the mail service or a private company ■ make (a product) available for purchase.

ship•ment ▸ n. the action of shipping goods: *logs waiting for shipment | shipments begin this month.*

■ a quantity of goods shipped; a consignment.

ship•ping ▸ n. ships considered collectively, esp. those in a particular area or belonging to a particular country.

■ the transport of goods by sea or some other means. ■ a charge imposed by a retail company to send merchandise to a customer.

shock ▸ n. a disturbance causing instability in an economy.

short ▸ adj. (of stocks or other securities or commodities) sold in advance of being acquired, with reliance on the price falling so that a profit can be made.

■ (of a broker, position in the market, etc.) buying or based on such stocks or other securities or commodities. ■ denoting or having a relatively early date for the maturing of a bill of exchange. ▸ n. a person who sells short.

■ (**shorts**) short-dated stocks.

short cov•er•ing ▸ n. the buying in of stocks or other securities or commodities that have been sold short, typically to avoid loss when prices move upward.

short-dat•ed ▸ adj. (of a stock or bond) due for early payment or redemption.

short-term•ism ▸ n. concentration on short-term projects or objectives for immediate profit at the expense of long-term security.

shrink•age ▸ n. an allowance made for reduction in the earnings of a business due to wastage or theft.

siege e•con•o•my ▸ n. an economy in which import controls are imposed and the export of capital is curtailed.

sight de•pos•it ▸ n. a bank deposit that can be withdrawn immediately without notice or penalty.

si•lent part•ner ▸ n. a partner not sharing in the actual work of a firm.

sim•ple ▸ adj. (**simpler, simplest**) (of interest) payable on the sum loaned only.

sin•gle-en•try ▸ adj. denoting a system of bookkeeping in which each transaction is entered in one account only.

sin•gle mar•ket ▸ n. an association of countries trading with each other without restrictions or tariffs.

sin•gle-source ▸ v. give a franchise to a single supplier for (a particular product).

sink•ing fund ▸ n. a fund formed by periodically setting aside money for the gradual repayment of a debt or replacement of a wasting asset.

sin tax ▸ n. informal a tax on items considered undesirable or harmful, such as alcohol or tobacco.

skim ▸ v. (**skimmed, skimming**) informal steal or embezzle (money), esp. in small amounts over a period of time.

skunk•works (also **skunk works**) ▸ plural n. [usu. treated as sing.] informal an experimental laboratory or department of a company or institution, typically smaller than and independent of its main research division.

slack ▸ adj. (of business) characterized by a lack of work or activity; quiet: *business was rather slack.*

slid•ing scale ▸ n. a scale of fees, taxes, wages,

etc., that varies in accordance with variation of some standard.

slo•gan ▸ n. a short and striking or memorable phrase used in advertising.

slow•down ▸ n. a decline in economic activity.

slump ▸ v. undergo a sudden severe or prolonged fall in price, value, or amount: *land prices slumped.*
▸ n. a sudden severe or prolonged fall in the price, value, or amount of something.
  ■ a prolonged period of abnormally low economic activity, typically bringing widespread unemployment.

small-cap ▸ adj. denoting or relating to the stock of a company with a small capitalization.

smart card ▸ n. a plastic card with a built-in microprocessor, used typically to perform financial transactions.

so•cial cred•it ▸ n. the economic theory that consumer purchasing power should be increased either by subsidizing producers so that they can lower prices or by distributing the profits of industry to consumers.

so•cial mar•ket e•con•o•my (also **social market**) ▸ n. an economic system based on a free market operated in conjunction with state provision for those unable to sell their labor, such as the elderly or unemployed.

so•cial se•cu•ri•ty ▸ n. any government system that provides monetary assistance to people with an inadequate or no income.
  ■ (**Social Security**) (in the US) a federal insurance program that provides benefits to retired persons, the unemployed, and the disabled.

soft ▸ adj. (of a market, currency, or commodity) falling or likely to fall in value.

soft loan ▸ n. a loan, typically one to a developing country, made on terms very favorable to the borrower.

so•go sho•sha ▸ n. (pl. same) a very large Japanese company that trades internationally in a wide range of goods and services.

sol•vent ▸ adj. having assets in excess of liabilities; able to pay one's debts.

spe•cial draw•ing rights (abbr.: **SDR**) ▸ plural n. a form of international money, created by the International Monetary Fund, and defined as a weighted average of various convertible currencies.

spe•cie ▸ n. money in the form of coins rather than notes.
–PHRASES **in specie** in coin.

spe•cif•ic ▸ adj. (of a duty or a tax) levied at a fixed rate per physical unit of the thing taxed, regardless of its price.

spec•u•late ▸ v. invest in stocks, property, or other ventures in the hope of gain but with the risk of loss.

spec•u•la•tive ▸ adj. (of an investment) involving a high risk of loss.
  ■ (of a business venture) undertaken on the chance of success, without a preexisting contract.

split ▸ v. (**splitting**; past and past part. **split**) issue new shares of (stock) to existing stockholders in proportion to their current holdings.
▸ n. short for STOCK SPLIT.

split shift ▸ n. a working shift comprising two or more separate periods of duty in a day.

spot ▸ n. denoting a system of trading in which commodities or currencies are delivered and paid for immediately after a sale.

spread ▸ n. the difference between two rates or prices.

squeeze ▸ n. a strong financial demand or pressure, typically a restriction on borrowing, spending, or investment in a financial crisis.

sta•bi•liz•er ▸ n. a financial mechanism that prevents unsettling fluctuation in an economic system.

stag ▸ n. a person who applies for shares in a new issue with a view to selling at once for a profit.

stag•fla•tion ▸ n. persistent high inflation combined with high unemployment and stagnant demand in a country's economy.

stake•hold•er ▸ n. a person with an interest or concern in something, esp. a business.
  ■ denoting a type of organization or system in which all the members or participants are seen as having an interest in its success.

stale ▸ adj. (of a check or legal claim) invalid because out of date.

stand•ard ▸ n. a system by which the value of a currency is defined in terms of gold or silver or both.

stand•ard of liv•ing ▸ n. the degree of wealth and material comfort available to a person or community.

stand•ing or•der ▸ n. an order for goods that remains in effect until cancelled.

stand•still a•gree•ment ▸ n. an agreement between two countries in which a debt owed by one to the other is held in abeyance for a specified period.
  ■ an agreement between a company and a bidder for the company in which the bidder agrees to buy no more shares for a specified period.

state•ment ▸ n. a document setting out items of debit and credit between a bank or other organization and a customer.

ster•ling ▸ n. British money: *prices in sterling are shown.*

stock ▸ n. the goods or merchandise kept on the premises of a business or warehouse and available for sale or distribution. ■ farm animals such as cattle, pigs, and sheep, bred and kept for their meat or milk; livestock. ■ the capital raised by a business or corporation through the issue and subscription of shares: *between 1982 and 1986, the value of the company's stock rose by 86%.*
  ■ (also **stocks**) a portion of this as held by an individual or group as an investment: *she owned $3000 worth of stock.* ■ (also **stocks**) the shares of a particular company, type of company, or industry: *blue-chip stocks.* ■ securities issued by the government in fixed units with a fixed rate of interest: *government gilt-edged stock.*
▸ adj. (of a product or type of product) usually kept in stock and thus regularly available for sale.
▸ v. have or keep a supply of (a particular product or type or product) available for sale.

–PHRASES **in (or out of) stock** (of goods) available (or unavailable) for immediate sale in a store.

stock ex•change ▸ n. a market in which securities are bought and sold: *the company was floated on the Stock Exchange.*
■ **(the Stock Exchange)** the level of prices in such a market.

stock•hold•er ▸ n. a shareholder.

stock in•dex fu•tures ▸ plural n. contracts to buy a range of shares at an agreed price but delivered and paid for later.

stock-in-trade ▸ n. the typical subject or commodity a person, company, or profession uses or deals in: *information is our stock-in-trade.*
■ the goods kept on hand by a business for the purposes of its trade.

stock mar•ket ▸ n. (usu. **the stock market**) a stock exchange.

stock op•tion ▸ n. a benefit in the form of an option given by a company to an employee to buy stock in the company at a discount or at a stated fixed price.

stock•out ▸ n. a situation in which an item is out of stock.

stock split ▸ n. an issue of new shares in a company to existing shareholders in proportion to their current holdings.

stop ▸ v. (**stopped, stopping**) instruct a bank to withhold payment on (a check).
–PHRASES **stop payment** instruct a bank to withhold payment on a check.

stop-loss ▸ adj. denoting or relating to an order to sell a security or commodity at a specified price in order to limit a loss.

strad•dle ▸ n. a simultaneous purchase of options to buy and to sell a security or commodity at a fixed price, allowing the purchaser to make a profit whether the price of the security or commodity goes up or down.

straight-line ▸ adj. of or relating to a method of depreciation allocating a given percentage of the cost of an asset each year for a fixed period.

straight time ▸ n. normal working hours, paid at a regular rate.

street ▸ n. (**the street**) used to refer to the financial markets and activities on Wall Street.

street name ▸ n. the name of a brokerage firm, bank, or dealer in which stock is held on behalf of a purchaser.

strike ▸ v. (past and past part. **struck**) (of employees) refuse to work as a form of organized protest, typically in an attempt to obtain a particular concession or concessions from their employer.
■ undertake such action against (an employer). (in financial contexts) reach (a figure) by balancing an account:
▸ n. a refusal to work organized by a body of employees as a form of protest, typically in an attempt to gain a concession or concessions from their employer.

strike pay ▸ n. money paid to strikers by their trade union.

strip ▸ v. (**stripped, stripping**) sell off (the assets of a company) for profit.

■ divest (a bond) of its interest coupons so that it and they may be sold separately.

strip mall ▸ n. a shopping mall consisting of stores and restaurants typically in one-story buildings located on a busy main road.

strong ▸ adj. (**stronger, strongest**) in a secure financial position.
■ (of a market) having steadily high or rising prices.

struc•tur•al un•em•ploy•ment ▸ n. unemployment resulting from industrial reorganization, typically due to technological change, rather than fluctuations in supply or demand.

sub•con•tract ▸ v. employ a business or person outside one's company to do (work) as part of a larger project.
■ (of a business or person) carry out work for a company as part of a larger project.
▸ n. a contract for a company or person to do work for another company as part of a larger project.

sub•con•trac•tor ▸ n. a business or person that carries out work for a company as part of a larger project.

sub•or•di•nat•ed debt ▸ n. a debt owed to an unsecured creditor that can only be paid, in the event of a liquidation, after the claims of secured creditors have been met.

sub•scribe ▸ v. apply for or undertake to pay for an offering of shares of stock.

sub•sid•i•ar•y ▸ adj. (of a company) controlled by a holding or parent company.
▸ n. (pl. **-ies**) a company controlled by a holding company.

sub•ten•ant ▸ n. a person who leases property from a tenant.

sun•rise in•dus•try ▸ n. a new and growing industry, esp. in electronics or telecommunications.

sun•set in•dus•try ▸ n. an old and declining industry.

su•per•an•nu•a•tion ▸ n. regular payment made into a fund by an employee toward a future pension.
■ a pension of this type paid to a retired person.
■ the process of superannuating an employee.

su•per•store ▸ n. a retail store, as a grocery store or bookstore, with more than the average amount of space and variety of stock.

su•per•tax ▸ n. an additional tax on something already taxed.

sup•ply ▸ n. (pl. **-ies**) the amount of a good or service offered for sale.
–PHRASES **supply and demand** the amount of a good or service available and the desire of buyers for it, considered as factors regulating its price.

sup•ply chain ▸ n. the sequence of processes involved in the production and distribution of a commodity.

sup•ply-side ▸ adj. denoting or relating to a policy designed to increase output and employment by changing the conditions under which goods and services are supplied, esp. by measures that reduce government involvement in the economy and allow the free market to operate.

sur•charge ▸ n. an additional charge or payment.
■ a charge made by assessors as a penalty for

false returns of taxable property. ■ the showing of an omission in an account for which credit should have been given.

▶v. exact an additional charge or payment from.

sur•plus ▶ n. an amount of something left over when requirements have been met; an excess of production or supply over demand.
■ an excess of income or assets over expenditure or liabilities in a given period, typically a fiscal year: *a trade surplus of $1.4 billion.* ■ the excess value of a company's assets over the face value of its stock.

sur•ren•der ▶ v. (of an insured person) cancel (a life insurance policy) and receive back a proportion of the premiums paid.

sur•ren•der val•ue ▶ n. the amount payable to a person who surrenders a life insurance policy.

sur•tax ▶ n. an additional tax on something already taxed, such as a higher rate of tax on incomes above a certain level.

sus•pense ac•count ▶ n. an account in the books of an organization in which items are entered temporarily before allocation to the correct or final account.

swap (also **swop**) ▶ n. an exchange of liabilities between two borrowers, either so that each acquires access to funds in a currency they need or so that a fixed interest rate is exchanged for a floating rate.

swap•tion ▶ n. an option giving the right but not the obligation to engage in a swap.

sweat eq•ui•ty ▶ n. informal an interest or increased value in a property earned from labor toward upkeep or restoration.

sweat•shop ▶ n. a factory or workshop, esp. in the clothing industry, where manual workers are employed at very low wages for long hours and under poor conditions.

swipe card ▶ n. a plastic card such as a credit card or ID card bearing magnetically encoded information that is read when the edge of the card is slid through an electronic device.

SWOT a•nal•y•sis ▶ n. a study undertaken by an organization to identify its internal strengths and weaknesses, as well as its external opportunities and threats.

syn•di•cate ▶ n. a group of individuals or organizations combined to promote some common interest.

▶v. (usu. **be syndicated**) control or manage by a syndicate.

syn•er•gy (also **synergism**) ▶ n. the interaction or cooperation of two or more organizations, substances, or other agents to produce a combined effect greater than the sum of their separate effects: *the synergy between artist and record company.*

tai•pan ▶ n. a foreigner who is head of a business in China or Hong Kong.

tare ▶ n. an allowance made for the weight of the packaging in order to determine the net weight of goods.

tar•iff ▶ n. a tax or duty to be paid on a particular class of imports or exports.
■ a list of these taxes. ■ a table of the fixed charges made by a business, esp. in a hotel or restaurant.

▶v. fix the price of (something) according to a tariff: *these services are tariffed by volume.*

tax ▶ n. a compulsory contribution to state revenue, levied by the government on workers' income and business profits or added to the cost of some goods, services, and transactions.

▶v. impose a tax on (someone or something).

tax•a•tion ▶ n. the levying of tax.
■ money paid as tax.

tax a•void•ance ▶ n. the arrangement of one's financial affairs to minimize tax liability within the law.

tax brack•et ▶ n. a range of incomes taxed at a given rate.

tax break ▶ n. informal a tax concession or advantage allowed by a government.

tax cred•it ▶ n. an amount of money that can be offset against a tax liability.

tax-de•duct•i•ble ▶ adj. able to be deducted from taxable income or the amount of tax to be paid.

tax e•va•sion ▶ n. the illegal nonpayment or underpayment of tax.

tax ex•ile ▶ n. a person with a high income or considerable wealth who chooses to live in a country or area with low rates of tax.

tax ha•ven ▶ n. a country or independent area where taxes are levied at a low rate.

tax loss ▶ n. a loss that can be offset against taxable profit earned elsewhere or in a different period.

tax•pay•er ▶ n. a person who pays taxes.

tax re•turn ▶ n. a form on which a taxpayer makes an annual statement of income and personal circumstances, used by the tax authorities to assess liability for tax.

tax shel•ter ▶ n. a financial arrangement made to avoid or minimize taxes.

tech•no•struc•ture ▶ n. [treated as sing. or pl.] a group of technologists or technical experts having considerable control over the workings of industry or government.

tel•e•mar•ket•ing ▶ n. the marketing of goods or services by means of telephone calls, typically unsolicited, to potential customers.

tel•e•phone bank•ing ▶ n. a method of banking in which the customer conducts transactions by telephone, typically by means of a computerized system using touch-tone dialing or voice-recognition technology.

tel•e•sales ▶ plural n. the selling of goods or services over the telephone.

tell•er ▶ n. a person employed to deal with customers' transactions in a bank.
■ an automated teller machine.

temp informal ▶ n. a temporary employee, typically an office worker who finds employment through an agency.

▶v. work as a temporary employee.

ten•der ▶ v. offer (money) as payment.
■ make a formal written offer to carry out work, supply goods, or buy land, shares, or another asset for a stated fixed price. ■ make such an offer giving (a stated fixed price).

▶n. an offer to carry out work, supply goods, or buy land, shares, or another asset at a stated fixed price.

–PHRASES **put something out to tender** seek offers to carry out work or supply goods at a stated fixed price.

ten•or ▸ n. the time that must elapse before a bill of exchange or promissory note becomes due for payment.

terms of trade ▸ plural n. the ratio of an index of a country's export prices to an index of its import prices.

think tank ▸ n. a body of experts providing advice and ideas on specific political or economic problems.

third mar•ket ▸ n. used to refer to over-the-counter trading in listed stocks outside the stock exchange.

third par•ty ▸ adj. of or relating to a person or group besides the two primarily involved in a situation: *third-party suppliers.*

thrift ▸ n. another term for SAVINGS AND LOAN.

tick ▸ n. the smallest recognized amount by which a price of the security or future may fluctuate.

tie-in ▸ n. denoting sales made conditional on the purchase of an additional item or items from the same supplier.

ti•ger ▸ n. (also **tiger economy**) a dynamic economy of one of the smaller eastern Asian countries, esp. that of Singapore, Taiwan, or South Korea.

tight mon•ey ▸ n. money or finance that is available only at high rates of interest.

till ▸ n. a cash register or drawer for money in a store, bank, or restaurant.

–PHRASES **have (or with) one's fingers (or hand) in the till** used in reference to theft from one's place of work.

time-and-mo•tion stud•y ▸ n. a procedure in which the efficiency of an industrial or other operation is evaluated.

time de•pos•it ▸ n. a deposit in a bank account that cannot be withdrawn before a set date or for which notice of withdrawal is required.

tomb•stone ▸ n. (also **tombstone advertisement** or **tombstone ad**) an advertisement listing the underwriters or firms associated with a new issue of securities.

ton-mile ▸ n. one ton of freight carried one mile, as a unit of traffic.

ton•nage ▸ n. shipping considered in terms of total carrying capacity: *the port's total tonnage.*

ton•tine ▸ n. an annuity shared by subscribers to a loan or common fund, the shares increasing as subscribers die until the last survivor enjoys the whole income.

top-heav•y ▸ adj. (of an organization) having a disproportionately large number of people in senior administrative positions.

trade ▸ n. the action of buying and selling goods and services. ■ a skilled job, typically one requiring manual skills and special training.
■ **(the trade)** [treated as sing. or pl.] the people engaged in a particular area of business.
▸v. buy and sell goods and services.
■ buy or sell (a particular item or product). ■ (esp. of shares or currency) be bought and sold at a specified price. ■ exchange (something) for something else, typically as a commercial transaction.

trade def•i•cit ▸ n. the amount by which the cost of a country's imports exceeds the value of its exports.

trade dis•count ▸ n. a discount on the retail price of something allowed or agreed between traders or to a retailer by a wholesaler.

trad•ed op•tion ▸ n. an option on a stock exchange or futures exchange which can itself be bought and sold.

trade•mark ▸ n. a symbol, word, or words legally registered or established by use as representing a company or product.
▸v. **(trademarked)** provide with a trademark.

trade name ▸ n. a name that has the status of a trademark. a name by which something is known in a particular trade or profession.

trade sur•plus ▸ n. the amount by which the value of a country's exports exceeds the cost of its imports.

trade-up ▸ n. a sale of an article in order to buy something similar but more expensive and of higher quality.

trade war ▸ n. a situation in which countries try to damage each other's trade, typically by the imposition of tariffs or quota restrictions.

trad•ing floor ▸ n. an area within an exchange or a bank or securities house where dealers trade in stocks or other securities.

trad•ing post ▸ n. a store or small settlement established for trading, typically in a remote place.

trad•ing stamp ▸ n. a stamp given by some stores to a customer according to the amount spent, and exchangeable in the appropriate number for various articles.

tranche ▸ n. a portion of something, esp. money: *they released the first **tranche of** the loan.*

trans•fer pay•ment ▸ n. a payment made or income received in which no goods or services are being paid for, such as a benefit payment or subsidy.

trans•na•tion•al ▸ n. a large company operating internationally; a multinational.

trav•el•er's check ▸ n. a check for a fixed amount that can be cashed or used in payment after endorsement with the holder's signature.

treas•ur•er ▸ n. a person appointed to administer or manage the financial assets and liabilities of a society, company, local authority, or other body.

treas•ur•y ▸ n. (pl. **-ies**) the funds or revenue of a government, corporation, or institution.
■ **(Treasury)** (in some countries) the government department responsible for budgeting for and controlling public expenditure, management of the national debt, and the overall management of the economy.

Treas•ur•y bill ▸ n. a short-dated government security, yielding no interest but issued at a discount on its redemption price.

Treas•ur•y bond ▸ n. a government bond issued by the US Treasury.

tri•al bal•ance ▸ n. a statement of all debits and credits in a double-entry account book, with any disagreement indicating an error.

tri•ple A (also **AAA**) ▸ n. the highest grading available from credit rating agencies.

trough ▸ n. a low level of economic activity.

trust ▸ n. a body of trustees.
■ an organization or company managed by trustees. ■ dated a large company that has or attempts to gain monopolistic control of a market.

trust•bust•er ▸ n. informal a person or agency employed to enforce antitrust legislation.

trust com•pa•ny ▸ n. a company formed to act as a trustee or to deal with trusts.

trust fund ▸ n. a fund consisting of assets belonging to a trust, held by the trustees for the beneficiaries.

turn•a•round ▸ n. the process of completing or the time needed to complete a task, esp. one involving receiving something, processing it, and sending it out again: *a seven-day turnaround.*
■ the process of or time taken for unloading and reloading a ship, aircraft, or vehicle.

turn•key ▸ adj. of or involving the provision of a complete product or service that is ready for immediate use.

turn•o•ver ▸ n. the amount of money taken by a business in a particular period.
■ the volume of shares traded during a particular period, as a percentage of total shares listed. the rate at which employees leave a workforce and are replaced.
■ the rate at which goods are sold and replaced in a shop.

un•au•dit•ed ▸ adj. (of financial accounts) not having been officially examined.

un•brand•ed ▸ adj. (of a product) not bearing a brand name: *unbranded computer systems.*

un•bun•dle ▸ v. market or charge for (items or services) separately rather than as part of a package. split (a company or conglomerate) into its constituent businesses, esp. before selling them off.

un•cap ▸ v. (**uncapped, uncapping**) remove a limit or restriction on (a price, rate, or amount).

un•cashed ▸ adj. (of a check or money order) not yet cashed.

un•charged ▸ adj. not charged to a particular account: *an uncharged fixed cost.*

un•cleared ▸ adj. (of a check) not having passed through a clearinghouse and been paid into the payee's account.

un•com•mer•cial ▸ adj. not making, intended to make, or allowing a profit.

un•com•pet•i•tive ▸ adj. (with reference to business or commerce) not competitive.

UNCTAD ▸ abbr. United Nations Conference on Trade and Development.

un•der•cap•i•tal•ize ▸ v. provide (a company) with insufficient capital to achieve desired results.

un•der•charge ▸ v. charge (someone) a price or amount that is too low.

un•der•con•sump•tion ▸ n. purchase of goods and services at a level lower than that of their supply.

un•der•cut ▸ v. (**-cutting;** past and past part. **-cut**) offer goods or services at a lower price than (a competitor).

un•der•de•vel•oped ▸ adj. (of a country or region) not advanced economically.

un•der•ground e•con•o•my ▸ n. the part of a country's economic activity that is unrecorded and untaxed by its government.

un•der•in•sured ▸ adj. (of a person) having inadequate insurance coverage.

un•der•per•form ▸ v. increase in value less than.

un•der•price ▸ v. sell or offer something at a lower price than (the competition).
■ sell or offer (something) at too low a price.

un•der•sell ▸ v. (past and past part. **-sold**) sell something at a lower price than (a competitor).

un•der•spend ▸ v. (past and past part. **-spent**) spend less than (a specified or allocated amount).

un•der•val•ue ▸ v. (**-values, -valued, -valuing**) underestimate the financial value of (something).

un•der•weight ▸ adj. (also **underweighted**) having less investment in a particular area than is considered desirable or appropriate.

un•der•write ▸ v. (past **-wrote;** past part. **-written**) sign and accept liability under (an insurance policy), thus guaranteeing payment in case loss or damage occurs.
■ accept (a liability or risk) in this way. (of a bank or other financial institution) engage to buy all the unsold shares in (an issue of new securities).
■ undertake to finance or otherwise support or guarantee (something).

un•earned in•come ▸ n. income from investments rather than from work.

un•earned in•cre•ment ▸ n. an increase in the value of land or property without labor or expenditure on the part of the owner.

un•ec•o•nom•ic ▸ adj. unprofitable.
■ constituting an inefficient use of money or other resources.

un•ec•o•nom•i•cal ▸ adj. wasteful of money or other resources; not economical.

un•em•ploy•a•ble ▸ adj. (of a person) not able or likely to get paid employment, esp. because of a lack of skills or qualifications.
▸ n. an unemployable person.

un•em•ployed ▸ adj. (of a person) without a paid job but available to work.

un•em•ploy•ment ▸ n. the state of being unemployed.
■ the number or proportion of unemployed people: *a time of high unemployment.* ■ short for **UN-EMPLOYMENT BENEFIT.**

un•em•ploy•ment ben•e•fit (also **unemployment compensation**) ▸ n. a payment made by a government or a labor union to an unemployed person.

un•en•cum•bered ▸ adj. free of debt or other financial liability.

un•freeze ▸ v. (past **unfroze;** past part. **unfrozen**) remove restrictions on the use or transfer of (an asset).

un•fund•ed ▸ adj. not funded, in particular:
■ not receiving public funds. ■ (of a debt) repayable on demand rather than having been

converted into a more or less permanent debt at fixed interest.

un•hedged ▸ adj. (of an investment or investor) not protected against loss by balancing or compensating contracts or transactions.

un•in•cor•po•rat•ed ▸ adj. (of a company or other organization) not formed into a legal corporation: *an unincorporated business.*

un•in•sur•a•ble ▸ adj. not eligible for insurance coverage.

un•in•sured ▸ adj. not covered by insurance.

un•is•sued ▸ adj. (esp. of shares of stock) not yet issued.

un•liq•ui•dat•ed ▸ adj. (of a debt) not cleared or paid off.

un•list•ed ▸ adj. denoting or relating to a company whose shares are not listed on a stock exchange.

un•mar•ket•a•ble ▸ adj. not marketable.

un•mer•chant•a•ble ▸ adj. not suitable for purchase or sale.

un•peg ▸ v. (**unpegged, unpegging**) cease to maintain a fixed relationship between (a currency) and another currency.

un•priced ▸ adj. having no marked or stated price.

un•quot•ed ▸ adj. not quoted or listed on a stock exchange: *an unquoted company.*

un•se•cured ▸ adj. (of a loan) made without an asset given as security.
■ (of a creditor) having made such a loan.

un•taxed ▸ adj. not subject to taxation.
■ (of an item, income, etc.) not having had the required tax paid on it.

up•front informal ▸ adv. (usu. **up front**) (of a payment) in advance.
▸ adj. (of a payment) made in advance.

up•mar•ket (also **up-market**) ▸ adj. & adv. upscale.

up•set price ▸ n. the lowest acceptable selling price for a property in an auction; a reserve price.

up•side ▸ n. [in sing.] an upward movement of stock prices.

u•til•i•ty ▸ n. (pl. **-ies**) a public utility.
■ stocks and bonds in public utilities.

val•or•ize ▸ v. raise or fix the price or value of (a commodity or currency) by artificial means, esp. by government action.

val•u•a•tion ▸ n. the monetary worth of something, esp. as estimated by an appraiser.

val•ue ▸ v. (**values, valued, valuing**) (often **be valued**) estimate the monetary worth of (something).

val•ue add•ed ▸ n. the amount by which the value of an article is increased at each stage of its production, exclusive of initial costs.
▸ adj. (**value-added**) (of goods) having features added to a basic line or model for which the buyer is prepared to pay extra.
■ (of a company) offering specialized or extended services in a commercial area.

val•ue-add•ed tax (abbr.: **VAT**) ▸ n. a tax on the amount by which the value of an article has been increased at each stage of its production or distribution.

val•ue a•nal•y•sis ▸ n. the systematic and critical assessment by an organization of every feature of

a product to ensure that its cost is no greater than is necessary to carry out its functions.

va•lu•ta ▸ n. the value of one currency with respect to its exchange rate with another.
■ foreign currency.

VAR ▸ abbr. value-added reseller, a company that adds extra features to products it has bought before selling them on. ■ value at risk, a method of quantifying the risk of holding a financial asset.

var•i•a•ble cost ▸ n. a cost that varies with the level of output.

var•i•ance ▸ n. (in accounting) the difference between expected and actual costs, profits, output, etc., in a statistical analysis.

VAT ▸ abbr. value added tax.

ve•loc•i•ty ▸ n. (pl. **-ies**) (also **velocity of circulation**) the rate at which money changes hands within an economy.

vend•ing ma•chine ▸ n. a machine that dispenses small articles such as food, drinks, or cigarettes when a coin, bill, or token is inserted.

ven•dor (also **vender**) ▸ n. a person or company offering something for sale, esp. a trader in the street.
■ a person or company whose principal product lines are office supplies and equipment.

ven•dor plac•ing ▸ n. a type of placing used as a method of financing a takeover in which the purchasing company issues its own shares as payment to the company being bought, with the prearranged agreement that these shares are then placed with investors in exchange for cash.

ven•ture ▸ n. a business enterprise involving considerable risk.

ven•ture cap•i•tal ▸ n. capital invested in a project in which there is a substantial element of risk, typically a new or expanding business.

ver•ti•cal ▸ adj. involving all the stages from the production to the sale of a class of goods.

ver•ti•cal in•te•gra•tion ▸ n. the combination in one company of two or more stages of production normally operated by separate companies.

ver•ti•cal mar•ket ▸ n. a market comprising all the potential purchasers in a particular occupation or industry.

vi•at•i•cal set•tle•ment ▸ n. an arrangement whereby a person with a terminal illness sells their life insurance policy to a third party for less than its mature value, in order to benefit from the proceeds while alive.

vic•to•ry bond ▸ n. a bond issued by a government during or immediately after a major war.

vis•i•ble ▸ adj. of or relating to imports or exports of tangible commodities: *the visible trade gap.*

vouch•er ▸ n. a small printed piece of paper that entitles the holder to a discount or that may be exchanged for goods or services.
■ a receipt.

wage dif•fer•en•tial ▸ n. the difference in earnings between workers with different skills in the same industry or between workers with similar skills in different industries or localities.

wage drift ▸ n. the tendency for the average level of wages actually paid to rise above wage rates through increases in overtime and other factors.

Wal•ras' law a law stating that the total value of goods and money supplied equals that of goods and money demanded.

ware•house ▸ n. a large building where raw materials or manufactured goods may be stored before their export or distribution for sale.
■ a large wholesale or retail store.
▸v. store (goods) in a warehouse.
■ place (imported goods) in a bonded warehouse pending the payment of import duty.

ware•house club ▸ n. an organization that operates from a large store and sells goods in bulk at discounted prices to business and private customers who must first become club members.

ware•hous•ing ▸ n. the practice or process of storing goods in a warehouse.

war•rant ▸ n. a document that entitles the holder to receive goods, money, or services.
■ a negotiable security allowing the holder to buy shares at a specified price at or before some future date.

war•ran•ty ▸ n. (pl. **-ies**) a written guarantee, issued to the purchaser of an article by its manufacturer, promising to repair or replace it if necessary within a specified period of time.

wa•ter ▸ n. capital stock that represents a book value greater than the true assets of a company.
▸v. (usu. **be watered**) increase (a company's debt, or nominal capital) by the issue of new shares without a corresponding addition to assets.

weak ▸ adj. not in a secure financial position.
■ (of prices or a market) having a downward tendency.

weight•ing ▸ n. an allocated proportion of an investment.

when-is•sued ▸ adj. of or relating to trading in securities that have not yet been issued.

whip•saw ▸ v. (past part. **-sawn** or **-sawed**) (usu. **be whipsawed**) informal subject to a double loss, as when buying a security before the price falls and selling before the price rises.

white goods ▸ plural n. large electrical goods used domestically such as refrigerators and washing machines, typically white in color.

white knight ▸ n. a person or company making an acceptable counteroffer for a company facing a hostile takeover bid.

white sale ▸ n. a store's sale of household linens.

whole-life ▸ adj. relating to or denoting a life insurance policy that pays a specified amount only on the death of the person insured.

whole•sale ▸ n. the selling of goods in large quantities to be retailed by others.
▸adv. being sold in such a way.
▸v. sell (goods) in large quantities at low prices to be retailed by others.

whol•ly-owned ▸ adj. denoting a company all of whose shares are owned by another company.

wind•fall prof•its tax (also **windfall tax**) ▸ n. a tax levied on an unforeseen or unexpectedly large profit, esp. one regarded to be excessive or unfairly obtained.

wind•ing ▸ n. (**winding up**) the process of closing down a company or a financial institution.

wire fraud ▸ n. financial fraud involving the use of telecommunications or information technology.

with•hold•ing tax ▸ n. the amount of an employee's pay withheld by the employer and sent directly to the government as partial payment of income tax.

work•ers' co•op•er•a•tive ▸ n. a business or industry owned and managed by those who work for it.

work•group ▸ n. a group within a workforce that normally works together.

work•ing cap•i•tal ▸ n. the capital of a business that is used in its day-to-day trading operations, calculated as the current assets minus the current liabilities.

write ▸ v. (past **wrote**; past part. **written**) underwrite (an insurance policy).
▸**write something off** cancel the record of a bad debt; acknowledge the loss of or failure to recover an asset.

write something up reduce the nominal value of stock or goods.

write-back ▸ n. the process of restoring to profit a provision for bad or doubtful debts previously made against profits and no longer required.

write-down ▸ n. a reduction in the estimated or nominal value of an asset.

write-off ▸ n. a cancellation from an account of a bad debt or worthless asset.

writ•er ▸ n. a broker who makes an option available for purchase or sells options.

write-up ▸ n. an increase in the estimated or nominal value of an asset.

xd ▸ abbr. ex dividend.

year end (also **year's end**) ▸ n. the end of the fiscal year.

yield ▸ v. (of a financial or commercial process or transaction) generate (a specified financial return).
▸n. the amount of money brought in, e.g., interest from an investment, revenue from a tax; return.

yield curve ▸ n. a curve on a graph in which the yield of fixed-interest securities is plotted against the length of time they have to run to maturity.

yield gap ▸ n. the difference between the return on government-issued securities and that on ordinary shares.

zai•ba•tsu ▸ n. (pl. same) a large Japanese business conglomerate.

ze•ro-based ▸ adj. (of a budget or budgeting) having each item costed anew, rather than in relation to its size or status in the previous budget.

ze•ro-cou•pon bond ▸ n. a bond that is issued at a deep discount to its face value but pays no interest.

Office Guide Bibliography

Abernathy, Frederick H. et al. *A Stitch in Time: Lean Retailing and the Transformation of Manufacturing—Lessons from the Apparel and Textile Industries*. New York: Oxford University Press, 1999.

Ackoff, Russell L. *Democratic Corporation: A Radical Prescription for Recreating Corporate America and Rediscovering Success*. New York: Oxford University Press, 1994.

Ackoff, Russell L. *Re-creating the Corporation: A Design of Organizations for the 21st Century*. New York: Oxford University Press, 1999.

Afuah, Allen. *Innovation Management: Strategies, Implementation, and Profits*. 2d ed. New York: Oxford University Press, 2003.

Akera, Atsushi, and Frederick Nebeker, eds. *From 0 to 1: An Authoritative History of Modern Computing*. New York: Oxford University Press, 2002.

Allen, David. *Getting Things Done: The Art of Stress-Free Productivity*. New York: Viking Press, 2001.

Allen, Judy. *Event Planning*. New York: John Wiley & Sons, 2000.

Allen, Thomas J., and Michael Scott Morton, eds. *Information Technology and the Corporation of the 1990s: Research Studies*. New York: Oxford University Press, 1991.

Alred, Gerald J. et al. *The Business Writer's Handbook*. New York: St. Martin's Press, 2000.

Altier, William J. *The Thinking Manager's Toolbox: Effective Processes for Problem Solving and Decision Making*. New York: Oxford University Press, 1999.

Angell, David, and Brent Heslop. *The Elements of E-mail Style*. Boston: Addison-Wesley Publishing Co., 1994.

Argenti, Paul A., and Janis Forman. *The Power of Corporate Communication: Crafting the Voice and Image of Your Business*. New York: McGraw-Hill, 2002.

Argyris, Chris. *Flawed Advice and the Management Trap*. New York: Oxford University Press, 2000.

Arthur, Michael B., and Denise M. Rousseau, eds. *The Boundaryless Career: A New Employment Principle for a New Organizational Era*. New York: Oxford University Press, 1996.

Ashby, Meredith D., and Stephen A. Miles, eds. *Leaders Talk Leadership: Top Executives Speak their Minds*. New York: Oxford University Press, 2002.

Axtell, Roger E. *Do's and Taboos of Hosting International Visitors*. New York: John Wiley & Sons, 1990.

Axtell, Roger E. *Do's and Taboos Around the World*. New York: John Wiley & Sons, 1993.

Axtell, Roger E. et al. *Do's and Taboos Around the World for Women in Business*. New York: John Wiley & Sons, 1997.

Barnes, A. James et al. *Law for Business*. New York: McGraw-Hill, 2002.

Bell, Arthur H. *Complete Business Writer's Manual: Model Letters, Memos, Reports and Presentations for Every Occasion*. Upper Saddle River, N.J.: Prentice Hall, 1991.

Bellingham, Richard. *The Manager's Pocket Guide to Virtual Teams*. Amherst, Mass.: HRD Press, 2001.

Benson, Laurie K. *The Manager's Pocket Guide to eCommunication*. Amherst, Mass.: HRD Press, 2000.

Bergeron, Bryan P., and Jeffrey Blander. *Business Expectations: Are You Using Technology to Its Fullest?* New York: John Wiley & Sons, 2002.

Bermont, Todd. *10 Insider Secrets to Job Hunting Success!* Chicago: 10 Step Corporation, 2001.

Bhidé, Amar V. *The Origin and Evolution of New Businesses*. New York: Oxford University Press, 2000.

Blake, Gary, and Robert W. Bly. *The Elements of Business Writing*. New York: Longman, 1992.

Blanchard, Kenneth H., and Sheldon Bowles. *Gung Ho! Turn On the People in Any Organization*. New York: William Morrow & Co., 1997.

Blanchard, Kenneth H. et al. *High Five! The Magic of Working Together*. New York: William Morrow & Co., 2000.

Boehme, Ann J. *Planning Successful Meetings and Events*. New York: AMACOM, 1998.

Bolland, Eric J., and Charles W. Hofer. *Future Firms: How America's High Technology Companies Work*. New York: Oxford University Press, 1998.

Bond, Alan J. *Over 300 Successful Business Letters for All Occasions*. Hauppauge, N.Y.: Barron's Educational Series, 1998.

Bontis, Nick, and Chun Wei Choo, eds. *The Strategic Management of Intellectual Capital and Organizational Knowledge*. New York: Oxford University Press, 2002.

Booher, Dianna. *To the Letter: A Handbook of Model Letters for the Busy Executive*. San Francisco: Jossey-Bass, 1998.

Bossidy, Larry et al. *Execution: The Discipline of Getting Things Done*. New York: Random House, 2002.

Buckingham, Marcus, and Donald O. Clifton. *Now, Discover Your Strengths*. New York: Free Press, 2001.

Byham, William C., and Jeff Cox. *Heroz: Empower Yourself, Your Coworkers, Your Company*. New York: Random House, 1995.

Carey, Dennis C., and Dayton Ogden. *CEO Succession*. New York: Oxford University Press, 2000.

Carnegie, Dale et al. *How to Win Friends and Influence People*. New York: Pocket Books, 1994.

Carnegie, Dale. *How to Develop Self-Confidence and Influence People by Public Speaking*. New York: Pocket Books, 1999.

Cavaiola, Alan A., and Neil J. Lavender. *Toxic Coworkers: How to Deal with Dysfunctional People on the Job*. Oakland: New Harbinger Publications, 2000.

Chan, Janis Fisher, and Diane Lutovich. *Professional Writing Skills*. San Anselmo, Calif.: Advanced Communication Designs Inc., 1997.

Chandler, Alfred D., and James W. Cortada. *A Nation Transformed by Information: How Information Has Shaped the United States from Colonial Times to the Present*. New York: Oxford University Press, 2000.

Choo, Chun Wei. *The Knowing Organization*. New York: Oxford University Press, 1998.

Collins, Jim. *Good to Great: Why Some Companies Make the Leap...and Others Don't*. New York: HarperCollins, 2001.

Cortada, James W. et al. *Into the Networked Age: How IBM and Other Firms Are Getting There Now*. New York: Oxford University Press, 1999.

Covey, Stephen R. *The 7 Habits of Highly Effective People*. New York: Simon & Schuster, 1990.

Craven, Robin E. et al. *Complete Idiot's Guide to Meeting and Event Planning*. Indianapolis: Alpha Books, 2001.

Culbert, Samuel A. *Mind-Set Management: The Heart of Leadership*. New York: Oxford University Press, 1996.

Curcio, Vincent. *Chrysler: The Life and Times of an Automotive Genius*. New York: Oxford University Press, 2001.

Cutcher-Gershenfeld, Joel et al. *Knowledge-Driven Work: Unexpected Lessons from Japanese and United States Work Practices*. New York: Oxford University Press, 1998.

Davenport, Thomas H., and Laurance Prusak. *Information Ecology: Mastering the Information and Knowledge Environment*. New York: Oxford University Press, 1997.

Davis, Jeannie, and Pat Landaker. *Beyond 'Hello': A Practical Guide for Excellent Telephone Communication and Quality Customer Service*. Aurora, Colo.: Now Hear This Inc. Publishing, 2000.

Delaney, Patrick R. et al. *Wiley GAAP 2003: Interpretation and Application of Generally Accepted Accounting Principles*. New York: John Wiley & Sons, 2002.

Diresta, Diane. *Knockout Presentations: How to Deliver Your Message with Power, Punch, and Pizzazz*. Worcester, Mass.: Chandler House Press, 1998.

Dodd, Annabel Z. *The Essential Guide to Telecommunications*. 3d ed. Upper Saddle River, N.J.: Prentice Hall, 2001.

Doeringer, Peter B. et al. *Startup Factories: Leading Edge Practices and Regional Advantage for High-Performing Firms*. New York: Oxford University Press, 2002.

Dornan, Andy. *The Essential Guide to Wireless Communications Applications*. Upper Saddle River, N.J.: Prentice Hall, 2000.

Doyle, Michael, and David Straus. *How to Make Meetings Work*. New York: Berkley Publishing Group, 1993.

Dresser, Norine. *Multicultural Manners: New Rules of Etiquette for a Changing Society*. New York: John Wiley & Sons, 1996.

Duarte, Deborah L., and Nancy Tennant Snyder. *Mastering Virtual Teams: Strategies, Tools, and Techniques That Succeed*. San Francisco: Jossey-Bass, 2000.

Dyer, Jeffrey H. *Collaborative Advantage: Winning Through Extended Enterprise Supplier Networks*. New York: Oxford University Press, 2000.

Dziak, Michael J. et al. *Telecommuting Success: A Practical Guide for Staying in the Loop While Working Away from the Office*. Indianapolis: JIST Publishing, 2001.

Eckhouse, Barry. *Competitive Communications: A Rhetoric for Modern Business*. New York: Oxford University Press, 1998.

Eisen, Peter J. *Accounting the Easy Way*. 3d ed. Hauppauge, N.Y.: Barron's Educational Series, 1995.

Ellsworth, Richard R. *Leading with Purpose: The New Corporate Realities*. Palo Alto, Calif.: Stanford University Press, 2002.

Emerson, Robert W., and John W. Hardwicke. *Business Law*. Hauppauge, N.Y.: Barron's Educational Series, 1997.

Fisher, Kimball, and Mareen Duncan Fisher. *The Distance Manager: A Hands On Guide to Managing Off-Site Employees and Virtual Teams*. New York: McGraw-Hill, 2000.

Freeman, R. Edward et al. *Environmentalism and the New Logic of Business*. New York: Oxford University Press, 2000.

Friedman, Stewart D., and Jeffrey H. Greenhaus. *Work and Family—Allies or Enemies? What Happens When Business Professionals Confront Life Choices*. New York: Oxford University Press, 2000.

Giuliani, Rudolph W., and Ken Kurson. *Leadership*. New York: Talk Miramax Books, 2002.

Gookin, Dan, and Rich Tennant. *Word 2002 for Dummies*. New York: John Wiley & Sons, 2001.

Griffin, Jack. *The Complete Handbook of Model Business Letters*. Upper Saddle River, N.J.: Prentice Hall, 1997.

Handfield, Robert B., and Ernest L. Nichols. *Streamlining: Using New Technologies and the Internet to Transform Performance*. New York: Palgrave, 2002.

Harris, Robert L. *Information Graphics*. New York: Oxford University Press, 2000.

Helfert, Erich A. *Techniques of Financial Analysis: A Guide to Value Creation*. New York: McGraw-Hill, 2002.

Hitt, Michael A. et al. *Mergers and Acquisitions: A Guide to Creating Value for Stakeholders*. New York: Oxford University Press, 2001.

Hoefling, Trina. *Working Virtually: Managing People for Successful Virtual Teams and Organizations*. Sterling, Va.: Stylus Publishing, 2001.

Horak, Ray et al. *Communications Systems and Networks*. New York: John Wiley & Sons, 2000.

Hoskisson, Robert E., and Michael A. Hitt. *Downscoping: How to Tame the Diversified Firm*. New York: Oxford University Press, 1994.

Huff, Anne Sigismund, and James Oran Huff. *When Firms Change Direction*. New York: Oxford University Press, 2001.

Ingebretsen, Mark. *Nasdaq: A History of the Market That Changed the World*. New York: Random House, 2002.

Jagpal, Sharan. *Marketing Strategy and Uncertainty*. New York: Oxford University Press, 1998.

Jean, Anna-Carin. *The Organizer: Secrets and Systems from the World's Top Executive Assistants*. New York: HarperCollins, 1998.

Johnson, Spencer, and Kenneth H. Blanchard. *The One Minute Manager*. New York: Berkley Publishing Group, 1983.

Johnson, Spencer, and Kenneth H. Blanchard. *Who Moved My Cheese?* New York: Penguin Putnam, 1998.

Katz, Ralph. *The Human Side of Managing Technological Innovation*. 2d ed. New York: Oxford University Press, 2003.

Kelsey, Dee, and Pam Plum. *Great Meetings! How to Facilitate Like a Pro*. Portland, Maine: Hanson Park Press, 1999.

Kleiner, Art, and George Roth. *Oil Change: Perspectives on Corporate Transformation*. New York: Oxford University Press, 2000.

Kostner, Jaclyn. *Bionic eTeamwork*. Chicago: Dearborn Trade Publishing, 2001.

Kravitz, Wallace W. *Bookkeeping the Easy Way*. 3d ed. Hauppauge, N.Y.: Barron's Educational Series, 1999.

Leana, Carrie R., and Denise M. Rousseau. *Relational Wealth: The Advantages of Stability in a Changing Economy*. New York: Oxford University Press, 2000.

Levine, John R., et al. *The Internet All-in-One Desk Reference for Dummies*. New York: John Wiley & Sons, 2000.

Linver, Sandy, and Jim Mengert. *Speak and Get Results: The Complete Guide to Speeches and Presentations That Work in Any Business Situation*. New York: Simon & Schuster, 1994.

Lipman-Blumen, Jean. *Connective Leadership: Managing in a Changing World*. New York: Oxford University Press, 2000.

Lipman-Blumen, Jean, and Harold J. Leavitt. *Hot Groups: Seeding Them, Feeding Them, and Using Them to Ignite Your Organization*. New York: Oxford University Press, 2001.

Lipnack, Jessica, and Jeffrey Stamps. *Virtual Teams: People Working Across Boundaries with Technology*. New York: John Wiley & Sons, 2000.

Longstaff, Patricia Hirl. *The Communications Toolkit: How to Build and Regulate Any Communications Business*. Cambridge, Mass.: MIT Press, 2002.

Lougheed, Lin. *Business Correspondence: Letters, Faxes, and Memos*. Boston: Addison-Wesley Publishing Co., 1993.

Lucas, Henry C. *Information Technology and the Productivity Paradox: Assessing the Value of Investing in IT*. New York: Oxford University Press, 1999.

Luftman, Jerry N., ed. *Competing in the Information Age: Strategic Alignment in Practice*. New York: Oxford University Press, 1996.

Martin, Joanne. *Cultures in Organizations: Three Perspectives*. New York: Oxford University Press, 1992.

Mathews, John A. *Dragon Multinational: A New Model for Global Growth*. New York: Oxford University Press, 2002.

McElhone, Alice Powers et al. *Mail It! High-Impact Business Mail from design to Delivery (Pitney Bowes Best Practices Guide)*. New Canaan, Conn.: Benchmark Publications Inc., 1996.

McGovern, Gerry, and Rob Norton. *Content Critical: Now Everyone's a Publisher, What Makes Your Content Better?* Upper Saddle River, N.J.: Prentice Hall, 2002.

McMillan, John. *Games, Strategies, and Managers: How Managers Can Use Game Theory to Make Better Business Decisions*. New York: Oxford University Press, 1996.

McNeilly, Mark R. *Sun Tzu and the Art of Business: Six Strategic Principles for Managers*. New York: Oxford University Press, 1996.

Miller, Paul, and Paul Bahnson. *Quality Financial Reporting*. New York: McGraw-Hill, 2002.

Miller, Robert F. *Running a Meeting That Works*. Hauppauge, N.Y.: Barron's Educational Series, 1997.

Miller, Samantha. *E-Mail Etiquette: Do's, Don'ts and Disaster Tales From People Magazine's Internet Manners Expert*. New York: Time Warner Books, 2001.

Miner, John B. *Organizational Behavior: Foundations, Theories, and Analyses*. New York: Oxford University Press, 2002.

Mitroff, Ian I. et al. *The Essential Guide to Managing Corporate Crises*. New York: Oxford University Press, 1996.

Morikawa, Hidemasa. *A History of Top Management in Japan: Managerial Enterprises and Family Enterprises*. New York: Oxford University Press, 2001.

Morrison, Terri. *Kiss, Bow, or Shake Hands*. Holbrook, Mass.: Bob Adams Publishers, 1995.

Nadler, David, and Michael Tushman. *Competing by Design: The Power of Organizational Architecture*. New York: Oxford University Press, 1997.

Nishiguchi, Toshihiro. *Managing Product Development*. New York: Oxford University Press, 1996.

Nonaka, Ikujiro, and Hirotaka Takeuchi. *The Knowledge-Creating Company: How Japanese Companies Create the Dynamics of Innovation*. New York: Oxford University Press, 1995.

Nonaka, Ikujiro, and Toshihiro Nishiguchi. *Knowledge Emergence: Social, Technical, and Evolutionary Dimensions of Knowledge Creation*. New York: Oxford University Press, 2001.

O'Shaughnessy, John. *Why People Buy*. New York: Oxford University Press, 1989.

Oster, Sharon M. *Modern Competitive Analysis*. 3d ed. New York: Oxford University Press, 1999.

Ostroff, Frank. *The Horizontal Organization: What the Organization of the Future Actually Looks Like and How It Delivers Value to Customers*. New York: Oxford University Press, 1999.

Pachter, Barbara. *Prentice Hall Complete Business Etiquette Handbook*. Upper Saddle River, N.J.: Prentice Hall, 1994.

Peiperl, Maury et al. *Career Creativity: Explorations in the Remaking of Work*. New York: Oxford University Press, 2002.

Perseus Publishing, and Daniel Goleman. *Business: The Ultimate Resource*. Cambridge, Mass.: Perseus Publishing, 2002.

Pfeffer, Jeffrey. *New Directions for Organization Theory: Problems and Prospects*. New York: Oxford University Press, 1997.

Piotrowski, Maryann V. *Effective Business Writing: A Guide for Those Who Write on the Job*. 2d ed. New York: HarperCollins, 1996.

Princeton Review. *Grammar Smart: A Guide to Perfect Usage*. New York: Random House, 2001.

Poole, Marshall Scott et al. *Organizational Change and Innovation Processes: Theory and Methods for Research*. New York: Oxford University Press, 2000.

Post, Peggy, and Peter Post. *The Etiquette Advantage in Business*. New York: Harper-Collins, 1999.

Rapp, William V. *Information Technology Strategies: How Leading Firms Use IT to Gain an Advantage*. New York: Oxford University Press, 2002.

Renshaw, Jean R. *Kimono in the Boardroom: The Invisible Evolution of Japanese Women Managers*. New York: Oxford University Press, 1999.

Ripin, Kathy M., and Leonard R. Sayles. *Insider Strategies for Outsourcing Information Systems: Building Productive Partnerships, Avoiding Seductive Traps*. New York: Oxford University Press, 1999.

Robek, Mary F. et al. *Information and Records Management: Document-Based Information Systems*. New York: McGraw-Hill, 1995.

Romney, Marshall B. *Accounting Information Systems*. Upper Saddle River, N.J.: Prentice Hall, 2002.

Rosenthal, Sandra B., and Rogene A. Buchholz. *Rethinking Business Ethics: A Pragmatic Approach*. New York: Oxford University Press, 1999.

Roth, George, and Art Kleiner. *Car Launch: The Human Side of Managing Change*. New York: Oxford University Press, 1999.

Rothwell, William J. *The Workplace Learner*. New York: AMACOM, 2002.

Scott, Susan. *Fierce Conversations: Achieving Success at Work & in Life, One Conversation at a Time*. New York: Viking Press, 2002.

Shepard, Steven. *Telecommunications Convergence: How to Profit from the Convergence of Technologies, Services, and Companies*. New York: McGraw-Hill, 2000.

Shockley-Zalabak, Pamela, and Sandra Buffington Burmester. *The Power of Networked Teams: Creating a Business Within a Business at Hewlett-Packard in Colorado Springs*. New York: Oxford University Press, 2001.

Smith, Lisa A. *Business E-Mail: How to Make It Professional and Effective*. San Anselmo, Calif.: Writing & Editing at Work, 2002.

Solomon, Robert C. *Ethics and Excellence: Cooperation and Integrity in Business*. New York: Oxford University Press, 1993.

Solomon, Robert C. *A Better Way to Think about Business: How Personal Integrity Leads to Corporate Success*. New York: Oxford University Press, 1999.

Sonnenfeld, Jeffrey. *The Hero's Farewell: What Happens When CEOs Retire*. New York: Oxford University Press, 1991.

Steuernagel, Robert. *The Cellular Connection: A Guide to Cellular Telephones*. New York: John Wiley & Sons, 2000.

Stickney, Clyde P., and Roman L. Weil. *Financial Accounting: An Introduction to Concepts, Methods, and Uses*. Mason, Ohio: South-Western Publications, 2002.

Stone, Bradford. *Uniform Commercial Code in a Nutshell*. Eagan, Minn.: West Group, 2001.

Strunk, Jr., William, and E.B. White. *The Elements of Style*. 4th ed. Boston: Allyn & Bacon, 2000.

Sutton, Michael J.D. *Document Management for the Enterprise: Principles, Techniques, and Applications*. New York: John Wiley & Sons, 1996.

Timm, Paul R. *How to Hold Successful Meetings: 30 Action Tips for Managing Effective Meetings*. Franklin Lakes, N.J.: Career Press, 1997.

Tracy, John A. *Accounting for Dummies*. New York: John Wiley & Sons, 2001.

Tushman, Michael L., and Philip C. Anderson. *Managing Strategic Innovation and Change: A Collection of Readings*. 2d ed. New York: Oxford University Press, 2003.

Van De Ven, Andrew H. et al. *The Innovation Journey*. New York: Oxford University Press, 1999.

Van De Ven, Andrew H. et al. *Research on the Management of Innovation: The Minnesota Studies*. New York: Oxford University Press, 2000.

Von Hippel, Eric. *The Sources of Innovation*. New York: Oxford University Press, 1994.

Von Krogh, Georg et al. *Enabling Knowledge Creation: How to Unlock the Mystery of Tacit Knowledge and Release the Power of Innovation*. New York: Oxford University Press, 2000.

Werhane, Patricia H. *Moral Imagination and Management Decision-Making*. New York: Oxford University Press, 1999.

Whelan, Jonathan. *e-mail@work*. Upper Saddle River, N.J.: Financial Times Prentice Hall, 2000.

Woods, Geraldine. *English Grammar for Dummies*. New York: John Wiley & Sons, 2001.

Zelazny, Gene. *Say It with Presentations: How to Design and Deliver Successful Business Presentations*. New York: McGraw-Hill, 1999.

Index